20.00

January 1988

To Mrs. Stra

with deep

Mark

THE PUBLIC FACE
OF ARCHITECTURE

THE PUBLIC FACE
OF ARCHITECTURE

Civic Culture and Public Spaces

Edited by

NATHAN GLAZER
MARK LILLA

THE FREE PRESS
A Division of Macmillan, Inc.
NEW YORK
Collier Macmillan Publishers
LONDON

The Free Press
A Division of Macmillan, Inc.
866 Third Avenue, New York, N.Y. 10022

Collier Macmillan Canada, Inc.

Printed in the United States of America

printing number

1 2 3 4 5 6 7 8 9 10

Library of Congress Cataloging-in-Publication Data

The Public face of architecture.

    Includes index.
    1. Public architecture—United States.   2. City
planning—United States—History—20th century.
I. Glazer, Nathan.   II. Lilla, Mark.
NA9050.5.P8   1987   725'.0973   86–33609
ISBN 0–02–911811–5

Contents

Introduction

NATHAN GLAZER AND MARK LILLA

Architecture, by its very nature, is a public matter. Whenever we consider buildings in their aesthetic, economic, or moral dimensions, we must be prepared, at the same time, to treat those dimensions in public terms: to see that buildings can also serve as public art, or as civic monuments, or as contributions to the social life of the city. Even the home, which might seem to exist solely for the private comfort and pleasure of the owner, will, except in the most rural setting, face pedestrians on a public street along with other homes. Architecture is "consumed" less by its owners than by the anonymous public that walks or drives by the facade, crosses the building lobby, or waits in the doctor's office.

If we do happen to think about the public nature of architecture today, it is most likely to be in terms of the constraints placed on builders and architects by government: building codes, zoning restrictions, set-back requirements, landmarks preservation. These public constraints seem to provoke less resentment than resignation from the architectural profession. The attitude, it seems, is that, just as buildings must accommodate themselves to the client's personal habits, or the commercial or religious nature of the activities they house, or to the budget available, so they must accommodate themselves to the often capricious demands of the citizenry and its elected officials. Yet when the profession attempts to treat architecture's "publicness" as an extraordinary *opportunity* to shape the way in which public life is conducted, and not just as a constraint on personal or corporate expression, it seems uncomfortable and its steps are unsure—less sure, certainly, than they were a century ago.

Our confusion in these matters is reflected only too clearly in the public spaces we have recently created for ourselves in the United States. The public face of architecture today is often painted and garish, tucked and crimped, and painfully lacking in the classical architectural elements of "firmness, commodity, and delight." It also, on closer inspection, demonstrates a false flaunting of public attractions. Today we encounter whole building complexes raised on pedestals, with inaccessible entries designed to ward off the casual public, and interior public delights (such as they are) reserved for those who can penetrate blank walls and find their way through garages.

It is encouraging, of course, to see people flocking to the spaces offered them, and there have been some notable successes in creating such spaces recently. Many new museums and museum extensions built in the last two decades are enormously popular—and with good reason, for they provide beautiful, spacious areas in which to share beautiful things with others. And the triumphs of the new urban public spaces for commerce—such as Boston's Quincy Market and its various imitators—cannot be denied. But in both cases the achievements of the present depend heavily on those of the past. The museum extensions built today often serve only to highlight the virtues of the original buildings, whose successes we no longer hope to replicate. And even the revitalized urban commercial centers often depend for their success on the restoration of older buildings and plazas.

If anything, the situation is worse when we consider those new buildings erected specifically for public business—city halls, courtrooms, public office buildings. How many of these structures can be compared with their predecessors built a century ago? Failures abound, it seems, in direct proportion to the actual involvement of the public and public officials. If we are to have any chance of encouraging good public architecture, the current wisdom runs, the public's role should be limited to property condemnation, leaving the design and management of grand public projects to private corporations and independent semi-public authorities. Our public institutions are not trusted to build well and grandly and economically, so to mollify a suspicious public those institutions must strip their buildings of all expensive trappings of style. The great public gestures of the past are carefully avoided—yet even this does not seem to reduce the expense.

Something is clearly amiss. But to understand fully the nature of this public problem, it is important to be aware of the difficult conditions under which all architecture and spaces are being shaped today. These include the enormous scale of modern building, which trivializes the details that characterized past great architecture; the disappearance of common conventions of building and design (even the anorexic conventions of the International Style, which at least created some unity and harmony in the cityscape); the decline of craftsmanship (along with the rise in its cost); the multiplicity of new materials challenging architects and designers, and tempting them too often into disastrous experiments; the enormous impact of the automobile, for whose accommodation the city fabric is steadily desiccated.

Attitudes toward cost have also changed, affecting government building projects and private institutional building for public use. In both cases, while we see no decline in the desire for grandeur and self-advertisement, we see excessive financial caution inspired by the greater hold that rational cost-benefit analysis has on the modern mind, and by the increasing democratic controls on those who make public and private building decisions. Who today could justify to his stockholders the building of a Pennsylvania Station or Grand Central Terminal? Who would justify today the extravagant Federal courthouses and post offices that were built in so many cities in the 19th and early 20th centuries? Since by any measure we are a much wealthier society today than when we put up those grand buildings, cost alone cannot explain our failures.

We must, for the most part, live with these conditions. It is hard to find the craftsmen who once could be given general directions in cutting and shaping details in wood or stone, or in arranging patterns in brick or tile. Our contemporary substitutes for the modestly paid artisans who once refined those wonderful buildings are a few highly-skilled restorers who can only hope to maintain or to copy the past. In any case, the huge scale of building today makes it virtually impossible to define details, and can reduce them to an annoying pastiche. This, too, is unlikely to change: no one will again build a university as small as Jefferson's University of Virginia. Nor will we give up the variety of materials that technology now makes available. The harmony of our cities will never again be shaped by the natural conditions (such as climate and geology) that once made brick the obvious building material in one region, stone or wood in another.

The democratization of our culture also has a subtle effect on our building since it has reduced the authority of a class with a common education and homogeneous tastes, and the autonomous power, to make decisions on public projects. Jefferson could build the University of Virginia with as much freedom and authority, it appears, as he built his own house, and the University was enormously popular. But we doubt whether we will ever have another Jefferson making such public decisions; and even where such power still exists, it is hardly executed with taste and discrimination. The splendor of Paris, for example, was created by the decisive royal and imperial decisions of the past, but imperiousness is no guarantee of good taste or good sense today. Witness, for example, a French President's government's threat to build a freeway on the Left Bank, or the glass pyramid now rising in the courtyard of the Louvre as the result of the decision of another French President.

These conditions affect all architecture today. But when we build *explicitly* for the public—either in constructing a privately-owned hotel, department store, or shopping center, or a publicly-funded capitol, courthouse, or city hall—conditions are still more troubling.

The most significant obstacle to effective public architecture may be the very substantial change that has taken place in the manner of public gathering. Camillo Sitte, whose theories had so much influence on town planning in Europe, was perhaps the first to note this:

> The significance of the public space in the middle of the city (a forum or a market place) has become an essentially different one to-

> day. Nowadays plazas seldom harbor great public festivities, and they see less and less daily use. . . . How different in ancient times! In those days the main plazas were of primary importance to the life of every city because such a great deal of public life took place in them: today not an open plaza but closed halls would be used for such purposes.

Much more has changed since Sitte wrote in 1889. Many of the public functions that once required public spaces have now gone, not only indoors, but into the private home. It is becoming difficult to attract great numbers to a major public function, since they can watch it more comfortably on television. And the automobile makes it an enormous challenge to bring them together in an urban space. Even our political party conventions, which could once be held in centrally-located structures such as New York's old Madison Square Garden, have been affected. Their scale now relegates them to huge convention centers built for commercial expositions, set off on some urban edge, surrounded by acres of parking.

Something, though, is amiss even when public functions are still conducted on the same scale as they were a hundred years ago, or indeed, as in antiquity. Fifty or a hundred thousand could gather in Rome for their spectacles; and the same number gather today in our cities, and for much the same reasons. And although there is an excitement in the actual presence of our fellow human beings that ensures we will always have an audience for games and contests, athletic as well as political, when we still do gather in this way there is a new concern: crime and disorder. There is always a fear of disorder when great crowds gather, but the decline in the power of common rules and in the homogeneity of the population inevitably increases these fears. Great public festivals must be more carefully prepared than in the past: barriers must be erected to guide the crowds, and policemen must be deployed. And when a well-known head of state or political leader is to speak to a large gathering, the fear of assassination and the need to protect against it introduce additional unease.

If the occasions of our public gatherings have changed, so have our purposes. They have, over the centuries, become less political, more commercial—to buy, to sell, to display, to bargain. We are a commercial republic, and it is not surprising that we allow the creation of our public space to be dominated by commercial interests. There seems to be less inhibition in accommodating grand commercial projects in the public space than in accommodating explicitly governmental projects, perhaps because we can attribute some economic value to such business ventures.

One hopeful development, however, is that the public increasingly controls just what those commercial interests may do. It determines what land and buildings can be condemned for large projects, and it protects old buildings and favors their rehabilitation. The public can, through the numerous powers public authorities have to safeguard the environment, play a role in determining conditions for design. Further, the public can bargain with private interests to get the space it seems unwilling to provide for itself by direct taxation. Local governments can trade off permission to build higher in order to obtain public arcades or theaters, and there is no evidence that this means of getting public space produces poorly designed or less useful public space than direct public measures. We have a more commercial public space today, but one increasingly shaped by public authorities.

These, then, are the difficult material and social conditions under which the public face of architecture is being shaped today. Yet it can be said with some confidence that, whatever other maladies we may suffer from, we are also in the grip of a deep intellectual confusion about the nature of public life that has paralyzed attempts to cope with those conditions. Beyond expense, beyond demographics, there is at the present time an astonishing absence of clear reflection among architects and critics about just what the public space *is*, and how architectural objects are meant to fill it. What, we must ask ourselves, is distinctive about a city hall, or a jury room, or a government office building? What are the differences between the activities taking place in streets, hotel lobbies, public parks, shopping malls, and the Washington Mall? What are the differences between private and public sculpture, and which objects are to be placed in the public space? These questions are absolutely central to the character of city life and the practice of architecture, but they are questions we seem unable to form (let alone answer) with any confident clarity today.

Clearly we need a kind of civic education that emphasizes the distinctive nature of these public questions in architecture, and we need to raise public and professional taste. Western democratic societies no longer have the design tastes of kings or despots or robber barons or civic aristocrats to rely on. In a democratic age civic and aesthetic education will be the final arbiters—the education of architects, planners, public officials, and private corporations, to be sure, but also the education of the general public, which now has the power to intervene at so many places in the process of planning and design.

While a single collection of essays cannot claim to deal exhaustively with the intellectual issues of public space, or set standards of taste, it can at least try to lay out the intellectual issues as we see them, and reclaim for them the centrality they deserve in current debates over the shape of the city. As outsiders to the architectural profession, we have been more than a little shocked to discover how confused the critics and architects themselves are on these matters, and how extremely difficult it is to find books and articles that treat such matters with the serious reflection they demand. While assembling this volume we were surprised to learn that some of the classic writings on public architecture and public spaces are not generally accessible, and that recent writings on the subject either evaporate into difficult theoretical discussions of style (modernism v. post-modernism, *ad nauseam*), or into highly detailed treatments of particular projects. Architecture and planning students, caught between reading the ever-increasing number of theoretical works and completing their own projects, seem not to be exposed to the great tradition of literate essays about public building, nor to some contemporary writers who see themselves working within that tradition. Bringing such essays together in one volume will, we hope, serve to place current architectural debate in its proper public context.

Civic education and the raising of taste seem like unimaginably difficult tasks. But in many ways they are already happening, as we see in the activities of the preservation movement. Would it be possible to tear down Pennsylvania Station today? We doubt it. Publicly-provided financial benefits for remodeling historic landmarks are in place, and have permitted the restoration and re-use of the

huge St. Louis railroad station; new means of legal intervention are available, as was demonstrated in the successful suit to prevent a tower from being placed on top of
Grand Central Terminal; and behind both we have a public
that appreciates architecture more, even if it can be bam-
boozled and confused by publicity and authority. We have,
as another barometer of the raising of taste, well-written
architectural guides to almost every major city. Hard as it
may be to believe, there were no such guidebooks to
American cities thirty years ago; it was as though only Europe had architecture.

Admittedly it is easier to educate taste to recognize the
virtues of the past than to educate it to make decisions regarding the future. Yet even here one sees signs of improvement, as the present learns to use the past. Architects, for reasons of taste and civic awareness, do not
ignore existing streets as cavalierly as they have in the past
thirty years. Some, no doubt, are still inspired by the idea
of wiping out the restraints imposed by streets to create
great superblocks, but most are willing to work with the
street, and to accept its limits and virtues.

This, at the very least, is a beginning. But we still have
a long way to go—intellectually and aesthetically, politically and professionally—if we are to improve the public
face of our architecture. The essays collected here make a
real, if modest, contribution to that effort. But, in the end,
an attentive and informed public will be the best guarantee
of good public building. Though this guarantee is not
much, we have no alternative in design, as in politics, but
to educate our masters.*

*This book began as a special issue of the quarterly *The Public Interest*
(Winter 1984), titled "Architecture and Public Spaces." A good number
of the articles assembled here were written for that issue. Others have
appeared in other issues of *The Public Interest*, and other selections have
been taken from some classic writing on public architecture and from
journals in which particularly perceptive analyses of the problems of
civic culture and public space have appeared.

I

PRINCIPLES OF PUBLIC SPACES

INTRODUCTION

Since the time of the ancient city-states, the role of public space in Western urban life has been an important social question, debated in philosophical, historical, and practical terms. The selections in this section explore these three separate dimensions of the question from several twentieth-century perspectives, and offer some general principles by which to assess our contemporary architecture and public spaces.

Hannah Arendt's celebrated book, *The Human Condition*, is the most recent sustained examination of the philosophical distinction between the public and private realms. In the selection reproduced here, she reflects on the public realm and how it may be distinguished from both the private and the social realms. The distinctive characteristics of the public realm, she writes, are two: it is what we hold in common, and it is what we make for ourselves. The public world is a shared world that overcomes our private isolation in order to achieve ''publicity'' in speech for the sharing of common experience. And this ''publicity'' in turn allows us to create our shared public world together, filling it with timeless, humanly-fabricated objects meant to serve more than one generation. Mass society has eroded this intergenerational public world, Arendt writes, leaving us within separate private worlds that are at once lonely and depressingly indistinguishable.

As regards architecture, Roger Scruton argues in ''Public Space and the Classical Vernacular'' that this public/private distinction in social life must be drawn resolutely by those in the public sphere, and can be expressed most clearly in the facades of buildings that divide street from home. Streets built in the classical idiom, as opposed to the modern, preserve publicness by treating the street as an end in itself, and not as a means only.

In *The Fall of Public Man*, Richard Sennett takes this philosophical public/private distinction and gives it psychological depth. The public space, he writes, grew in importance between the fall of Rome and the eighteenth century, but has been in decline since the rise of bourgeois life and secularism in the nineteenth. Since then we have grown psychologically accustomed to the supremacy of "intimate" private life, the consequences of which may be seen in the "dead public spaces" of our modern architecture that reflect and reinforce our isolation and self-absorption.

The historical rise of the modern public space is traced in selections from the work of Camillo Sitte, Lewis Mumford, J.B. Jackson, and Walter Benjamin. Sitte's *City Planning according to Artistic Principles* (1889) emphasized the distinctiveness of the public realm in ancient life and the nature of its organic growth over the centuries. Sitte was disturbed by the dissolution of the physical public/private boundary in European cities and the decline of the communal activity once staged in plazas. He lays much of the blame at the feet of nineteenth-century planners who, in the pursuit of pure geometric "symmetry," removed public sculptures from their places and destroyed the subjective enjoyment of irregular "proportion." The selection from Mumford's *The City in History* emphasizes the extraordinary adaptability of the informal, organic character of medieval planning. The sensitivity to geographical and social irregularities displayed in medieval towns meant that the public/private distinction was never strictly maintained: cathedrals were surrounded with private dwellings, and public streets were maintained by private residents. Jackson's essay, "The Discovery of the Street," shows how the street was "discovered" as the first public space as markets grew to meet rising trade in the later medieval period. New streets broke up the strict divisions between urban quarters, allowing frequent—we might say "cosmopolitan"—encounters with the whole city. Benjamin, in these Marxist reflections on the public spaces of Paris, brings this survey up to the nineteenth century. His three short selections from "Paris, Capital of the Nineteenth Century" trace the rise of arcades, world fairs, and Haussmann's grand boulevards as signs of the growing cultural dominance of the bourgeoisie in the Western public sphere.

Practical discussions of architecture in the public sphere are to be found throughout this volume, but a selection from Jane Jacobs's *The Death and Life of Great American Cities* is included here because her empirical reflections have in fact become principles for the serious student of cities. With an almost anthropological eye, she gives a ''thick description'' of the public functions of modern city streets, and shows how, if an unplanned mix of uses is allowed to develop, those streets can still provide the public experience.

1

The Public Realm: The Common

HANNAH ARENDT

The term "public" signifies two closely interrelated but not altogether identical phenomena:

It means, first, that everything that appears in public can be seen and heard by everybody and has the widest possible publicity. For us, appearance—something that is being seen and heard by others as well as by ourselves—constitutes reality. Compared with the reality which comes from being seen and heard, even the greatest forces of intimate life—the passions of the heart, the thoughts of the mind, the delights of the senses—lead an uncertain, shadowy kind of existence unless and until they are transformed, deprivatized and deindividualized, as it were, into a shape to fit them for public appearance. The most current of such transformations occurs in storytelling and generally in artistic transposition of individual experiences. But we do not need the form of the artist to witness this transfiguration. Each time we talk about things that can be experienced only in privacy or intimacy, we bring them out into a sphere where they will assume a kind of reality which, their intensity notwithstanding, they never could have had before. The presence of others who see

From Hannah Arendt, The Human Condition *(Chicago: University of Chicago Press, 1958), pp. 50–58. Copyright © 1958 by The University of Chicago.*

what we see and hear what we hear assures us of the reality of the world and ourselves, and while the intimacy of a
fully developed private life, such as had never been known
before the rise of the modern age and the concomitant decline of the public realm, will always greatly intensify and
enrich the whole scale of subjective emotions and private
feelings, this intensification will always come to pass at the
expense of the assurance of the reality of the world and
men.

Indeed, the most intense feeling we know of, intense
to the point of blotting out all other experiences, namely,
the experience of great bodily pain, is at the same time the
most private and least communicable of all. Not only is it
perhaps the only experience which we are unable to transform into a shape fit for public appearance, it actually de-
prives us of our feeling for reality to such an extent that we
can forget it more quickly and easily than anything else.
There seems to be no bridge from the most radical subjectivity, in which I am no longer "recognizable," to the outer
world of life. Pain, in other words, truly a borderline experience between life as "being among men" (*inter homines
esse*) and death, is so subjective and removed from the
world of things and men that it cannot assume an appearance at all.

Since our feeling for reality depends utterly upon appearance and therefore upon the existence of a public
realm into which things can appear out of the darkness of
sheltered existence, even the twilight which illuminates
our private and intimate lives is ultimately derived from
the much harsher light of the public realm. Yet there are a
great many things which cannot withstand the implacable,
bright light of the constant presence of others on the public
scene; there, only what is considered to be relevant, worthy of being seen or heard, can be tolerated, so that the irrelevant becomes automatically a private matter. This, to
be sure, does not mean that private concerns are generally
irrelevant; on the contrary, we shall see that there are very
relevant matters which can survive only in the realm of the
private. For instance, love, in distinction from friendship,
is killed, or rather extinguished, the moment it is displayed
in public. ("Never seek to tell thy love / Love that never
told can be.") Because of its inherent worldlessness, love
can only become false and perverted when it is used for

political purposes such as the change or salvation of the world.

What the public realm considers irrelevant can have such an extraordinary and infectious charm that a whole people may adopt it as their way of life, without for that reason changing its essentially private character. Modern enchantment with "small things," though preached by early twentieth-century poetry in almost all European tongues, has found its classical presentation in the *petit bonheur* of the French people. Since the decay of their once great and glorious public realm, the French have become masters in the art of being happy among "small things," within the space of their own four walls, between chest and bed, table and chair, dog and cat and flowerpot, extending to these things a care and tenderness which, in a world where rapid industrialization constantly kills off the things of yesterday to produce today's objects, may even appear to be the world's last, purely humane corner. This enlargement of the private, the enchantment, as it were, of a whole people, does not make it public, does not constitute a public realm, but, on the contrary, means only that the public realm has almost completely receded, so that greatness has given way to charm everywhere; for while the public realm may be great, it cannot be charming precisely because it is unable to harbor the irrelevant.

Second, the term "public" signifies the world itself, in so far as it is common to all of us and distinguished from our privately owned place in it. This world, however, is not identical with the earth or with nature, as the limited space for the movement of men and the general condition of organic life. It is related, rather, to the human artifact, the fabricaton of human hands, as well as to affairs which go on among those who inhabit the man-made world together. To live together in the world means essentially that a world of things is between those who have it in common, as a table is located between those who sit around it; the world, like every in-between, relates and separates men at the same time.

The public realm, as the common world, gathers us together and yet prevents our falling over each other, so to speak. What makes mass society so difficult to bear is not the number of people involved, or at least not primarily, but the fact that the world between them has lost its power to gather them together, to relate and to separate them. The weirdness of this situation resembles a spiritualistic séance where a number of people gathered around a table might suddenly, through some magic trick, see the table vanish from their midst, so that two persons sitting opposite each other were no longer separated but also would be entirely unrelated to each other by anything tangible.

Historically, we know of only one principle that was ever devised to keep a community of people together who had lost their interest in the common world and felt themselves no longer related and separated by it. To find a bond between people strong enough to replace the world was the main political task of early Christian philosophy, and it was Augustine who proposed to found not only the Christian "brotherhood" but all human relationships on charity. But this charity, though its worldlessness clearly corresponds to the general human experience of love, is at the same time clearly distinguished from it in being something which, like the world, is between men: "Even robbers have between them [*inter se*] what they call charity." This surprising illustration of the Christian political principle is in fact very well chosen, because the bond of charity between people, while it is incapable of founding a public realm of its own, is quite adequate to the main Christian principle of worldlessness and is admirably fit to carry a group of essentially worldless people through the world, a group of saints or a group of criminals, provided only it is understood that the world itself is doomed and that every activity in it is undertaken with the proviso *quamdiu mundus durat* ("as long as the world lasts"). The unpolitical, non-public character of the Christian community was early defined in the demand that it should form a *corpus*, a "body," whose members were to be related to each other like brothers of the same family. The structure of communal life was modeled on the relationships between the members of a family because these were known to be non-political and even antipolitical. A public realm had never come into being between the members of a family, and it was therefore not likely to develop from Christian community life if this life was ruled by the principle of charity and nothing else. Even then, as we know from the history and the rules of the monastic orders—the only communities in which the principle of charity as a political device was ever tried—the danger that the activities undertaken under "the necessity of present life" (*necessitas vitae praesentis*) would lead by themselves, because they were performed in the presence of others, to the establishment of a kind of counterworld, a public realm within the orders themselves, was great enough to require additional rules and regulations, the most relevant one in our context being the prohibition of excellence and its subsequent pride.

Worldlessness as a political phenomenon is possible only on the assumption that the world will not last; on this assumption, however, it is almost inevitable that worldlessness, in one form or another, will begin to dominate the political scene. This happened after the downfall of the Roman Empire and, albeit for quite other reasons and in very different, perhaps even more disconsolate forms, it seems to happen again in our own days. The Christian abstention from worldly things is by no means the only conclusion one can draw from the conviction that the human artifice, a product of mortal hands, is as mortal as its makers. This, on the contrary, may also intensify the enjoyment and consumption of the things of the world, all manners of intercourse in which the world is not primarily understood to be the *koinon*, that which is common to all. Only the existence of a public realm and the world's subsequent transformation into a community of things which gathers men together and relates them to each other depends entirely on permanence. If the world is to contain a public space, it cannot be erected for one generation and planned for the living only; it must transcend the life-span of mortal men.

Without this transcendence into a potential earthly immortality, no politics, strictly speaking, no common world and no public realm, is possible. For unlike the common good as Christianity understood it—the salvation of one's soul as a concern common to all—the common world is what we enter when we are born and what we leave behind when we die. It transcends our lifespan into past and future alike; it was there before we came and will outlast our brief sojourn in it. It is what we have in common not only with those who live with us, but also with those who were here before and with those who will come after us. But such a common world can survive the coming and going of the generations only to the extent that it appears in

public. It is the publicity of the public realm which can absorb and make shine through the centuries whatever men
may want to save from the natural ruin of time. Through
many ages before us—but now not any more—men entered the public realm because they wanted something of
their own or something they had in common with others to
be more permanent than their earthly lives. (Thus, the
curse of slavery consisted not only in being deprived of
freedom and of visibility, but also in the fear of these obscure people themselves "that from being obscure they
should pass away leaving no trace that they have existed.") There is perhaps no clearer testimony to the loss
of the public realm in the modern age than the almost complete loss of authentic concern with immortality, a loss
somewhat overshadowed by the simultaneous loss of the
metaphysical concern with eternity. The latter, being the
concern of the philosophers and the *vita contemplativa*,
must remain outside our present considerations. But the
former is testified to by the current classification of striving
for immortality with the private vice of vanity. Under modern conditions, it is indeed so unlikely that anybody
should earnestly aspire to an earthly immortality that we
probably are justified in thinking it is nothing but vanity.

The famous passage in Aristotle, "Considering human
affairs, one must not . . . consider man as he is and not
consider what is mortal in mortal things, but think about
them [only] to the extent that they have the possibility of
immortalizing," occurs very properly in his political writings. For the *polis* was for the Greeks, as the *res publica* was
for the Romans, first of all their guarantee against the futility of individual life, the space protected against this futility and reserved for the relative permanence, if not immortality, of mortals.

What the modern age thought of the public realm, after the spectacular rise of society to public prominence,
was expressed by Adam Smith when, with disarming sin-
cerity, he mentions "that unprosperous race of men commonly called men of letters" for whom "public admiration
. . . makes always a part of their reward . . . , a considerable part . . . in the profession of physic; a still greater perhaps in that of law; in poetry and philosophy it makes almost the whole." Here it is self-evident that public
admiration and monetary reward are of the same nature

and can become substitutes for each other. Public admiration, too, is something to be used and consumed, and status, as we would say today, fulfils one need as food fulfils another: public admiration is consumed by individual vanity as food is consumed by hunger. Obviously, from this viewpoint the test of reality does not lie in the public presence of others, but rather in the greater or lesser urgency of needs to whose existence or non-existence nobody can ever testify except the one who happens to suffer them. And since the need for food has its demonstrable basis of reality in the life process itself, it is also obvious that the entirely subjective pangs of hunger are more real than "vainglory," as Hobbes used to call the need for public admiration. Yet, even if these needs, through some miracle of sympathy, were shared by others, their very futility would prevent their ever establishing anything so solid and durable as a common world. The point then is not that there is a lack of public admiration for poetry and philosophy in the modern world, but that such admiration does not constitute a space in which things are saved from destruction by time. The futility of public admiration, which daily is consumed in ever greater quantities, on the contrary, is such that monetary reward, one of the most futile things there is, can become more "objective" and more real.

As distinguished from this "objectivity," whose only basis is money as a common denominator for the fulfilment of all needs, the reality of the public realm relies on the simultaneous presence of innumerable perspectives and aspects in which the common world presents itself and for which no common measurement or denominator can ever be devised. For though the common world is the common meeting ground of all, those who are present have different locations in it, and the location of one can no more coincide with the location of another than the location of two objects. Being seen and being heard by others derive their significance from the fact that everybody sees and hears from a different position. This is the meaning of public life, compared to which even the richest and most satisfying family life can offer only the prolongation or multiplication of one's own position with its attending aspects and perspectives. The subjectivity of privacy can be prolonged and multiplied in a family, it can even become so strong that its weight is felt in the public realm; but this family "world" can never replace the reality rising out of the sum total of aspects presented by one object to a multitude of spectators. Only where things can be seen by many in a variety of aspects without changing their identity, so that those who are gathered around them know they see sameness in utter diversity, can worldly reality truly and reliably appear.

Under the conditions of a common world, reality is not guaranteed primarily by the "common nature" of all men who constitute it, but rather by the fact that, differences of position and the resulting variety of perspectives notwithstanding, everybody is always concerned with the same object. If the sameness of the object can no longer be discerned, no common nature of men, least of all the unnatural conformism of a mass society, can prevent the destruction of the common world, which is usually preceded by the destruction of the many aspects in which it presents itself to human plurality. This can happen under conditions of radical isolation, where nobody can any longer agree with anybody else, as is usually the case in tyrannies. But it may also happen under conditions of mass society or mass hysteria, where we see all people suddenly behave as though they were members of one family, each multiplying and prolonging the perspective of his neighbor. In both instances, men have become entirely private, that is, they have been deprived of seeing and hearing others, of being seen and being heard by them. They are all imprisoned in the subjectivity of their own singular experience, which does not cease to be singular if the same experience is multiplied innumerable times. The end of the common world has come when it is seen only under one aspect and is permitted to present itself in only one perspective.

2

Public Space and the Classical Vernacular

ROGER SCRUTON

A consideration of "public space" should begin by defining terms. Contained within this pair of words are two
ideas of the utmost importance—that of public-ness and
that of space—and it is arguable that a failure to understand them has been responsible for many of the recent disasters in town planning, both in Europe and in America.

The public is to be contrasted with the private. In the
private sphere a man is his own master, within the limits
prescribed for him by morality and law. At the same time,
and paradoxically, he is closely constrained by domestic
circumstances. His projects, rhythm, time, and companionship reflect the immediate demands of intimacy and
the obligations of family life. In public he may breathe
more freely, but in private the needs of his spouse, parents, and children tie him by an overriding law.

The public is a sphere of broad and largely unplanned
encounter. No individual is sovereign in this sphere, but
each, on entering it, renounces the right to dictate the
terms upon which he communes and conflicts with others.
His projects are subject, not to the discipline of domestic

From The Public Interest, *Winter 1984, pp. 5–16. Copyright © 1984 by*
National Affairs, Inc.

affection, but to the vacillating opposition of adversaries and fools. His time and rhythm are to a great extent his own, but they are also forced into a flexibility which they need not otherwise acquire. If a person is to advance in the public sphere it is either in opposition to others, or in agreement with them. The purpose of civil government is to ensure that agreement is the norm.

In *The Philosophy of Right*, Hegel drew a contrast between family and civil society, arguing that each is necessary to the development of the individual, and that neither is complete until fully embodied in the impartial legislation of a state. In the family the ruling principle is piety: respect, love, and obedience towards the spirit of the hearth. My family exists only partly by my choice, and forms the immovable condition of my existence. The love that I owe to it stems, not from contract, but from the obligations of human gratitude. By contrast, civil society is the sphere of choice, and its ruling principle is contract or agreement—the faculty whereby we move peaceably among our fellows, making concessions, earning advantages, and agreeing on terms.

On the basis of that distinction, we may add further substance to the idea of the public. In entering the public sphere, the individual exchanges the security, inevitability, and obligation of family life for the uncertainty and fluidity of civil society. In this realm the individual cannot be sovereign, and he moves in a world resistant to his purposes. At the same time he enjoys a freedom that he cannot enjoy in private. The immovable obligations of the hearth are replaced by the wayward and transient obligations of contract, through which the individual secures the cooperation of strangers in the ends and means of his existence.

The public world can exist only if sustained by the assent of those who enter it, and by a prescriptive state strong enough to resolve conflicts. Civil society therefore requires both the state, which administers justice, and the virtue in the common citizen that makes government possible. People must abide by the norms of justice, and treat one another, in Kant's famous words, "not as means only, but also as ends." The most important sign that they are prepared to do this is their obedience to a code of manners. Good manners are the formalized expression of the ruling virtue of civil society—the virtue of ''respect for persons,'' as agents able freely to bind themselves to strangers, despite, and because of, the fact that they owe no debt of gratitude or love. Another name for this virtue is ''civility.'' Civility is the essential condition for the building of a public world.

In sketching the distinction between the private and the public I have used political concepts, for the distinction is to be understood in political terms. What I have said is of course contentious, but I hope that it serves to suggest that the idea of the public is not only complex, but also essential to a full understanding of the human condition. Architecture, which draws in tangible forms the boundary between the private and the public, is therefore a major component of political order, which leaves indelible marks upon the civil society whose space it defines. It is, as Ruskin remarked in *The Seven Lamps of Architecture*, the most political of the arts. In what follows I shall discuss the ways in which architecture both defines the space of human action, and also endows that space with a public character.

CREATED SPACE VS. NATURAL SPACE

This brings me to the second term: ''space.'' This does not refer to the physical dimension studied by the geometer, which exists everywhere and in unlimited quantities. Nor does it refer simply to the space perceived and understood by human beings through observation and movement—the ''phenomenological space'' of the psychologist and the philosopher. It refers rather to the perceived boundaries, created by human labor, which mark out the areas of our world. A space is made public by the nature of its boundary. It is a space into which anyone may enter, and from which anyone may depart, without the consent of strangers, and without any declaration—however tacit—of a justifying purpose. The boundary which creates a public space is both permeable and open to our public uses. A truly public architecture is one which attempts to record and symbolize the condition of civil life, by reminding us at every juncture of our freedom to engage in it. It is an architecture which possesses the virtue of civility. We must attempt, therefore, to understand the kind of boundary which such an architecture erects.

The boundaries of the private are, in a sense, easier to define. They consist in shelter and protection, and in the intimate vigilance of inner walls. The inner walls of a house are the most important sign of the domestic life that takes place in it. The color scheme, pictures, and ornaments tell us how the occupant perceives the boundaries of the family. For some, these boundaries open into another, larger world. For others, they provide a mirror, which points always inward, to the security of home.

The boundaries of the public are more fluid and variable. Their purpose is not to bear the imprint of a single life, but to remain open to all life that may legitimately claim their protection. For the most part, a public space is confined by facades, external walls, and railings. However, one should not forget that most important of all public spaces, the church, mosque, or temple, in which an interior is devoted to public use and made open and available to all. In the church or mosque the roof is really the sky made close to us, and the walls move out from the worshipper, signifying not confinement, but the infinite vastness of God's creation. I shall be concerned not with public buildings, but with the spaces defined by their external walls. Hence I shall not comment on the use and design of churches. It should be borne in mind, therefore, that my remarks will be incomplete, and that I will have avoided one of the most important problems which confronts the architect of public space: the problem of the public *interior*. I shall consider only those public spaces which are also "outside." Furthermore, I shall refrain from discussing either squares or open markets, although, as will be seen, both are extremely pertinent to my theme. Instead I propose to concentrate on the street, as the most basic of public exteriors.

The wild countryside may be open to unlimited human movement, but it has no point of contact with the private world, no point at which to announce its public purpose. It is "unbounded," not because it goes on forever, but because its perimeter has no mark. Lacking a boundary, it lacks the character of public-ness, for it lacks social stigma altogether. Nature is neither private nor public, but merely beyond society.

Nevertheless, nature presents us with experiences that we cannot forgo. We may stroll in it, and our movements are not in any obvious way constricted by it; nor does it declare in all its features, "Private Property, Keep Out." We also long for nature, and are prepared to go far in order to reach it. As a result, there has emerged a very important idea of public space. According to this idea, which has been extremely influential in modern planning, a public space is primarily a substitute for nature. Under the baneful tutelage of Ebeneezer Howard, Lewis Mumford, and Le Corbusier, the park has become accepted as a paradigm; it is the area in the heart of a city where the citizen can walk freely. Underlying this idea is a peculiar view of civil association: Our primary civil need, it is supposed, is to escape from the pressures of others, and in the park we become free, by becoming free of others. We then commune effortlessly with the birds and the trees, refresh our weary faculties, and rid our systems of the physical and moral poison of urban life.

THE PRIMACY OF THE STREET

In a distinguished and familiar book, Jane Jacobs has argued that the emphasis on parks displays a concealed hostility to the city and its works.[1] The logical conclusion of this hostility—the tower block rising without neighbors out of a park without streets—was embraced by Le Corbusier, and preached to the world with an inflammatory rhetoric equal to that of Lenin and Hitler. The result lies everywhere about us—dead trodden wastes, crowned by concrete slums, places as unfriendly and dangerous as they are ugly, places, to put it succinctly, in which public life has been extinguished, and in which the partitions that secure what is private are no longer walls but barricades. I believe that the moral of Miss Jacobs's treatise must be learned by every architect and planner. Cities do indeed need public spaces. It is not *space*, however, but *public-ness* that is the principal requirement. Space does not become public merely by ceasing to be private, or by being provided in quantities that no private purpose requires. Moreover, when there is no public space, private space too is threatened.

People can live without parks, but not without streets; they can live without greenery, but not without accessible windows and doors. The street is the most important of open public spaces, and the task of constructing a street is the most important that any planner may face. Anyone who has studied the ruins of Ephesus or Pergae will quickly appreciate the immense energy and skill that the Romans devoted to this task. One may naturally doubt that the civic virtues which inspired the glories of Roman architecture, and which produced such a harmony between the private and the public in all aspects of government and law, could either be renewed or widely appreciated in our equalizing age. But it is important to see that the classical vernacular styles which the Romans perfected, and which have lasted until recent times, were, by their good manners, the greatest single reason for the existence in our cities of genuine public space. Everywhere, in Europe and America, the pedestrian confronts Roman architecture, whose forms and details speak a public language that he understands. In studying this language we shall gain insight into our subject. Its first important aspect is the street, construed as an assembly of facades.

Jane Jacobs has persuasively argued that the emphasis on parks, and the neglect of streets, is a product of a planning mentality. In order to grasp the problem, the planner divides human life into isolated functions. He then proceeds to ''decontaminate'' these functions, to isolate them one from the other, and to assign areas to each. The house, the street, the park, the industrial precinct—each becomes (in Le Corbusier's revealing word) a ''machine,'' for the satisfaction of some human use. Here you eat, there you shop, here you take exercise, there you rest. The result, however, is chaos. The individual retreats into that lonely apartment in the tower block which, being surrounded by no public world with which to contrast its inner isolation, cannot achieve the true security of private life. The private and the public are alike objective forms of moral order, but in this ''decontaminated'' world there can be no objective order. All is subjectivity, the isolated and unjustified ''I want,'' built upon itself in a thousand repetitions.

By contrast, Miss Jacobs tellingly describes the true life of the street—the diversity of functions and the tacit cooperation which people spontaneously achieve when doors and windows bring them into constant contact. The street has eyes which guard it, tongues which instruct it, hands which help it; it is a busy sphere of human understanding, whose perimeters are also the points of entry into private worlds. Naturally, there are good streets and bad streets, peaceful streets and violent streets. And the mere existence of a street can hardly suffice to guarantee the good behavior and social cooperation of its residents. Nevertheless, it is surely reasonable to suppose that, insofar as architecture has any role to play in supporting the social life of those who live with it, the street of congenial facades must inevitably offer more basic nourishment than the block of dead corridors.

PLANNING FOR SPONTANEITY

It is not difficult to see the parallel between Miss Jacobs's criticism of urban planning, and the modern criticisms of socialist planning—and it is worth emphasizing the common utopian inspiration that caused socialism and modern architecture to be, for a while, confused.[2] F.A. Hayek (who is, I think, the most thoroughgoing critic of the planned economy) argues in roughly the following way: The business of producing and distributing what is necessary for survival is a collective task, and can be successfully accomplished only with the help of collective knowledge.[3] This knowledge is not theoretical but practical; it consists in a myriad of responses and skills that, in motivating people to their own projects, secure also the advantage of society as a whole. The "tacit knowledge" of individuals is a social affair. It is stored, so to speak, in the spontaneous institutions of civil society, and in no institution more effectively than in that of the market. The participant in a free market is prompted spontaneously to act in a manner that secures the efficient transfer of goods. The tacit knowledge contained in this social institution could never be translated into a rational plan, for a plan must inevitably destroy the knowledge that it is meant to embody, by destroying the conditions for its exercise. The true failure of the planned economy is therefore epistemological: The plan pretends to a knowledge which it cannot embody, and which indeed cannot exist except in the concrete form of social practice.

It is not difficult to recognize in Hayek's description of the market a further embellishment of the Hegelian idea of society. Civil society is a sphere of spontaneous cooperation under contract. Contract here includes the multitude of hardly observable niceties of tacit agreement, whereby business is conducted between strangers. According to Hayek, this aspect of civil society depends upon a store of tacit knowledge which it also creates. And what is true of the market might be true of civil society generally. If that were so, then we could see Miss Jacobs's criticism of the "decontaminated" plan as reflecting a philosophy of the "public." The public order depends upon a complex pattern of practical knowledge. The attempt to embody this knowledge in a plan is doomed to failure, for the plan is epistemologically incompetent. The tacit knowledge upon which social order depends is lost, just so soon as that social order is broken down into disaggregated functions, and presented as a theoretical problem. Jacobs's critique then becomes, like Hayek's, a special case of the conservative critique of utopianism—the critique which originated in Burke's defense of "prejudice," and which culminated in theories of politics and economics which have at last gained common currency.

Many of Hayek's disciples have been tempted by his argument to conclude that it is better to have no planning whatsoever, and to consign our destiny to a regimen of "spontaneous" social interaction. This conclusion is, I believe, dangerous. The conditions of "spontaneous order" belong to an age when populations were small, immobile, uninstructed, and, above all, bound by a moral order that contained their ambitions within the limits of peaceful coexistence. These conditions no longer prevail. We must now apply our minds to the question of survival, and, although it is surely the height of folly to tamper with those natural institutions which the Hayekians defend, it is also equally foolish to consign our future entirely to their operation. A conscious effort must be made so as to defend a "spontaneous order" that can no longer defend itself. To think that our plans will inevitably destroy that order is to imagine that they must inevitably overreach their epistemological competence.

But this need not be so. Consider the skill of cycling. To know how to ride a bicycle is to possess a piece of practical knowledge which resides in the will and readiness of the body, and could not be acquired merely by studying the theory of the bicycle. At the same time, someone who studies the theory may learn to design a better bicycle— one that leads to the acquisition of better and more efficient skills. Thus practical and theoretical knowledge may coexist about a single theme, the second providing part of the foundation of the first.

Likewise there may be plans which attempt neither to displace practical knowledge, nor to make it explicit, but simply to understand and improve the conditions from which it grows. Indeed, there have been successful premeditations in which human ingenuity attempted to supplement the spontaneous order of social existence by providing more propitious circumstances for its exercise. No better example exists than the detailed plans exhibited by the streets of Ephesus and Pergae—plans motivated by the desire to provide a fitting background to civil life. What is required, I believe, is not the abolition of planning, but the abolition of the "planning mentality" which sees every problem in terms of a set of disaggregated tasks.

OUR "ALIENATED" CITIES

This "planning mentality" is deficient, not only for the reasons offered by Miss Jacobs, but for another, and perhaps deeper, reason. It sees the human world in terms of a clear dichotomy between ends and means. The "rational" plan is the one which involves the right choice of means to given ends. And the ends themselves are specified in functional terms. We need light, air, food, exercise. To each of these functions is assigned a mechanism for its fulfillment. This way of thinking causes the city itself to be divided up into ends and means. There are parks, theaters, churches, restaurants, in which our common purposes are accomplished. These, therefore, are the true public spaces, to which we proceed and in which we find our fulfillment. If the park has become so important in modern planning it is because of a libertarian idea of human ends. Ends must not be imposed on people. On the contrary, people must be free to discover them for themselves. The park, unlike the church, does not bear the imprint of any particular set of values. It is a place to which all may go and seek, in recreation, the peculiar satisfaction that they covet. The park is essentially "open to our uses," providing the background to every individual aim. In short, it is not so much a public space as an open arena, in which the modern individualist may roam freely, pursuing his private satisfactions. It is a place of "outdoor privacy"—or rather "subjectivity," since to call this privacy is once again to presuppose the constraints of an objective order.

Both the libertarian morality, and the underlying conception of rationality, serve to devalue the street. The street is seen essentially as a means, a conduit through which we proceed, either to other means (such as the place of work) or to our true ends, in park or theater or home. The most important feature of a street becomes its quality as a conduit. Does it permit easy, rapid circulation? The result of attempting to answer that question in the affirmative can be seen in acres of American cities—deserts stormed by squads of motor cars, in which the desire for easy circulation has, paradoxically, so increased the distances between every human objective as to confine people for hours on end in the forced privacy of a motor car. This solution was in fact recommended by Le Corbusier. The Real Presence of the *Ville Radieuse* is downtown Los Angeles.

It is the mark of rational beings that the ends of their conduct cannot be divorced from the means. Ends and means interpenetrate, and each rational activity can be seen, now as the one, now as the other. There are, of course, activities that are no more than means, and can be seen in no other way. These used to be called "drudgery," although deference to Marx requires us to use the expression "alienated labor." The correct "restoration of man to himself" is not the replacement of work by leisure, but the provision of better work—work which is not merely a means, but also an end. Such work, which treats the laborer as an end, has the virtue of civility. Similarly, the correct way to plan a street is not as a means of access to other things, but as an end in itself—a place that can be enjoyed for its own sake. The diversifying and mingling of functions that Miss Jacobs recommends may indeed form a part of this enterprise. Far more important, however, is the provision of a human boundary—walls and facades that lend themselves to human purposes, and can be perceived immediately in human terms. The classical idiom is devoted to the perfection of civil boundaries. It is an idiom of facades, junctures, and progressions. It defines space effectively, precisely because it is in itself something more than space, something more than the abstract language of geometry.

LONDON AND THE CLASSICAL VERNACULAR

By "classical" I mean the pattern-book vernacular which we have inherited directly from eighteenth-century building, and indirectly from Rome. The purpose of the pattern book was to solve the problems of the wall: what size and shape of aperture, what divisions, mouldings and string courses, what architraves, porticoes, and keystones. The idea was simple: The builder adopted a repeatable vocabulary of recognizable forms, each with an established visual meaning. He was thereby able to fit houses, shops and factories neatly together, so as to soothe the eye of the pedestrian, and retain a reassuring human vigilance in the street. Now, the most important part of every building is the facade, since this is the part which everyone may see. The classical idiom generates facades in conformity with the elementary rules of politeness.[4] The resulting street invariably has the character of a public space, in which people are encouraged to linger at will, for it has the character of civility.

The classical idiom does not so much impose unity, as make diversity agreeable. The London street in which I live contains houses of every shape and size, arranged behind facades that stand politely beside one another. The porticoes are identical, as are the window frames—each being cobbled together from standard parts. No house obtrudes into the path of the pedestrian, but each meets the pavement with obvious signs of welcome. The windows, crowned by moulded architraves, have that kind of half-smiling look which permits you to glance into them; the flight of steps softens the approach to the door, and provides a useful area of neutral ground between the public and the private; the portico shelters the visitor, and also alerts him to the proportions of the interior hall. The walls fall into the areas protected by heavy iron railings. These railings provide pleasant knobs which people clutch as they stand in conversation, and upon which children hang in play. At the corner of the block stands a house without an area; here the wall joins the pavement through a lightly moulded skirting, which protects the stucco and creates an agreeable fugue of parallel lines. The English are not given to sitting on doorsteps, or to standing about. Nevertheless, their movements in this street have a markedly leisurely quality, and when, as on the occasion of Prince Charles's marriage, we gathered together for a party, the orderly windows and the porticoes seemed to provide protection, and endowed our comings and goings with a naturalness that they could hardly have acquired in a park, or in any other place that was not so agreeably overlooked by accessible entrances.

Around me are many such streets, built on the edge of Kensington Park. My walks take me, not into the park—although let me not disparage it—but into these streets, which have so inexhaustible a fascination for a Londoner. It is not so much the human life and human opportunities that are attractive—although these are present in abundance. It is the architecture, which retains a human presence around all who walk before its walls. These vital and vivid boundaries create a vital and vivid space. The politeness of the style—the refusal to outrage or to defy—reminds one constantly of the ideal condition of society, in which people seek not to confront but to cooperate, and in which conversation takes the place of command. Walls, which divide space, also create it. And it is the discipline of the wall which is the pride of the classical vernacular. We linger where walls invite us, and hurry where they exclude us. Plate glass facades leave us over-exposed to observation from those behind them. Blank concrete screens seal us off from whatever they contain. A street must avoid all such extremes. It must provide us with walls that are pierced, and openings that are civil and friendly.

North Kensington was not planned—or at least it was planned only in the most rudimentary fashion. Beyond Kensington Park there are few public spaces in the modern planner's sense of the term—only long strings of streets like mine, clustered around Ladbroke Grove and Portobello Road, some with large communal gardens, some devoid of vegetation altogether. Yet this part of London is eminently public. It has lent itself to every form of human industry, both commerce and manufacture. It has also lent itself to human leisure. At the moment of writing, it is invaded by the annual carnival. Blacks from all the London Boroughs ride through the streets in colorful floats, and fill the air with the sound of steel bands. These streets are frequented in equal measure by the aimless and the purposeful, for they are bounded by surfaces that concede the validity of civil life. The classical wall, which is humanly proportioned, safe, gregarious, and quietly vigilant, constantly reminds the pedestrian that he is not alone, that he is in a world of human encounter, and that he must match the good manners of the wall which confines and guides him.

NOTES

1. Jane Jacobs, *The Death and Life of Great American Cities* (New York: Random House, 1961).

2. Consider in particular the "socialist" inspiration of Ebeneezer Howard's "Garden City," and the far more sinister Leninism of the Bauhaus, and in particular of its second director, Hannes Meyer. See Andrew Saint, *The Image of the Architect* (New Haven: Yale University Press, 1983), chap. 6.

3. F.A. Hayek, *Studies in Philosophy, Politics and Economics* (New York: Simon and Schuster, 1974). The argument is conveniently summarized by John Gray, "Hayek as a Conservative Thinker," *Salisbury Review* 4 (Summer, 1983).

4. See A. Trystan Edwards, *Good and Bad Manners in Architecture* (London: Philip Allen, 1924), especially chap. 1, "Civic Values."

3

The Public Domain

RICHARD SENNETT

Modern times are often compared to the years the Roman Empire went into decline: Just as moral rottenness is supposed to have sapped Rome's power to rule the West, it is said to have sapped the modern West's power to rule the globe. For all the silliness of this notion, it contains an element of truth. There is a rough parallel between the crisis of Roman society after the death of Augustus and present-day life; it concerns the balance between public and private life.

As the Augustan Age faded, Romans began to treat their public lives as a matter of formal obligation. The public ceremonies, the military necessities of imperialism, the ritual contacts with other Romans outside the family circle, all became duties—duties in which the Roman participated more and more in a passive spirit, conforming to the rule of the *res publica*, but investing less and less passion in his acts of conformity. As the Roman's public life became bloodless, he sought in private a new focus for his emotional energies, a new principle of commitment and belief. This private commitment was mystic, concerned with escaping the world at large and the formalities of the *res publica* as part of that world. This commitment was to various Near Eastern sects, of which Christianity gradually be-

From Richard Sennett, The Fall of Public Man *(New York: Knopf, 1977), pp. 3–5, 12–17. Copyright ©1974, 1976 by Richard Sennett. Reprinted by permission of Alfred A. Knopf, Inc.*

came dominant; eventually Christianity ceased to be a spiritual commitment practiced in secret, burst into the world, and became itself a new principle of public order.

Today, public life has also become a matter of formal obligation. Most citizens approach their dealings with the state in a spirit of resigned acquiescence, but this public enervation is in its scope much broader than political affairs. Manners and ritual interchanges with strangers are looked on as at best formal and dry, at worst as phony. The stranger himself is a threatening figure, and few people can take great pleasure in that world of strangers, the cosmopolitan city. A *res publica* stands in general for those bonds of association and mutual commitment which exist between people who are not joined together by ties of family or intimate association; it is the bond of a crowd, of a ''people,'' of a polity, rather than the bonds of family or friends. As in Roman times, participation in the *res publica* today is most often a matter of going along, and the forums for this public life, like the city, are in a state of decay.

The difference between the Roman past and the modern present lies in the alternative, in what privacy means. The Roman in private sought another principle to set against the public, a principle based on religious transcendence of the world. In private we seek out not a principle but a reflection, that of what our psyches are, what is authentic in our feelings. We have tried to make the fact of being in private, alone with ourselves and with family and intimate friends, an end in itself.

Modern ideas about the psychology of this private life are confused. Few people today would claim that their psychic life arises by spontaneous generation, independent of social conditions and environmental influences. Nevertheless, the psyche is treated as though it has an inner life of its own. This psychic life is seen as so precious and so delicate that it will wither if exposed to the harsh realities of the social world, and will flower only to the extent that it is protected and isolated. Each person's self has become his principal burden; to know oneself has become an end, instead of a means through which one knows the world. And precisely because we are so self-absorbed, it is extremely difficult for us to arrive at a private principle, to give any clear account to ourselves or to others of what our personalities are. The reason is that, the more privatized the psyche, the less it is stimulated, and the more difficult it is for us to feel or to express feeling.

The post-Augustan Roman's pursuit of his private, Oriental gods was separated in his mind from the public world. He finally imposed those gods upon the public world, by subjugating military law and social custom to a higher, clearly different principle. Under the modern code of private meaning, the relations between impersonal and intimate experience have no such clarity. We see society itself as "meaningful" only by converting it into a grand psychic system. We may understand that a politician's job is to draft or execute legislation, but that work does not interest us until we perceive the play of personality in political struggle. A political leader running for office is spoken of as "credible" or "legitimate" in terms of what kind of man he is, rather than in terms of the actions or programs he espouses. The obsession with persons at the expense of more impersonal social relations is like a filter which discolors our rational understanding of society; it obscures the continuing importance of class in advanced industrial society; it leads us to believe community is an act of mutual self-disclosure and to undervalue the community relations of strangers, particularly those which occur in cities. Ironically, this psychological vision also inhibits the development of basic personality strengths, like respect for the privacy of others, or the comprehension that, because every self is in some measure a cabinet of horrors, civilized relations between selves can only proceed to the extent that nasty little secrets of desire, greed, or envy are kept locked up.

The advent of modern psychology, and of psychoanalysis in particular, was founded on the faith that in understanding the inner workings of the self *sui generis,* without transcendental ideas of evil or of sin, people might free themselves from these horrors and be liberated to participate more fully and rationally in a life outside the boundaries of their own desires. Masses of people are concerned with their single life-histories and particular emotions as never before; this concern has proved to be a trap rather than a liberation. . . .

In a sense, I am turning around the argument David Riesman made in *The Lonely Crowd.* Riesman contrasted an inner-directed society, in which men pursued actions and made commitments based on goals and sentiments they felt within themselves, to an other-directed society, in which these passions and commitments depend on what people sense to be the feelings of others. Riesman believed American society, and in its wake Western Europe, was moving from an inner- to an other-directed condition. The sequence should be reversed. Western societies are moving from something like an other-directed condition to an inner-directed condition—except that in the midst of self-absorption no one can say what is inside. As a result, confusion has arisen between public and intimate life; people are working out in terms of personal feelings public matters which properly can be dealt with only through codes of impersonal meaning. . . .

AN ILLUSTRATION: DEAD PUBLIC SPACE

Intimate vision is induced in proportion as the public domain is abandoned as empty. On the most physical level, the environment prompts people to think of the public domain as meaningless. This is in the organization of space in cities. Architects who design skyscrapers and other large-scale, high-density buildings are among the few professionals who are forced to work with present-day ideas of public life, such as they are, and indeed are among the few professionals who of necessity express and make these codes manifest to others.

One of the first pure International School skyscrapers built after World War II was Gordon Bunshaft's Lever House on Park Avenue in New York. The ground floor of Lever House is an open-air square, a courtyard with a tower rising on the north side, and, one story above the ground, a low structure surrounding the other three sides. But one passes from the street underneath this low horseshoe to penetrate to the courtyard; the street level itself is dead space. No diversity of activity takes place on the ground floor; it is only a means of passage to the interior. The form of this International-type skyscraper is at odds with its function, for a miniature public square revivified is declared in form, but the function destroys the nature of a public square, which is to intermix persons and diverse activities.

This contradiction is part of a greater clash. The International School was dedicated to a new idea of visibility in the construction of large buildings. Walls almost entirely of glass, framed with thin steel supports, allow the inside and the outside of a building to be dissolved to the least point of differentiation; this technology permits the achievement of what S. Giedion calls the ideal of the permeable wall, the ultimate in visibility. But these walls are also hermetic barriers. Lever House was the forerunner of a design concept in which the wall, though permeable, also isolates the activities within the building from the life of the street. In this design concept, the aesthetics of visibility and social isolation merge.

The paradox of isolation in the midst of visibility is not unique to New York, nor are the special problems of crime in New York a sufficient explanation of the deadness of public space in such a design. In the Brunswick Centre built in the Bloomsbury section of London and in the Defense office complex being built on the edge of Paris, the same paradox is at work, and results in the same dead public area.

In the Brunswick Centre two enormous apartment complexes rise away from a central concrete concourse; the apartment buildings are stepped back story after story, so that each looks like a Babylonian terrace city sited on a hill. The terraces of the Brunswick Centre apartments are covered in glass for the most part; thus the apartment dweller has a greenhouse wall letting in a great deal of light and breaking down the barrier between inside and outside. This permeation of the house and the outside is curiously abstract; one has a nice sense of the sky, but the buildings are so angled that they have no relationship to, or view out on, the surrounding buildings of Bloomsbury. Indeed, the rear end of one of the apartment blocks, faced in solid concrete, gives on, or rather ignores, one of the most beautiful squares in all of London. The building is sited as though it could be anywhere, which is to say siting shows its designers had no sense of being anywhere in particular, much less in an extraordinary urban milieu.

The real lesson of Brunswick Centre is contained in its central concourse. Here there are a few shops and vast areas of empty space. Here is an area to pass through, not to use; to sit on one of the few concrete benches in the concourse for any length of time is to become profoundly uncomfortable, as though one were on exhibit in a vast empty hall. The ''public'' concourse itself is raised several feet above street level. Everything has been done, again, to isolate the public area of Brunswick Centre from accidental street incursion, or from simple strolling, just as the siting of the two apartment blocks effectively isolates those who inhabit them, from street, concourse, and square. The visual statement made by the detailing of the greenhouse wall is that the inside and the outside of a dwelling have no differentiation; the social statement made by the concourse, the siting of the complex, and the ramps is that an immense barrier separates "within" the Brunswick Centre from "without."

The erasure of a live public space contains an even more perverse idea—that of making space contingent upon motion. In the Defense Center, as with Lever House and Brunswick Centre, the public space is an area to move through, not to be in. At Defense, the grounds around the mass of office towers which compose the complex contain a few stores, but the real purpose is to serve as a pass-through area from car or bus to office building. There is little evidence that the planners of Defense thought this space to have any intrinsic value, that people from the various office blocks might want to remain in it. The ground, in the words of one planner, is "the traffic-flow–support-nexus for the vertical whole." Translated, this means that the public space has become a derivative of movement.

The idea of space as derivative from motion parallels exactly the relations of space to motion produced by the private automobile. One does not use one's car to see the city; the automobile is not a vehicle for touring—or, rather, it is not used as such, except by joyriding adolescent drivers. The car instead gives freedom of movement; one can travel, uninhibited by formal stops, as in the subway, without changing one's mode of motion, from bus, subway, or elevated to pedestrian movement, in making a journey from place A to place B. The city street acquires, then, a peculiar function—to permit motion; if it regulates motion too much, by lights, one-ways, and the like, motorists become nervous or angry.

Today, we experience an ease of motion unknown to any prior urban civilization, and yet motion has become the most anxiety-laden of daily activities. The anxiety comes from the fact that we take unrestricted motion of the individual to be an absolute right. The private motorcar is the logical instrument for exercising that right, and the effect on public space, especially the space of urban street, is that the space becomes meaningless or even maddening unless it can be subordinated to free movement. The technology of modern motion replaces being in the street with a desire to erase the constraints of geography.

Thus does the design concept of a Defense or a Lever House coalesce with the technology of transportation. In both, as public space becomes a function of motion, it loses any independent experiential meaning of its own.

"Isolation" has so far been used in two senses. First, it means that the inhabitants or workers in an urban high-density structure are inhibited from feeling any relationship to the milieu in which that structure is set. Second, it means that as one can isolate oneself, in a private automobile, for freedom of movement, one ceases to believe one's surroundings have any meanings save as a means toward the end of one's own motion. There is a third, rather more brutal sense of social isolation in public places, an isolation directly produced by one's visibility to others.

The design idea of the permeable wall is applied by many architects within their buildings as well as on the skin. Visual barriers are destroyed by doing away with office walls, so that whole floors will become one vast open space, or there will be a set of private offices on the perimeter with a large open area within. This destruction of walls, office planners are quick to say, increases office efficiency, because when people are all day long visually exposed to one another, they are less likely to gossip and chat, more likely to keep to themselves. When everyone has each other under surveillance, sociability decreases, silence being the only form of protection. The open-floor office plan brings the paradox of visibility and isolation to its height, a paradox which can also be stated in reverse. People are more sociable, the more they have some tangible barriers between them, just as they need specific places in public whose sole purpose is to bring them together. Let us put this another way again: Human beings need to have some distance from intimate observation by others in order to feel sociable. Increase intimate contact and you decrease sociability. Here is the logic of one form of bureaucratic efficiency.

Dead public space is one reason, the most concrete one, that people will seek out on intimate terrain what is denied them on more alien ground. Isolation in the midst of public visibility and overemphasis on psychological transactions complement each other. To the extent, for instance, that a person feels he must protect himself from the surveillance of others in the public realm by silent isolation, he compensates by baring himself to those with whom he wants to make contact. The complementary relation exists because here are two expressions of a single, general transformation of social relations. . . .

THE CHANGES IN THE PUBLIC DOMAIN

The history of the words "public" and "private" is a key to understanding this basic shift in the terms of Western culture. The first recorded uses of the word "public" in English identify the "public" with the common good in society; in 1470, for instance, Malory spoke of "the emperor Lucyos . . . dictatour or procurour of the publyke wele of Rome." Some seventy years later, there was added a sense of "public" as that which is manifest and open to general observation. Hall wrote in his *Chronicle* of 1542, "Their inwarde grudge could not refrayne but crye out in places publicke, and also private." "Private" was here used to mean privileged, at a high governmental level. By the end of the 17th Century, the opposition of "public" and "private" was shaded more like the way the terms are now used. "Public" meant open to the scrutiny of anyone, whereas "private" meant a sheltered region of life defined by one's family and friends; thus Steele, in an issue of the *Tatler* in 1709, "These effects . . . upon the publick and private actions of men," and Butler in the *Sermons* (1726), "Every man is to be considered in two capacities, the private and the publick." To go "out in publick" (Swift) is a phrase based on society conceived in terms of this geography. The older senses are not entirely lost today in English, but this 18th Century usage sets up the modern terms of reference.

The meanings accorded *le public* in French show something similar. Renaissance use of the word was largely in terms of the common good and the body politic; gradually *le public* became also a special region of sociability. Erich Auerbach once made a thorough study of this more modern definition of "the public," first appearing in France in the middle of the 17th Century, as it was related to the public that was the audience for plays. The theatrical public was referred to in the time of Louis XIV by the catch-phrase *la cour et la ville,* the court and the city. Auerbach discovered that this theatrical public in fact consisted of an elite group of people—an obvious finding in terms of court life, not so obvious in terms of urban life. *La ville* of 17th Century Paris was a very small group, whose origins were non-aristocratic and mercantile, but whose manners were directed to obscuring this fact, not only out of shame but in order to facilitate interchanges with the court.

The sense of who "the public" were, and where one was when one was out "in public," became enlarged in the early 18th Century in both Paris and London. Bourgeois people became less concerned to cover up their social origins; there were many more of them; the cities they inhabited were becoming a world in which widely diverse groups in society were coming into contact. By the time the word "public" had taken on its modern meaning, therefore, it meant not only a region of social life located apart from the realm of family and close friends, but also that this public realm of acquaintances and strangers included a relatively wide diversity of people.

There is a word logically associated with a diverse urban public, the word "cosmopolitan." A cosmopolite, in the French usage recorded in 1738, is a man who moves comfortably in diversity; he is comfortable in situations which have no links or parallels to what is familiar to him. The same sense of the word appeared in English earlier than in French, but was not much employed until the 18th Century. Given the new terms of being out in public, the cosmopolitan was the perfect public man. An early English usage foreshadowed the commonplace sense of the word in 18th Century bourgeois society. In one of Howell's *Letters* (1645), he wrote, "I came tumbling out into the World, a pure Cadet, a true Cosmopolite, or born to Land, Lease, House, or Office." Without inherited wealth or uninherited feudal obligation, the cosmopolitan, whatever his pleasure in worldly diversity, of necessity must make his way in it.

"Public" thus came to mean a life passed outside the life of family and close friends; in the public region diverse, complex social groups were to be brought into ineluctable contact. The focus of this public life was the capital city.

These changes in language were correlated with conditions of behavior and terms of belief in the 18th Century cosmopolis. As the cities grew, and developed networks of sociability independent of direct royal control, places where strangers might regularly meet grew up. This was the era of the building of massive urban parks, of the first attempts at making streets fit for the special purpose of pedestrian strolling as a form of relaxation. It was the era in which coffeehouses, then cafes and coaching inns, became social centers; in which the theater and opera houses became open to a wide public through the open sale of tickets rather than the older practice whereby aristocratic patrons distributed places. Urban amenities were diffused out from a small elite circle to a broader spectrum of society, so that even the laboring classes began to adopt some of the habits of sociability, like promenades in parks, which were formerly the exclusive province of the elite, walking in their private gardens or ''giving'' an evening at the theater.

In the realm of necessity as in the realm of leisure, patterns of social interaction grew up which were suited to exchange between strangers and did not depend on fixed feudal privileges or monopolistic control established by royal grant. The 18th Century urban market was unlike its late medieval or Renaissance predecessors; it was internally competitive, those selling in it vying for the attention of a shifting and largely unknown group of buyers. As the cash economy expanded and modes of credit, accounting, and investment became more rationalized, business was carried on in offices and shops and on an increasingly impersonal basis. It would, of course, be wrong to see either the economy or the sociability of these expanding cities replacing at a stroke older modes of business and pleasure. Rather they juxtaposed still-surviving modes of personal obligation with new modes of interaction, suited to a life passed amidst strangers under conditions of poorly regulated entrepreneurial expansion.

Nor would it be correct to imagine that forging a social bond suited to an expanding city and expanded bourgeois class was either painless or just. People anxiously sought to create modes of speech, even of dress, which would give order to the new urban situation, and also demarcate this life from the private domain to the new urban situation, and also demarcate this life from the private domain of family and friends. Often in their search for principles of public order they resorted to modes of speech, dress, or interaction logically suited to a vanishing era, and tried to force these modes to signify under new and antipathetic conditions. In the process many inequities of late medieval society, now transplanted to alien terrain, became all the more painful and oppressive. There is no need to romanticize the public life of the *ancien régime* cosmopolis to appreciate it; the attempt to create a social order in the midst of confusing and chaotic social conditions at one and the same time brought the contradictions of the *ancien régime* to a point of crisis and created positive opportunities for group life which have yet to be understood.

As in behavior, so in belief, the citizens of the 18th Century capitals attempted to define both what public life was and what it was not. The line drawn between public and private was essentially one on which the claims of civility—epitomized by cosmopolitan, public behavior—were balanced against the claims of nature—epitomized by the family. They saw these claims in conflict, and the complexity of their vision lay in that they refused to prefer the one over the other, but held the two in a state of equilibrium. Behaving with strangers in an emotionally satisfying way and yet remaining aloof from them was seen by the mid-18th Century as the means by which the human animal was transformed into a social being. The capacities for parenthood and deep friendship were seen in turn to be natural potentialities, rather than human creations; while man *made* himself in public, he *realized* his nature in the private realm, above all in his experiences within the family. The tensions between the claims of civility and the rights of nature, epitomized in the divide between public and private life in the cosmopolitan center, not only suffused the high culture of the era but extended into more mundane realms. These tensions appeared in manuals on child-rearing, tracts on moral obligation, and common-sense beliefs about the rights of man. Together, public and private created what would today be called a ''universe'' of social relations.

The struggle for public order in the 18th Century city, and the tension between the claims of public and private life, constituted the terms of a coherent culture, though there were, as there are in any period, exceptions, deviations, and alternative modes. But a balance of public and private geography in the Enlightenment did exist, and against it there stands out in relief the fundamental change in the ideas of public and private which followed upon the great revolutions at the end of the century and the rise of a national industrial capitalism in more modern times.

Three forces were at work in this change. They were, first, a double relationship which industrial capitalism in the 19th Century came to have with public life in the great city; second, a reformulation of secularism beginning in the 19th Century which affected how people interpret the strange and the unknown; third, a strength which became a weakness, built into the structure of public life itself in the *ancien régime*. This strength meant that public life did not die an instantaneous death under the weight of political and social upheaval at the end of the 18th Century. The public geography prolonged itself into the 19th Century, seemingly intact, in fact changing from within. This inheritance affected the new forces of secularism and capitalism as much as they were at work on it. The transformation of public life can be thought of as parallel to the collapse which comes to athletes who have been especially strong, so that they survive beyond youth with seemingly undiminished powers, and then all at once make manifest the decay which has been continuously eroding the body from within. Because of this peculiar form of survival, the signs of *ancien régime* publicness are not so far from modern life as might at first be imagined.

The double relation of industrial capitalism to urban public culture lay first in the pressures of privatization which capitalism aroused in 19th Century bourgeois society. It lay second in the ''mystification'' of material life in public, especially in the matter of clothes, caused by mass production and distribution.

The traumas of 19th Century capitalism led those who had the means to try to shield themselves in whatever way possible from the shocks of an economic order which neither victors nor victims understood. Gradually the will to control and shape the public order eroded, and people put more emphasis on protecting themselves from it. The family became one of these shields. During the 19th Century the family came to appear less and less the center of a particular, nonpublic region, more an idealized refuge, a world all of its own, with a higher moral value than the public realm. The bourgeois family was idealized as life wherein order and authority were unchallenged, security of material existence could be a concomitant of real marital love, and the transactions between members of the family would brook no outside scrutiny. As the family became a refuge from the terrors of society, it gradually became also a moral yardstick with which to measure the public realm of the capital city. Using family relations as a standard, people perceived the public domain not as a limited set of social relations, as in the Enlightenment, but instead saw public life as morally inferior. Privacy and stability appeared to be united in the family; against this ideal order the legitimacy of the public order was thrown into question.

Industrial capitalism was equally and directly at work on the material life of the public realm itself. For instance, the mass production of clothes, and the use of mass-production patterns by individual tailors or seamstresses, meant that many diverse segments of the cosmopolitan public began in gross to take on a similar appearance, that public markings were losing distinctive forms. Yet virtually no one believed that society was becoming thereby homogenized; the machine meant that social differences—important differences, necessary to know if one were to survive in a rapidly expanding milieu of strangers—were becoming hidden, and the stranger more intractably a mystery. The machine production of a wide variety of goods, sold for the first time in a mass-merchandising setting, the department store, succeeded with the public not through appeals to utility or cheap price, but rather by capitalizing on this mystification. Even as they became more uniform, physical goods were endowed in advertising with human qualities, made to seem tantalizing mysteries which had to be possessed to be understood. "Commodity fetishism," Marx called it; he was only one among many who were struck by the confluence of mass production, homogeneity of appearance, and yet the investing in material things of attributes or associations of intimate personality.

The interaction of capitalism and public geography thus pulled in two directions; one was withdrawal from the public into the family, the other was a new confusion about the materials of public appearance, a confusion

which, however, could be turned to a profit. It might therefore be tempting to conclude that industrial capitalism
alone caused the public realm to lose legitimacy and coher-
ence, but the conclusion would be inadmissible even on its
own terms. What after all prompted people to believe
these physical goods, so uniform, could have psychological associations? Why believe in a thing as though it were
human? The fact that this belief was profitable for a few
does not explain why it should be held by a multitude.

This question involves the second force which changes
the public life inherited from the *ancien régime,* a change in
the terms of belief about worldly life. This belief is secularity. As long as the secular is thought opposed in some way
to the sacred, the word becomes one-dimensional and
fixed. It is better used as the imagery and symbols which
make things and people in the world understandable. I
think the following definition best: secularity is the conviction before we die of why things are as they are, a conviction which will cease to matter of itself once we are dead.

Secular terms changed drastically from the 18th to the
19th Century. "Things and people" were understandable
in the 18th Century when they could be assigned a place in
the order of Nature. This order of Nature was not a physical, tangible thing, nor was the order ever encapsuled by
worldly things. A plant or a passion occupied a place in the
order of Nature but did not define it in miniature and
whole. The order of Nature was therefore an idea of the
secular as the transcendental. Not only did this idea per-
meate the writing of scientists and other intellectuals, it
reached into such daily affairs as attitudes toward the dis
cipline of children or the morality of extramarital affairs.

The secularism which arose in the 19th Century was of
a wholly antithetical sort. It was based on a code of the immanent, rather than the transcendent. Immediate sensation, immediate fact, immediate feeling, were no longer to
be fitted into a pre-existent scheme in order to be understood. The immanent, the instant, the fact, was reality in
and of itself. Facts were more believable than system—or,
rather, the logical array of facts became a system; the 18th
Century order of Nature in which phenomena had a place
but in which Nature transcended phenomena was thus
overturned. This new measure of what could serve as materials for belief ruled psychology as much as it ruled the

study of physical objects. By 1870 it appeared plausible to study ''an emotion'' as having a self-contained meaning, if one could find out all the tangible circumstances in which ''the emotion'' appeared and the tangible signs through which ''the emotion'' made itself manifest. No circumstance or sign could therefore be ruled out, a priori, as irrelevant. In a world where immanence is the principle of secular knowledge, everything counts because everything might count.

This restructuring of the code of secular knowledge had a radical effect on public life. It meant that appearances in public, no matter how mystifying, still had to be taken seriously, because they might be clues to the person hidden behind the mask. Any appearance a person made was in some way real, because it was tangible; indeed, if that appearance were a mystery, all the more reason for taking it seriously: on what grounds, a priori, would one put it out of mind, on what grounds discriminate? When a society dedicates itself to the principle of things having meanings in themselves, it thus introduces an element of profound self-doubt into its cognitive apparatus, for any exercise of discrimination may be a mistake. Thus arose one of the great and enriching contradictions of the 19th Century; even as people wanted to flee, to shut themselves up in a private, morally superior realm, they feared that arbitrarily classifying their experience into, say, public and private dimensions might be self-inflicted blindness.

To fantasize that physical objects had psychological dimensions became logical in this new secular order. When belief was governed by the principle of immanence, there broke down distinctions between perceiver and perceived, inside and outside, subject and object. If everything counts potentially, how am I to draw a line between what relates to my personal needs and what is impersonal, unrelated to the immediate realm of my experience? I must therefore draw no distinction between categories of objects and of sensations, because in distinguishing them I may be creating a false barrier. The celebration of objectivity and hard-headed commitment to fact so prominent a century ago, all in the name of Science, was in reality an unwitting preparation for the present era of radical subjectivity.

If the impact of industrial capitalism was to erode the sense of public life as a morally legitimate sphere, the impact of the new secularity was to erode this sphere by a contrary route, posing to mankind the dictum that nothing which arouses sensation, puzzlement, or simple notice may be excluded a priori from the realm of the private life of a person, or be bereft of some psychological quality important to discover. However, capitalism and secularism together still provide only an incomplete view of what agents of change were at work on the public domain, or rather a distorted picture. For the sum of these two forces would have added up to complete social and cognitive disaster. All the familiar catastrophic clichés—alienation, dissociation, etc.—would have to be trundled out. Indeed, if the story of how a public dimension was shattered stopped at this point, we should expect that there would have occurred among the bourgeoisie massive upheavals, political storms, and rages of a sort equal in passion, if different in substance, to those which socialists hoped would arise among the 19th Century urban proletariat.

The very extension of an established urban culture into the world of these new economic and ideological forces counterbalanced them, and maintained some semblance of order for a time in the midst of very painful and contradictory emotions. Historians promote blindness about this inheritance. When they speak of a revolution being a "watershed," or the coming of industrial capitalism as being a "revolution," they often suggest to the imagination of their readers that beforehand there was one society, that during the revolution society stopped, and that afterward a new society began. This is a view of human history based on the life cycle of the moth. Nowhere, unfortunately, has the chrysalis theory of human history reigned to worse effect than in the study of the city. Phrases like "the urban-industrial revolution" and "the capitalist metropolis" (employed by writers of contrary political views) both suggest that before the 19th Century the city was one thing, after capitalism or modernism did its work, entirely another. The error is more than that of failing to see how one condition of life blurs into another; it is a failure to understand both the reality of cultural survival and the problems this legacy, like any inheritance, creates in a new generation.

The bourgeoisie continued to believe that "out in public" people experienced sensations and human relations which one could not experience in any other social setting or context. The legacy of the *ancien régime* city was united to the privatizing impulses of industrial capitalism in another way. Out in public was where moral violation occurred and was tolerated; in public one could break the laws of respectability. If the private was a refuge from the terrors of society as a whole, a refuge created by idealizing the family, one could escape the burdens of this ideal by a special kind of experience, one passed among strangers, or, more importantly, among people determined to remain strangers to each other.

The public as an immoral domain meant rather different things to women and men. For women, it was where one risked losing virtue, dirtying oneself, being swept into ''a disorderly and heady swirl'' (Thackeray). The public and the idea of disgrace were closely allied. The public for a bourgeois man had a different moral tone. By going out, in public, or ''losing yourself in public,'' as the phrase occurred in ordinary speech a century ago, a man was able to withdraw from those very repressive and authoritarian features of respectability which were supposed to be incarnate in his person, as father and husband, in the home. So that for men, the immorality of public life was allied to an undercurrent of sensing immorality to be a region of freedom, rather than of simple disgrace, as it was for women. For instance, in the restaurants of the 19th Century, a lone, respectable woman dining with a group of men, even if her husband were present, would cause an overt sensation, whereas the dining out of a bourgeois man with a woman of lower station was tacitly but studiously avoided as a topic of conversation among any of those near to him. For this same reason, the extramarital liaisons of Victorian men were sometimes conducted more publicly than one would in retrospect imagine, because they occurred in a social space which continued to be far away from the family; they were ''outside,'' in a kind of moral limbo.

Moreover, by the middle of the last century, experience gained in the company of strangers came to seem a matter of urgent necessity in the formation of one's personality. One's personal strengths might not develop if one did not expose oneself to strangers—one might be too inexperienced, too naïve, to survive. In the child-rearing manuals and primers for juveniles of the 1870's or 1880's, we encounter again and again the contradictory themes of avoidance of worldly perils in the company of strangers and the command to learn so thoroughly the dangers of the world that one becomes strong enough to recognize these hidden temptations. In the *anciene régime,* public experience was connected to the formation of social order; in the last century, public experience came to be connected to the formation of personality. Worldly experience as an obligation for self-development appeared in the great monuments of the last century's culture, as well as in its more everyday codes of belief; the theme speaks in Balzac's *Illusions Perdues,* in Tocqueville's *Souvenirs,* in the works of the social Darwinists. This pervasive, painful, unreasonable theme was the conjunction of a surviving belief in the value of public experience with the new secular creed that all experiences may have an equal value because all have an equal, potential importance in forming the self.

We need finally to ask what hints we have in ordinary experience at the present time of the transformations which occurred in the last century. In what ways do seemingly abstract forces like privatization, commodity fetishism, or secularism bear upon our lives? Within the realm of current beliefs about personality itself, four of these connections with the past can be discerned.

THE PAST IN THE PRESENT

In ordinary language today, people speak of doing "unconsciously" or making an "unconscious" slip which reveals their true feelings to someone else. No matter that the usage is meaningless in any strict psychoanalytic sense. What it reveals is a belief in the involuntary disclosure of emotion, and that belief took form in the last century as the weighting of public and private life became imbalanced. By the end of the last century, the notion of the involuntary disclosure of character states showed itself most clearly in the flourishing practice of phrenology—the reading of character from the physical shape of the head—and the Bertillon measurements in criminology, by which psychologists attempted to identify future criminals through cranial and other physical traits. In both, what a person is psychologically was thought to show both physically and involuntarily; personality is a state not subject to

guided, sure shaping. In more refined notions, like that of
Darwin's, transitory emotional states were also thought to
be involuntarily disclosed; indeed, much early psychoanalytic investigation was based on a principle derived from
Darwin—namely, that primary process could be studied in
adults because it escaped adult control and will. At a
broader level, in the high Victorian era people believed
their clothes and their speech disclosed their personalities;
they feared that these signs were equally beyond their
power to mold, but would instead be manifest to others in
involuntary tricks of speech, body gesture, or even how
they adorned themselves.

The result was that the line between private feeling and
public display of it could be erased beyond the power of
the will to regulate. The boundary between public and private was no longer the work of a resolute human hand;
thus, even as the separate reality of the public realm remained believable, its governance no longer seemed a social act. What is today popularly misnamed "unconscious" behavior was foreshadowed by these ideas of
involuntary disclosure of character in public.

The second trace of the 19th Century crisis lies in ordinary political speech today. We are likely to describe as a
"credible" or "charismatic" or "believable" leader someone who can make appeals to groups whose interests are
alien to his own beliefs, constituency, or ideology. In modern politics it would be suicide for a leader to insist: Forget
about my private life; all you need to know about me is
how good a legislator or executive I am and what action I
intend to take in office. Instead, we get excited when a
conservative French President has dinner with a working-
class family, even though he has raised taxes on industrial
wages a few days before, or believe an American President
is more "genuine" and reliable than his disgraced predecessor because the new man cooks his own breakfast. This
political "credibility" is the superimposition of private
upon public imagery, and, again, it arose in the last century as a result of the behavioral and ideological confusions between these two realms.

Psychological imagery, it has already been noted, was
superimposed on things for sale in public. The same sort
of process began in the behavior or politicians in front of
street crowds, first strikingly manifest in the revolutions of

1848. What was perceived when people watched someone behave in public was his intentions, his character, so that the truth of what he said appeared to depend on what kind of person he was. If the person observed on these terms in public was a politician, this superimposition had a profoundly anti-ideological effect, in the pure political sense of that word. How can a view of social ills or the vision of a better society ever signify in and of itself, and motivate sustained action, if its believability depends on how much an audience at a given moment sympathizes with the character of the man who champions the cause? Under these conditions, the system of public expression became one of personal representation; a public figure presents to others what he feels, and it is this representation of his feeling which arouses belief. This superimposition of private upon public had a particularly strong appeal among bourgeois audiences, but to the extent that others lower in the social scale could be made to believe in its terms, there could occur class domination through the imposition of bourgeois canons of ''respect'' for a genuine personality. In short, the present-day ideas of ''authenticity'' in public have their root in an anti-ideological weapon, one which began to be used in the last century in the warfare between the classes.

The third connection involves the defense mechanisms people used one hundred years ago against their own belief in involuntary disclosure of character and against the superimposition of public and private imagery. By an odd route, these defenses came to encourage people to elevate artistic performers to the special status as public figures which they occupy today.

If one can't help showing what one feels, and if the truth of any emotion, statement, or argument in public depends on the character of the person speaking, how are people ever to avoid being fathomed? The only sure defense is to try to keep oneself from feeling, to have no feelings to show. Today, the repressiveness of Victorian society is condemned as a mixture of social snobbishness and sexual fear. But behind these motivations, there was something, if not more appealing, at least more understandable. In a milieu where sensation and feeling, once aroused, are thought to be displayed beyond the power of the will to conceal them, withdrawal from feeling is the only means of keeping some measure of invulnerability. For instance, people tried to shield their characters from others by wearing as little as possible jewelry, lace, or trimmings of an unusual kind, so as not to draw attention to themselves; this was one of the reasons why only a few machine dies for clothes were popular at any one time, although technically a variety of patterns might easily have been employed on the same machines.

At the same time that people sought to appear as unremarkable as possible, they began to demand that in the theater clothes be exact indicators of the characters, histories, and social positions of the *dramatis personae*. In the historical plays performed in midcentury, the actors were supposed to represent exactly what a medieval Danish prince or Roman imperator was supposed to look like; in melodrama, costume and stage gesture became so stylized that by looking at a man entering the stage with rapid, mincing steps you could instantly tell he was the villain before he had spoken a word. More generally, in a performing art, unlike life, one was to see a person strongly declared, see personality regnant. The actor and musician rose in social status far beyond the level of servanthood which they occupied in the *ancien régime*. The performer's social rise was based on his declaration of a forceful, exciting, morally suspect personality, wholly contrary to the style of ordinary bourgeois life, in which one tried to avoid being read as a person by suppressing one's feelings.

In this society on its way to becoming intimate—wherein character was expressed beyond the control of the will, the private was superimposed on the public, the defense against being read by others was to stop feeling—one's behavior in public was altered in its fundamental terms. Silence in public became the only way one could experience public life, especially street life, without feeling overwhelmed. In the mid-19th Century there grew up in Paris and London, and thence in other Western capitals, a pattern of behavior unlike what was known in London or Paris a century before, or is known in most of the non-Western world today. There grew up the notion that strangers had no right to speak to each other, that each man possessed as a public right an invisible shield, a right to be left alone. Public behavior was a matter of observation, of passive participation, of a certain kind of voyeurism. The "gastronomy of the eye," Balzac called it; one is open to everything, one rejects nothing a priori from one's purview, provided one needn't become a participant, enmeshed in a scene. This invisible wall of silence as a right meant that knowledge in public was a matter of observation—of scenes, of other men and women, of locales. Knowledge was no longer to be provided by social intercourse.

The paradox of visibility and isolation which haunts so much of modern public life originated in the right of silence in public which took form in the last century. Isolation in the midst of visibility to others was a logical consequence of insisting on one's right to be mute when one ventured into this chaotic yet still magnetic realm.

To speak of the legacy of the 19th Century's crisis of public life is to speak of broad forces such as capitalism and secularism on the one hand and of these four psychological conditions on the other: involuntary disclosure of character, superimposition of public and private imagery, defense through withdrawal, and silence. The obsessions with selfhood are attempts to work out these conundrums of the last century, by denial. Intimacy is an attempt to solve the public problem by denying that the public exits. As with any denial, this has only made the more destructive aspects of the past the more firmly entrenched. The 19th Century is not yet over.

4

Monuments and Plazas

CAMILLO SITTE

In the south of Europe and especially in Italy, where ancient cities have partially preserved their original layout and many civic customs have long survived unchanged—occasionally to the present—the public squares of cities have in many respects remained true to the type of the old forum down to modern times.

A considerable share of public life continued, after all, to take place in the plazas; because of this there persisted some measure of their public significance as well as many natural relationships between the squares and the monumental structures that framed them. The functions of the agora or forum on the one hand and the marketplace on the other were maintained—as was the desire to unite outstanding buildings at these major points in the city and to embellish these proud centers of the community with fountains, monuments, statues, other works of art, and tokens of historic fame. Plazas decorated in this sumptuous manner were still the pride and joy of the independent towns of the Middle Ages and Renaissance; here people

From George R. Collins and Christiane Crasemann Collins, Camillo Sitte: The Birth of Modern City Planning. *With a translation of the 1889 German edition of his* City Planning according to Artistic Principles *(New York: Rizzoli, 1986), pp. 151–154, 156–157, 185–190. Copyright © 1986 Rizzoli International Publications, Inc.*

trafficked, public celebrations took place, plays were put
on, state proceedings were carried out, laws proclaimed,
and so on. In Italy according to the size or importance of
the community two or three such principal squares, seldom only one, served these various practical purposes;
thus the distinction between ecclesiastical and secular authority (with which Antiquity had been unconcerned in
this connection) tended to find expression even in plazas.
As a result, there developed as independent types the cathedral square (usually including baptistery, campanile,
and bishop's palace), the secular main square (the Signoria) and, besides these two, the Mercato. The Signoria
functions as a forecourt for the princely residence and in
addition is surrounded with palaces of local grandees and
embellished with historic memorials and monuments. Frequently one finds a loggia for the bodyguards or municipal
guards developed architecturally in some fashion or other,
and combined with it or set up separately, an elevated terrace for promulgation of laws and for public announcements. We see the most handsome example of this in the
Loggia dei Lanzi in Florence. In the marketplace there
stands, almost without exception, the town hall—an arrangement which can also be observed in all towns north
of the Alps. A fountain with its basin, as grand as the
means will allow, is also never missing here; it often still
exists today as the "market fountain," although the gay
activities of vending have long since been shut up in the
glass-and-iron bird cage of a market hall.

All this, sketchily outlined, is witness to an active con-
tinuance of public life on open plazas. Indeed, artistic
treatment of this theme was attempted in these later times,
even up to the point of creating true works of art similar to
the Acropolis of Athens. The Piazza del Duomo in Pisa is
such a masterpiece of city building—an acropolis for Pisa
(Figure 1). Here is brought together everything that the
burghers of the town were able to produce in the way of
large-scale and lavish churchly art: the magnificent cathedral, the campanile, the baptistery, the incomparable
Campo Santo; anything profane or commonplace is excluded. This plaza, secluded from the world yet decked
out abundantly with the most noble works of the human
spirit, produces an overpowering effect; even a person of
moderate artistic sensibilities cannot escape the compel-

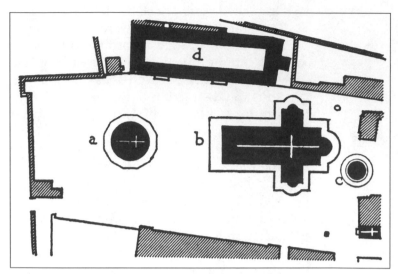

FIGURE 1. *Pisa: Piazza del Duomo, a. Baptistery—b. Cathedral—c. Leaning Tower —d. Campo Santo.*

ling and powerful impression it evokes. There is nothing here to distract our attention; nothing that reminds us of the daily hustle and bustle. In contemplating the venerable façade of the cathedral, we are not annoyed by any obtrusive little tailor shop, by the confusion of a café, or by the shouts of drivers and porters. Peace prevails, and the totality of effect assists our spirit to enjoy and comprehend the works of art accumulated in this place.

The purity of the cathedral square of Pisa is, to be sure, almost unique, although there are others that come close to it: the siting of San Francesco at Assisi, of the Certosa at Pavia, etc. In general, modern times are not exactly in favor of creating such pure chords, but prefer instead contrapuntal works, as it were. Thus the categories enumerated before (the cathedral square, the Signoria, and the marketplace), all too frequently merge together in every conceivable combination. The same thing occurs with city planning—even in the homeland of antique art—that happens with the palace and house. The last two do not continue to develop a single basic motif, but combine the archetype of the northern hall structure with that of the southern patio house. Ideas and stylistic tendencies mingle variously as soon as peoples themselves intermix; a feeling for the simple prototype becomes more and more lost. That which remained intact the longest was the institution of the market-place and its ever-present fountain as a constant adjunct to the town hall. It is well known how many splendid city views in the North are owing to this combination. . . .

A word of explanation is necessary at this point. In this investigation it is not our intention to recommend that every picturesque beauty of old town plans be used for modern purposes, because especially in this area the saying applies: "necessity breaks iron" [*Not bricht Eisen*]. That which is essential for hygienic or other compelling reasons has to be carried out, even at the cost of any number of pictorial motifs. But this in turn must not prevent us from studying carefully all features of the planning of old cities—even the merely picturesque—and establishing parallels to modern conditions. In this way we consider the problem from its artistic basis so that we can determine with certainty what might still be salvageable, and retainable as a heritage, of the beauties of old town planning. It then remains to be noted precisely which of the motifs used by our ancestors we can still employ today. However, we must emphasize, purely theoretically for the moment, *that in the Middle Ages and the Renaissance there still existed a vital and functional use of the town square for community life and also, in connection with this, a rapport between square and surrounding public buildings.* Meanwhile in our day plazas are, at most, used as parking lots, and any artistic relationship between them and their buildings has almost totally vanished. Missing today near the parliament buildings is the colonnaded agora; near universities and cathedrals, a respectful silence; near town halls, the crowds of people and all the busyness of market life. In short, we miss activity exactly where in Antiquity it was most animated, that is, around the great public buildings. So it turns out that all that we have stressed so far as characteristic of the enchantment of old plazas is today absent. . . .

The ancients also placed their statues around the edges of their public spaces; we do the opposite. . . .

Perhaps the most dramatic example of modern folly in this respect is offered by the story of Michelangelo's *David*, which took place in Florence, the homeland and the exemplar of old monumental splendor. The huge marble statue was standing in front of the masonry wall of the Palazzo Vecchio to the left of the main entrance—on the spot chosen by Michelangelo himself. One can wager with surety that no modern commission would have chosen this place: public opinion would consider the choice of such an apparently inferior and inauspicious location to be either a joke or a madness. However, Michelangelo selected it, and he is supposed to have understood something of these matters. The statue remained there from 1504 until 1873. All those who still had a chance to see this unique masterpiece at such an unusual spot can testify to the tremendous impact it produced at precisely this location. Contrasted with the relative intimacy of its corner of the plaza, and readily compared with people walking by, the giant statue seemed actually to grow in dimension. One could not imagine anything better to set off all the lines of the body than the background of the dark and monotonous, yet powerfully rusticated masonry of the palace. This effect can still be partially appreciated in the large Alinari photograph. Since that time the *David* has stood in a room of the Accademia under a specially constructed glass cupola, amongst plaster casts, photographs, and color prints of Michelangelo's works—as a model for artists and as an object of research for historians and critics. It takes a special mental effort to overcome the well-known deadening effects of the art-prison called "museum," in order to arrive at a real appreciation of the noble work. But this still did not satisfy the enlightened artistic taste of the time. *David* was also cast in bronze in the original size, and was put on a high pedestal in the wide, open Piazzale Michelangelo on the Viale dei Colli above Florence—precisely in the geometric center, of course. In front spreads a beautiful panorama; behind, cafés; to the side, a parking place; right through it runs a Corso; and all around it, the rustling leaves of the Baedekers. At this spot the statue is absolutely ineffective, and one often hears the opinion expressed that its dimensions do not exceed human size. So Michelangelo really did understand more about placing his statue: our predecessors have always been more competent in these matters than we are today.

The decisive difference in this case between past and present is that we always look for places as magnificent as possible for every little statue, thus diminishing its effect instead of augmenting it, as could be done by means of the neutral background that a portraitist would choose for his heads under the circumstances.

Another point in closely related to this. As was demonstrated, the ancients placed their monuments and statues around their plazas and against walls. Eloquent evidence of this is offered by views of the Signoria in Florence. At the walls around a square there is ample space for hundreds of statues, all of which will be well situated because they find a favorable background there (as pointed out in the case of the *David*). But nowadays we consider only the center of the plaza suitable, thus permitting no more than one installation, no matter how large the square. If, however, the plaza is irregular so that its center cannot be determined geometrically, we are unable to install even a single monument and the plaza must remain entirely vacant for all time.

THE IRREGULARITIES OF OLD PLAZAS

A very special emphasis is placed nowadays on straight thoroughfares of interminable length and particularly on the absolute regularity of public squares. This is, however, quite unimportant, and the whole effort is expended uselessly—at least as far as artistic aims are concerned.

Let us look at the Piazza Eremitani at Padua (Figure 2),

FIGURE 2. *Padua: Piazza degli Eremitani. [From Martin]*

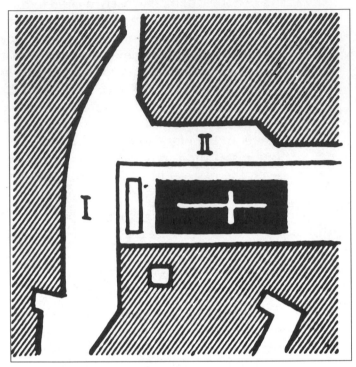

FIGURE 3. *Syracuse. I. Piazza del Duomo.—II. Piazza Minerva*

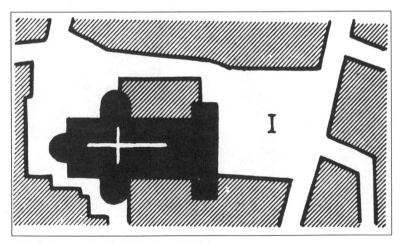

FIGURE 4. *Padua: Piazza del Duomo (I)*

FIGURE 5. *Palermo: Piazza S. Francesco*

the Piazza del Duomo at Syracuse (Figure 3) and at Padua (Figure 4), and S. Francesco at Palermo (Figure 5). The reason for the quite typical irregularity of these old plazas lies in their gradual historical development. One can generally assume that there once was a practical basis for each of the odd curvatures, be it a water channel which has long since ceased to run, or a road, or a building of the shape in question.

It is generally realized from personal experience that these irregularities do not have an unpleasant effect at all, but on the contrary, they enhance naturalness, they stimulate our interest, and, above all, they augment the picturesque quality of the tableau. Less understood probably is how extreme these irregularities can become before they are recognized as such—or are considered to be unpleasant—because to do so requires a close comparison with the ground plan. Every town offers examples enough of this, for one is always inclined to overlook slanted lines, to consider oblique or obtuse junctures as being right-angled—in short, to idealize nature's deviations in our pursuit of strict regularity.

Anyone who examines the plans of his own town for skewed angles and plazas will discover that they have lived

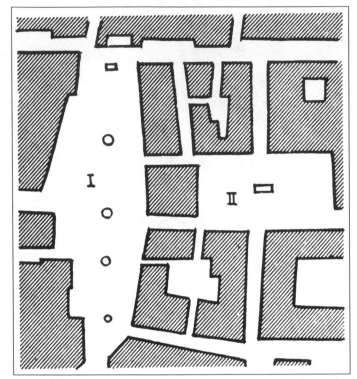

FIGURE 6. *Verona. I. Piazza Erbe.—II. Piazza dei Signori*

in his memory as being more or less regular and straight-lined. Here are only some better known plazas as examples: the famous Piazza Erbe of Verona (Figure 6) is certainly remembered by many, whether from reality or from pictures. However, one is seldom aware of the great irregularity of this plaza; that the plaza has a remarkably uneven outline has scarcely ever been noticed. This is quite natural because nothing is harder than to reconstruct the plan of a plaza from a perspective view of it, or even more from one's memory—especially when one was not concerned with this particular aspect at that moment, but was only joyfully taking in all the beautiful things which there abound.

No less curious is the discrepancy between the actual plan and the mental image of the Piazza S. Maria Novella in Florence (Figure 7). The plaza is actually five-sided, but is rememberd as being four-sided (certainly not by every traveler, but frequently, as has been testified to). This ap-

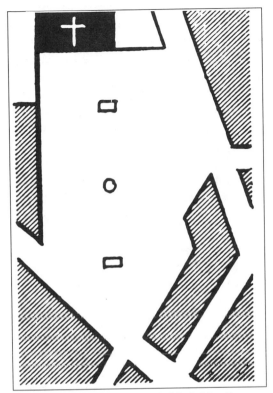

FIGURE 7. *Florence: Piazza S. Maria Novella*

parently arises from the fact that in actuality one is able to
see only three sides of the plaza at once, the juncture of the
other two always remaining unseen behind the back of the
observer. However, one easily deceives oneself as to the
right-angled or obtuse-angled relationship of these three
sides (particularly when one is, as usual, not paying special attention) because such judgment is based exclusively
on a perspective view, and an exactitude in measurement
of the true angle by eye alone is difficult even for the expert
who is giving his full attention to it. Thus this plaza is a
real puzzler for the eye because of the optical illusion it
produces. Yet of what merit is an exactly regular plan in
comparison with these phenomena?

It is strange that the really wildly irregular plazas of old
towns often do not look bad at all, while an irregular corner in a modern layout invariably appears very unattractive. This is due to the fact that the irregularity of old plan-

ning is almost always of a kind that one notices only on paper, overlooking it in reality; and the reason for this is that old planning was not conceived on the drafting board, but instead developed gradually *in natura,* allowing for all that the eye notices *in natura* and treating with indifference that which would be apparent only on paper. . . .

Striving for symmetry has become quite the rage. Nowadays the term symmetry is on the tongue of every barely educated person, and everybody feels called upon to give an opinion on such difficult artistic problems as those of town planning because he has at his fingertips the single decisive rule—symmetry. The word is Greek, yet it can be easily demonstrated that all of Antiquity understood something quite different by it than we do and was not acquainted with the modern theoretical concept of symmetry—that is, of a mirror-image likeness of right to left. Whoever has taken the trouble to investigate the meaning of the word "symmetry" throughout the fragments of Greek and Latin writings on art will know that it always expressed something for which we today lack a term. We can therefore not translate the old word *symmetria* without paraphrasing it. Even Vitruvius could only describe, not translate it: "*Symmetria* is a *proper agreement* between the members of the work itself, and *relation* between the different parts and the whole general scheme, in accordance with a certain part selected as standard."* For this reason Vitruvius's terminology vacillates constantly, except where he preserves the Greek word *symmetria* itself. A few times he uses *proportio* instead of it and thus comes closest to its true meaning, but he chooses this word reluctantly for, as he says himself, symmetry only emerges from *proportio*: "They [the principles of symmetry] are due to proportion, in Greek αναλογια."** Actually proportion and symmetry were essentially one and the same for the ancients, with only this difference: under proportion in architecture was understood merely a certain generally

*Item *symmetria* est ex ipsius operis membris *conveniens consensus* ex partibusque separatis ad universae figurae speciem ratae partis *responsus.* Book I, Chapter II, paragraph 4. [Translation above is Morgan's. Italics are Sitte's.]
**. . . *Proportio,* quae graece αναλογια dicitur. Book III, Chapter I, paragraph 1. [Morgan translation.]

pleasing quality of relationship based on feeling (for example, that of the height of a column to its thickness) whereas symmetry involved the same relationship but expressed precisely in numbers. This meaning of the concept also persisted throughout the Middle Ages. It was when real architectural drawings began to be developed in the lodges of the Gothic masters and one became more and more concerned with symmetrical axes in the modern sense that one also became increasingly conscious of the theoretical notion of an identity of right and left. For this new concept the old word was chosen, and thus its meaning changed. Already the writers of the Renaissance used it in this sense. Since then the idea of symmetry has conquered the world. Symmetrical axes get to be ever more frequent in ground plans, and from plans they move to plazas and streets, conquering one sphere after another, until they stand out as the only cure or arcanum. All our so-called aesthetic town-planning ordinances illustrate this weak, meager, and unfortunate taste. Everybody agrees about the need for aesthestic regulations, but as soon as something specific is to be said, utter helplessness replaces their original enthusiasm. The tiny mouse brought forth by the mountain is symmetry—universally accepted as necessary and incontrovertible. So, for instance, the Bavarian building regulations of 1864 demand as their main aesthetic requirement that in façades everything should be avoided "that might offend *symmetry* or *morality*," it being apparently left open to interpretation which of the two would be considered the greater offense.

5

The Medieval Town

LEWIS MUMFORD

In general, there were three basic patterns of the medieval town, which corresponded to their historic origin, their geographic peculiarities, and their mode of development. Behind these urban patterns were still older rural ones, such as we find in the "street" village, the crossroads village, the commons village, and the round village, which could be represented graphically by $\approx$, $+$, $\#$, and 0.

The towns that remained from Roman days usually retained their rectangular system of block platting, in the original center, modified by the building of a citadel or a monastery, which might alter the even parcelling out of the plots. Towns that grew by slow stages out of a village or a group of villages lying under a monastery or a castle would conform more closely to topography, changing slowly generation by generation, often preserving in their plan features that were products of historic accident rather than conscious choice.

This second kind of town is often regarded as the sole truly medieval type: some historians even deny the title of plan to its actual conformation. Those who refer to the winding streets of such a town as mere tracings of the cowpath do not realize that the cow's habit of following contours usually produces a more economical and sensible layout on hilly sites than any inflexible system of straight streets. Finally, many medieval towns were designed in advance for colonization: frequently, though not always, these would be laid out on a strict checkerboard plan, with a central place left open for the market and public assembly. All three modes were medieval. In separation or combination they produced an inexhaustible variety of forms.

At the very beginning of the Middle Ages one discovers, indeed, a certain partiality for the regular, geometric plan, with the rectangle as the basis of subdivision: see the ideal ground plan for the monastery of St. Gall in the ninth century. Kenneth Conant has shown, too, that the original buildings of Cluny were set in rectangular formation, within a three-hundred-foot square. Plainly Oswald Spengler's interpretation of the checkerboard plan as purely the product of the final hardening of a culture into a civilization is an unsupportable generalization. But though a geometric layout was more characteristic of freshly founded towns, it did not always follow that, as in the classic bastide of Montpazier, it would be coupled with a rectangular outline for the city as a whole. Sometimes the rectangles are placed within a circular bounding wall; sometimes, as at Montségur or Cordes in France, a basically rectangular plan was intelligently adapted to the contours and natural boundaries of the site.

I emphasize these points because the checkerboard or gridiron plan has been subject to a constant stream of misleading speculation and interpretation. Sometimes such plans are referred to as peculiarly American or New World types; sometimes, in the face of the brilliant precommunist Peiping, as a synonym for dullness. Even town-planning theorists have made such errors, largely because of their failure to grasp the difference, familiar to students of biology, between homologous and analogous forms. A similar form does not necessarily have a similar significance in a different culture; again, similar functions may produce quite different forms. As we have seen the rectangle meant one thing to an Etruscan priest, another to Hippodamos, a third to the Roman legionary, spading his camp for the night, and a fourth to the City Plan Commissioners for New York in 1811, seeking to provide in advance the maximum number of building lots. To the first, the rectangle might symbolize cosmic law; to the last, it meant simply the most favorable possibilities for real-estate speculation.

There is indeed a sound reason for thinking of medieval plans as usually more informal than regular. This was because rugged rocky sites were more frequently utilized, for they had decisive advantages for defense until effective cannon fire became possible in the sixteenth century. Since streets were not adapted to wheeled traffic and neither water pipes nor sewage drains needed to be provided for, it was more economical to follow nature's contours than to attempt to grade them down: note the tilt of the broad market place in Siena. By building on barren hilly sites, moreover, the thrifty citizens did not encroach on the richer agricultural bottom land.

In organic planning, one thing leads to another, and what began as the seizure of an accidental advantage may prompt a strong element in a design, which an a priori plan could not anticipate, and in all probability would overlook or rule out. Many of the surviving irregularities in medieval towns are due to streams that have been covered over, trees that were later cut down, old balks that once defined rural fields. Custom and property rights, once established in the form of lots, boundaries, permanent rights of way, are hard to efface.

Organic planning does not begin with a preconceived goal: it moves from need to need, from opportunity to opportunity, in a series of adaptations that themselves become increasingly coherent and purposeful, so that they generate a complex, final design, hardly less unified than a pre-formed geometric pattern. Towns like Siena illustrate this process to perfection. Though the last stage in such a process is not clearly present at the beginning, as it is in a more rational, non-historic order, this does not mean that rational considerations and deliberate forethought have not governed every feature of the plan, or that a deliberately unified and integrated design may not result.

Those who dismiss organic plans as unworthy of the name of plan confuse mere formalism and regularity with purposefulness, and irregularity with intellectual confusion or technical incompetence. The towns of the Middle Ages confute this formalistic illusion. For all their variety, they embody a universal pattern; and their very departures and irregularities are usually not merely sound, but often subtle, in their blending of practical need and esthetic insight.

Each medieval town grew out of a unique situation, presented a unique constellation of forces, and produced, in its plan, a unique solution. The consensus is so complete as to the purposes of town life that the variations in detail only confirm the pattern. That consensus makes it look, when one views a hundred medieval plans in succession, as if there were in fact a conscious theory that guided this townplanning. The agreement was deeper than that. But toward the close of the Middle Ages, the rationale of this planning was expressed by the highly reflective intelligence of Leone Battista Alberti, in his "De Re Edificatori."

Alberti was in many ways a typical medieval urbanist. In his concern for functionalism, the localization of business, curved streets, "he did no more," as Lavedan observes, "than register approval of what he saw under his eyes." Even when Alberti justifies the continuously curving street, with its gently blocked yet ever-changing vistas, he was only giving conscious expression to something his predecessors recognized and valued, too. The slow curve is the natural line of a footwalker, as anyone can observe if he looks back at his tracks in the snow across an open field, unless he has consciously tried to overcome this tendency. But the pleasure in that curve, once laid out by the pedestrian, is what gives character to medieval building, on such a consummate piece of late-medieval and renascence building as the High Street in Oxford. There a single tree whose branches jut out beyond the building line enriches the picture more than would a whole arcade of streets.

The other source of the organic curves in the medieval town was the emphasis on its central core. Lavedan goes so far as to say that "the essential fact of medieval urbanism is the constitution of the city in such a fashion that all the lines converge toward a center, and that the contour is usually circular: this is what contemporary theorists call the radio-concentric system." Unfortunately, the term radio-concentric calls to mind the spider web. What one finds, rather, in most towns, is a central quarter or core, surrounded by a series of irregular rings, which have the effect of enclosing and protecting the core, while, by devious passages, approaching more closely to it. Where there is something that approximates a continuous circular street, it is almost surely the indication of a wall that has been torn down. Even in a little town like Bergues, as seen in Blaeu's great Atlas, with its almost geometric precision in its central core, only three streets come together at the center. The resulting plan is generated by the two opposing forces of attraction and protection: the public buildings and open places find security behind a labyrinth of streets, through which the knowing foot nevertheless easily penetrates. It is only with the baroque planners who worked to overcome the medieval pattern that the street drives headlong into the town center, as in the asterik plan—though Alberti himself, as it happens, anticipated this new scheme, which symbolized the collection of public power in a centralized institution or a despotic prince.

The determining elements in the medieval plan hold both for an old town on a Roman foundation, like Cologne, or for a new town like Salisbury. The wall, the gates, and the civic nucleus determine the main lines of circulation. As for the wall, with its outside moat, canal, or river, it made the town an island. The wall was valued as a symbol as much as the spires of the churches: not a mere military utility. The medieval mind took comfort in a universe of sharp definitions, solid walls, and limited views: even heaven and hell had their circular boundaries. Walls of custom bounded the economic classes and kept them in their place. Definition and classification were the very essence of medieval thinking: so that philosophic nominalism, which challenged the objective reality of classes, and presented a world of unrelated atoms and disconnected events, was as destructive to the medieval style of life as cannonballs proved to be to the walls of the town.

The psychological importance of the wall must not be forgotten. When the portcullis was drawn and the town gate were locked at sundown, the city was sealed off from the outside world. Such enclosure helps create a feeling of unity as well as security. It is significant—and a little disturbing—that in one of the rare modern communities where people have lived under analogous conditions, namely in the atomic-research community at Oak Ridge, the protected inhabitants of the town grew to value the "secure" life within, free from any sort of foreign invasion or even unauthorized approach—though it meant that their own comings and goings were under constant military surveillance and control.

But once again, in the medieval community, the wall built up a fatal sense of insularity: all the more because the poor state of road transport increased the difficulties of communication between towns. As so often happened in urban history before, defensive unity and security reversed their polarity and passed over into anxiety, fear, hostility, and aggression, especially when it seemed that a neighboring city might prosper at its rival's expense. Recall Florence's shameless assaults on Pisa and Siena! This isolationism was in fact so self-defeating that it gave sanction to forces of exploitation and aggression, both in Church and in State, that sought at least to bring about some more inclusive unity, by turning the all too solid wall into a more etherialized frontier boundary, outlining a far wider province.

One may not leave the wall without noting the special function of the town gate: far more than a mere opening, it was a "meeting place of two worlds," the urban and the rural, the insider and the outsider. The main gate offered the first greeting to the trader, the pilgrim, or the common wayfarer; it was at once a customs house, a passport office and immigration control point, and a triumphal arch, its turrets and towers often vying, as in Lübeck, with those of the cathedral or town hall. Wherever the river or traffic slows down, it tends to deposit its load: so it would be usually near the gates that the storehouses would be built, and the inns and taverns congregate, and in the adjoining streets the craftsmen and merchants would set up their shops.

Thus the gate produced, without special zoning regulations, the economic quarters of the city; and since there was more than one gate, the very nature of traffic from different regions would tend to decentralize and differentiate the business areas. As a result of this organic disposition of functions, the inner area of the city was not burdened by any traffic except that which its own needs generated. The original meaning of "port" derives from this portal; and the merchants who settled in this port were once called "porters," till they passed the name on to their menial helpers.

Finally, one must not forget an ancient function of the

wall, which came back in the Middle Ages: it served as an open promenade for recreation, particularly in the summer. Even when the walls were no more than twenty feet high, they gave a point of vantage over the surrounding countryside, and permitted one to enjoy summer breezes that might not penetrate the city.

No town plan can be adequately described in terms of its two-dimensional pattern; for it is only in the third dimension, through movement in space, and in the fourth dimension, through transformation in time, that the functional and esthetic relationships come to life. This holds particularly for the medieval city; for the movement it generated led not merely through horizontal space, but upwards; and to understand the plan one must take in the mass and profile of its dominant structures: especially the disposition of the nuclear components, the Castle, the Abbey or Friary, the Cathedral, the Town Hall, the guild hall. But if one building may be taken as the key structure in the medieval town plan, it is the Cathedral; so much so that Braunfels even suggests that the master builders in charge of the Cathedral also, in fact, excercised a pervasive influence over other public buildings.

With certain notable exceptions, the dominant medieval buildings did not exist in empty spaces; still less did one approach them along a formal axis. That type of space came in with the sixteenth century, as in the approach to Santa Croce in Florence; and it was only with the nineteenth century that urban "improvers" who were incapable of appreciating the medieval system of town planning removed the smaller structures that crowded around the great Cathedrals, to create a wide parklike area, like that in front of Notre Dame in Paris: bleak staring emptiness. This undermines the very essence of the medieval approach: the secrecy and the surprise, the sudden opening and the lift upwards, the richness of carved detail, meant to be viewed near at hand.

Esthetically, a medieval town is like a medieval tapestry: the eye, challenged by the rich intricacy of the design, roams back and forth over the entire fabric, captivated by a flower, an animal, a head, lingering where it pleases, retracing its path, taking in the whole only by assimilating the parts, not commanding the design at a single glance.

For the baroque eye, that medieval form is tortuous and the effort to encompass it is tedious; for the medieval eye, on the other hand, the baroque form would be brutally direct and over-unified. There is no one "right" way to approach a medieval building: the finest face of the Chartres cathedral is the southern one; and though perhaps the best view of Notre Dame is from across the Seine, in the rear, that view, with its engirdling green, was not opened up till the nineteenth century.

Yet there are exceptions. There is a handful of minsters—to say nothing of countless village churches—that are free-standing buildings, set in the midst of an open green, quite detached from the busy life of the town: Salisbury and Canterbury are almost suburban in their free use of space and greenery, while Pisa's Campo Santo is equally detached and open. Often an original graveyard accounts for such openness.

In the main, the great church is central to the town, in every sense but a geometric one; and since it drew to itself the largest crowds, it needed a forecourt to provide for the entrance and exit of the worshippers. With the theological orientation of the church, its altar pointing toward the East, the church would often be set at a non-conforming angle to a more regular pattern of streets. When one finds the marketplace either spreading in front of the cathedral, or opening a wedge or a square for itself nearby, one must not assign to these institutions the same values they have today: it was the market that was occasional, while it was the church whose services were constant and regular. As with the original growth of the city, the market settles close to the church because it is there that the inhabitants most frequently come together.

One must think of the church, indeed, as one would now think of a "community center": not too holy to serve as a dining hall for a great festival, as a theater for a religious play, as a forum where the scholars in church schools might stage oratorical contests and learned disputes on a holiday, or even, in the early days, as a safe-deposit vault, behind whose high altar deeds or treasures might be deposited, safe from all but the incorrigibly wicked.

In one manner or another, a constant procession of people, alone, or by twenties or by thousands, wound through the streets to the portals of the church. Here is where one set out on one's journey; here is where one returned. If it were otherwise, how could one account for the riches lavished on the building of a Bamberg, a Durham, an Amiens, a Beauvais, an Assisi, in communities of ten thousand inhabitants or less. Such communities today, with all our mechanized facilities and capital accumulation, would find it hard to raise funds for a pre-fabricated parish house, bought at a discount.

As for the open places of the medieval city, even the big marketplaces and cathedral places were anything but formal squares. More often than not, in towns of organic growth, the marketplace would be an irregular figure, sometimes triangular, sometimes many-sided or oval, now saw-toothed, now curved, seemingly arbitrary in shape because the needs of the surrounding buildings came first and determined the disposition of the open space. Though sometimes the market may be but a widened street, there are other examples, in Brussels or Bremen, in Perugia or Siena, where the proportions of the place are ample: big enough not merely for many stalls, but for public gatherings and ceremonies. The marketplace recaptured, in fact, the function of the earliest forum or agora.

In the marketplace the guilds set up their stages for the performance of the mystery plays; here the savage punishment of criminals or heretics would take place, on the gallows or at the stake; it was here that at the end of the Middle Ages, when the serious occupations of feudalism were transformed into urban sports, that great tourneys would be held. Often one marketplace will open into another subordinate place, connected by a narrow passage: Parma is but one of many examples. The dry goods and hardware market was usually separated for very natural reasons from the provisions market. Many a square we now admire purely for its noble architectural frame, like the Piazzetta San Marco in Venice, originally was carved out for a utilitarian purpose—in this case a meat market.

Apart from the cathedral and, sometimes, the town hall, where mass and height were important symbolic attributes, the medieval builder tended to keep to modest human dimensions. Almshouses would be founded for seven or ten men; convents might begin with the apostolic dozen; and instead of building a single hospital for the entire town, it was commoner to provide a single hospital for the entire town, it was commoner to provide a small one for every two or three thousand people. So, too, the parish churches multiplied throughout the growing town, instead of letting a few big edifices wax at the center. In London in the twelfth century, according to Fitz Stephen, there were 13 conventual and 126 smaller churches, for a population of possibly 25,000 people; and Stow notes some three centuries later from two to seven churches in each of the twenty-six wards.

This decentralization of the essential social functions of the city not merely prevented institutional overcrowding and needless circulation: it kept the whole town in scale. The loss of this sense of scale, in the oversized burgher houses of the north, or in the crazily competitive fortress towers of Bologna or San Gimignano was a symptom of social pathology. Small structures, small numbers, intimate relations—these medieval attributes gave the town special qualitative attributes, as against large numbers and mass organizations, that may help account for its creativity.

The street occupied in the medieval town a quite different place than in an age of wheeled transportation. We usually think of urban houses as being ranged along a line of pre-determined streets. But on less regular medieval sites, it would be the other way about: groups of trades or institutional buildings would form self-contained quarters or "islands," with the building disposed without relation to the public ways outside. Within these islands, and often outside, the footways marked the daily goings and comings of the inhabitants. The notion of a "traffic network" was as absent as constant wheeled traffic itself. "Islands" formed by the castle, the monasteries or colleges, the specialized industrial section of the more advanced towns, like the Arsenal at Venice, interrupted the closer pattern of small scale residential blocks.

In medieval new towns, the charters often distinguished between traffic streets—traffic being mainly carts—and lesser streets; and in uniform Montpazier, as centuries later in Philadelphia, the houses had a two-street frontage, one on a broad street twenty-four feet wide and one on an alley seven feet wide. But in general, the street was a line of communication for pedestrians, and their utility for wheeled transport was secondary. Not merely were the streets narrow and often irregular, but sharp turns and closures were frequent. When the street was narrow and twisting, or when it came to a dead end, the plan broke the force of the wind and reduced the area of mud.

Not by accident did the medieval townsman, seeking protection against winter wind, avoid creating such cruel wind-tunnels as the broad, straight street. The very narrowness of medieval streets made their outdoor activities more comfortable in winter. But likewise, in the south, the narrow street with broad overhangs protected the pedestrian against both rain and the sun's direct glare. Small variations in height and building material and rooftop profile, and variations in window openings and doorways gave each street its own physiognomy.

Though Alberti favored straight and broad streets for noble and powerful cities, to increase their air of greatness and majesty, he wrote a most perceptive apology for the older medieval type of winding street. "Within the heart of the town," he observed, "it will be handsomer not to have them strait, but winding about several ways, backwards and forwards, like the course of a river. For thus, besides by appearing so much longer, they will add to the idea of the greatness of the town, they will likewise be a great security against all accidents and emergencies. Moreover, this winding of the streets will make the passenger at every step discover a new structure, and the front door of every house will directly face the middle of the street; and where as in larger towns even too much breadth is unhandsome and unhealthy, in a smaller town it will be both healthy and pleasant to have such an open view from every house by means of the turn of the street." No one, not even Camillo Sitte, has done better justice to the esthetics of medieval town planning.

The medieval town thus had a character in its residential quarters that the blank walls of a classic Greek city, for example, certainly lacked. But the town enjoyed still another happy feature, perhaps carried over from the ancient city: for frequently the street would be edged on each side with an arcade, which formed the open end of a shop. This gave better shelter than even a narrow open street, and one finds it not merely in France and Italy, where it might in fact be a conscious continuation or resumption of the classic portico, but in towns like Innsbruck in Austria, in the street leading up to Das Goldene Dachl. One must not forget how important physical protection against the weather was, for the stalls and booths of handicraftsmen and merchants were not generally put behind glass till the seventeenth century; in fact, the greater part of the business of life, even cooking, was conducted more or less outdoors. The closed narrow street, the arcaded front, and the exposed shop were in fact complementary. Not till cheap glass enclosed the second could new conceptions of town planning open up the first.

One further feature of the street must be noted: its paving. Some three centuries before wheeled vehicles became common, the street lost its natural underfooting. Paving for the pedestrian came in as early as 1185 in Paris, 1235 in Florence, and 1310 in Lübeck; indeed, by 1339 all of Florence was paved; while by the end of the fourteenth century even in somewhat backward England, William Langland could use the figure "as common as the pavement to every man that walketh." Often these early improvements applied only to a single important street, and the movement spread so slowly that it did not reach Landshut in Bavaria till 1494, though that other great technical innovation, window glass, was used by South Bavarian farmers, according to Heyne, in the thirteenth century. In the hands of the medieval pavior, paving became an art, often repeating in stone the pattern of the mower's scythe; while in Venice, the color and line of the pavement adds to the magnificence of St. Mark's plaza itself.

The provision and care of paving reminds one of another feature about the management of the medieval town: here again it was association that had a public basis, while physical organization was, more often than not, on a private basis. Certainly this applies to paving, lighting, and the piped water supply. By the sixteenth century the first two were usually mandatory; but they were carried out by the private householder for his particular private property. The cleaning of streets likewise remained for long a private concern: a custom that lingered beyond the nineteenth century in London, in the institution of the crossing sweeper, who disappeared only with the banishment of the horse. (Medieval practice, curiously, still usually applies to the building and maintenance of sidewalks.) Under the paving act that prevailed in Northampton in 1431, the municipal authorities had the power to order the owners of the property to pave and keep in repair the street in front of their houses and adjoining property, but ''no property owner was compelled to extend the pavement into the street above thirty feet, so it became the duty of the town to pave the market and similar wide places.''

Note one more feature: the neighborhood unit and the functional precinct. In a sense, the medieval city was a congeries of little cities, each with a certain degree of autonomy and self-sufficiency, each formed so naturally out of common needs and purposes that it only enriched and supplemented the whole. The division of the town into quarters, each with its church or churches, often with a local provision market, always with its own local water supply, a well or a fountain, was a characteristic feature; but as the town grew, the quarters might become sixths, or even smaller fractions of the whole, without dissolving into the mass. Often, as in Venice, the neighborhood unit would be identified with the parish and get its name from the parish church: a division that remains to this day.

This integration into primary residential units, composed of families and neighbors, was complemented by another kind of division, into precincts, based on vocation and interest: thus both primary and secondary groups, both *Gemeinschaft* and *Gesellschaft*, took on the same urban pattern. In Regensburg, as early as the eleventh century, the town was divided into a clerical precinct, a royal precinct, and a merchant's precinct, corresponding thus to the chief vocations, while craftsmen and peasants must have occupied the rest of the town. To this constellation, university towns, like Toulouse or Oxford, would also add their college precincts, each relatively self-contained; while as convents and nunneries were drawn into the city, a movement that went on steadily from the thirteenth to the eighteenth century, a scattering of conventual precincts, different from the cathedral precinct, would likewise follow, adding their gardens and open spaces, however private, to the sum total of open spaces in the city. In London, the Inns of Court, like The Temple, formed still another kind of enclosed precinct.

The significance of the functional precinct has been too tardily recognized, even by planning theorists: in fact, perhaps the first modern planners to have done justice either to the historic form or its modern variations were Henry Wright and Clarence Stein. But these precincts were the first translation of the spatial qualities of the sacred precinct of the original city into the vernacular of everyday life. At the present moment, when the very existence of the city today is threatened by the overexpansion of wheeled traffic, the tradition of the medieval precinct, released from the street and the major traffic artery, comes back as a new form at a higher point in the spiral of development.

One cannot leave the medieval city, in its unity and diversity, without asking a final question about its planning: how far was it pursued as a conscious effort to achieve order and beauty? In formulating an answer, it is easy to overestimate both spontaneity and accidental good looks, and to forget the rigor and system that were fundamental qualities in the education of both scholar and craftsman. The esthetic unity of the medieval town was not achieved any more than its other institutions without effort, struggle, supervision, and control.

No doubt most of the supervision was personal; most of the agreements probably came from face-to-face discussions of interested parties, which left no record behind. But we know that when the Town Hall of Siena was built in the fourteenth century, the municipal government ordered that the new buildings put up on the Piazza del Campo should have windows of the same type. And though much work remains to be done in medieval archives to bring out all the functions of the Town Architect, we know, too, that in Italy the office was an old one. We need not doubt Descartes in his "Discourse on Method" when he observes that "there have been at all times certain officers whose duty it is to see that private buildings contributed to public ornament."

What the nineteenth-century admirer of medieval art regarded as the result of effortless spontaneity and artless unconsciousness was done in fact with method and conscious intention in urban planning, precisely as any other art is carried through. Lavedan, it is true, in his admirable appreciation of the medieval town, is inclined to regard its beauty as a mere by-product of its practical and symbolic concerns. But the city was no more innocent of intentional esthetic order than it was of geometric order, though its discipline was pliant enough to allow for the new, the spontaneous, the different.

As a result, the same "medieval" town plan could, by the eighteenth century, hold together Romanesque, High Gothic, Florid, Renascence, and Baroque structures, often jostling together on the same street, without any dulling of the esthetic moment: indeed, with just the contrary effect. The esthetic mixture corresponded with the historic social complex. This was a mode of planning that met the requirements of life, and yielded to change and innovation without being shattered by it. In the deepest sense of the words it was both functional and purposeful, for the functions that mattered most were those of significance to man's higher life.

Under such a canon of planning, no one was tempted to deny either the old form that still served well, or the new form that represented a new purpose; and instead of wiping out buildings of different styles in order to make them over wholesale in the fashionable stereotype of the passing moment, the medieval builder worked the old and the new into an ever richer pattern. The bastard estheticism of a single uniform style, set within a rigid town plan, arbitrarily freezing the historic process at a given moment, was left for a later period, which valued uniformity more than universality, and visible power more than the invisible processes of life.

6

The Discovery of the Street

J.B. JACKSON

The image of the contemporary city, the sign or logo which all of us know how to interpret, is a blend of cartographic abstraction and aerial view. It is a grid pattern of streets on a plain background, a criss-cross of lines, for that is all of the city we need recognize.

To the men of the Middle Ages, the most familiar image of the city was a conventionalized cluster of towers and bastions and roofs, vertical in feeling, so tightly compacted that there was no indication of the streets and spaces within it.

The gradual supplanting of that essentially architectural image (with its flatland, upwards-directed view) by our own remote view *down* from outer space is one measure of how our perception of the city has changed. It is also a measure of how, over the centuries, the city itself has changed, by the creation of public spaces—roads, streets, avenues, squares—to give it a new form and articulation.

To us an obvious difference between a rural and an urban environment is the density of the road or street network. If we perceive the city less in terms of architecture

From J.B. Jackson, The Necessity for Ruins, and Other Topics *(Amherst: The University of Massachusetts Press, 1980), pp. 55–66. Copyright © 1980 by J.B. Jackson.*

than in terms of communication, it is because we usually experience it by moving through an elaborate system of arteries that has priority over the environment of buildings; and we are justified in perceiving the city in this manner because we sense that our economic and social system—even our notions of urban environmental systems—depend in a large measure upon the existence of streets and roads and highways as means of movement and communication and of orientation.

Yet, given a different economy, a different social order, given also an esthetic unawareness of public spaces, is the arterial system (as we know it) inevitable? A community, whatever its size and sophistication, which travels on foot, transports its wares by beasts of burden, a community whose daily movements are no more extensive than the journey to work, to church, to market, to neighbors can usually get along well with a flexible and informal network of alleys, blind alleys, flights of steps, and paths. It is charming to pass through such a labyrinth of tunnels and sunlit spaces, between blank walls and gardens and open fields, part private, part public. Well into the Middle Ages the European town knew nothing else, just as until a half century ago the Moslem towns of the Near East knew nothing else, and as many traditional American Indian communities know it still.

The emergence of the city as a system of public squares and streets harks back to a time when the medieval town began to acquire a political and territorial identity. Only in a very limited sense can the European city be seen as a continuation of the Roman city—even though it may have occupied the same site and retained not only the walls and fortification but the alignment of its principal street or thoroughfare. Spatially as well as politically and economically the European city evolved in its own unique manner.

The few small towns on the continent which survived the collapse of the Roman Empire and the repeated Barbarian invasions did so largely because their fortifications provided shelter and security for the population scattered throughout the immediate countryside and because the more powerful nobles, as well as the bishops, chose them as headquarters for their administration. The earliest urban populations were therefore likely to be composed of two very distinct elements: the rural dependents of a feudal lord living in the half-ruined city much as they might have lived in their rural villages; and a body of educated and disciplined monks, priests, scholars who comprised the court or staff of the bishop or lord. These two elements not only occupied separate areas of the town—the castle and the cathedral versus the working and farming or gardening area—but were ruled by different codes of law.

Another reason for the partial survival of some of the Roman cities was their location: on what was left of the old roads and at established river crossings or landing places. To travelling merchants, who managed to survive the almost complete disruption of society after the 5th Century and continued to maintain contacts throughout Europe and the Near East, these riverside communities, however small and poor, offered a place to rest and to store their wares—salt, spices, weapons, honey, oil, and furs. For most of the year the merchants were far away, but their annual reappearance was often an occasion for a fair and a certain amount of trading. In time they established permanent headquarters outside the city walls near the waterfront; this merchants' village was known in northern Europe as a *vicus*—as evident in such place names as Brunswick, Norwich, Greenwich. In the 7th Century riverside London was known as Lundenwik. In western Europe the usual term for this merchants' settlement was *portus*, from which of course we derive our word for harbor. The traders, foreign or otherwise, were made welcome. Their village—actually little more than a collection of storehouses and shelters—was recognized as part of the town even if outside its walls, and in time the Crown granted the merchants their own separate legal status and their own courts. It was characteristic of the age that the Merchants' Law applied to persons only, not to the village itself; it was only in the 12th Century that it acquired a territorial character.

The advent of the *vicus*, the merchants' quarter, marked the beginning of a new development: the multiplication not so much of districts or sections in the town as of legally defined groups. The lords in the castle, the bishop and his clerical staff, had their special law; so did the feudal working population dependent on those centers of power. There was a special law for outsiders—individuals who lived and worked in the town but who were not burghers or citizens; a law for visitors, a law for Jews, and of course a law for the burghers or citizens themselves. The craftsmen and small local merchants eventually managed to free themselves from their feudal ties and to become associated with the merchants, thereby sharing *their* legal status. Even the workers and craftsmen who settled immediately outside the city walls had a status of their own.

What held each of these various groups together was mutual dependence or a common objective: territorial identification was rare. "The boundaries of these political unities, manors, feudal states, kingdoms are not yet fixed," writes Jacques Ellul. "There are therefore very few established structures. The milieu in which men live and in which institutions develop . . . is based on the relationship between man and man. . . . It is toward the end of the 11th century that the situation changes completely."

Perhaps the first evidence we have of this change—of the city evolving from a fluid assembly of legally defined groups or orders into a composition of well-defined spaces—is the appearance in the 11th Century in one northern European town after another of a recognizable, permanent marketplace. In earlier times merchants periodically offered their wares for sale in the *vicus* or in any sufficiently wide street, and local craftsmen joined them, though their production was scanty. But a combination of economic and political circumstances fostered the creation of distinct, centrally located spaces for this sort of activity. The surrounding villages, in the 11th Century, began to produce a surplus of vegetables, livestock, certain raw materials that they sought to dispose of in the nearest town; the town craftsmen likewise produced more than their feudal lords could consume, and merchants discovered that the town, now grown larger, offered a respectable outlet for their goods.

Thus the marketplace came into existence. At first little more than a widened street or open space in the *vicus*, it then moved into the town itself to be nearer its customers and sources of supply; and finally in the 11th Century, in many of the numerous new towns laid out in central Europe and France and England, we see a rectangular public place, often in the very center, where regular markets could be held. And eventually there are several markets—

livestock market, grain market, crafts market, even hay market, wood market, etc.

These public spaces, undoubtedly the first planned and designed public spaces to appear in the European city, were of course the creation of the civic authorities—a recognition not only of the importance of the mercantile and craft interests, but also of the fact that they demanded recognition in terms of space. This is what the geographer Vance terms the *process of congregation*: ''The activities that grow up in limited areas of specialization drawn into a congregation by the internalizing linkages among them. . . . A few persons doing a particular thing, normally congregate, but not in an obvious congregation. When numbers are increased to the point they present a really extensive pattern, then a geographical congregation is to be seen.''

Several features of the medieval market are worth noting. First, it was usually located in the center of the town, not in front of the cathedral or the castle, but as often as possible—particularly in the designed new towns of the 11th and 12th Centuries—at the intersection of the two main streets or highways. It was located, in other words, where workaday activity was concentrated and where many related businesses and occupations naturally congregated: workshops, storage facilities, inns, taverns, brothels. The market by its nature attracted out-of-town visitors, men looking for work, pedlars, entertainers, preachers, and peasants in town for the day. If in subsequent periods the marketplace became the location of public buildings and the houses of guilds, it still remained what it originally was: a secular space identified with the everyday business of making a living and spending money. It is *not* the medieval equivalent of the Classical forum, and medieval records usually refer to it not as *forum* but as *mercatus*.

In Classical cities the forum was a space from which merchants and craftsmen were usually excluded and which was reserved for a superior order of citizens: for political action and the exchange of ideas. Unlike the Classical city, the European city has always had more than one focal point: the castle or palace or cathedral or the university corresponded to the forum; the marketplace corresponded to those spaces in the contemporary city where transients and natives, buyers and sellers, workers and employers, people in search of pleasure and excitement all foregathered—an essential environment, which, in one shape or another, has persisted to this day.

The emergence of the marketplace in the 11th Century was significant of several developments in the medieval landscape: the importance of the merchant and craftsman in the economic life of the town was thereby recognized and given form; the self-awareness of the town or city fostered an awareness of environments, of the feasibility of planning and creating environments for special activities or groups of people. Was there perhaps also a technological significance? Did the marketplace begin to assume importance when means of transportation improved? Ever since 1924, when the French historian Lefebvre de Noëttes started to investigate the development of horse harnesses in Europe and especially the introduction of the horse collar, archeologists and historians of medieval culture have been debating the impact of those innovations. In Greece and Rome and until probably some time in the 10th Century in western Europe, men harnessed their horses to the plow or wagon by means of a collar which all but strangled the animal when the load was heavy. The new style horse collar removed the pressure from the windpipe and placed it on the shoulder blades of the horse. What ensued from this new kind of harness (which probably originated in Asia and was copied by European farmers in the Dark Ages) was the greater use of the horse as an animal of traction, in preference to the stronger but slower and less enduring ox.

In describing what he calls ''The Discovery of Horsepower,'' Lynn White enumerates some of the very far-reaching consequences of the introduction of the new type horse harness. ''We still know very little in detail about the improvement of wagons which followed the invention of modern harness, the development of pivoted front axles, adequate brakes, whipple-trees, and the like. . . . But beginning with the first half of the twelfth century we find a large, horsedrawn, four wheeled 'longa caretta' capable of hauling heavy loads, and by the middle of the thirteenth century a wagon normally had four wheels. . . . In still another way the new harness affected the life of the northern peasants. . . . [In the 13th Century] not only were peasants moving to neighboring cities while still going out each day to their fields: villages were absorbing the inhabitants of the hamlets in their vicinity. With the employment of the horse both for ploughing and for hauling, the same amount of time spent going to and from the fields would enable the peasant to travel a greater distance. . . . Deep in the Middle Ages this 'urbanization' of the agricultural workers laid the foundation for the change in focus of Occidental Culture from country to city which has been so conspicuous in recent centuries." He notes still another consequence, of particular importance to towns: "Not only merchants but peasants were now able to get more goods to better markets."

Our generation has reason to know what the introduction of a new and more versatile vehicle can mean to a town or city. No doubt the introduction of wagon traffic in the early medieval town was gradual, but when it became possible to harness horses in tandem—one in front of the other—and when the pivoted front axle allowed wagons to negotiate sharper curves, then something began to happen to the town. The marketplace, first of all, was crowded with wagons maneuvering and parking. In certain regions where lumber was transported by wagon from the nearby forests the space needed for the maneuvering of the wagons and teams was extensive. "The great spaces have a monumental character," says a writer on the medieval towns of southern Bavaria. "The first impression on the visitor is astonishing and unforgettable. At the time of their creation this expanse was absolutely necessary, and can only be explained by the extensive freight traffic of the Middle Ages that needed a great deal of room. In front of the business establishments there had to be enough room for parking, for loading and unloading. The increase in traffic on market days had to be taken into account, and also the traffic passing through the town."

The new kind of traffic had its effect on the layout of the market, and even country roads leading into town were given attention; those living along their margins had to help in their maintenance. In town the important streets—often those inherited from the Roman Empire—were periodically repaired, and the ruts and holes made by wagons eliminated.

But the increasingly vital role played by the street in the medieval town derived less from its use by wagons than from the growth of the town itself; streets were laid out or widened and extended to regulate real estate activity and make land available in the form of lots. It seems likely that the market was the first formally designated open public space to appear in the medieval town, and that the artificially created street came later, largely as a result of the greater concentration of activity around the marketplace. Both spaces had their Classical predecessors; both were re-invented, as it were, at about the same period: the 11th Century. But the laying out of new streets involved a good deal more than traffic; it involved the orderly expansion of the town, new concepts of land ownership and taxation, and in the long run a new way of defining the town, and a new, more horizontal image.

In the 11th Century there were probably no more than a hundred communities north of the Alps that could qualify as cities, and with the exception of London and Paris and Cologne and one or two other places in the Lowlands none had more than two or three thousand inhabitants; most were little more than large villages.

Small size did not prevent them from playing their essential role as focal points in the landscape, nor from being proudly conscious that they were centers of authority and wealth, and symbols of Christian culture. Oblivious to their actual form and appearance, they saw themselves as miniature versions of a celestial prototype: a walled city divided by two intersecting streets into four quarters. A historian of the early medieval city calls our attention to the way in which the age perceived a cruciform layout even when it did not in fact exist. He cites a description of the English town of Chester, written in 1195. ''It offers what is surely the most complete definition of a medieval city layout. Twice the author indicates the cross symbolism of the place: once in the city itself in the intersection of the streets that divide it into four quarters and produces four gates (just as the mystery of the Cross fulfills the double law of the Covenant in the four evangelists) and then in the four monasteries outside the city. . . . The planned circle or outer ring of churches is the hallmark of [the early medieval] town. That it was planned and that the circle with the central castle or 'burg' was to be perceived as a unit is attested to in eleventh and twelfth century sources. . . . The loosely distributed surrounding suburban churches . . . located on conspicuous topographical features transform the town and its surroundings into a Divine landscape [*Gotteslandschaft*] whose silhouette, even at a distance, announces the religious nature of the place . . . it was characteristic of the early medieval town that it emphasized its vertical image.''

This is probably why the medieval artist in depicting such towns showed only those buildings—castle, cathedral, churches, fortifications—which were built of stone and which reinforced the image of the town as a collection of towers.

But the facts of the case were very different. Towns were not neatly divided into four quarters nor were they compact; and permanent, stone structures were few. The castle, the cathedral, the market, represented separate and distinct centers of activity, and beyond them the town was little more than small groups of flimsy dwellings, gardens and orchards; even within the boundaries of the town or city there were totally empty, unused stretches of land. The scale was astonishingly small: Cambridge with a population of less than three thousand had no less than thirteen parishes.

In the 11th Century the average dwelling in a town was very similar to the peasant village dwelling—a small and primitive structure of wood and clay and straw. These buildings were usually huddled together in compounds, grouped in close-packed neighborhoods, according to family ties, ethnic background, or feudal allegiance. These temporary shelters were so little thought of and accorded so little dignity that the punishment for many civil offenses was the destruction of the offender's dwelling. In times of war the houses of the poor were often torn down as a defense measure, for fear that the attackers would set fire to them and destroy the whole town. Each such compound or precinct stood apart, so that the early town resembled a collection of tight neighborhoods, not unlike the Oriental town divided according to clans or tribes and only partially penetrated by blind alleys and passages. What streets existed in this mosaic of communities were narrow and crooked and led to the center of town or the place of work, not to neighboring precincts. The two intersecting streets or roads leading to the outside world had an entirely different character.

The 11th Century saw the emergence of a new kind of urban plan, based not simply on the dominance of a small number of important buildings and streets but on the street as a direct link between the private domain—home or place of work—and the life of the town. There is some debate as to how this developed, and where. Evidence indicates that, in northern France during the first decades of the century, when a town was expanding the landowners determined the location of streets in order to produce an orderly and profitable subdivision into lots—a practice followed in England after the Conquest. On the other hand designed streets became common in central Europe at about the same time, when merchants were granted land for building houses near the marketplace. Streets devoted to one particular craft or trade became common. In any case the discovery of the street as a determinant of city growth and development had by the end of the century produced increasingly orthogonal town patterns, based on right angles and perpendicular lines—most conspicuous in the bastides or artificial, fortified medieval towns of southern France and in the so-called colonial towns of central and eastern Germany.

We, who live in towns and cities where the system of streets not only provides an armature for the whole built environment but affects much of our view of the world, cannot easily recognize the extent of that medieval revolution. Its most fundamental result was the destruction of the former arrangement of self-contained neighborhoods and precincts and the integration of every dwelling, every resident into the life of the town or city. The house or workshop now had direct and permanent contact and communication with the public and was related to a public space. It created a new kind of community.

Almost at once the town authorities recognized the street as a versatile tool for exerting control. In one town after another ordinances regulated the height of buildings, the pitch of their roofs, their construction, even their design, which had to be suited to the social standing of the occupants. City building plans were detailed. When a highly placed citizen of Lucerne wanted to build ''a simple and inexpensive house'' on his own land he was informed that according to the town plan a "handsome residence" had to be built. In the additions to existing towns and in most of the new towns the dimensions of the lot were prescribed, and all houses were taxed on the basis of their frontage. The fact that each house owned half the width of the street in front of it encouraged each business or each household to expand its activities into the street and to use the space for its convenience. As a consequence the civic authorities legislated questions of health and safety.

Finally what the street did to the medieval town was introduce a more precise system of linear measurements in the sale or purchase or assessment of land, so that land came to be seen as a commodity.

The esthetic consequences of the building of streets were scarcely less revolutionary. People learned to perceive a new kind of public space where previously they had merely seen a succession of alleys and passageways, a crooked interval between houses. Now they discovered a continuous space with a quality—and eventually with a name—of its own. What had been two rows of heterogeneous structures now became the walls of a spatial unit. From the beginning therefore the street served to catalyze the confusion of houses and spaces of the early medieval town, introducing concepts of architectural orientation and harmony, and even façade. At the same time the street undoubtedly destroyed one visible bond between town and village. Speaking of the development of the European city, Spengler mentions, "the courses of the streets, straight or crooked, broad or narrow; the houses low or tall, bright or dark, that in all Western cities turn their façades, *their faces,* and in all Eastern cities turn their backs, blank wall and railing, toward the street. . . . And these stone visages that have incorporated in their light world the humanness of the citizen himself and, like him, are all eye and intellect—how distinct the language of form that they talk, how different from the rustic drawl of the landscape!

It was in this tentative and almost unconscious manner that the street in our European-American landscape began a career that became increasingly spectacular and then culminated in the freeway. Imperceptibly and over many generations our vision of the city shifted from the cluster of towers and spires to the perspective of avenues and streets and uniform-size lots. The celestial model, never easy to discern in the dark medieval spaces among stone walls and crowded huts, has been at last forgotten; the map, the diagram, the coordinates are what help us make sense of the city.

7

Paris, Capital of the Nineteenth Century

WALTER BENJAMIN

The waters are blue and the vegetation pink;
The evening sweet to behold;
People are out walking. Great ladies promenade;
and behind them walk the small ladies.
  —Nguyen-Trong-Hiep: *Paris, Capital of France* (1897)

FOURIER, OR THE ARCADES

De ces palais les colonnes magiques
A l'amateur montrent de toutes parts
Dans les objets qu'étalent leurs portiques
Que l'industrie est rivale aux arts.
  —*Nouveaux tableaux de Paris* (1828)

Most of the Paris arcades are built in the decade and a half after 1822. The first condition for this new fashion is the boom in the textile trade. The *magasins de nouveauté*, the first establishments to keep large stocks of goods on their premises, begin to appear, precursors of the department stores. It is the time of which Balzac wrote, "The great poem of display chants its many-colored strophes from the Madeleine to the Porte-Saint-Denis." The arcades are a center of trade in luxury goods. In their fittings art is brought in to the service of commerce. Contemporaries never tire of admiring them. They long remain a center of attraction for foreigners. An *Illustrated Guide to Paris* said: "These arcades, a recent invention of industrial luxury, are glass-roofed, marble-walled passages cut through whole blocks of houses, whose owners have combined in this

From Walter Benjamin, "Paris, Capital of the Nineteenth Century," in Reflections, *ed. Peter Demetz (New York: Harcourt Brace Jovanovich, 1978), pp. 146–149, 151–153, 159–162. English translation copyright © 1978 by Harcourt Brace Jovanovich, Inc. Reprinted by permission of the publisher.*

speculation. On either side of the passages, which draw their light from above, run the most elegant shops, so that an arcade of this kind is a city, indeed, a world in miniature." The arcades are the scene of the first gas lighting.

The second condition for the construction of the arcades is the advent of building in iron. The Empire saw in this technique an aid to a renewal of architecture in the ancient Greek manner. The architectural theorist Bötticher expresses a general conviction when he says, "with regard to the artistic form of the new system, the formal principle of the Hellenic style" should be introduced. *Empire* is the style of revolutionary heroism for which the state is an end in itself. Just as Napoleon failed to recognize the functional nature of the state as an instrument of domination by the bourgeois class, neither did the master builders of his time perceive the functional nature of iron, through which the constructive principle began its domination of architecture. These builders model their pillars on Pompeian columns, their factories on houses, as later the first railway stations are to resemble chalets. "Construction fills the role of the unconscious." Nevertheless the idea of the engineer, originating in the revolutionary wars, begins to assert itself, and battle is joined between constructor and decorator, Ecole Polytechnique and Ecole des Beaux-Arts.

In iron, an artificial building material makes its appearance for the first time in the history of architecture. It undergoes a development that accelerates in the course of the century. The decisive breakthrough comes when it emerges that the locomotive, with which experiments had been made since the end of the twenties, could only be used on iron rails. The rail becomes the first prefabricated iron component, the forerunner of the girder. Iron is avoided in residential buildings and used in arcades, exhibition halls, stations—buildings serving transitory purposes. Simultaneously, the architectonic scope for the application of glass expands. The social conditions for its intensified use as a building material do not arrive, however, until a hundred years later. Even in Scheerbart's "glass architecture" (1914) it appears in utopian contexts.

Chaque époque rêve la suivante.
        —Michelet, *Avenir! Avenir!*

Corresponding in the collective consciousness to the forms of the new means of production, which at first were still dominated by the old (Marx), are images in which the new is intermingled with the old. These images are wishful fantasies, and in them the collective seeks both to preserve and to transfigure the inchoateness of the social product and the deficiencies in the social system of production. In addition, these wish-fulfilling images manifest an emphatic striving for dissociation with the outmoded—which means, however, with the most recent past. These tendencies direct the visual imagination, which has been activated by the new, back to the primeval past. In the dream in which, before the eyes of each epoch, that which is to follow appears in images, the latter appears wedded to elements from prehistory, that is, of a classless society. Intimations of this, deposited in the unconscious of the collective, mingle with the new to produce the utopia that has left its traces in thousands of configurations of life, from permanent buildings to fleeting fashions.

This state of affairs is discernible in Fourier's utopia. Its chief impetus comes from the advent of machines. But this is not directly expressed in his accounts of it; these have their origin in the morality of trade and the false morality propagated in its service. His phalanstery is supposed to lead men back to conditions in which virtue is superfluous. Its highly complicated organization is like a piece of machinery. The meshing of passions, the intricate interaction of the *passions mécanistes* with the *passion cabaliste,* are primitive analogies to machinery in the material of psychology. This human machinery produces the land of milk and honey, the primeval wish symbol that Fourier's utopia filled with new life.

In the arcades, Fourier saw the architectonic canon of the phalanstery. His reactionary modification of them is characteristic: whereas they originally serve commercial purposes, he makes them into dwelling places. The phalanstery becomes a city of arcades. Fourier installs in the austere, formal world of the Empire the colorful idyll of Biedermeier. Its radiance lasts, though paled, till Zola. He takes up Fourier's ideas in *Travail,* as he takes leave of the arcades in *Thérèse Raquin.* Marx defends Fourier to Carl Grün, emphasizing his "colossal vision of man." He also draws attention to Fourier's humor. And in fact Jean Paul in *Levana* is as closely related to Fourier the pedagogue as Scheerbart in his "glass architecture" is to Fourier the utopian. . . .

GRANDVILLE, OR THE WORLD EXHIBITIONS

> *Oui, quand le monde entier, de Paris jusqu'en Chine,*
> *O divin Saint-Simon, sera dans la doctrine,*
> *L'âge d'or doit renaitre avec tout son éclat,*
> *Les fleuves rouleront du thé, du chocolat;*
> *Les moutons tous rôtis bondiront dans la plaine,*
> *Et les brochets au bleu nageront dans la Seine;*
> *Les épinards viendront au monde fricassés,*
> *Avec des croûtons frits tout au tour concassés.*
> *Les arbres produiront des pommes en compotes*
> *Et l'on moissonnera des cerricks et des bottes;*
> *Il neigera du vin, il pleuvera des poulets,*
> *Et du ciel les canards tomberont aux navets.*
>
> —Lauglé and Vanderbusch, *Louis et le Saint-Simonien* (1832)

World exhibitions are the sites of pilgrimages to the commodity fetish. ''Europe is on the move to look at merchandise,'' said Taine in 1855. The world exhibitions are preceded by national industrial exhibitions, the first of which takes place in 1798 on the Champ-de-Mars. It proceeds from the wish ''to entertain the working classes, and becomes for them a festival of emancipation.'' The workers stand as customers in the foreground. The framework of the entertainment industry has not yet been formed. The popular festival supplies it. Chaptal's speech on industry opens this exhibition. The Saint-Simonists, who plan the industrialization of the earth, take up the idea of world exhibitions. Chevalier, the first authority in the new field, is a pupil of Enfantin and editor of the Saint-Simonist journal, *Globe*. The Saint-Simonists predicted the development of the world economy, but not of the class struggle. Beside their participation in industrial and commercial enterprises about the middle of the century stands their helplessness in questions concerning the proletariat. The world exhibitions glorify the exchange value of commodities. They create a framework in which commodities' intrinsic value is eclipsed. They open up a phantasmagoria that people enter to be amused. The entertainment industry facilitates this by elevating people to the level of commodities. They submit to being manipulated while enjoying their alienation from themselves and others. The enthronement of merchandise, with the aura of amusement surrounding it, is the secret theme of Grandville's art. This is reflected in the discord between its utopian and its cynical elements. Its subtleties in the presentation of inanimate objects correspond to what Marx called the "theological whims" of goods. This is clearly distilled in the term *spécialité*—a commodity description coming into use about this time in the luxury industry; under Grandville's pencil the whole of nature is transformed into *spécialités*. He presents them in the same spirit in which advertising—a word that is also coined at this time—begins to present its articles. He ends in madness.

Fashion: My dear Mr. Death!
       —Leopardi, *Dialogue Between Fashion and Death*

The world exhibitions build up the universe of commodities. Grandville's fantasies extend the character of a commodity to the universe. They modernize it. Saturn's ring becomes a cast-iron balcony on which the inhabitants of the planet take the air in the evening. The literary counterpart of this graphic utopia is presented by the book of the Fourierist natural scientist Toussenal. Fashion prescribes the ritual according to which the commodity fetish wishes to be worshiped; Grandville extends fashion's claims both to the objects of everyday use and to the cosmos. By pursuing it to its extremes he discloses its nature. This resides in its conflict with the organic. It couples the living body to the inorganic world. Against the living it asserts the rights of the corpse. Fetishism, which is subject to the sex appeal of the inorganic, is its vital nerve. The cult of commodities places it in its service.

On the occasion of the 1867 World Exhibition, Victor Hugo issues a manifesto: *To the Peoples of Europe.* Earlier, and more unambiguously, their interests had been represented by the French workers' delegations, the first of which had been sent to the London World Exhibition of 1851, and the second, consisting of seven hundred and fifty representatives, to that of 1862. The latter was of indirect importance for the foundation of the International Workingmen's Association by Marx. The phantasmagoria of capitalist culture reaches its most brilliant display in the World Exhibition of 1867. The Empire is at the height of its power. Paris reaffirms itself as the capital of luxury and fashion: Offenbach sets the rhythm of Parisian life. The operetta is the ironic utopia of the capital's lasting rule. . . .

HAUSSMANN, OR THE BARRICADES

J'ai le culte de Beau, du Bien, des grandes choses,
De la belle nature inspirant le grand art,
Qu'il enchante l'oreille ou charme le regard;
J'ai l'amour du printemps en fleurs: femmes et roses.
    —Baron Haussmann, *Confession d'un lion devenu vieux*

The blossomy realm of decoration,
Landscape and architecture's charm
And all effects of scenery repose
Upon perspective's law alone.
    —Franz Böhle, *Theatrical Catechism*

Haussmann's urban ideal was of long perspectives of streets and thoroughfares. This corresponds to the inclination, noticeable again and again in the nineteenth century, to ennoble technical necessities by artistic aims. The institutions of the secular and clerical dominance of the bourgeoisie were to find their apotheosis in a framework of streets. Streets, before their completion, were draped in canvas and unveiled like monuments. Haussmann's efficiency is integrated with Napoleonic idealism. The latter favors finance capital. Paris experiences a flowering of speculation. Playing the stock exchange displaces the game of chance in the forms that had come down from feudal society. To the phantasmagorias of space to which the *flâneur* abandons himself, correspond the phantasmagorias of time indulged in by the gambler. Gambling converts time into a narcotic. Lafargue declares gaming an imitation in miniature of the mysteries of economic prosperity. The expropriations by Haussmann call into being a fraudulent speculation. The arbitration of the Court of Cassation, inspired by the bourgeois and Orleanist opposition, increases the financial risk of Haussmannization. Haussmann attempts to strengthen his dictatorship and to place Paris under an emergency regime. In 1864 he gives expression in a parliamentary speech to his hatred of the rootless population of big cities. The latter is constantly increased by his enterprises. The rise in rents drives the proletariat into the suburbs. The *quartiers* of Paris thus lose their individual physiognomies. The red belt is formed. Haussmann gave himself the name of "artist in demolition." He felt himself called to his work and stresses this in his memoirs. Meanwhile, he estranges Parisians from their city. They begin to be conscious of its inhuman character. Maxime du Camp's monumental work *Paris* has its origin in this consciousness. The *Jérémiades d'un Haussmannisé* give it the form of a biblical lament.

The true purpose of Haussmann's work was to secure the city against civil war. He wanted to make the erection of barricades in Paris impossible for all time. With such intent Louis-Philippe had already introduced wooden paving. Yet the barricades played a part in the February Revolution. Engels studies the technique of barricade fighting. Haussmann seeks to prevent barricades in two ways. The breadth of the streets is intended to make their erection impossible, and new thoroughfares are to open the shortest route between the barracks and the working-class districts. Contemporaries christen the enterprise "strategic embellishment."

Fais voir, en déjouant la ruse,
O République, à ces pervers
Ta grande fuce de Méduse
Au milieu de rouges éclairs.
            —Workers' song (about 1850)

The barricade is resurrected in the Commune. It is stronger and better secured than ever. It stretches across the great boulevards, often reaching the height of the first floor, and covers the trenches behind it. Just as the *Communist Manifesto* ends the epoch of the professional conspirator, the Commune puts an end to the phantasmagoria that dominates the freedom of the proletariat. It dispels the illusion that the task of the proletarian revolution is to complete the work of 1789 hand in hand with the bourgeoisie. This illusion prevailed from 1831 to 1871, from the Lyons uprising to the Commune. The bourgeoisie never shared this error. The struggle of the bourgeoisie against the social rights of the proletariat has already begun in the Great Revolution and coincides with the philanthropic movement that conceals it, attaining its fullest development under Napoleon III. Under him is written the monumental work of this political tendency: Le Play's *European Workers*. Besides the covert position of philanthropy, the bourgeoisie was always ready to take up the overt position of class struggle. As early as 1831 it recognizes, in the *Journal des Débats*, "Every industrialist lives in his factory like the plantation owners among their slaves." If, on the one hand, the lack of a guiding theory of revolution was the undoing of the old workers' uprisings, it was also, on the other, the condition for the immediate energy and enthusiasm with which they set about establishing a new society. This enthusiasm, which reached its climax in the Commune, for a time won over to the workers the best elements of the bourgeoisie, but in the end led them to succumb to their worst. Rimbaud and Courbet declare their support for the Commune. The Paris fire is the fitting conclusion to Haussmann's work of destruction.

My good father had been in Paris.
     —Karl Gutzkow, *Letters from Paris* (1842)

Balzac was the first to speak of the ruins of the bourgeoisie. But only Surrealism exposed them to view. The development of the forces of production reduced the wish symbols of the previous century to rubble even before the monuments representing them had crumbled. In the nineteenth century this development emancipated constructive forms from art, as the sciences freed themselves from philosophy in the sixteenth. Architecture makes a start as constructional engineering. The reproduction of nature in photography follows. Fantasy creation prepares itself to become practical as commercial art. Literature is subjected to montage in the *feuilleton*. All these products are on the point of going to market as wares. But they hesitate on the brink. From this epoch stem the arcades and interiors, the exhibitions and panoramas. They are residues of a dream world. The realization of dream elements in waking is the textbook example of dialectical thinking. For this reason dialectical thinking is the organ of historical awakening. Each epoch not only dreams the next, but also, in dreaming, strives toward the moment of waking. It bears its end in itself and unfolds it—as Hegel already saw—with ruse. In the convulsions of the commodity economy we begin to recognize the monuments of the bourgeoisie as ruins even before they have crumbled.

8

The Uses of Sidewalks: Contact

JANE JACOBS

Reformers have long observed city people loitering on busy corners, hanging around in candy stores and bars and drinking soda pop on stoops, and have passed a judgment, the gist of which is: "This is deplorable! If these people had decent homes and more private or bosky outdoor place, they wouldn't be on the street!"

This judgment represents a profound misunderstanding of cities. It makes no more sense than to drop in at a testimonial banquet in a hotel and conclude that if these people had wives who could cook, they would give their parties at home.

The point of both the testimonial banquet and the social life of city sidewalks is precisely that they are public. They bring together people who do not know each other in an intimate, private social fashion and in most cases do not care to know each other in that fashion.

Nobody can keep open house in a great city. Nobody wants to. And yet if interesting, useful and significant contacts among the people of cities are confined to acquaintanceships suitable for private life, the city becomes stultified. Cities are full of people with whom, from your viewpoint, or mine, or any other individual's, a certain degree of contact is useful or enjoyable; but you do not want them in your hair. And they do not want you in theirs either.

In speaking about city sidewalk safety, I mentioned how necessary it is that there should be, in the brains behind the eyes on the street, an almost unconscious assumption of general street support when the chips are down—when a citizen has to choose, for instance, whether he will take responsibility, or abdicate it, in combating barbarism or protecting strangers. There is a short word for this assumption of support: trust. The trust of a city street is formed over time from many, many little public sidewalk contacts. It grows out of people stopping by at the bar for a beer, getting advice from the grocer and giving advice to the newsstand man, comparing opinions with other customers at the bakery and nodding hello to the two boys drinking pop on the stoop, eying the girls while waiting to be called to dinner, admonishing the children, hearing about a job from the hardware man and borrowing a dollar from the druggist, admiring the new babies and sympathizing over the way a coat faded. Customs vary: in some neighborhoods people compare notes on their dogs; in others they compare notes on their landlords.

Most of it is ostensibly utterly trivial but the sum is not trivial at all. The sum of such casual, public contact at a local level—most of it fortuitous, most of it associated with errands, all of it metered by the person concerned and not thrust upon him by anyone—is a feeling for the public identity of people, a web of public respect and trust, and a resource in time of personal or neighborhood need. The absence of this trust is a disaster to a city street. Its cultivation cannot be institutionalized. And above all, *it implies no private commitments.*

I have seen a striking difference between presence and absence of casual public trust on two sides of the same wide street in East Harlem, composed of residents of roughly the same incomes and same races. On the old-city side, which was full of public places and the sidewalk loitering so deplored by Utopian minders of other people's leisure, the children were being kept well in hand. On the project side of the street across the way, the children, who had a fire hydrant open beside their play area, were behaving destructively, drenching the open windows of houses with water, squirting it on adults who ignorantly walked on the project side of the street, throwing it into the windows of cars as they went by. Nobody dared to stop them. These were anonymous children, and the identities behind them were an unknown. What if you scolded or stopped them? Who would back you up over there in the blind-eyed Turf? Would you get, instead, revenge? Better to keep out of it. Impersonal city streets make anonymous people, and this is not a matter of esthetic quality nor of a mystical emotional effect in architectural scale. It is a matter of what kinds of tangible enterprises sidewalks have, and therefore of how people use the sidewalks in practical, everyday life.

The casual public sidewalk life of cities ties directly into other types of public life, of which I shall mention one as illustrative, although there is no end to their variety.

Formal types of local city organizations are frequently assumed by planners and even by some social workers to grow in direct, common-sense fashion out of announcements of meetings, the presence of meeting rooms, and the existence of problems of obvious public concern. Perhaps they grow so in suburbs and towns. They do not grow so in cities.

Formal public organizations in cities require an informal public life underlying them, mediating between them and the privacy of the people of the city. We catch a hint of what happens by contrasting, again, a city area possessing a public sidewalk life with a city area lacking it, as told about in the report of a settlement-house social researcher who was studying problems relating to public schools in a section of New York City:

Mr. W___ [principal of an elementary school] was questioned on the effect of J___ Houses on the school, and the uprooting of the community around the school. He felt that there had been many effects and of these most were negative. He mentioned that the project had torn out numerous institutions for socializing. The present atmosphere of the project was in no way similar to the gaiety of the streets before the project was built. He noted that in general there seemed fewer people on the streets because there were fewer places for people to gather. He also con-

tended that before the projects were built the Parents Association had been very strong, and now there were only
very few active members.

Mr. W____ was wrong in one respect. There were not
fewer places (or at any rate there was not less space) for
people to gather in the project, if we count places deliberately planned for constructive socializing. Of course there
were no bars, no candy stores, no hole-in-the-wall *bodegas*,
no restaurants in the project. But the project under discussion was equipped with a model complement of meeting
rooms, craft, art and game rooms, outdoor benches, malls,
etc., enough to gladden the heart of even the Garden City
advocates.

Why are such places dead and useless without the
most determined efforts and expense to inveigle users—
and then to maintain control over the users? What services
do the public sidewalk and its enterprises fulfill that these
planned gathering places do not? And why? How does an
informal public sidewalk life bolster a more formal, organizational public life?

To understand such problems—to understand why
drinking pop on the stoop differs from drinking pop in the
game room, and why getting advice from the grocer or the
bartender differs from getting advice from either your
next-door neighbor or from an institutional lady who may
be hand-in-glove with an institutional landlord—we must
look into the matter of city privacy.

Privacy is precious in cities. It is indispensable. Perhaps it is precious and indispensable everywhere, but
most places you cannot get it. In small settlements everyone knows your affairs. In the city everyone does not—
only those you choose to tell will know much about you.
This is one of the attributes of cities that is precious to
most city people, whether their incomes are high or their
incomes are low, whether they are white or colored,
whether they are old inhabitants or new, and it is a gift of
great-city life deeply cherished and jealously guarded.

Architectural and planning literature deals with privacy in terms of windows, overlooks, sight lines. The idea
is that if no one from outside can peek into where you
live—behold, privacy. This is simple-minded. Window pri-

vacy is the easiest commodity in the world to get. You just pull down the shades or adjust the blinds. The privacy of keeping one's personal affairs to those selected to know them, and the privacy of having reasonable control over who shall make inroads on your time and when, are rare commodities in most of this world, however, and they have nothing to do with the orientation of windows.

Anthropologist Elena Padilla, author of *Up from Puerto Rico,* describing Puerto Rican life in a poor and squalid district of New York, tells how much people know about each other—who is to be trusted and who not, who is defiant of the law and who upholds it, who is competent and well informed and who is inept and ignorant—and how these things are known from the public life of the sidewalk and its associated enterprises. These are matters of public character. But she also tells how select are those permitted to drop into the kitchen for a cup of coffee, how strong are the ties, and how limited the number of a person's genuine confidants, those who share in a person's private life and private affairs. She tells how it is not considered dignified for everyone to know one's affairs. Nor is it considered dignified to snoop on others beyond the face presented in public. It does violence to a person's privacy and rights. In this, the people she describes are essentially the same as the people of the mixed, Americanized city street on which I live, and essentially the same as the peple who live in high-income apartments or fine town houses, too.

A good city street neighborhood achieves a marvel of balance between its people's determination to have essential privacy and their simultaneous wishes for differing degrees of contact, enjoyment or help from the people around. This balance is largely made up of small, sensitively managed details, practiced and accepted so casually that they are normally taken for granted.

Perhaps I can best explain this subtle but all-important balance in terms of the stores where people leave keys for their friends, a common custom in New York. In our family, for example, when a friend wants to use our place while we are away for a week end or everyone happens to be out during the day, or a visitor for whom we do not wish to wait up is spending the night, we tell such a friend that he can pick up the key at the delicatessen across the street. Joe Cornacchia, who keeps the delicatessen, usually has a dozen or so keys at a time for handing out like this. He has a special drawer for them.

Now why do I, and many others, select Joe as a logical custodian for keys? Because we trust him, first, to be a responsible custodian, but equally important because we know that he combines a feeling of good will with a feeling of no personal responsibility about our private affairs. Joe considers it no concern of his whom we choose to permit in our places and why.

Around on the other side of our block, people leave their keys at a Spanish grocery. On the other side of Joe's block, people leave them at the candy store. Down a block they leave them at the coffee shop, and a few hundred feet around the corner from that, in a barber shop. Around one corner from two fashionable blocks of town houses and apartments in the Upper East Side, people leave their keys in a butcher shop and a bookshop; around another corner they leave them in a cleaner's and a drug-store. In unfashionable East Harlem keys are left with at least one florist, in bakeries, in luncheonettes, in Spanish and Italian groceries.

The point, wherever they are left, is not the kind of ostensible service that the enterprise offers, but the kind of proprietor it has.

A service like this cannot be formalized. Identifications . . . questions . . . insurance against mishaps. The all-essential line between public service and privacy would be transgressed by institutionalization. Nobody in his right mind would leave his key in such a place. The service must be given as a favor by someone with an unshakable understanding of the difference between a person's key and a person's private life, or it cannot be given at all.

Or consider the line drawn by Mr. Jaffe at the candy store around our corner—a line so well understood by his customers and by other storekeepers too that they can spend their whole lives in its presence and never think about it consciously. One ordinary morning last winter, Mr. Jaffe, whose formal business name is Bernie, and his wife, whose formal business name is Ann, supervised the small children crossing at the corner on the way to P.S. 41, as Bernie always does because he sees the need; lent an umbrella to one customer and a dollar to another; took custody of two keys; took in some packages for people in the next building who were away; lectured two youngsters who asked for cigarettes; gave street directions; took custody of a watch to give the repair man across the street when he opened later; gave out information on the range of rents in the neighborhood to an apartment seeker; listened to a tale of domestic difficulty and offered reassurance; told some rowdies they could not come in unless they behaved and then defined (and got) good behavior; provided an incidental forum for half a dozen conversations among customers who dropped in for oddments; set aside certain newly arrived papers and magazines for regular customers who would depend on getting them; advised a mother who came for a birthday present not to get the ship-model kit because another child going to the same birthday party was giving that; and got a back copy (this was for me) of the previous day's newspaper out of the deliverer's surplus returns when he came by.

After considering this multiplicity of extra-merchandising services I asked Bernie, "Do you ever introduce your customers to each other?"

He looked startled at the idea, even dismayed. "No," he said thoughtfully. "That would just not be advisable. Sometimes, if I know two customers who are in at the same time have an interest in common, I bring up the subject in conversation and let them carry it on from there if they want to. But oh no, I wouldn't introduce them."

When I told this to an acquaintance in a suburb, she promptly assumed that Mr. Jaffe felt that to make an introduction would be to step above his social class. Not at all. In our neighborhood, storekeepers like the Jaffes enjoy an excellent social status, that of businessmen. In income they are apt to be the peers of the general run of customers and in independence they are the superiors. Their advice, as men or women of common sense and experience, is sought and respected. They are well known as individuals, rather than unknown as class symbols. No; this is that almost unconsciously enforced, well-balanced line showing, the line between the city public world and the world of privacy.

This line can be maintained, without awkwardness to anyone, because of the great plenty of opportunities for public contact in the enterprises along the sidewalks, or on the sidewalks themselves as people move to and fro or deliberately loiter when they feel like it, and also because of the presence of many public hosts, so to speak, proprietors of meeting places like Bernie's where one is free either to hang around or dash in and out, no strings attached.

Under this system, it is possible in a city street neighborhood to know all kinds of people without unwelcome entanglements, without boredom, necessity for excuses, explanations, fears of giving offense, embarrassments respecting impositions or commitments, and all such paraphernalia of obligations which can accompany less limited relationships. It is possible to be on excellent sidewalk terms with people who are very different from oneself, and even, as time passes, on familiar public terms with them. Such relationships can, and do, endure for many years, for decades; they could never have formed without that line, much less endured. They form precisely because they are by-the-way to people's normal public sorties.

"Togetherness" is a fittingly nauseating name for an old ideal in planning theory. This ideal is that if anything is shared among people, much should be shared. "Togetherness," apparently a spiritual resource of the new suburbs, works destructively in cities. The requirement that much shall be shared drives city people apart.

When an area of a city lacks a sidewalk life, the people of the place must enlarge their private lives if they are to have anything approaching equivalent contact with their neighbors. They must settle for some form of "togetherness," in which more is shared with one another than in the life of the sidewalks, or else they must settle for lack of contact. Inevitably the outcome is one or the other; it has to be; and either has distressing results.

In the case of the first outcome, where people do share much, they become exceedingly choosy as to who their neighbors are, or with whom they associate at all. They have to become so. A friend of mine, Penny Kostritsky, is unwittingly and unwillingly in this fix on a street in Baltimore. Her street of nothing but residences, embedded in an area of almost nothing but residences, has been experimentally equipped with a charming sidewalk park. The sidewalk has been widened and attractively paved, wheeled traffic discouraged from the narrow street roadbed, trees and flowers planted, and a piece of play sculpture is to go in. All these are splendid ideas so far as they go.

However, there are no stores. The mothers from nearby blocks who bring small children here, and come here to find some contact with others themselves, perforce go into the houses of acquaintances along the street to warm up in winter, to make telephone calls, to take their children in emergencies to the bathroom. Their hostesses offer them coffee, for there is no other place to get coffee, and naturally considerable social life of this kind has arisen around the park. Much is shared.

Mrs. Kostritsky, who lives in one of the conveniently located houses, and who has two small children, is in the thick of this narrow and accidental social life. "I have lost the advantage of living in the city," she says, "without getting the advantages of living in the suburbs." Still more distressing, when mothers of different income or color or educational background bring their children to the street park, they and their children are rudely and pointedly ostracized. They fit awkwardly into the suburbanlike sharing of private lives that has grown in default of city sidewalk life. The park lacks benches purposely; the "togetherness" people ruled them out because they might be interpreted as an invitation to people who cannot fit in.

"If only we had a couple of stores on the street," Mrs. Kostritsky laments. "If only there were a grocery store or a drug store or a snack joint. Then the telephone calls and the warming up and the gathering could be done naturally in public, and then people would act more decent to each other because everybody would have a right to be here."

Much the same thing that happens in this sidewalk park without a city public life happens sometimes in middle-class projects and colonies, such as Chatham Village in Pittsburgh for example, a famous model of Garden City planning.

The houses here are grouped in colonies around shared interior lawns and play yards, and the whole development is equipped with other devices for close sharing, such as a residents' club which holds parties, dances, reunions, has ladies' activities like bridge and sewing parties, and holds dances and parties for the children. There is no public life here, in any city sense. There are differing degrees of extended private life.

Chatham Village's success as a "model" neighborhood where much is shared has required that the residents be similar to one another in their standards, interests and backgrounds. In the main they are middle-class professionals and their families.* It has also required that residents set themselves distinctly apart from the different people in the surrounding city; these are in the main also middle class, but lower middle class, and this is too different for the degree of chumminess that neighborliness in Chatham Village entails.

The inevitable insularity (and homogeneity) of Chatham Village has practical consequences. As one illustration, the junior high school serving the area has problems, as all schools do. Chatham Village is large enough to dominate the elementary school to which its children go, and therefore to work at helping solve this school's problems. To deal with the junior high, however, Chatham Village's people must cooperate with entirely different neighborhoods. But there is no public acquaintanceship, no foundation of casual public trust, no cross-connections with the necessary people—and no practice or ease in applying the most ordinary techniques of city public life at lowly levels. Feeling helpless, as indeed they are, some Chatham Village families move away when their children reach junior high age; others contrive to send them to private high schools. Ironically, just such neighborhood islands as Chatham Village are encouraged in orthodox planning on the specific grounds that cities need the talents and stabilizing influence of the middle class. Presumably these qualities are to seep out by osmosis.

People who do not fit happily into such colonies eventually get out, and in time managements become sophisticated in knowing who among applicants will fit in. Along with basic similarities of standards, values and backgrounds, the arrangement seems to demand a formidable amount of forbearance and tact.

City residential planning that depends, for contact among neighbors, on personal sharing of this sort, and that cultivates it, often does work well socially, if rather

*One representative court, for example, contains as this is written four lawyers, two doctors, two engineers, a dentist, a salesman, a banker, a railroad executive, a planning executive.

narrowly, *for self-selected upper-middle-class people.* It solves easy problems for an easy kind of population. So far as I have been able to discover, it fails to work, however, even on its own terms, *with any other kind of population.*

The more common outcome in cities, where people are faced with the choice of sharing much or nothing, is nothing. In city areas that lack a natural and casual pubic life, it is common for residents to isolate themselves from each other to a fantastic degree. If mere contact with your neighbors threatens to entangle you in their private lives, or entangle them in yours, and if you cannot be so careful who your neighbors are as self-selected upper-middle-class people can be, the logical solution is absolutely to avoid friendliness or casual offers of help. Better to stay thoroughly distant. As a practical result, the ordinary public jobs—like keeping children in hand—for which people must take a little personal initiative, or those for which they must band together in limited common purposes, go undone. The abysses this opens up can be almost unbelievable.

For example, in one New York City project which is designed—like all orthodox residential city planning—for sharing much or nothing, a remarkably outgoing woman prided herself that she had become acquainted, by making a deliberate effort, with the mothers of every one of the ninety families in her building. She called on them. She buttonholed them at the door or in the hall. She struck up conversations if she sat beside them on a bench.

It so happened that her eight-year-old son, one day, got stuck in the elevator and was left there without help for more than two hours, although he screamed, cried and pounded. The next day the mother expressed her dismay to one of her ninety acquaintances. "Oh, was that *your* son?" said the other woman. "I didn't know whose boy he was. If I had realized he was *your* son I would have helped him."

This woman, who had not behaved in any such insanely calloused fashion on her old public street—to which she constantly returned, by the way, for public life—was afraid of a possible entanglement that might not be kept easily on a public plane.

Dozens of illustrations of this defense can be found wherever the choice is sharing much or nothing. A thor-

ough and detailed report by Ellen Lurie, a social worker in
East Harlem, on life in a low-income project there, has this
to say:

> It is . . . extremely important to recognize that for considerably
> complicated reasons, many adults either don't want to become in-
> volved in any friendship-relationships at all with their neighbors,
> or, if they do succumb to the need for some form of society, they
> strictly limit themselves to one or two friends, and no more. Over
> and over again, wives repeated their husband's warning:
> "I'm not to get too friendly with anyone. My husband doesn't
> believe in it."
> "People are too gossipy and they could get us in a lot of trou-
> ble."
> "It's best to mind your own business."
> One woman, Mrs. Abraham, always goes out the back door of
> the building because she doesn't want to interfere with the people
> standing around in the front. Another man, Mr. Colan . . . won't
> let his wife make any friends in the project, because he doesn't
> trust the people here. They have four children, ranging from 8 years
> to 14, but they are not allowed downstairs alone, because the par-
> ents are afraid someone will hurt them.* What happens then is that
> all sorts of barriers to insure self-protection are being constructed
> by many families. To protect their children from a neighborhood
> they aren't sure of, they keep them upstairs in the apartment. To
> protect themselves, they make few, if any, friends. Some are afraid
> that friends will become angry or envious and make up a story to
> report to management, causing them great trouble. If the husband
> gets a bonus (which he decides not to report) and the wife buys
> new curtains, the visiting friends will see and might tell the man-
> agement, who, in turn, investigates and issues a rent increase. Sus-
> picions and fear of trouble often outweigh any need for neighborly
> advice and help. For these families the sense of privacy has already
> been extensively violated. The deepest secrets, all the family skele-
> tons, are well known not only to management but often to other
> public agencies, such as the Welfare Department. To preserve any
> last remnants of privacy, they choose to avoid close relationships
> with others. This same phenomenon may be found to a much
> lesser degree in non-planned slum housing, for there too it is often
> necessary for other reasons to build up these forms of self-protec-
> tion. But, it is surely true that this withdrawing from the society of
> others is much more extensive in planned housing. Even in En-
> gland, this suspicion of the neighbors and the ensuing aloofness
> was found in studies of planned towns. Perhaps this pattern is
> nothing more than an elaborate group mechanism to protect and
> preserve inner dignity in the face of so many outside pressures to
> conform.

Along with nothingness, considerable "togetherness"
can be found in such places, however. Mrs. Lurie reports
on this type of relationship:

---

*This is very common in public projects in New York.

> Often two women from two different buildings will meet in the
> laundry room, recognize each other; although they may never have
> spoken a single word to each other back on 99th Street, suddenly
> here they become ''best friends.'' If one of these two already has a
> friend or two in her own building, the other is likely to be drawn
> into that circle and begins to make her friendships, not with
> women on her floor, but rather on her friend's floor.
>
> These friendships do not go into an ever-widening circle. There
> are certain definite well-traveled paths in the project, and after a
> while no new people are met.

Mrs. Lurie, who works at community organization in
East Harlem, with remarkable success, has looked into the
history of many past attempts at project tenant organization. She has told me that ''togetherness,'' itself, is one of
the factors that make this kind of organization so difficult.
''These projects are not lacking in natural leaders,'' she
says. ''They contain people with real ability, wonderful
people many of them, but the typical sequence is that in
the course of organization leaders have found each other,
gotten all involved in each others' social lives, and have
ended up talking to nobody but each other. They have not
found their followers. Everything tends to degenerate into
ineffective cliques, as a natural course. There is no normal
public life. Just the mechanics of people learning what is
going on is so difficult. It all makes the simplest social gain
extra hard for these people.''

Residents of unplanned city residential areas that lack
neighborhood commerce and sidewalk life seem sometimes to follow the same course as residents of public projects when faced with the choice of sharing much or nothing. Thus researchers hunting the secrets of the social
structure in a dull gray-area district of Detroit came to the
unexpected conclusion there was no social structure.

The social structure of sidewalk life hangs partly on
what can be called self-appointed public characters. A
public character is anyone who is in frequent contact with
a wide circle of people and who is sufficiently interested to
make himself a public character. A public character need
have no special talents or wisdom to fulfill his function—
although he often does. He just needs to be present, and
there need to be enough of his counterparts. His main
qualifications is that he *is* public, that he talks to lots of different people. In this way, news travels that is of sidewalk
interest.

Most public sidewalk characters are steadily stationed in public places. They are storekeepers or barkeepers or the like. These are the basic public characters. All other public characters of city sidewalks depend on them—if only indirectly because of the presence of sidewalk routes to such enterprises and their proprietors.

Settlement-house workers and pastors, two more formalized kinds of public characters, typically depend on the street grapevine news systems that have their ganglia in the stores. The director of a settlement on New York's Lower East Side, as an example, makes a regular round of stores. He learns from the cleaner who does his suits about the presence of dope pushers in the neighborhood. He learns from the grocer that the Dragons are working up to something and need attention. He learns from the candy store that two girls are agitating the Sportsmen toward a rumble. One of his most important information spots is an unused breadbox on Rivington Street. That is, it is not used for bread. It stands outside a grocery and is used for sitting on and lounging beside, between the settlement house, a candy store and a pool parlor. A message spoken there for any teen-ager within many blocks will reach his ears unerringly and surprisingly quickly, and the opposite flow along the grapevine similarly brings news quickly in to the breadbox.

Blake Hobbs, the head of the Union Settlement music school in East Harlem, notes that when he gets a first student from one block of the old busy street neighborhoods, he rapidly gets at least three or four more and sometimes almost every child on the block. But when he gets a child from the nearby projects—perhaps through the public school or a playground conversation he has initiated—he almost never gets another as a direct sequence. Word does not move around when public characters and sidewalk life are lacking.

Besides the anchored public characters of the sidewalk, and the well-recognized roving public characters, there are apt to be various more specialized public characters on a city sidewalk. In a curious way, some of these help establish an identity not only for themselves but for others. Describing the everyday life of a retired tenor at such sidewalk establishments as the restaurant and the *bocce* court, a San Francisco news story notes, ''It is said of Meloni that because of his intensity, his dramatic manner and his life-long interest in music, he transmits a feeling of vicarious importance to his many friends.'' Precisely.

One need not have either the artistry or the personality of such a man to become a specialized sidewalk character—but only a pertinent speciality of some sort. It is easy. I am a specialized public character of sorts along our street, owing of course to the fundamental presence of the basic, anchored public characters. The way I became one started with the fact that Greenwich Village, where I live, was waging an interminable and horrendous battle to save its main park from being bisected by a highway. During the course of battle I undertook, at the behest of a committee organizer away over on the other side of Greenwich Village, to deposit in stores on a few blocks of our streets supplies of petition cards protesting the proposed roadway. Customers would sign the cards while in the stores, and from time to time I would make my pickups.* As a result of engaging in this messenger work, I have since become automatically the sidewalk public character on petition strategy. Before long, for instance, Mr. Fox at the liquor store was consulting me, as he wrapped up my bottle, on how we could get the city to remove a long abandoned and dangerous eyesore, a closed-up comfort station near his corner. If I would undertake to compose the petitions and find the effective way of presenting them to City Hall, he proposed, he and his partners would undertake to have them printed, circulated and picked up. Soon the stores round about had comfort station removal petitions. Our street by now has many public experts on petition tactics, including the children.

Not only do public characters spread the news and learn the news at retail, so to speak. They connect with each other and thus spread word wholesale, in effect.

A sidewalk life, so far as I can observe, arises out of no mysterious qualities or talents for it in this or that type of population. It arises only when the concrete, tangible facilities it requires are present. These happen to be the same facilities, in the same abundance and ubiquity, that are re-

---

*This, by the way, is an efficient device, accomplishing with a fraction of the effort what would be a mountainous task door to door. It also makes more public conversation and opinion than door-to-door visits.

quired for cultivating sidewalk safety. If they are absent, public sidewalk contacts are absent too.

The well-off have many ways of assuaging needs for which poorer people may depend much on sidewalk life— from hearing of jobs to being recognized by the head-waiter. But nevertheless, many of the rich or near-rich in cities appear to appreciate sidewalk life as much as anybody. At any rate, they pay enormous rents to move into areas with an exuberant and varied sidewalk life. They actually crowd out the middle class and the poor in lively areas like Yorkville or Greenwich Village in New York, or Telegraph Hill just off the North Beach streets of San Francisco. They capriciously desert, after only a few decades of fashion at most, the monotonous streets of "quiet residential areas" and leave them to the less fortunate. Talk to residents of Georgetown in the District of Columbia and by the second or third sentence at least you will begin to hear rhapsodies about the charming restaurants, "more good restaurants than in all the rest of the city put together," the uniqueness and friendliness of the stores, the pleasures of running into people when doing errands at the next corner—and nothing but pride over the fact that Georgetown has become a specialty shopping district for its whole metropolitan area. The city area, rich or poor or in between, harmed by an interesting sidewalk life and plentiful sidewalk contacts has yet to be found.

Efficiency of public sidewalk characters declines drastically if too much burden is put upon them. A store, for example, can reach a turnover in its contacts, or potential contacts, which is so large and so superficial that it is socially useless. An example of this can be seen at the candy and newspaper store owned by the housing cooperative of Corlears Hook on New York's Lower East Side. This planned project store replaces perhaps forty superficially similar stores which were wiped out (without compensation to their proprietors) on that project site and the adjoining sites. The place is a mill. Its clerks are so busy making change and screaming ineffectual imprecations at rowdies that they never hear anything except "I want that." This, or utter disinterest, is the usual atmosphere where shopping center planning or repressive zoning artificially contrives commercial monopolies for city neighborhoods. A store like this would fail economically if it had competition. Meantime, although monopoly insures the financial success planned for it, it fails the city socially.

Sidewalk public contact and sidewalk public safety, taken together, bear directly on our country's most serious social problem—segregation and racial discrimination.

I do not mean to imply that a city's planning and design, or its types of streets and street life, can automatically overcome segregation and discrimination. Too many other kinds of effort are also required to right these injustices.

But I do mean to say that to build and to rebuild big cities whose sidewalks are unsafe and whose people must settle for sharing much or nothing, *can* make it *much harder* for American cities to overcome discrimination no matter how much effort is expended.

Considering the amount of prejudice and fear that accompany discrimination and bolster it, overcoming residential discrimination is just that much harder if people feel unsafe on their sidewalks anyway. Overcoming residential discrimination comes hard where people have no means of keeping a civilized public life on a basically dignified public footing, and their private lives on a private footing.

To be sure, token model housing integration schemes here and there can be achieved in city areas handicapped by danger and by lack of public life—achieved by applying great effort and settling for abnormal (abnormal for cities) choosiness among new neighbors. This is an evasion of the size of the task and its urgency.

The tolerance, the room for great differences among neighbors—differences that often go far deeper than differences in color—which are possible and normal in intensely urban life, but which are so foreign to suburbs and pseudosuburbs, are possible and normal only when streets of great cities have built-in equipment allowing strangers to dwell in peace together on civilized but essentially dignified and reserved terms.

Lowly, unpurposeful and random as they may appear, sidewalk contacts are the small change from which a city's wealth of public life may grow.

Los Angeles is an extreme example of a metropolis

with little public life, depending mainly instead on contacts of a more private social nature.

On one plane, for instance, an acquaintance there comments that although she has lived in the city for ten years and knows it contains Mexicans, she has never laid eyes on a Mexican or an item of Mexican culture, much less ever exchanged any words with a Mexican.

On another plane, Orson Welles has written that Hollywood is the only theatrical center in the world that has failed to develop a theatrical bistro.

And on still another plane, one of Los Angeles' most powerful businessmen comes upon a blank in public relationships which would be inconceivable in other cities of this size. This businessman, volunteering that the city is ''culturally behind,'' as he put it, told me that he for one was at work to remedy this. He was heading a committee to raise funds for a first-rate art museum. Later in our conversation, after he had told me about the businessmen's club life of Los Angeles, a life with which he is involved as one of its leaders, I asked him how or where Hollywood people gathered in corresponding fashion. He was unable to answer this. He then added that he knew no one at all connected with the film industry, nor did he know anyone who did have such acquaintanceship. ''I know that must sound strange,'' he reflected. ''We are glad to have the film industry here, but those connected with it are just not people one would know socially.''

Here again is ''togetherness'' or nothing. Consider this man's handicap in his attempts to get a metropolitan art museum established. He has no way of reaching with any ease, practice or trust some of his committee's potentially best prospects.

In its upper economic, political and cultural echelons, Los Angeles operates according to the same provincial premises of social insularity as the street with the sidewalk park in Baltimore or as Chatham Village in Pittsburgh. Such a metropolis lacks means for bringing together necessary ideas, necessary enthusiasms, necessary money. Los Angeles is embarked on a strange experiment: trying to run not just projects, not just gray areas, but a whole metropolis, by dint of ''togetherness'' or nothing. I think this is an inevitable outcome for great cities whose people lack city public life in ordinary living and working.

II

CIVIC
ARCHITECTURE

INTRODUCTION

Beginning in the Renaissance, and continuing for some time thereafter, it was common practice in architectural treatises to call all non-ecclesiastical building ''civic'' (or ''civil'') architecture. It was thought that there was a unified manner through which to approach all public and private buildings, since they both made up the secular city: simple homes and *palazzi*, courts and corn exchanges.

Today we have difficulty thinking of the city as this unified whole: we came to separate the study of public and private architecture (often ignoring the former), or, under the influence of the modern movement, erected buildings that express little relation to their social purposes. While there is greater interest today in the architecture of the public place, J.B. Jackson writes in ''Forum Follows Function'' that that place has undergone a transformation in the United States. Whereas European public places always had a civic character that framed political activities and speech within a pre-existing political community, the American public space has increasingly surrendered that civic quality in favor of more gregarious, relaxed, informal social interaction. That interaction does indeed go on—in parks, sports arenas, flea markets—but it is no longer political.

In their essays, William Hubbard, Moshe Safdie, and Donlyn Lyndon attempt to define the elements of a civic architecture that might still play that earlier, political role. Hubbard's ''A Meaning for Monuments'' examines the Vietnam Veterans Memorial in Washington from this perspective, and finds that the original design fails to serve as a truly political monument because its pure geometric form and list of individual names do not speak to us collectively as all successful icons do. Modern monuments, like modern architecture generally, are mute, Hubbard insists, and do not give us the opportunity to reflect intelligently as we do before an articulate monument. (In an epilogue, however, he finds that the figurative statues subsequently placed nearby do allow the original monument to speak, and powerfully.)

In ''Collective Significance,'' Safdie treats the question of ''monumentality'' more abstractly, as those elements that define the city and reflect its political and social hierarchy—either through slow evolution, or through conscious composition. Our modern cities lack this monumentality, this self-definition, for more than architectural reasons: our architecture simply reflects the fact that we live in a democratic political and economic culture that rebels against such physical embodiments of hierarchy. We can "read" the civic life of the city through its architecture; and when any monumental skyscraper can be placed in the shadow of another built alongside by another developer, this reflects a great deal about our levelling politics.

Looking back over the history of civic buildings and public places in "Public Buildings: Symbols Qualified by Experience," Lyndon finds that the most successful are those that do not treat themselves as simple monuments to institutional purpose. The most memorable—from the Rue de Rivoli, to the Massachusetts State House, to the new Beverly Hills Civic Center—are conscious of their interaction with their physical environment and with the ways they will be used in everyday life. When they are conceived in this way, turning outward from the work done inside, they are able to embody civic purposes.

The final three essays examine different types of American civic buildings and how they affect our conception of the political order. Michael A. Scully's "The Triumph of the Capitol" gives a short history of the U.S. Capitol Building and how it successfully defined the architecture, planning, and monuments of Washington for many generations. This dominance lasted through the years of the City Beautiful movement in this century, but Washington architecture became less political and monumental in the face of the anonymous, non-monumental building program of the International Style, and has yet to recover. Charles T. Goodsell's "The City Council Chamber: From Distance to Intimacy" traces the history of that building type through three eras that, Goodsell feels, increasingly came to reflect greater intimacy between governors and governed. This less hierarchical, more democratic style can be welcomed, but he also wonders whether it reduces the legitimate authority of public officials. This same concern is reflected in Allan Greenberg's "Symbolism in Architecture: Courtrooms," which examines the interaction between symbolism and functionalism in courtroom design. Since a purely functional approach does not lead to any clearly superior design solution, Greenberg maintains that the institutional symbolism of the court as an embodiment of the rule of law should be the principle from which the designer approaches his formal solution.

9

Forum Follows Function

J. B. JACKSON

When we hear mention of political spaces and their value, what comes to mind is the familiar space—plaza or market or town square or forum—where we gather to enjoy the company of others and pass the time of day. It would be hard to find a community without such a space: alive and full of action, with people buying and selling, talking and listening, walking and looking about, or merely resting. Sometimes the space is the civic center, ornate and immense, sometimes it is nothing more than an empty lot or a wide space in the street. It is always enjoyable, and instinct tells us that a public space of one kind or another is essential to any community.

But there is a great variety in the way these public spaces are used, and a great variety in the groups of people who use them. In a political landscape they play a very different role than they do in a landscape like that of contemporary America. Architectural and urban historians often analyze them as works of art, and indeed that is what many of them seem to be, but it is their social function that we should look at first of all. In his book *Town and Square*

From J.B. Jackson, Discovering the Vernacular Landscape *(New Haven: Yale University Press, 1984), pp. 16–21. Copyright © 1984 by Yale University Press.*

Paul Zucker defines the space as one "which makes a community a community and not merely an aggregate of individuals . . . a gathering place for the people, humanizing them by mutual contact, providing them with a shelter against the haphazard traffic, and freeing them from the tension of rushing through a web of streets."

Here is a characteristically modern definition of the public square: a place of passive enjoyment, a kind of playground for adults, and it says a good deal about how slack our current definition of community can be. Zucker and many others are content to describe the public square strictly in terms of gregariousness: how it offers a spatial experience shared by a heterogeneous public which will sooner or later go its separate ways; an urban form which acts to draw people together and give them a momentary pleasure and sense of well-being. No one should underestimate those benefits, but in the political landscape the public square serves an entirely different purpose. It is assumed that those who come there are *already* aware that they are members of the community, responsible citizens, and that on occasion they will participate in public discussions and take action on behalf of the community.

True, every traditional public square has served several ends: marketplace, a place of business and a place of informal sociability and amusement, a place for pageantry. The agora in Athens, far from being architecturally impressive, was a jumble of crowded downtown streets and irregular open spaces where shrines and altars, public buildings and monuments stood in the midst of workshops, market stalls, and taverns. For Athenians of conservative tastes, as R. E. Wycherley reminds us, "the agora was the haunt of the dregs of the populace, the home of idleness, vulgarity and gossip." Aristotle, who thought of the agora chiefly as a place for discussion and the exchange of ideas, described in *The Politics* his ideal public square: All commercial activities and all merchants and vendors were to be exiled to another part of town. "Nothing here [in the agora] may be bought or sold, and no member of the lower order may be admitted unless summoned by the authorities. . . . The market proper, where buying and selling are done, must be in quite a separate place, conveniently situated both for goods sent up from the harbor and for people coming in from the country."

Aristotle's suggestions were ignored in antiquity, but they seem to have inspired some of the features of the Spanish colonial towns laid out according to the Laws of the Indies. Their produce market was located outside the plaza, and the presence of Indians was strictly controlled.

To see one of these traditional public squares in action, or better yet to take part in the action, is one of the greatest pleasures the tourist can know. Nothing is more festive than the corso in a Mexican plaza after dark, with the band playing, the women strolling clockwise around the square while the men go counterclockwise. And what is more colorful than a Moslem market or bazaar? No wonder every American wishes we had more such places in our cities. An eminent architect has gone so far as to say that the plaza is the basis of civilization and that our failure to have examples is a sign of American decadence. But there are those who have grown weary of our cult of the plaza as the solution to all our urban problems. Robert Venturi holds that "architects have been bewitched by a single element in the Italian landscape: the piazza. . . . [They] have been brought up on Space, and enclosed space is the easiest to handle.

I am inclined to agree, though my objection to the contemporary American plaza derives from a suspicion that most of its proponents do not really understand what it is. They think of it as an environment, a stage set, yet it has always been something much more worthwhile than that. It was, and in many places still is, a manifestation of the local social order, of the relationship between citizens and between citizens and the authority of the state. The plaza is where the role of the individual in the community is made visible, where we reveal our identity as part of an ethnic or religious or political or consumer-oriented society, and it exists and functions to reinforce that identity.

That is one reason for learning to perceive the urban public space not simply in esthetic or environmental terms, but in terms of history. When we do that we discover that there are many different kinds of squares, each with its own ideology, its own origin often at odds with its everyday appearance. Urbanists and architects, in keeping with that fascination with Space that Venturi decries, praise the immense, open, unencumbered space or plaza of the Pueblo villages of the Southwest as the perfect center for the fostering of community interaction. But the fact of the matter is, the Pueblo plaza is primarily the site of periodic religious ceremonies, and its focal point is a shrine called the World Navel, the place of communication with the ancestral spirits. Casual sociability—at least until recently—was confined to the flat roofs of the surrounding houses.

Every traditional public space, whether religious or political or ethnic in character, displays a variety of symbols, inscriptions, images, monuments, not as works of art but to remind people of their civic privileges and duties—and tacitly to exclude the outsider. The Roman Forum was cluttered with such reminders, and though the colonial New England town was hostile to public art it nevertheless contained a number of powerful symbols, impossible to misinterpret: the church with its steeple and bell, its front door covered with public notices and decrees; the whipping post, the stocks, the graveyard, and sometimes the tree ceremoniously planted by the first settlers. All of these served to tell those who came to the church services or town meeting or to the militia drill that they were part of a tight-knit religious community and had obligations. The public space was not for relaxation or environmental awareness; it was for *civic* awareness.

As we might expect, the ideal public square in the political landscape has a strong architectural quality. It occupies the most prestigious location in the principal town and is surrounded by politically significant buildings: law court, archives, treasury, legislative hall, and often military headquarters and jail as well. The space itself is adorned with statues of local heroes and divinities, monuments to important historic events. All important ceremonies are enacted here. Typical of the political emphasis on boundaries, the area is well defined by markers and has its own laws and its own officers. Finally, it is here in the agora or forum that history is made visible and where speech becomes a political instrument, eloquence a form of political action.

What is the origin of this space dedicated to public debate and public visibility? Jean-Pierre Vernant in his studies of historical psychology traces the evolution of the agora from the practice of the special warrior class of ancient Greece of periodically assembling in military formation—

in a circle, that is to say—to discuss matters of common concern. One after another, the men step into the circle and freely express themselves. When each has finished, he steps back and another takes his place and says his piece. The circle is thus a place of free speech and debate. In the course of time this agora (the word means "assembly") becomes the meeting of all qualified citizens; they too debate matters of common interest. Vernant comments: "[T]he human group creates this image of itself: along with the private dwellings there is a center where public affairs are discussed, and this center represents everything that is 'common,' the collectivity as such. In this center all persons are on a footing of equality, no one is inferior to anyone else. . . . We here see the birth of a society in which the relationships between man and man are perceived as identical, symmetrical, interchangeable. . . . It could be said that by having access to this circular space known as the agora, citizens become part of a political system based on balance, symmetry, reciprocity."

Vernant goes on to speculate on how this notion of equality and interchangeability may well have inspired Hippodamus to create the grid city plan of identical, interchangeable blocks.

In seventeenth-century France something resembling a new political landscape emerged, and there, in consequence, the public square became a work of art—a place where the social hierarchy could display itself to best advantage. We Americans later produced our own version—less elaborate, no doubt, but more faithful to the classic prototype. For more than half a century after the Revolution we remained loyal to the national political landscape of identical, interchangeable townships all centered on the county seat with its courthouse square. I have suggested elsewhere how that tradition lingered longer in the South than in other regions. The memory of the classical public space as the place of oratory and as the safeguard of democracy died hard, and no longer than seventy-five years ago we undertook to bring it back to life—statues, colonnades, and fountain—in the grandiose form known as the City Beautiful. Civic centers in San Francisco, Denver, Washington, and other cities still testify to its brief popularity.

I think we have finally come to recognize that we no

longer know how to use the traditional public space as an effective political instrument, and that we need a wide choice of very different kinds of public space. No one has written more perceptively on the matter than William H. Whyte. In a recent article telling of his extensive research into how such spaces are used in New York, he makes it plain that what we now want most of all is an agreeable "environmental" experience. The most popular, most frequented plazas and small parks are those which (he says) provide an agreeable microclimate, easy accessibility, some sensational object like a piece of sculpture or a display of flowing water, and which (this is most essential) allow people to sit comfortably and relax. "What attracts people most," he concludes, ". . . are other people." But what does other people mean? Those with whom (to use Aristotle's phrase) we can exchange "moral or noble ideas"? No; "other people" more often than not in this new urban space seems to mean voices and color and movement and fleeting impressions. People have become elements of animation in a pleasantly planned environment, and we are social beings merely to the extent that we want to be "at one" with that particular environment.

These contemporary urban parks, I cannot help feeling, are the last poor remnants of what was once an almost sacred space, but in our rejection of their political function we presage not the end of civilization but the end of one chapter. We are better off than we suppose; our landscape has an undreamed of potential for public spaces of infinite variety. When we look back a century, or even a half century, we realize how many new public or common spaces have appeared in our towns and cities, spaces where people come together spontaneously and without restraint. I am thinking of how the role of the college campus has changed, even in my own day. A half century ago it was a jealously guarded academic grove, surrounded by a fence and looked upon by the public with a mixutre of envy and contempt. It now plays a leading role in the cultural life of all classes in the community. In the high school auditorium many smaller communities not only come in contact with ideas but discuss them in meetings. The sports arena belongs in a different class, but in one respect it is the legitimate successor of the agora or forum: it is where we demonstrate local loyalties—loudly as the Greeks would have done and with gestures. The flea market is a new and unpredictable public space and so is the strip. If their humanizing function seems doubtful that may be because they have yet to develop, but even now there can be no doubt as to their popularity.

It is next to impossible to enumerate all the new spaces we are using and enjoying together. Wherever we look we see a new one: the cluster of campers in a recreation area, the Sunday meetings of classic car buffs in the empty parking lots of supermarkets, outdoor revivals, protest parades, stamp collectors' markets, family reunions, and the picnics of the sons and daughters of Iowa—all of them public, all of them fulfilling in one manner or another the needs once met in a single, consecrated space.

In the meantime the obsolete courthouse is demolished and replaced by a parking garage, and a giant Calder mobile takes the place of the statue to a Civil War general, and downtown, the victim of urban renewal, waits to be restored. What is left of the old political landscape vanishes, space by space, but as yet we have no name for the one which is taking form around us. . . .

10

A Meaning for Monuments

WILLIAM HUBBARD

Upon first seeing the Vietnam Veterans Memorial in Washington, D.C., columnist James J. Kilpatrick reacted with these words:

> We walked . . . and gradually the long walls of the monument came into view. Nothing I had heard of or written had prepared me for the moment. I could not speak. I wept. There are the names. The names! . . . For twenty years I have contended that these men died in a cause as noble as any cause for which a war was ever fought. Others have contended, and will always contend, that these dead were uselessly sacrificed in a no-win war that should never have been waged at all. Never mind. . . .

The experience of the names is an emotion that unites us all.

Indeed it is the impact of the names that overwhelms. The names of the dead and missing, nearly 58,000 of them, carved into a wall of mirror-polished black granite folded at the center to form a wide splay, one leg pointing at the Lincoln Memorial, the other toward the Washington Monument. The wall itself is set into the earth, its top edge exactly level with the flat ground behind, the earth in front scooped away in a gentle slope to reveal the names. The scooping, ten feet deep at the point of the splay, slopes gradually upward to rejoin the surrounding land at the

From The Public Interest, *Winter 1984, pp. 17–30. Copyright © 1984 by National Affairs, Inc.*

ends of the wall, some two hundred feet away. The feeling, upon entering the precinct of the monument, is one of descending into a shallow bowl in the earth, the ground held back by this tapering dam of black granite.

PRIVATE GRIEF AND PUBLIC MONUMENTS

On my first visit to the memorial, walking that slow descent into the earth along the face of the wall, I too wept. It was indeed the names, the names beyond counting. As I walked, and stood, and moved on again, I passed and was passed by the people who had come that day to find the names of friends or kin, or simply to see this memorial to the war that had touched us all in some way or another. Those of us who had come to see simply stood and ran our eyes over the length and height of the wall. But those who had come to find—they had a more pointed mission. They could be seen kneeling or standing before one particular spot in the wall, staring long at one name out of the thousands, their eyes welling with tears. We others allowed a circle of distance around each of these solitary mourners lost in their thoughts, keeping our own shared thoughts to a quiet murmur.

We talked, stranger to stranger, of the names—first of their number, but then of their arrangement—not alphabetical nor by hometown nor by military unit nor by any of those chance groupings by which we are arranged in life. Not by those, but by the final, personal ordering of the moment of death. The names begin on one side of the fold in the wall, with the first soldier lost in 1959. They continue in columns, moment by moment and year by year, out to the end of that wall, to resume at the far end of the other wall, continuing on until the last moment of the war in 1975, back at the fold where the sequence began, the last name joined to the first. We talked, in whispers, and pondered this, the way the names returned upon themselves, closing the circle they had formed in their progression outward and back.

And we realized, in that pondering, how the monument spoke to the memories of the private grievers. This wall of names arranged by date of death encompassed the private reality, and not the corporate enterprise, of war. That reality, for those kneeling in thought, must have been one of sequential loss, of one particular friend taken at one particular moment, over and again until the circle closed and all who had been sent away were gathered in again.

Even those of use who sought no particular death found ourselves reading individual names and, unbidden, imagining the places and the circumstances of their deaths. When we encountered, in the seeming randomness, a sequence of alphabetical arrangement, we knew that here were the men of a single platoon, wiped out together in a single engagement.

So many moments! Each movement of our gaze was a movement through time. A glance up and down carried us through weeks. Walking the length of the wall carried us through months and years. We made that slow journey with faces turned toward the wall, toward the names; we could not look elsewhere. It was only as the wall slipped below eye level, as we ascended, that we were able to look around again at the surrounding land. Then we realized, in that looking, that we were slowly returning to level ground, slowly coming out from that reverie of loss.

In that ascent, through and out from time, we remembered the feeling of the war at home: the slow, almost imperceptible descent into the conflict, the equally slow—agonizingly slow—diminuendo by which we left. In that remembering, we realized anew that, whatever the character of our days at home, here was the character of time in Vietnam, lives taken one by one, moment by moment by moment.

After a long time, I walked away from the precinct of the monument and stood looking back at the milling crowd arrayed along its length, and I recalled the controversies that had surrounded its design. ''A black ditch of shame,'' it was called, its V-shape a reminder of the years of protest. As I weighed those objections against my own deeply-touched emotions, the thought came to me, as it had to others, that surely this memorial, of such emotional power, had put those objections finally to rest.

But had it really? The objections to the monument were, in essence, that it did not glorify the war in ways that other monuments had—the Iwo Jima Monument being one frequently-cited example. Now clearly a monument equating Vietnam with World War II, implying that the Vietnam War had been conducted for the same noble purposes, had

been supported with equal fervor, had had the same import for the people and the nation—such a monument
would have been a sham, a lie. But behind that call for a
glorification is the assumption that a monument—any
monument—should make concrete some shared idea
about the thing it commemorates, that a war memorial in
particular should embody some resolved way of thinking
about the war it commemorates. In short, a monument
should *speak*. In that sense, the objections stand unad-
dressed: The Vietnam monument does not speak. Indeed
the designer, Maya Ying Lin, has said that she intended a
monument that "would not tell you how to think" about
the Vietnam War.

To feel that a monument should speak seems a reasonable opinion to hold. But what follows from it? What is in-
cumbent upon *us* to do if we are to have monuments—and,
by extension, public buildings—that speak to us?

READING AND "RE-KNOWING"

To answer such a question we must first ask how monuments and buildings once spoke when there were people
to listen. Probably the most commonly-cited examples of
buildings that speak are the great Gothic cathedrals,
whose windows and statuary were "the bibles of the illit-
erate peasants." The idea that the iconographical decoration of Gothic churches was read "like a book" is certainly
commonly held, but like many such ideas it is unexamined
and, in this case, fundamentally wrong. How did people
read those stained glass windows?

Take, for example, the famous windows at Chartres. In
one window of the nave there is a panel depicting this
scene: A man is kneeling with his head on a chopping
block, and over him stands his executioner, sword up-
raised. But the executioner's attention is distracted: He is
looking over his shoulder at a sheep that is butting him
from the rear. Watching over this curious scene is another
man, looking out from what appears to be a guard-box.
What on earth (or in heaven) are we to make of this scene?
The guidebooks, of course, can tell us. This is the story of
Simon Magus, a false prophet who, according to legends
current in Gothic Europe, competed with St. Peter for the
attention of the early Christians in Rome. To prove his di-

vinity, Simon Magus offered to have himself executed before the Emperor Nero. But before the blade fell, Simon changed himself into a lamb and so was saved. Knowing that, we can see how the window depicts the tale (and the humor with which it does so), but how would a person of the time, without a guidebook, have fathomed the window's message? He might have begun with the knowledge that each of the great windows in that section of the nave depicted stories of the life of an individual apostle. Looking up and down the height of this particular window, some image might have triggered the thought, "This window could be the one for the apostle Peter." Lighting then on the image of the lamb and the executioner, the peasant would have thought: "Yes, there is the story of Simon Magus. This must indeed be the window of Peter. Now what other stories of Peter are depicted in this window?"

This is a far cry from the way we read books. The method is more nearly one of formulating a hypothesis from one scanty piece of evidence and then testing that hypothesis against other pieces of evidence for confirmation or refutation. The crucial difference between icon-reading and book-reading is that icons do not do what books can do, which is to impart to us something we do not know. Rather, icons give us the scantest of hints—hints which, by a leap of the imagination, elicit from our memory something we already know. In contrast to book-reading, the power of icon-reading consists in letting us "re-know" something in a new, perhaps more profound, way. The point, though, is that the re-knowledge does not come easily to us, like words off a page. It requires work and speculative imagination.

And it can be done, even today, although the opportunities are extremely rare. One instance is the narthex of St. Thomas Church in New York City, which was remodeled in the 1940s into a memorial for the dead of World War II. A visitor without a guidebook could know that the narthex is such a memorial by the lighted Book of the Dead in a side niche and by the coats of arms of the Allied powers set into the floor. But if the visitor were to play the part of modern-day Gothic peasant and look around him, he might notice, in the corners of the room, four carved brackets—one showing a man blowing clouds from his mouth, another bracket formed out of flame-like arabesques—and the hypothesis might come upon him that here were the four elements of ancient physics: air, fire, earth, and water. Checking out the other two corners would confirm his hypothesis, but if our visitor's imagination were truly working, he might make the leap between ancient physics and modern physics and, in that leap, come to re-know in a new and more profound way the manner in which World War II was finally won. That re-knowledge, thrust upon him in this place, would call upon him to contemplate his role, and the role of his church, both in that conflict and in the nuclear world that has existed since.

THE LANGUAGE OF ICONS

That is how a powerful icon speaks. And it is by that same process that buildings can communicate with us. Buildings can communicate in at least four ways, each way in its turn being a little more meaningful and thus requiring of us a little more work of the imagination.

On the simplest level, a building can merely denote the identity of the institution housed inside. This denotation is often done with a coat of arms or some similar iconographical device. But it may also happen that the building itself is shaped to tell us those things This shaping might be subtle, as at the Harvard Club in New York; the building is done in a brick Georgian style, anomalous for that part of Manhattan but reminiscent of much of the architecture of the Harvard campus. Or the shaping might be extreme, as in the case of the New York Yacht Club, where each of the main bay windows has the look of the stern of those eighteenth-century sailing ships familiar to us from movies like *Mutiny on the Bounty* or *Peter Pan*.

A building can also go a little farther and attempt to say something about what this institution ''does for a living.'' Every city has such buildings—the headquarters for the light and power company adorned with Venetian lanterns, the old meat market with a frieze of bulls' and rams' heads, the newspaper building with its globe of the world. The Daily News Building in New York has such a globe, a huge contraption set in a well in the lobby, revolving slowly under a black glass dome of outer space—telling us clearly that the work of this institution is to bring the world to us.

A building can go one step farther and voice an ideology: It can propose to us what this institution means (or wants to mean) to society. Over the entrance to the same Daily News Building is an immense low-relief sculpture panel depicting multitudes of people doing their various jobs, with the inscription "Because He made so many of them." Clearly this newspaper has set an institutional goal for itself: It will not merely convey the news of the world, it will aspire to direct that news toward the common people, for whom God showed His love by making so multitudinous.

The final step in this progression is the building that propounds to us an aspiration that exists apart from an institutional "owner." In such a situation the building talks not only about the role an institution plays in society, but also about how society itself ought ideally to be organized, the ideas which ought ideally to govern society's operation. This is what a monument traditionally does. Buildings too can take on this aspirational role, as at Thomas Jefferson's University of Virginia campus, where students and professors are grouped together around a space leading to the central library. Jefferson intended that this arrangement be not merely a model for the physical layout of universities, but that it stand as a model for how life in a university ought to be organized, with students and teachers meeting on common ground to share and increase knowledge. And by holding before us the accomplished fact of life lived according to such an ideal, the university would stand as an ideal toward which the society at large might aspire.

REPAYING THE IMAGINATION

But buildings only rarely get the chance to speak about the whole of society. This propounding of cultural ideals is more often the province of monuments. Take, for example, the Virginia War Memorial to the dead of the World Wars, which stands on a bluff above the James, the great river that traverses the length of the state. The memorial has the form of a high, wide corridor, roofed and open at both ends. One flank of the corridor, on the side away from the river, is solid stone; the other is completely glass, upon which are etched the names of all those who died in the wars. Through this glass wall of names one sees a broad sweep of the James, and in the distance the state's capital city. Set in the floor at the base of this glass wall are relics from each of the battles: a canteen from Chateau-Thierry, a shell casing from Iwo Jima, a bayonet from Normandy—the common equipment of common soldiers. Looking up from that detritus of war through the screen of names at the great river of the state, one again realizes that these people went to faraway places so that we, standing here, might continue to have and enjoy this beautiful land.

The memorial thus tells us not just *that* these people died, or even how or where they died. It offers us a reason *why* they died. To each of us who either feels the loss of a loved one or contemplates such a loss, it offers a pattern into which that loss can be fit and so made sense of and more easily lived with. That pattern does not take the form of a recounting of the facts of the war: We know, intellectually, the real nature of wars, just as we know the real nature of life in a university or of reporting in a newspaper. The pattern is, rather, an ideal about wars and sacrifice—an ideal state of affairs which daily reality will always fall short of, but which can serve as a standard, a yardstick upon which each remembered occurrence, in its near or far distance from the ideal, can be arrayed and so be felt to have a place, contributing in large or small measure to the attainment of that ideal.

I cite this particular monument not because it is so distinguished (it is not) but because its message is so readily accessible to our ordinary understanding. It requires no esoteric knowledge, no difficult research for us to grasp and then to feel what is being symbolized here, only our common knowledge and our active imagination. But also required is that there be a graspable message there that *repays* imagination. When we think of recent monuments or memorials or public sculpture, the memory that most often comes to mind is not the experience of imaginative revelation but an opaque frustration. Recent public memorials and sculpture seem so often to take the form of abstract objects or minimalist shapes. We have all confronted such objects, and try as we might—staring long at them, walking slowly around or through them—our imagination draws a blank. We might notice an interesting pattern of shadows or a piquant play of shapes, but those impressions seem such meager fare, insufficient repayment for our efforts of imagination.

Take, for example, the monument erected in Dallas to commemorate the assassination of President Kennedy—a large hollow cube lifted off the ground and open to the sky, with a vertical slit cut out of the center of two opposite sides. We enter in through those slits, feel the enclosure and the sky, see the narrowed views of the scene where the murder took place. But nothing re-tells us of the terrible feelings we all shared on that day. There is no offered pattern by which we might make sense of those feelings, or draw some lesson or guidance or even solace from the events of that day. The monument, for all of its memorializing intentions, does not seem to be about the assassination of a President but about the feeling of enclosed space and the play of light on hard surfaces. The speaking it does is addressed not to our minds and hearts but to our bodies and eyes.

OUR INARTICULATE ARTS

In that respect, this and other abstract monuments are not so very different from the modern buildings we encounter daily. There too the message being spoken is about shape and shadow, not about what institution is housed inside or what it does, much less what it aspires to. It is, in that precise sense, an *inarticulate* architecture, and the public environments that result are likewise mute: They do not tell us, as cities once did, of how our institutions relate to one another (those pregnant juxtapositions like that in New York where the homes of the leading newspapers glared across a park at Tammany-run City Hall). Our public spaces now speak only about the physical shapes of those spaces and the ways that light moves across and through them.

How did architecture get this way? The true answer to that question is complex, but in large part modern architecture followed the path blazed first by modern art. Like architecture, art before modernism spoke of human affairs. When one encountered a work of art, one would encounter (in addition to the play of shape and light) some puzzle of human conduct: What is happening in that scene? What would I do and think and feel if I were there?

And what does that say about the way I live in the here and now?

But the moderns set themselves a different task. They wanted artworks that would not be *about* things in the world but would themselves *be* things in the world. They did not want to create scenes and shapes that reminded us of places and things we had previously encountered in the world; they wanted to present us with scenes and shapes wholly unlike any we had ever encountered, so that we could contemplate the invented qualities of those new works—shapes never before experienced, configurations of color and light never before seen. To accomplish this goal, art had constantly to contend with our propensity, ingrained through centuries of encounters with art, to try to link artworks with the remembered world. And so, one by one, art concocted strategies to thwart that propensity, to prevent us from connecting the art-experience with human experience. It does not go too far to say that art wanted to render itself irrelevant to human experience, so that we could more completely have and be moved by the art experience.

In at least part of this effort, art can be said to have succeeded. We do indeed no longer connect the experience of art with life as lived in the world. The idea that we would seek, in art, guidance for the conduct of human affairs that proposition now sounds strange to our ears. The question that now arises, though, is: Have we, in this divorce, become able to attend more closely to, and derive sustenance from, the experience of shape and light that art offers? There the answer is equivocal. Some can and do derive intense feeling from the contemplation of form and color, but many people (in whose number I must count myself) have the feelings but find they are not deeply moved by them. What we find in the case of all but the most powerful abstract artworks is that the kind of feelings we get are not so very different from the feelings we get in the presence of the best graphic design—movie titles, say, or big magazine spreads. We get the visual, sometimes visceral, "rush" of a wholly new, never-before-experienced arrangement of color and form.

This experience leads many to feel that the frame of mind that takes in and appreciates the best graphics and product design is the appropriate frame of mind for "taking in'' artworks. They know that they have gotten the full measure of the one; nothing tells them that they have gotten the full measure of the other. Aestheticians have noted this phenomenon (European theorists call it ''the consumption of culture''—treating art as if it were a consumer product). They have seen how easily artworks that try to become special, almost magical objects can become merely objects like any other. And they have carefully pointed out the cues by which we can know which works are fine art and which are mere graphics or packaging. But I, for one, cannot rid my mind of that Gothic peasant, and an art that, in its form, told one that here was an object to be pondered.

Our art, for so many years now, has not possessed that quality. It does not hold out to us recognizable puzzles from human experience that cause us to stop, ponder, and not rest until we can answer them. Nor do we encounter the questions that architecture, ''Mother of the Arts,'' once raised. We now come to architecture with the same frame of mind that ''takes in''—readies itself for a visceral impact and feels it has gotten full measure when that impact hits.

THE MEANING OF MONUMENTS

Little wonder, then, that the sheer emotional impact of the Vietnam Veterans Memorial satisfies us. Not having the idea that artworks can provide guidance in human dilemmas, we do not sense the absence of such guidance here. We take from the monument not a resolution of our conflicting emotions over the war, but an intensified, vivified version of those emotions.

But is this, you must ask, so very bad? Is this not a sufficient role for a memorial? Or, at the very least, are we done any harm by such monuments, by such art? I cannot help but believe that our interests are indeed harmed when art abandons the field of human affairs, because that abandonment leaves the field in the sole possession of *words*. Having bought art's definition of itself, we can conceive of no other way to think about the conduct of our lives except with words.

This is not to deny the power of words, but to recognize that thinking with words is only one of the ways we think. Not to avail ourselves of those other ways of thinking, to have our conduct determined by words alone, is to risk a way of life in fundamental conflict with what we are. Art—and in this context the art of monuments—can provide a counterbalance to the weight of words in our lives.

What monuments have traditionally done is embody an idea important to those who erected them. That is what Jefferson did with his idea of an ideal academic society, and what the builders of the Virginia War Memorial did for their ideas of war and sacrifice. But a monument endures beyond its time, holds that idea before us, in our time, and asks us to contemplate that idea—turn it over in our heads, stand it next to our own experiences and ask if it still applies. Do people and institutions act as they do out of allegiance to this idea? And if they do, do I want people and institutions to keep on doing those things? Do I want them to do those things out of allegiance to this idea, knowing what that might entail? And if people and institutions do not act in accord with this idea, would I wish them to? In short: Do I want this idea, and all it might entail, to be an operative force in our society?

Monuments confront us with that choice. They tell us that people like ourselves once chose to affirm a certain set of ideals, but in that telling, they remind us that we too must face the decision of which ideals to affirm. Monuments thus set before us the task of reassessing our values. And they do it by giving us both the means to criticize and the reason for doing so. By asking us to contemplate imaginatively the ideas they embody, monuments prod us to think through the implications of our social ideals. Through the free contemplation which they engender, we can know an idea more wholly—see more clearly and feel more deeply both the dangers and the glories to which it might lead. In that sensing of both danger and glory we have a surer means, a firmer basis for judging.

But in that sensing we also feel, if we are alive to it, the evanescence of an idea. For to sense the consequences of an idea is to realize that those consequences can only come to pass through our actions. And to realize *that* is to realize that, without our taking action, ideas engender nothing. Monuments tell us that the moment we become unwilling to do the actions that an idea entails, at that moment the idea dies: It becomes a "form," a thing to be paid lip service, or a target of cynicism.

In this call to contemplation and action, monuments put before us the task of keeping our values and aspirations aligned with our desires and needs. When such monuments stand among us, they act as a counter to the experience that can so dominate our daily lives—not as a goad, but as a call to hold on only to those values and aspirations whose consequences we freely choose to bear. In this very real sense, then, monuments call us to keep ourselves free: free from the demagoguery of ideas whose consequences we could not support, free from the brutish life of sheer expedience.

That is a very real necessity for monuments. And that is an equally real necessity for buildings that bespeak the nature of the institutions they house. A public environment that articulates ideas is an environment that lets us know which ideas we must support and, sometimes, which ideas we must contend against.

LIVING WITH OUR IDEALS

I did not quite finish my story of the Virginia War Memorial. A few years ago that memorial was extended, to include relics of the battles of Vietnam and the names of those Virginians who died there. Looking now, out through *those* names at the green banks of the James, a question arises: Did these soldiers really die that we might continue to have and enjoy this great land? And the answer, which we cannot avoid, is: No, they did not. But within that answer lies the true question to be asked: Is the defense of this land the *only* justification we will accept for sending young men and women to death in faraway places?

I am certain of the necessity for asking that question, continually and repeatedly throughout all our lives. But I am just as certain that I do not have the wisdom to frame an answer. Aided so far only by words, we have not been able to find an answer we can share. Perhaps if we could open ourselves to the kinds of thoughts that monuments can engender, our imaginations could supply an answer we could live with—and live by.

EPILOGUE, 1985

In November of 1984 an addition to the Vietnam Veterans Memorial was unveiled, a group of three soldiers in combat gear sited across a clearing from the original granite walls. When, a month afterward, I visited the augmented memorial, I wept again. But I also shuddered. To describe the reason for that reaction, though, requires a description of the monument itself.

With its landscaping now complete, one approaches the precincts of the memorial from the direction of The Mall. A path moves gently through a sparsely wooded glade, makes a gradual turn, and then splits to form an island of turf on which the soldiers stand. By its dividing we are invited to walk around the soldiers, and in our walk to see them in two aspects: from the front, we see them against the backdrop of the wooded glade; from the rear, we stand ourselves in the glade, looking with them across the clearing at the black wall of names in the distance. Thus, even when standing before them, we both feel them emerging (as we have emerged) from the woods out into the clearing, and feel (because we too have seen it) what they are looking at. We thus can imagine ourselves standing in their places, seeing what they see, feeling what they feel.

This feeling of ourselves-in-their-place is underscored by the realism of their depiction. In the heft and sag of their combat boots we can feel the implacable suck of mud pulling at our feet. In the many folds and wrinkles of their battle-fatigues we can imagine the character of the steamy days and nights they have spent on patrol.

It is their composition, though, that speaks to us most directly. The central soldier of the three stands stock-still, pinning the group to the spot. The soldiers on either side are leaning forward. Their forward movement, though, is checked by the way they stand slightly behind the central soldier: they could not move forward without brushing his shoulders in their passage. And they seem to sense this: both of them extend a hand behind the back of the central figure. These outstretched hands fuse the three into an indivisible whole. Artistically, the gestures of each would be incongruous without the presence of the other two. But psychologically, these gestures let us know that these men have been together for some time, have gotten to know each other's patterns of movement and cast of mind. These three have been through peril together and have learned to trust and depend upon each other. These are not just three soliders but three buddies, with unspoken bonds tested by combat and found equal to the test.

The three soldiers thus give a psychological reality to the abstraction of the names on the wall. They awake in us the memory of specific emotions that we have had in time of stress or actual danger. Through them we are able to take the generalized emotions the wall engenders and connect them to specific emotions we have felt in the course of our lives. But because the figures also evoke soldiery, through them we are able also to forge a connection in our minds between these specific war-engendered emotions and all wars. And in this way they give us a way of *re-seeing* all wars in a new way.

Re-seeing the world has always been one of the prime functions of art. The signal accomplishment of this dual work, the soldiers and the wall, is that it is the *ensemble* that engenders in us this re-seeing. Neither work, by itself, accomplishes the task as fully as the two conjoined.

This is a profound accomplishment. We had previously assumed that modern and traditional art could not easily coexist, so fundamentally different were their premises. The nearest we had approached to a combining of the two modes was that the one would stand in critique of the other. The paradigm example was the modern abstract sculpture placed before the traditional decorated building. The sculpture, in its abstractness, would make us aware of the decorative, "speaking" quality of the building and the stories and ideas its figures and carvings depicted. The building, with its conventionalized forms, would make us aware of how unconventional were the forms of the sculpture, how much those forms could be enjoyed simply for themselves and not for what they had to "say."

This ensemble, though, shows us that both figurative and non-figurative art can engender in us real human thoughts and emotions. The ensemble tells us that the gap between the modern and the traditional can be closed, that we are now able to view the two modes as our common heritage. We no longer need to have the two only in counterpoint, thereby leaving the split intact, indeed exploiting it. We can now have the two conjoined in a single work, the whole indivisible, the one unimaginable without the other.

Part of why this is so is that in his three soldiers the sculptor Frederick Hart has produced a very nearly "transparent" work of art. In modernism the imperative has always been that an artist explore a personal formal agenda, that the form of each work be a brave working-out of the formal concerns raised in previous work. To a degree remarkable in an age which so demands such personal expression, Hart has divested the work of all signs of his personal formal concerns. It is utterly without idiosyncrasy or personal formal exploration. Like the artists of old, he has subordinated his personal style to the interpretation of an idea.

Which is not to say that it is not an artistically *knowing* work. Hart knows and has used the lessons of art technique adumbrated by the masters of figurative art. The figures are just above life-size so that they will *appear* to us life-size (unlike George Segal's plaster casts or Wayne Hanson's mannequins, which always appear a bit smaller than ourselves). And he has raised them up off the plane where we walk just enough that they appear not to inhabit our space, and so are freed to stand not completely in our time and daily circumstances. The composition remarked earlier is likewise a device learned from previous artworks: The postures of the three figures make each impinge on the others so that we sense first not the individual character of each soldier but feel instead the relationship that binds them.

But in his use of the lessons of art history, Hart has not, again to his credit, given us three figures from art class, those Michelangelesque titans in postures of Renaissance *contrapposto*, torsos twisted in dynamic opposition to limbs and heads. Those gestures, we have been told, were derived from close observation of how people in that era carried and displayed themselves. Hart has closely observed how young men of *this* day carry themselves. Their postures are like nothing so much as the postures of the basketball court, arms outstretched in the body-attitude that guards against the feints of an oncoming opponent, the weight of the body forward over the balls of the feet so as to be able to move in any direction in response to an opponent's actions. These are the postures of only our time.

And, seeing these soldiers in such postures, we know that these are people like ourselves, not abstracted symbols of humanity, but real American boys of the late twentieth century. That is the "transparency" of Hart's sculpture. We know these boys not through the filter of art history but through the camera-eye of our own daily seeing. We feel we know these boys. We have met, in our daily lives, people so like them.

Feeling that way, we feel ourselves qualified to feel, too, privy to their thoughts. One imagines the three having just stepped out of the cover of the forest into the dangerous opening of a clearing. Their postures show that they are apprehensive. They remember the times when their buddies have met death upon advancing from cover (a memory of death made visible to us in the wall they face). But still they do courageously advance. From what source does their courage come? Not from generals nor the machinery of war, nor from support from home or the government, nor from moral certitude that their cause is just. All of these have failed them. (We know this failure from our memory of the war, but we—and those who will come after us with no memory of the war—can also read this from the fact that symbols of such props to courage are nowhere to be seen in the precinct of the memorial.) No, the only sure guard that makes their courage possible is the camaraderie of their fellow soliders. On that and only on that can they rely.

And indeed in this war—perhaps in all wars—that camaraderie is the only virtue that survives untainted. One's commanding officers screw up, the Army is riddled with absurdities, the government's motives are tainted, even loved ones never fully understand. Only one's buddies know what it is like, only they can act and remember with authenticity. Only they, with their precise knowledge and feeling, can be relied upon to do and say what is needed at the moment a soldier most needs it.

With the addition of these three figures—with the *completion* of this monument—the Vietnam Veterans Memorial becomes the truest of our war memorials, the only one without hypocrisy or inauthenticity. It states, with a clarity that brings shudders, that in the tainted enterprise of war, the greatest virtue is camaraderie. Not valor, not duty, not moral certitude. All those virtues will, in the conduct of war, be compromised. Only camaraderie will endure, pure and worthy of unabashed memory.

This memorial, built by veterans alone in the face of misunderstanding, indifference, and opposition, with no substantial help from officialdom, impels us to realize that central fact of war. It is, again, our purest monument. And in its implacable purity, it is a challenge to all our platitudes and abstractions about combat. It does not say, "Wage no more war." It says to us: Know, deeply know, what combat is. And weigh that knowledge when next you consider embarking on the enterprise of war.

11

Collective Significance

MOSHE SAFDIE

The origin of city was rooted in ritual, worship, government, and administration. The city came into being as a place where those elements and institutions were physically singled out amidst the general fabric of buildings. Monumentality in its elemental sense is the articulation of a network of spaces and particular buildings that give the city legibility. It is that network of significant buildings and public places, and the connections between them, that has always given the city perceptible order, a sense of location for the people within it, a sense of structure, and a much needed hierarchy. In their striving for legibility and their desire to give significance and importance to certain buildings the builders of cities have relied on their visual imagination. From time immemorial, they were concerned with two closely related issues: the choice of what to single out and the means by which to make it significant.

The means that are usually associated with achieving monumentality are scale, order, repetition (often simplistic repetitions, sometimes complex rhythms), and certainly unity. Often we associate the monumental with the unfragmented; or, as popularly considered, the monu-

From the Harvard Architectural Review, *Spring 1984, pp. 87–97. Copyright © 1984 by Moshe Safdie.*

mental tends to be symmetrical, axial, sometimes ornate and elaborate. But in spite of these commonly accepted associations, my hypothesis is that there are two distinct architectural traditions or attitudes that have generated monumentality. These differing attitudes prevail from the design of individual buildings to the design of public spaces and parts of cities. For convenience, we can call these, in a somewhat oversimplified manner, "evolved" and "composed" traditions of the creation of monumentality.

Evolved monumentality, as the term suggests, has its roots in the morphological expression of the structure of cities. Its central characteristic is that it resorts to a language of architecture that is adaptable. There is a connection in evolved monumentality between the design of the simplest shelter and the most significant structure, a connection between the architecture of a house and the architecture of a temple, between the most ordinary and the sublime. Building form is generated by a response to materials and to the processes of building. It reinforces and illustrates Richard Sennett's hypothesis that one of the characteristics of design that achieves the so-called open city is the ability of a layperson to understand and feel the physical coming together of the materials that constitute buildings and public spaces.

Another characteristic of evolved monumentality is that design is generated responsively to the forces of nature. Climate, orientation, light, site, terrain, even gravity, all resonate with building form. Most significantly in this tradition there is rarely a conflict between responsiveness to the needs of the user, in its broadest sense, and formal composition.

My use of the word *morphological* in connection with *evolved* monumentality is partly pictorial and partly literal. In the usual, dictionary sense, forms in nature evolve to respond to a set of survival requirements. As we examine each organism in nature we can trace the connection between its form and the elements necessary for its survival; its form is the result of evolution. Monumentality, in the sense of singling out significant places and buildings of the city, is an inevitable, evolutionary facet of city form.

The pictorial connection has to do with the fact that if we examine complex organisms, we recognize in them a hierarchy which is beyond, say, the cellular amalgamation of bacteria or simple life forms. If we examine the human body, the hierarchy is fascinating: the spine; the head; and the brain; the eyes; all with very distinct roles. The skeleton with the ribs growing out of the spine, the brain contained by the skull and supported by the neck bones, etc. Add to this the muscle tissues and nerve systems and so on, and you find an inevitable connection to city. One can substitute a human body with that of a dinosaur. Both demonstrate a hierarchy which results from the very specific roles each part of the organism plays and the necessity for connecting them into a living system. The beauty of the spine and its significance has to do with its role connecting the brain to the body and supporting the frame and containing communications, in this case nerve messages.

The analogy is dangerous if taken too literally, but it is nevertheless, in the pictorial sense, suggestive of the hierarchy which is reminiscent of cities. A plan or an aerial photograph of a city in which there is no sense of hierarchy, a presence of elements with specific roles, is suspect. The idealized utopian plans produced for cities during the this century, be they the grid plan of Chandigarh or the Ville Radieuse or some of the more banal large-scale suburban subdivisions, have something fundamental missing. That sense of hierarchy, of specific role playing, is missing, and the result is the absence of monumentality.

Monumentality in architecture, both evolved and composed, transcends the morphological—in the general sense of form derived in response to survival. Culture cannot be explained in morphological terms: a man tattoos his body with ornate patterns or tears his lip and pushes ivory into it, a woman spends hundreds of hours embroidering a dress that would fulfill its purely survival role if the cloth were simply wrapped around the body to keep it warm. Hence, at the level of culture, issues of psychic satisfaction, fears, superstitions, worship, dreams, and hopes transcend the normal morphological terminology. In the realm of culture, we must therefore recognize the different mechanisms by which people have sought to satisfy certain aspirations related to celebration, significance, and the importance of their institutions.

In Eastern cultures, there is intimate connection in the design, and hence the forms, of the sublime and the ordinary. In other cultures a distinct polarization has evolved between the sublime and the ordinary. In Chinese, Japanese, and Moslem architecture (in particular that of Iran), the means of building, the system of decoration and embellishment, extend from a farmhouse to a mosque, from a little domestic shelter to a great palace. In the West, particularly from the late Renaissance on, a certain schizophrenia has evolved. One approach is applied to the ordinary, another to the significant. Ordinary farmhouses built in fifteenth-century Tuscany utilized a visual language different from palaces built at the same time. The schizophrenia grows with time until the criteria used to design ordinary shelter, which is subject to the forces of economy, survival in its elementary sense, climate, building processes, and so on, and the criteria applied to the design of a church, which is dominated by intellectual traditions, are very different.

The ordinary Chinese farmhouse uses wood framing and bearing walls. A similar framing system is used for a palace or temple, but it is made more complex, not because the spans and the scale of construction are bigger, but for effect. Whereas a simple joint between two pieces of wood is deemed appropriate for the house, a more complex way of joining two or three pieces of wood that is more expressive or playful is developed. In the Temple of the Heavens in Peking, a language of decoration is applied so that not only is the juncture of two pieces of wood elaborate and exaggerated, but the ends of every piece are painted with symbols and colors. The coloring system does not attempt to obliterate the clarity of the symphony of structural expression, but rather it exaggerates it and sings its song or, as Kenneth Frampton puts it, it celebrates "the poetics of construction." A similar analysis could be made of a Japanese temple or an Iranian mosque. To achieve an impressive facade, in a conceptual sense, the architect considers the spatial framework, the treatment of surfaces within rooms, and the treatment of the face of the building as inseparable elements.

In contrast, in the baroque a separation is created between the mode of building and its visual language. Bearing walls, the framing system, the mode of construction give way to an applied visual pattern. A borrowed language of pilasters, cornices, elaborate elements of other times, can be legitimately applied; furthermore, they are distorted at will. In other words, they are not even applied with any sense of restriction related to their origins. They are considered free game for manipulation. The difference between this manner of construction and the wood framing of the Chinese palace is fundamental. In one, there is always a feeling for the process through which a building technique or architectural motif evolved, a sense of the origin of things. In the other case, origins are irrelevant. A language is adopted with a sense of anarchic freedom.

These differences in attitude are not limited to East and West. They have, in various periods, emerged in the West; a Baroque church, for example, reflects different attitudes than does a Gothic cathedral. The Gothic tradition demonstrated an almost tongue-in-cheek competition between humans and the natural constraints set upon them. In some ways, there is a similarity between the Gothic saga and space exploration—stretching human capabilities to the limit. Buildings are built and they collapse (and Gothic architects surely had their experience of collapsed cathedrals); but by stretching ingenuity and building skills, they achieved a new experience—space, light, lightness, balance. Works of art, of decoration and embellishment, are designed to highlight that experience. Every sculpture, every gargoyle, every stained-glass window, every molding is designed to intensify the experience. The sense of light coming through the great apertures between the flying buttresses would be less dramatic if the apertures were white glass. The elaborate pattern that tells a story about a part of Christian history increases the sense of light penetration, the sense of movement of sun in sky. Similarly, we go to the moon, apart from our curiosity, to stretch to the limit our technical capabilities, to intensify our experience of nature.

In the baroque church, the means and the attitudes are different. There is a kind of defeatism or pessimism about extending building skills. Instead, the baroque concentrates on effect that does not contend with the process of building or with natural forces. If the builders of Hagia Sophia did their best to stretch gravity and construction techniques to achieve a spatial experience, the builders of, say, the Neumann Church gave up on those terms altogether, perhaps because they felt that manipulating an applied visual language is more cost-effective or because, in a profound sense, it gave them more satisfaction. Perhaps their psyches were stimulated by the manipulations of a painter's world, by being in a three-dimensional painting so to speak, than by the type of tension created between humans and nature in a Gothic structure.

Composed monumentality is generally achieved by the imposition or application of a visual, formal order. We often associate it with the classic or neoclassic (but even a brief scrutiny of classical Greek architecture demonstrates that its origins are not Greek). For laypeople, Beaux Arts axial planning is equated with classicism. When it is pointed out that a typical axial plan of the Beaux Arts tradition of the eighteenth century differs fundamentally from the planning of the Acropolis or Delphi, laypeople are at first surprised. The adaptability to site and the asymmetries created because of site, the multiplicity of axes responding to an array of both site and ritual constraints, are not present in the simplistic axial Beaux Arts plans. A temple sitting on the edge adapts itself to the rock and does not obliterate the rock in order to be symmetrical to another temple on the other side of the Acropolis.

In the seventeenth and eighteenth centuries architects became intimidated by axial concepts. A good example is perhaps the Louvre, where in spite of the long period of its realization and the variations in details of facades, all the way from the first to the last phase the architects were restrained by the axial arrangement that had been established at the outset.

Even more fundamental to composed monumentality is the fact that the elementary needs that relate to the livability of a building or a public space are sacrificed to meet preconceived formal objectives. The formal language of composed monumentality is generally detached from and not founded on building processes and materials. It often attempts to ignore the reality or constraints of site and context. One has the feeling that if Baron Haussmann had traveled to Venice, he would have straightened out the Grand Canal. Composed monumentality is often holistic and simplistic in its formal concepts and generally tends to be externally and superficially applied to achieve its means. It is pictorial, treating architecture as a medium toward communicating nonarchitectural ideas (power, authority, discipline). It is often pure, simple imagery: it is more often symmetrical than not; it is often axial.

I suggest that the development of axial planning might

have been influenced by the development of modern war equipment. The connection exists at two levels. We know, for example, that the adaptive medieval patterns of many cities, Paris being the most well known example, were modified and transformed into axial arrangements, motivated by the need of control and of efficient movement of troops. There is an acknowledged connection that movement of troops generated, in part, a formal vocabulary. Furthermore, the notion of sequence experienced in the use of modern weapons must have had a very profound impact on the visual perception of people. Warfare in premodern times was primarily the random shooting off of rocks and ballistae, the use of bows and arrows in a projectile sense, and the phalanx movements of masses of troops. Modern warfare consists of the target, the aiming mechanism, and the trigger as a direct connection of points A, B, C. The movement of the trigger, once on axis, results in the hitting of the object. The similarity to the visual experience of boulevard, obelisk, concave temple or palace, and domed rotunda, all on axis, is suggestive.

Axial plans were another effective way of taking aim. One takes aim with a weapon, one takes aim with architecture; the obelisk and the boulevard and the semicircle and the dome are in sequence, and it is quite clear what is important in the city.

This notion of monumentality of repetitive colonades and axial monuments led to certain conclusions during the emergence of the modern movement. As Giedion said about monumentality, ''The recipe is always the same: take some curtains of columns and put them in front of any building, whatever its purpose and to whatever consequence it may lead.''

But much more can be made of distinguishing the different attitudes about monumentality. Evolved monumentality is man designing in God's image, or alternatively, man designing in nature's image—the city as an extension of nature, in harmony with nature. There is a fundamental humility to this tradition that is omnipresent in indigenous architecture; and there is a sense that one treats one's fellow beings as equals.

Composed monumentality is man designing so as to dominate nature, to defy nature. Composed monumentality is fundamentally egocentric, often godless, although we often produce buildings in the name of God. It has been a useful tool manipulated by totalitarian and authoritarian regimes. A confession of this attitude is found in a statement made by Pope Nicholas V, as quoted by Paulsson: "On his death-bed he told his cardinals that the church had need of monumentality not for the sake of the wise and the learned who understood in any case, without its aid, but for the *turbae populorum* whose feeble faith is always in danger and can only be strengthened through the magnificence of what they see."

It is time to challenge the popular view that monumentality is synonymous with manipulation, power, and domination, an interpretation that Paulsson to conclude: "Monumentality is not desirable. . . . The totalitarian society has always taken monumentality into its service to strengthen its power over people, the democratic society in conformity with its nature is antimonumental. . . . Intimacy not monumentality should be the emotional goal." If monumentality is the essential means of creating meaning for and giving legibility to the city, one cannot embrace this conclusion. The legible city depends on the delicate balance and differentiation between the routine and the significant (the ordinary and the monumental). The understanding of the difference between these two traditions leads to important lessons about the evolution and issues facing architecture today.

One such contemporary issues is monumentality's intrinsic dependence on discipline. Throughout history there have been different forms of discipline. In the past it was primarily economic; no matter how much a peasant would want to achieve the monumentality of a palace in a family dwelling, he could not. His adobe hut in the city of Sumer could not achieve the magnificence of the ziggurat of the temple or the palace. That does not mean that the peasant didn't attempt in some way to distinguish himself, say by decoratively carving the house door. Today, economic constraints no longer apply because economic means are distributed in an unpatterned way, and many people have the means to attempt to be important.

Discipline, however, did not primarily rely on economic constraints in the past. In eighteenth-century China, for example, the color red was reserved for royalty. The massive walls that were built around compounds and houses and palaces were the only ones painted red. This subtle and elementary means of achieving significance depended on voluntary discipline. If others painted their houses red, the distinction of royal construction would be lost. In fact, if everybody started painting their houses any color they wished to, including red, the royal architect would have to find a new means, perhaps less subtle and more elaborate, to achieve the same measure of monumentality and distinction. We must relate that observation to our own times. Some relatively modest means could be used to achieve significance and monumentality for the buildings appropriate in our own culture to be so singled out. However, in the absence of restraint or some code of good behavior, the means have to get increasingly elaborate. If every outhouse can be a temple (to use the example of Philip Johnson), then we have to use more and more elaborate methods to achieve monumentality; at some point, this is self-defeating, because all becomes chaos. Our culture is now at a point in its evolution where the preconditions for a legible city are impossible because the minimum accepted constraint does not exist between that which is significant and that which is not. Our culture is therefore *a priori* and by definition fated to anarchic chaos. Achieving legibility in the city is an impossible task until the values of economic and social restraint are reestablished.

The exploration of these values is not without paradoxes: buildings that related to governments and to religion seem to have been made significant, whether the government was a Greek democracy or a Roman imperial dictatorship. Today the situation is very different because there is no consensus about what should be singled out as significant nor is there any clarity as to what means are appropriate. A corporation has wealth, as does government and private individuals. This situation leads to visual chaos.

Another paradox is the visual consequence of the culture of egalitarianism. One can make a case that it is egalitarianism that makes it possible for every corporate chairman or man of wealth to throw his muscle around in the monuments he builds for himself. It is inherent in the notion of equality of opportunity. One can, therefore, make the case that the chaos we experience is not a negative phenomenon but, on the contrary, an inevitable (desirable?) consequence. The chaos becomes the characteristic that differentiates the city of our time from the architecture of a hierarchical society. Affluence leads to inevitable arbitrariness. The notion that you can make buildings out of glass regardless of where they are built, be it in Saudi Arabia or Montreal, is a specific example where climate, lifestyle, availability of materials, are simply ignored. As a minimum objective, a monumental building must shed the arbitrary. Beyond that is the deeper meaning of an architecture responsive to people's needs.

We must search for an architecture that is concerned with people's needs as the most elementary and uncompromisable ingredient. People's needs are also people's dreams, but they have to be *people's* dreams and not our own private dreams. We must attempt to achieve buildings of significance that have universal, collective meaning. They have to come from an understanding of the collective, not only from an understanding of the collective, not only from an understanding of self. We place too much emphasis on self. We miss the essence of the collective in our narcissistic focus.

Since monumentality deals with dream, memory, and, hence, symbol, it is the most profound aspect of architecture as the formal and visual expression of culture. It is a mirror of our values, of how society functions. But that sets an enormous responsibility on the architect to determine what constitutes a meaningful, relevant, and truthful symbol of the society in which he or she builds. The tragedy of the recent decades in architecture is that we have come to recognize collectively and by consensus the shortcomings of the architecture of the modern movement in the early part of the century in its response to the need for symbol and cultural expression, but we have not lost touch with the whole question of appropriateness and relevance.

Architecture must be rooted in building process. It is the one quality through the entire history of building that has brought pleasure and wholesomeness to building. It is the fundamental element of the language of architecture. We must draw on history to fully appreciate this.

If we have even modest faith in democracy and any vision of an egalitarian world, then we owe it to ourselves to explore monumentality in the city in our own terms.

The burning question is: What are the limits of the value of the historic experience? The political scientist, tracing the evolution of human thought through the centuries, would certainly present a picture of a positive evolutionary sequence, not a recycled process but one in which there is a nonrepetitive sequence toward change. We begin in a world of slavery and we are presently, whether practicing it or not, at the U.N. Declaration of Human Rights. Today, we reject slavery. We begin with the society administered by autocratic powers, sometimes by consensus, sometimes by imposition, and we move toward a world that attempts to be governed democratically by consensus or majority rule.

These are positive steps in the development of society. It is absolutely inevitable that they lead to a parallel development in the design of cities. It is a truism that the design of a public place of government in the democratic United States is, in nature, fundamentally different from the design of a public place of government in imperial Rome. If it comes to pass that we recognize similarity in solutions adapted today for this kind of place, we must be suspicious, because something has changed in the relationship of people to government and of people to each other, and architecture must express it.

One must not underestimate the enormous differences between the political structures of the past and of today. The entire relationship between ruler and ruled has been transformed. One can reasonably assume, therefore, that this new era should generate its own urban forms. In a period in which architects are turning to the past for lessons and inspiration, there is a danger that the significance of the differences between past and present is overlooked. In making models of the forms of buildings and places created by societies that were governed and administered very differently from our governing structures, there is the obvious danger that we do not explore adequately the appropriate expression for today's situation, particularly as it concerns monumentality. There is no question about the trend. The political order of our time is new. It is maybe a century old. Hence, we are still at the beginning of the exploratory phase of understanding its formal urban and architectural implications. Richard Sennett in his Graduate School of Design lecture series outlined a framework for such investigation: What is appropriate for the design of urban places in a democracy?

We have not yet understood the challenge with all its paradoxes, let alone come up with responses. My concern for the current general tendency in architecture is that because of the great interest in looking back there is a tendency to fail to discover the new meaning our own culture gives to these questions.

If monumentality in the city is the balance between the ordinary and the significant, then it is going to take a tremendous amount of civility, restraint, and modesty to create this balance. Certain communities have been prepared to take positions about that. Washington, D.C. is a city in which the decision as to what is significant and what is not is decided by the public. Other communities (like Houston) pride themselves on allowing the whim, ambitions, and idiosyncrasy of every individual to be publicly displayed. The typical office tower is also a case in point; it is a mistaken notion that the office building gives the city monumentality. The skyscraper is monumental when it is the first one there; it is certainly noticeable, but it will not give our cities the legibility we seek. It is quite understandable that every corporate president thinks of himself or herself as Zeus and the building constructed for his or her corporation as a temple of Zeus. Considering the general state of our culture, this attitude is quite understandable. It is less understandable that most architects jump to the occasion. The question about what is significant and is worthy of being made significant and what must be kept ordinary is difficult. When an office building stands alone, it might have some elements of monumentality, but, as can be seen in Chicago with its scores of big buildings, one has to go to all kinds of measures to be noticed—and always with the knowledge that somebody is going to come after and be noticed a bit more. The chaos implied seems unacceptable.

The legibility of the city depends on the public domain as the connective framework between individual buildings. This is exemplified in the agora and the markets of the past, but it does not exist today. We are unable to connect buildings as part of the urban experience. The Galeria in Houston, the grand space of Philip Johnson's IDS building in Minneapolis, the great spaces created by Portman are an attempt to respond to our desire for public places worthy of the kind of urban life that we want. But, by definition, built as individual pieces, they are introverted and, hence, they are private and not connectable. They cannot become that which ties together the buildings of significance in the city. There is no alternative but to find a way in which the public domain, the streets or the square or whatever new term it will acquire, is designed as the place that connects the pieces.

The solution is to rediscover what is appropriate. Every time we draw a line, we should ask ourselves, "Is it appropriate?" When a student designing for Jerusalem, one of the great sacred cities of the world, proposes a colonnaded street, 500 columns long, double columns on each side, and explains that at the end of this axis is a tourist hotel, you know that somewhere we, the teachers, have misled our students.

Italo Calvino in *Invisible Cities* talks about the city of dreams. The hero, Calvino's teller of tales, spends his life searching for the city of his dream. He searches and searches for a city "where buildings have spiral staircases encrusted in sea shells . . . where the foreigner hesitating between two women always encounters a third." Finally he arrives at the city of his dreams in old age—he has searched for it all his life—and then Calvino tells us "in the square there is a wall where the old men sit and watch the young go by." He is seated in a row with them— "desires are already memories."

Let not our desires be degraded to memories.

12

Public Buildings: Symbols Qualified by Experience

DONLYN LYNDON

The notebook on which I write this, purchased in the supermarket of a small town in Michigan, has a picture on the cover that perhaps illustrates our condition. The rendering is gruesome to my untutored eye: a murky brown, cellar-like space inhabited by three figures, mutants of some grotesque sort that appear to be engaged in a musical performance. One is bright blue and vaguely elephantine, the other two are of sickly yellow and brown hues, malformed on the top but each distinctly two-legged and upright, both with giant-toed feet planted firmly and flatly on the ground. There are four distinctly recognizable items in the picture: a masonry arch in the background, two microphones that receive the attentions of the two upright figures, and a pair of spotlights at the feet of the central celebrity figure. Three almost recognizable items appear: something very like a clarinet that one figure holds to an indistinct portion of its upper anatomy, an electrical junction box, and a metallic relief panel that bears the features of a man's face, two hands, and the mid-parts of a belted torso. A bright red line traces a frame around the picture

From The Public Interest, *Winter 1984, pp. 77–97. Copyright © 1984 by National Affairs, Inc.*

and emblazons the headline "Return of the Jedi" across the top.

I say "perhaps" this illustrates our condition because I have never seen a Star Wars film, so the popular meanings of these figures escape me entirely, just as the nuances of architecture escape many. The plight I have in mind, however, is our participation in a culture wherein the morbid fascination of a mutant world can be counted on to elicit shared recognition from millions of consumers (in this case purchasers of rather low-grade notepaper), while there is virtually no agreement regarding the nature of a shared public place or how we should use our resources to build an environment that has benefits for the public. If we would believe my notebook cover, the shared constants in our world today are electronics (microphone and switches), celebrity status (spotlights), music, and the sheltering arch. Music gives hope, and to an architect the arch, at least, is reassuring.

ARCHITECTURE BETWEEN PAST AND FUTURE

Once upon a time architecture was the big production; architects (or craftsmen much like them) transformed ordinary buildings into magical monuments, places that formed the consciousness of generations, buildings that, through a tremendous investment of skill and labor, commanded the imagination of a people. Nothing in recent memory has had this effect, with the possible exception of Mr. Blanding's Dream House—and there the imaginative skills were invested in words and film, not bricks, mortar, or even clapboards. Architecture is hard put to compete for public loyalty with the distributive capacity of the media.

Still, great places persist, and our passion for visiting them has become the basis for an international industry. Borobudur, the Arc de Triomphe, Taj Mahal, Big Ben— these have become the trademarks of TWA. Yet the experience of place, we are told by critics, has become yet another packaged consumer item, with tightly-controlled tourist expectations. TWA can exploit great monuments from the part because we yearn, now more than ever, to be part of something more than our immediate present. And we have been taught to believe that we can have it cheaply, complete with "frequent flyer" bonuses.

Real places have a power over the mind because they are the locus of our actions; the events of our lives are connected with the settings in which they take place. Places take on meanings through our participation in them. Private places develop an intimacy of association that nurtures individual identity; public places must of necessity bring together elements that reflect or can support common bonds. The paths to commonality are by no means straight and narrow. Places matter to us because we come to care about them; we have a telling experience there—a smile from a friend, a lesson from a parent, a dance with a stranger—and the place becomes imbued with association. Or we recognize the investments that others have made in the place and admire their efforts—examine the craftsmanship of masonry set in place centuries ago, study the proportions of a carefully-determined facade, delight in the festoons of a festival that mark the presence of traditional public ceremony, connect ourselves with the past by taking part in a procession that takes its very form from the shape of a historical place.

J.B. Jackson, in his provocative essay "The Necessity for Ruins," characterized the traditional civic monument as the measure of our obligation to the past and commitment to the future—of a society's intention to live up to the standards and ideals of a significant event or great person. We seem now to have an entirely different conception of the national indebtedness—we pass on to our children the obligations that we are unwilling to meet ourselves. Unmanageable radioactive waste is but the most arrogant of our legacies, a telling symbol of our careless disregard for the future.

What does all this have to do with the architecture of public buildings? How might it influence the designs, the decision to build, or the appreciation of public places? There are three propositions I would submit for consideration:

1. All buildings should be seen as opportunities to build the city—as fragments of a covenant with the future.
2. It is necessary to beware of the exploitive ingenuity of our time; the impulse to make celebrities and the widespread diffusion of photographic images may subvert the search for places that can gather genuine public significance.

3. Public architecture should be given a mandate that exceeds that of private building. That mandate should include considerations of place, of the dignity of persons, and of the connection with a larger, more enduring order than that which characterizes the market.

Consideration of the public interest in building must of course proceed from a position regarding the nature of the public and in what measure it stands in independence from the aggregate of private interests. Architects (myself included) are characteristically befuddled on this issue. Property rights in American cities are now hopelessly entangled with issues that bear on the financial management of cities. Our fractured political structure intersects with a complex, interconnected economic structure to make the center city into a Monopoly gameboard. We have no coherent vision of how to build to public benefit because modern government is for most a contingent force, a qualifier, rather than an embodiment of purpose.

BUILDING AND BUREAUCRACY

There are several ways in which a building may be considered public. First, it may be privately owned, though open to the public as shops generally are, and therefore constitute a significant segment of what may be considered the public realm. Second, it may be constructed with public funds as a general-use facility such as a parking garage, for instance, or public works in general. Third, it may house a publicly-funded special institution such as a hospital, school, or library. Fourth, it may be a place in which to ''be public''—a stadium, meeting hall, or plaza. Fifth, it may be a government building, expected to represent the public interest as well as to house its functionaries.

Buildings of the first sort—such as shops, department stores, theaters, even churches—are public in that they are accessible to the public at large and make up a large part of the spatial realm that is generally used, even though their ownership and control are distinctly private. These, the spaces that are contiguous with the public rights-of-way, are the most ubiquitous definers of the public realm. If they are obscure, devoid of information, ''dead on the street,'' they will structure an environment that is lifeless, one that is not only tiresome, but that conveys a disregard for the lively exchange between people that lies at the base of democratic life.

This day-to-day lively exchange is not generally understood today as a way of knowing, as the arena for understanding our society and recognizing the diversity of initiatives that are the fruits of a secular, free society (though this was suggested by Robert Venturi's haunting phrase, ''Main Street is almost all right''). It is also not generally recognized that this environment comes about through a form of public design, by way of street patterns, lot dispositions, zoning regulations, building and sign ordinances, and so on. The regulations and ordinances that implement these designs are usually commonplace, based on dimly-perceived presumptions about the nature of the public realm, and seldom examined in term of their predicted outcome in the form of the city—except insofar as they are generally expected to contribute to a certain tidiness in the relations between buildings and activities.

The bureaucratic mind, dedicated as it is to control and prediction, is not comfortable with the untidy. Places which come under the predominant influence of government and financial institutions tend to become emotionally arid, with little opportunity to find or express personal insight or initiative. Such places instead become the domains of material expression, expensive, hard places where investment is geared more to maintenance than to the proffering of enjoyment or even enlightenment for the many. The center of Austin, Texas, is an excellent though not exceptional case in point. Situated in a beautiful location, with abundant landscaping and rolling land around, the ambitious and dignified capitol grounds are surrounded by a band of government agencies and financial institutions that have denuded the landscape, and forged in its stead a place that is hard and overscaled, strewn with monuments to power and endurance. These buildings have simple messages that, once received, sustain no further scrutiny, yet bear down upon us as we pass, imposing themselves on the daily public life of Austin's citizens.

In contrast to this we might place the Rue de Rivoli in Paris, a Napoleonic vision extended with a real sense of purpose several generations later by Haussmann's bureaucracy. Situated next to the Louvre and the Tuileries gardens, its uniform architectural cadence is juxtaposed for part of its stretch against great buildings recalling great events, then opens to the side of a grand park filled with carefully-measured trees. The tiny little shops that inhabit this magnificent bit of public scenery gain perspective from their confrontation with a larger, more-differentiated area beyond. This was an instance of government architects setting the frame, then leaving private initiative to fill out the internal organization of the shops and residences. The regulated order of the Rue de Rivoli facade mediates between the disorderly initiatives of the marketplace and the regal ambitions for a controlled place of resort. The sharp, built boundary for the two is far more effective than the antiseptic indifference that is generally fostered by state control now, when the architect's magical artifice is suspect, if not absent.

What works in the shade of the Louvre and opposite a grand gravelled park should not too easily be seen as a model transferable to other parts of the city, let alone to other cultures. Yet it is a clear, readily-imagined example of the use of building form to suit both civic purpose and private interests. And it is a form that was initially imagined with the pleasures of an encompassing scene, albeit not the specific interests of previous landholders, in mind. What matters here is the willingness and authority to design the physical connections between things, rather than leaving their juxtaposition to be softened by intervening space—in the manner that still dominates the American design imagination.

The design of mental and physical connections between the buildings of government and the places of which they are a part has been a long time coming in the United States. Buildings for public use were few in the days of the founding, and often linked with the marketplace. Gradually most public buildings were elaborated into a symbolic formula that was almost immune to local qualification. However, a string of particularized American examples indicates the opportunity to make buildings here that can carry public meanings not only through conventional symbols but also through a complex engagement with everyday life. We can follow the trail of these conceptual changes on the two coasts, first in Boston and then in various spots in California, with a brief stop at Lincoln, Nebraska en route.

MASSACHUSETTS: FROM COLONY TO COMMONWEALTH

The earliest town hall in Boston, no longer extant, was associated with the market, like many of the first city halls in Europe. It was perched over an open porch that offered shelter for the exchange of goods in a none-too-favorable climate. This pattern was continued in a refined form in Faneuil Hall, a place of public assembly donated to the town by a wealthy merchant, and in which much of the rhetoric leading to the American Revolution was first sounded. It harbored meat and provisions stores on its ground floor until very recently, when they were replaced by shops selling ice cream and old photographs of Boston. The meeting hall remains, however, a beautiful, light-filled, balconied room now used for special occasions and tourist visits. Conceived initially as a part of the marketplace—because that is where the citizenry gathered— Faneuil Hall now lends its name to a revitalized market area. The markets form a lively public place, though now the shops are more an entertainment than a vital source of either food or income. The real trading takes place elsewhere—in land, options, and interest—and the citizenry is too numerous (or too uninterested) to gather anywhere, except in fun. Here, as in the more affluent shopping centers, the experience of shopping, complete with jugglers, musicians, banners, and flowers, has become street theater of the most engaging sort. Buying our bread has become a circus.

Buildings for the state have followed a different path. The Old State House, built in 1712 as the home of the Colonial government, was constructed on the site of the original town hall (Figure 1). It is a simple volume, large for its time (though dwarfed now), and made gracious by embellishments. An elegantly formed lantern towers several stories above its center, proudly announcing its landmark status. This status is conferred not only by civic purpose but by its location at the most important crossing in Boston. One end of the building faces down State Street, out Long Wharf to the sea and to England beyond, and the other end opens through a simple porch onto the road that connected the peninsula on which Boston was founded to the mainland beyond. The State Street end is elaborated by statues of a lion and a unicorn bracketing the facade ga-

FIGURE 1. *Old State House, Boston, Mass. (1712) (Photo: Alice Wingwall)*

ble as emblems of the crown, and by an amply-proportioned door frame and balcony that project from the second level to make a place suitable for proclamations and pronouncements. This face of the Old State House is a perfect representation of government by decree and was a logical focus for protest. Not surprising, then, that it set the scene for the Boston Massacre.

The Boston State House, designed in 1795 by Charles Bulfinch for the Commonwealth of Massachusetts, represents government in an entirely different way (Figure 2). It presents a broad, accessible side to the populus, not a narrow declaratory end, and its facade is graced by what was

FIGURE 2. *Charles Bulfinch's State House, Boston, Mass. (1795) (Photo: Alice Wingwall)*

then a spectacular porch, surely broad enough to hold the entire legislative assembly. The tall lantern is here replaced by a gleaming dome, unmistakably a landmark, lodged high on Beacon Hill, the summit of the peninsula. Here are the embodied aspirations of a new beginning (with, to be sure, a Tory cast). The building is set out with a grandeur that was simply unknown in that place at that time, calling forth an intention to reach the levels of sophistication only then emerging in England, and to do so with an expansiveness worthy of the new Commonwealth. The building reads as a complex unity, with the Senate and Governor's chambers in wings to either side, and the House of Representatives resplendent beneath the dome. The whole is accessible through a broad arcade at the ground level and is given an extraordinary sense of largesse by the tall columns that measure out the aforementioned porch above. The porch is adjacent to the assembly rooms on the second floor—aloof still, but nonetheless expansive and inviting to the mind.

The State House was subsequently enlarged, keeping pace with the prosperity and complexity of the Commonwealth. The successive stages are instructive. The first expansions were minor pragmatic additions to the rear of the building that provided some extra space and convenience. In the last decade of the nineteenth century a major expansion transformed the nature of the building, absorbing the original into a vast brick palace that extended across the crest of the hill. It was executed, however, in the Classical motifs established in the original building, slightly updated to suit the sensibility of a later generation. The extended building provides a new and grander room for the House of Representatives, a great amount of office space, rows of corridor in which to lobby, rooms memorializing the Civil War, and an array of broad internal stairs connecting the various places of office and assembly to a carriage portico that is formed underneath the buildings as it bridges over Mt. Vernon Street. What is of principal note in this stage of expansion is that the architect, Charles Brigham, used a great deal of ingenuity in accommodating the expanded scope of government, yet he worked within a formal vocabulary that is a direct continuation of the traditions adopted by Bulfinch nearly a century before. Note too that the business of governance (conducted in top hats, we may suppose) was a principal activity to be accommodated by the extension.

The Brigham addition was not the end of the State House expansion story. During World War I another addition was undertaken, this by less adventurous architects, Chapman, Sturgis & Andrews. They were perhaps embarrassed by the bravura of Brigham's transformation, for they designed their addition as two wings forming courts to either side of the Bulfinch State House, completely isolating it from the addition. Their buildings also refer to the Classical traditions, but in a vapid, modestly-scaled manner that leaves the original State House in clear command. Here the heritage of Bulfinch's design is considered an antique to be cherished and displayed rather than a guiding force in the contemporary imagination.

The elements of the Bulfinch design are similar to those which characterize the national Capitol and which were in turn emulated by the majority of state capitols: a balanced three-part composition with a crowning dome at the center and a large portico facing broadside, executed in a version of the Classical protocols for form that trace back through England, France, and Italy, to Rome and thence to Greece. The lineage of these forms is so complex that they have been, at various times, associated with the Enlightenment (as here), Greek democracy, republican virtue, and Roman imperialism—to say nothing of Renaissance idealism and, more notoriously, fascism.

SAN FRANCISCO AND THE IMPERIAL STYLE

Roman imperialism was probably closest to the mark at the turn of the century, a period bracketed, for our purposes, by the Columbian Exposition in Chicago in 1893 and the Panama Pacific International Exposition in San Francisco in 1915. The former created a nationwide thirst for grand Classical orders and sweeping vistas, while the latter implanted freely-interpreted stucco versions of imperial grandeur by the side of San Francisco Bay, where one fragment still stands. The dome of the Palace of Fine Arts, designed by Bernard Maybeck, has been recast in concrete to mark one section of the city and to hover permanently over the imaginations of its citizens.

The City Beautiful movement, prompted by the 1893 Exposition, led to a spate of civic centers, as architects and politicians sought ways to make government investment serve more than isolated purposes. In 1915, along with the Exposition, San Francisco erected a city hall worthy to be a state capitol (or at least a French war monument). It is the centerpiece of an ambitious scheme for a civic center that now includes a library, opera house, civic auditorium, concert hall and museum, a state office building, and a federal building (Figure 3). Most recently a symphony hall has been added, a suitable coda to the inclination towards epic visions that the civic center represents.

The San Francisco Civic Center, though much admired for the singleminded skill with which it was executed, remains incomplete and largely unpleasant. It founders on the inherent limits of a vision of public life that is cast only in institutional terms. The refinements of civic aspiration and established culture were meant to be unsullied by commerce (or rabble-rousers) and are instead surrounded by automobiles and haunted by vagrants. The spaces of

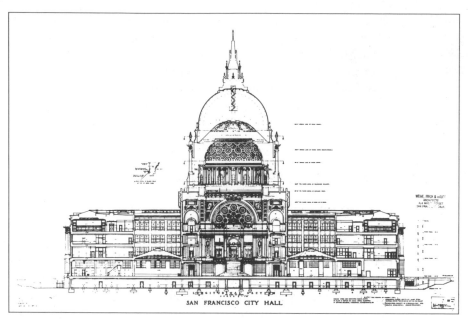

FIGURE 3. *Plan for San Francisco City Hall (1915) (Bakewell and Brown, Architects),*
Courtesy, The Bancroft Library

the Center, designed solely for effect and cut through by
wide streets, are simply too large for the foggy wind-swept
reality of San Francisco. As symbol they suffer, for their
significance is not reinforced by experience. Despite rows
of clipped trees, they are unpleasant to be around and they
make no satisfactory connection with the form of the adjoining city. The possible exceptions are the various performance halls which are closely packed across the back of
the complex, divided from it by Van Ness Avenue, but
linked thereby to a major artery of the city. These places of
performance and assembly do provide a number of differing occasions to visit the Center but they are mostly institutions of elite interest; even the attendant cafes and bookstores are relegated to areas outside the Center, leaving a
dark void in front of City Hall, an arbored expanse that
seems at night rather like an urban version of Sherwood
Forest.

The crowning glory of the City Hall is a grand rotunda,
an ornate dome that marks the center of the domain. Inside this rotunda the experience of the place is intensely
concentrated, with elaborate and spirited decorations arrayed about the surfaces of the dome and surrounding col-

onnades, and enormous medallions in the four corners of the dome's supporting structure that are carved with allegorical figures. (Though comely, these figures may be as obscure to many citizens as the Jedi are to me.) Recently the American Institute of Architects held a Beaux Arts Ball, a black tie and costume celebration inside the rotunda, with dancing up and down the magnificent great stair that descends from the civic rooms on the second floor to the floor of the rotunda. It was a splendid way of appropriating a civic symbol to personal experience, but only for the professional society and its friends and patrons who were willing and able to pay the rather hefty price of admission. For some there were also grim echoes of 1960, when the local newspapers carried full-page photographs of protestors being washed down the stairs with fire hoses.

NEBRASKA AND SANTA BARBARA: NEW DEPARTURES

During the next phase of building for public institutions, the decades following World War I, the Classical formula was adopted with numbing regularity, but two new departures did take place. One had to do with forging new formal means to express the aspirations of government; the other was involved with shaping urban complexes in a gentler, more approachable manner that paid closer attention to local context. The former is best represented by Bertram Grosvenor Goodhue's great tower for the unicameral Nebraska State Capitol. The other is marvelously illustrated by the Santa Barbara County Court House. They serve different levels of government, but also pose different conceptions of how public buildings are to be built.

Goodhue's capital, like many others, sits on its own block of land and may be approached from all sides (Figure 4). Unlike most others, however, it abandons the specific emblems of dome and portico and three-part division in favor of a single monumental shaft that stands as a marker, large enough to be seen from miles around as a centering beacon. From its top a heroically-sized figure of the sower appears to cast seeds to the wind. The tower is very handsomely shaped, with carefully sculpted modulations as it rises from a broad mass of office and assembly rooms at the base to the slim, largely useless but expres-

FIGURE 4. *State Capitol, Lincoln, Neb. (Photo: Ted Kirk)*

sive tower. The tower easily captures the imagination. Here, in the plains of Nebraska, this one draws on the wonder of New York, city of towers, then still a promising vision of the new world.[1]

The architects of the Santa Barbara County Court House took a very different tack, surely prompted by the site and climate and the nature of county government. The building has no distinct form. Its rooms and open corridors are instead ranged around the edge of a county-scaled courtyard, like a thick wall open on the end to views of the surrounding town and mountains. This too eschews the traditional elements of building ordinarily associated with government. The forms used here associate rather with an

FIGURE 5. *Arch of Santa Barbara County Court House (1929) (Photo: Gerald Allen & Associates)*

imagined Spanish past. It is a glorified *hacienda* built on a scale that Spanish California never knew. Hispanic architecture had been officially adopted shortly before as the appropriate model to use in rebuilding Santa Barbara after its partial destruction in an earthquake. The court house is in this adopted style, but in other ways as well it is almost the opposite of the San Francisco example. There are almost none of the overt, conventional symbols of government; the memorability of the place has to do with your experience in it. The court becomes a center of experience in the town because it is nicely made and can be richly inhabited. It fosters the dignity of all who enter there. Registering these qualities can lead to a respect for the place and for the government that it represents. The most overt symbol is itself one that refers to the larger setting—a grand arch that forms the entry, not into the building, but into the courtyard, with a magnificent view of the Santa Barbara mountains framed through the opening as you pass under it (Figure 5). This is a building that serves its purposes by reminding us of the place to which it belongs.

BEVERLY HILLS: THE CONTEMPORARY MOOD

A competition held in the summer of 1982 for a civic center for Beverly Hills, California, tells much about the current situation regarding the design of public buildings. It was forthrightly intended to be an act of city-building, and the new buildings were clearly intended to supplement rather than replace the existing city hall. The present building, designed in 1931, has a nine story tower and is rendered in vaguely Hispanic motifs. It lacks the expressive power of the Nebraska State Capitol and fails to create the evocative ambience of the Santa Barbara County Court House, but has nonetheless attracted the affections and allegiance of its citizens. The program was intended to reorganize and expand the facilities that house various services of government—fire and police departments, a jail, library, and meeting hall—and to provide a large parking facility that would serve both these activities and the adjacent merchants, providing, meanwhile, a revivified sense of civic pride and a valuable thrust of new development at the lesser end of the business district. Six architectural firms were invited to enter a limited competition for the project, each firm one that has achieved national recognition for innovative design. It was a highly select list that included only two architects from California and none that could be expected to treat the commission in a routine manner. The competition was managed with uncommon thoroughness. Each firm was paid a fee to develop initial designs and to present them in models and drawings with cost estimates. These were then examined carefully and in minute detail by representatives of each of the agencies to be housed and by the professional adviser. They were also placed on public display with opportunity for comments from the citizenry. Each of the schemes was reviewed by a jury consisting of several distinguished architects, a landscape architect, and an architectural critic. The professional jury then selected one scheme to be recommended to the City Council for approval. City Council action followed some weeks later and was unanimous in approving the jury's choice of the entry prepared by Charles W. Moore and the Urban Innovations Group of UCLA. Work is now proceeding through contract documents to construction with minor revisions.

An examination of the several entries to the competition reveals that many of the attitudes and problems previously discussed still establish the context in which architectural decisions are made for a project of this sort. How to treat the existing building, what forms to use in the new architecture, how civic buildings might best relate to the spaces and activities around them, how most effectively to use the taxpayers' money to shape a segment of the city— all these considerations were added to the functional considerations of city facilities.

One of the principal decisions to be made was how to reconcile the desire for a unified civic center with the divisive reality of the site, which straddled two sides of a street and had the city hall on one side and most of the available space on the other. Two of the schemes accepted this division and fronted it with colonnades, leaving the city hall to stand more or less on its own, accompanied in one case by a formal park, in the other by a fire station. Two other schemes closed the street, linking the city hall tower and the auxiliary facilities by a great, shapely-terraced mall. Two bridged the street, one with an independent, fantastically-shaped building, the other (Charles Moore's) with a long wing that arches over the street, linking the new structure to the old. The significant difference in Moore's scheme, however, is that the divisive geometry of the existing street axis is subordinated by more powerful architectural themes, themes that unify the site and transform it into a place of special significance.

The themes that Moore develops are akin to those of the Santa Barbara County Court House (not coincidentally, since he was the first to introduce this precedent into contemporary discussions of architectural theory). As with its Santa Barbara ancestor, the most important elements of the Beverly Hills complex are open spaces shaped by the buildings (Figure 6). In this case a series of three open courtyards, elliptical in configuration, are lined up along a pedestrian axis that cuts diagonally across the site. The central and largest of these courts is formed around the intersection of diagonal axis and existing cross street. It creates an automobile arrival court that serves also as entry to the public parking structure. The courtyards are given their shape by tall surrounding arcades which also house a succession of ramps, stairs, and passages that accommo-

FIGURE 6. *Model of Charles Moore's Design for Beverly Hills Civic Center (Photo: Courtesy City of Beverly Hills)*

date the various types of pedestrian movement that are required and encouraged by the site.

Whereas Charles Brigham, in his extension to the Boston State House, adopted with only slight modifications the formal vocabulary of Bulfinch's original design—the classical columns, pilasters, and pediments—Moore has taken the vocabulary of the early Beverly Hills City Hall and made it more scenic, even cinematographic. The fundamental proportions and sizes of the earlier building are used again in the new design, the height of the main mass of the building controls the height of the new structures, the bay spacing of elements along the wall is the same, and the new structure, like the old, is made of concrete and decorated sparingly with tiles. The differences are that the arcades and passages are for everyday use, not just for ritual observances such as reviewing parades and receiving dignitaries, and they are not only for the business of government (Figure 7). These arcades are cinematographic in

FIGURE 7. *Artist's Conception of Moore's Civic Center Scheme (Rendering by William Hersey)*

that they encourage the moving, roaming eye and the gliding step; they will engage the users of the place as participants in, not only observers of, the admittedly-staged drama of the civic center. The pleasures of being there are meant to become fused with the connotations of civic pride and the protections and services provided by good government. The risk of the scheme is that it depends on the experience of these places being pleasant, on there being enough civic pride and good management to maintain them well and to make a continuing investment in the landscape of the place. Without care they can become a fresco of bad government.

Though none of the other competitors used building elements that closely resembled those of the original building, they all used the older building in a rigidly symbolic way. In each case they isolated it as a singular presence on the site, allowing its form to dominate the entire complex, and treating it with the isolated respect that makes the old feel alien. They have made their proposed new buildings skillfully, in some cases using the familiar symbols of civic grandeur, colonnades, and well-formed piazzas, though stripped of superfluous Classic refine-

FIGURE 8. *Model of Moshe Safdie's Design for Beverly Hills Civic Center (Photo: Ruth Nadel)*

ments. In two instances the whole site was transformed into terraced hanging gardens. In one, Moshe Safdie's much-admired scheme, a block-long reflecting pool is centered on the city hall tower, and the other building forms are so completely hidden by terraces and pavilions that the older building looms larger than life over a scene of Shangri-La splendor (Figure 8). The Moore scheme, while building in a manner consistent with the initial city hall, does not make it an iconic object. Instead, it makes a larger place which is very distinct, filled both with useful facilities and experiential incident, for which the city hall tower is but the most visible and familiar landmark. It extends, where others would embalm, the significance of the 1930s building.

In most of the schemes presented to the City Council the dominant images were of physical connection—arcades, colonnades, sweeping terraces. Frank Gehry, the

FIGURE 9. *Model of Frank Gehry's Design for Beverly Hills Civic Center (Photo: Ruth Nadel)*

other Californian, posed the only alternative concept (Figure 9). The various elements of his scheme were disposed around the site as isolated buildings jostling against each other as though competitors in a land speculation venture. For Gehry, as for many others, this seems to have been the archetypal "Los Angeles" scheme, the ultimate westward expression of freedom of opportunity. These are discrete approachable eccentric buildings untroubled by any subordinating vision, using the consolidated municipally-owned site as so many building plots to be exploited. The proposal has an ingratiating charm, an appearance at once familiar and make-believe. However, like so many restored Old Towns, it strains credulity as it attempts to be beguiling. What the Gehry scheme misses (most likely with intention) is that part of the "California quest" and "American dream" which sought not only opportunity, but solace—which longed to find a place where the land and the sun could, with some vision (and a little northern California water), be fashioned into Arcadian splendor. That dream, no less than the "City Upon a Hill" that led the founders of Boston, requires a covenant—if not with God or nature, then with ourselves.

RESTORING THE CIVIC PACT

The public places that we build help express the nature of that implicit social pact we make with each other. That civic pact should include a respect for the places in which we live, a commitment to continue building a city to which we can all belong, and a determination to infuse public architecture with a sense of human dignity.

To embody all this in building requires attending to more than the pragmatic and circumstantial. It requires a sense of human purpose. And it needs an ability and willingness to use the mysteries of the sympathetic imagination to reach beyond the confines of institutional definition—to know the character of places and the many ways we can inhabit them. The architect's goal should be to embody an understanding of the public weal through building in a way that captures the mind, as symbols must, yet allows a freedom and complexity of individual experience. Then it becomes possible to make connections between individual interests and common values. In great architecture, each subsequent generation will see not only the interests and aspirations of our time, but its own interests and those of its heirs as well.

NOTE

1. Coincidentally, as Richard Oliver has observed in his book on Goodhue, both Wallace Harrison and Raymond Hood, principal architects in the development of Rockefeller Center, earlier worked for Goodhue on the Nebraska State Capitol. There they acquired some of the formal ideas later used to design one of the finest and most influential office complexes in the world, an instance of city-building on a large scale. Working with the towering office blocks and the theaters, plazas, and ground level shops, they give expressive force to a complex of unprecedented dimension. Harrison in turn was a member of the United Nations design team, where the massive administrative block of the Secretariat has become a dominating symbol, with the softly formed General Assembly building placed to one side at its base; the whole isolated from its surroundings—a manager's view of government.

13

The Triumph
of the Capitol

MICHAEL A. SCULLY

Two newspapers of the period, in Maryland and Boston, published the same account, datelined Georgetown, September 21, 1793: "On Wednesday last one of the grandest Masonic processions took place, for the purpose of laying the cornerstone of the Capitol of the United States. . . . The procession marched two abreast, in the greatest solemn dignity, with music playing, drums beating, colors flying and spectators rejoicing." The stern General Washington, by then President, laid a silver plate, on top of a cut stone, in a hole in the ground, on a hill called Jenkins' Heights that overlooked a swamp. In the next 200 years, a hundred such ceremonies in every part of the globe would express the hopes of decolonized peoples against the smirk of history. So much hope, and so little reason to be hopeful. Here was the first of them, and typically, it chose for the site of its capital city—its Brasilia—a marshy wilderness.

What was in Washington's mind that day? Let us assume he saw a mall, a great plaza stretching from that hill two and a half miles to the Potomac, for that was the plan. And if he could not have foreseen, precisely, the Pennsylvania veteran with his yellow VFW tee-shirt, plaid jacket, and baseball cap I saw recently treading the Capitol

From The Public Interest, *Winter 1984, pp. 99–115. Copyright © by National Affairs, Inc.*

grounds, or the two score families with craned-up necks standing beneath the Capitol rotunda, let us assume he foresaw their children's eyes, bulging in amazement at what is theirs.

GRANDEUR, SIMPLICITY, AND CONVENIENCE

What would sit atop that hill, that "pedestal waiting for a monument," as the city's planner, Charles Pierre L'Enfant, had called it? Only recently had it been decided.

On March 24, 1792 an advertisement appeared in the *Gazette of the United States* offering "a premium of a lot in the city" and "$500, or a medal of that value" to the person who produced the "most approved" plan for the Capitol. (A similar offer was made at about the same time, soliciting plans for the "President's House.") The advertisement listed specifications for rooms to be included in the design. There was to be a conference room and a room for Representatives, each large enough to accommodate 300 persons. The instructions called for a lobby or antechamber to the Representatives' room, and another to the Senate room, which itself was to measure 1,200 square feet. These rooms and lobbies were to be "full of elevation." In addition to these, the solicitation mandated "twelve rooms of 600 square feet each for committee rooms and clerks, to be half the elevation" of the major rooms and lobbies.

A dozen or more plans were received in the four months allowed by the advertisement, none of them judged wholly satisfactory by the Commissioners of the District of Columbia—who kept in frequent communication with President Washington. Indeed, one of the principal historians of the city, H. Paul Caemmerer, notes that Washington took "personal interest in the selection of the design." So much so, says Caemmerer, that, "In fact the decision seems to have rested almost entirely with him."

Three plans were returned to their authors with requests for revisions, but by the end of August 1792 there was still no plan thought satisfactory. The Commissioners then engaged a French immigrant, Stephen Hallet—whose plan had interested the Commissioners—to prepare a new design. Hallet moved to Washington and began to work on a new plan, which by the next January he still had not completed.

In the meantime another design had been offered, and in early February 1793 the Commissioners noted their general satisfaction with it. Caemmerer described the architect in a paper delivered to the Columbia Historical Society in 1943:

> . . . Dr. William Thornton, a 'physician, architect, poet, and horse-racer,' born in the West Indies and trained abroad, a man of culture and technical bent of mind, who was living in Philadelphia, heard of the competition for a capitol building while visiting his native town of Tortola. Architecture was his avocation, and in 1789 he had won a competition for the first public library to be erected in the country in Philadelphia.

Thus Thornton's design was selected, and with a number of alterations—many lobbied for by Hallet, who for a time was supervisor of construction—Thornton's plan was built. The design was of a modified Palladian style.

In March 1793, Thornton arrived in the city of Washington. He brought with him a letter of introduction from President Washington to the Commissioners. (The seat of government was then still in Philadelphia.) Washington wrote of the Thornton design that "Grandeur, simplicity, and convenience appear to be so well combined in this plan of Dr. Thornton's." If anything Jefferson was even more effusive: "The grandeur, simplicity, and beauty of the exterior, the propriety with which the departments are distributed, and the economy in the mass of the whole structure, recommend this plan." Wrote Jefferson somewhat later, "Thornton's plan had captivated the eyes and the judgment of all. It is simple, noble, beautiful, excellently arranged, and moderate in size." And, Jefferson noted, "among its admirers none are more decided than he whose decision is most important"—meaning, of course, Washington.

Several years ago, a group that included several distinguished scholars toured the Capitol. Entering the old Senate chamber—recently refurbished—one of the party, a noted historian, said in a kind of whispered gasp, "My, they *really* knew what a republic was all about." Washington's and Jefferson's descriptions of Thornton's plan demonstrate as much: beauty, yet simplicity; grandeur, yet moderation in size; convenience and economy of mass. Even with its subsequent changes and expansions, more than enough truth remains in these first words of approval to set the Capitol apart. Other of Washington's buildings, most from necessity and some from deficient sensibility, violate these prescriptions. Yet the Capitol remains too measured for the potentate, too grand for the populist—the product of an epoch that at once proclaimed republican government and remembered the appropriateness, even to self-governing men and women, of lofty sentiments.

"IT IS A SIGN"

In 1803, Benjamin Henry Latrobe, one of American's few professionally-trained architects at that time, succeeded William Thornton as architect. Latrobe undertook refinements and expansions in the Thornton design. The Capitol dome was completed. Changes were made in Thornton's design for the East portico, and a dramatic departure was taken from Thornton's scheme for the West facade. Yet Latrobe's work, a decade in the making, was finished only a short time before the British sacked Washington in 1814 and—after great effort—managed to set the Capitol ablaze. Frustrated in their initial attempts, British troops finally piled chairs and desks and set them ablaze beneath the Capitol rotunda. The hemisphere, then made of wood and masonry, collapsed. When the architect returned to Washington in 1815, little was left of his Capitol: two burnt and ransacked ends, connected by a demolished and burnt-out middle. It was, said Latrobe, "a most magnificent ruin."

For the next two years, Latrobe supervised a reconstruction that included enlargement of the Senate chamber and redesign of the old House chamber (now Statuary Hall). After a disagreement with the Commissioner of Public Buildings in 1817, however, Latrobe was replaced by another architect—the first American-born Capitol architect—Charles Bulfinch of Boston. Bulfinch had traveled widely throughout the United States and Europe after graduating from Harvard in 1781. Architecture had begun as an avocation for him, but financial setbacks forced him to turn to it as a source of income. By the time he was enlisted as the third architect of the Capitol, he had designed the Massachusetts State House (1795), the New South Church (1814), and the Lancaster Meeting House (1816–17). Lonelle Aikman, author of the U.S. Capitol Historical Society's guide to the Capitol, describes Bulfinch's Washington tenure this way:

To Bulfinch goes the credit for completing the Capitol as Thornton and Latrobe had planned it. He worked out the remaining structural details of the Senate and House chambers. . . . and Bulfinch carried through the building's long-planned central portion, including its east and west fronts, and a central Rotunda covered by a low copper-sheathed dome.

Bulfinch remained in Washington for thirteen years, by which time his work was completed and Congress had abolished the position of Capitol architect. Not until 1851 would there be another. By then, the nation's expansion to 26 states—which meant the Senate's growth to 52 members and the House's to more than eleven score—necessitated an enlargement of the Capitol. An appropriation of $100,000 was passed, and work begun on the expansion of the Capitol into the building that—despite some changes in the intervening century—we know today.

New wings were constructed for the House and Senate, with the old chambers coming to serve as walkways connecting the two wings and the Rotunda. Above all, literally and figuratively, there was the new Capitol dome, which made use of a new technology, and was the masterstroke of the fourth Capitol architect, Thomas Ustick Walter.

E.J. Applewhite, the author of *Washington Itself*, an outstanding guide to the city, describes the architectural lineage of the dome, and the symbolic importance it had from its origin:

> In the depths of the Civil War, Lincoln was criticized for continuing the construction of the Capitol, but his response was resolute: "If the people see the Capitol going on," he said, "it is a sign we intend the Union shall go on." So Walter and Meigs [of the Army Corps of Engineers] worked on the dome without stint, employing cast iron because it was fireproof and because it was stronger, lighter, and more versatile than stone. They took as their models Paris's Pantheon and Invalides, and also St. Isaac's Cathedral in Leningrad, completed in 1842 with one of the first great cast iron domes in Europe. Their accomplishment at the Capitol was a considerable technical tour de force, for they applied the only real innovation in dome engineering between the coffered masonry domes of Rome and the Renaissance and the pre-stressed concrete and geodesic domes of today.
>
> The Capitol dome is Baroque in silhouette and scale. The cast iron structural elements of the outer shell are not concealed behind a veneer, although they are partially disguised as molded arches and columns with Corinthian capitals. It is Baroque in its huge mass, and in its complex and expansive composition that dominates the sweeping vistas of the Mall; its self-confidence derives from an exuberance restrained with dignity. Some guides will tell

you that the 36 columns around the base are for the 36 states of the Union at the time it was built and that the 13 columns of the lantern atop the dome stand for the original colonies—which are nice thoughts, but in fact there were only 32 states when the dome was completed and the lantern has only 12 columns.[1]

The dome—actually, there are inner and outer domes trussed to withstand the stresses of climate-caused expansions and contractions—weighs 9 million pounds and stands 285 feet above the eastern plaza. Thomas Crawford's statue of Freedom sits atop the dome, ten platinum-tipped lightning rods fixed to her shoulders and helmet. The drum of the dome, reminiscent of the drum of St. Peter's in Rome, is extended at its base beyond the structural supports of Bulfinch's dome, which in Walter's design still carry most of the structure's weight.

Still to come are decades of improvement. Inside, the great Brumidi painted, "to make beautiful the Capitol of the one country on earth in which there is liberty." Outside, the nation's greatest landscape architect, Frederick Law Olmsted, had, by the time of Brumidi's death in 1880, undertaken the landscaping of the grounds and the addition of the walkways and sweeping stairways that lead from Pennsylvania Avenue up the West front of the Capitol.

There would be other artists, and in time other changes. Filippo Costaggini would work for eight years following Brumidi's death on the dome's circular frieze. Sixty-five years later, Allyn Cox would begin to close the 31-foot gap unfinished by Costaggini. Seven giant paintings of historic scenes would hang inside the Rotunda, to remind us of such tidal events as the Pilgrims' embarkation, the surrender of Cornwallis, and Washington resigning his commission in 1783. Still to come were statues from every state, so many that they now clutter the halls. They are inspiring, or pious, or lifelike, or stiff, or ugly. And there have been changes, the most important being the extension of the East Front of the Capitol by some 32 feet in 1959 and 1960, a favorite project of House Speaker Sam Rayburn. (Extension was first proposed by Walter, as its defenders testily remind us.) Another major alteration, that of the West facade, has been a smoldering, occasionally flaming, controversy for over two decades. Wrote Wolf von Eckardt of this Rayburn expansion plan:

The vastly enlarged marble version was to extend the old building
by up to 88 feet and to house cafeterias for tourists, truck-loading
platforms and hideaway offices for deserving members. This folly
was to cost $58 million in 1969 dollars.

   It would have destroyed not only the Capitol's earliest history,
but also its most endearing feature—the grand terraces that gracefully elevate the building above the mall and which were designed
almost 100 years ago by Frederick Law Olmsted, America's greatest
landscape architect.

A later plan, by the current Architect of the Capitol,
George M. White, would have considerably shrunk the
Rayburn plan, left Olmsted's terraces alone, and yet added
160,000 square feet to the structure. Recently, the Congress
opted for restoration of the West facade, rather than expansion. This leaves the Rayburn House Office Building, the
most notable reminder of that legislator's taste in public
buildings.

At least in a general way, each of the eras of Washington architecture has a representative on Capitol Hill. Yet in
almost every case, be the building triumphant or medio-
cre, grand and efficient or gross and inefficient, its style is
mediated by the appropriate prejudice that Capitol Hill is
of a piece, and the Capitol is its centerpiece.

The great exception, of course, is the Library of Congress. Twenty-four years from its design to its completion,
its construction delayed by more than a decade of hag-
gling, it was conceived in an era different from the one in
which it was born. The Library of Congress is the only
Capitol Hill building that might be said to compete with
the Capitol. It has, for example, its own dome. Its facing is
a purple-gray granite. When it opened in 1897, its features
were derided by at least one architectural critic; in the decades that followed, such words would be applied to it
as "a dreadful medley" and "overlavish." Franklin
Roosevelt ("gingerbread," he said) wanted it resurfaced
and its dome removed. In the last decade of its construction, an important new movement was taking shape ("The
City Beautiful"), and within a half-dozen years of the Library's completion the L'Enfant Plan for Washington—dis-
regarded for decades—would be reinstituted, and it would
matter that this Italian Renaissance palace of knowledge
completely blocked L'Enfant's planned vista from Pennsylvania Avenue Southeast to the Capitol and beyond to the
Mall. Designed eight years after Lincoln's assassination,

completed three years before Dreiser's *Sister Carrie*, there it sits.

Wrote Dreiser of Carrie's lovers, they were ''the titled ambassadors of comfort and peace, aglow with their credentials. It is but natural that when the world which they represented no longer allured her, its ambassadors should be discredited.'' The original Library of Congress building *is* an ambassador from a gilded age (19 artists worked on its 112 murals, 22 sculptors on its embellishments), but as with an old, perhaps once-wanton ambassador, all is by now forgiven—his antique courtliness is cherished in the era of the un-held door.

"THE CITY BEAUTIFUL"

To both Capitol Hill and the city generally, no movement of architectural sensibility mattered more than the City Beautiful Movement, which lasted from the 1890's to the First World War. Represented in Washington by the McMillan Commission in 1901, it was chiefly influenced by Daniel H. Burnham, architect of Union Station, advisor to the Commission, and initiator of the enormously influential Chicago Exposition in 1893, which had fixed attention on architecture and city beautification.

In the second of her two volumes on the history of the city of Washington, Constance McLaughlin Green describes the McMillan Commission's importance both to the city and the City Beautiful Movement:

> The fame of the members appointed to the commission added weight to their recommendations; every American concerned with ''city beautiful'' knew of architects Daniel Burnham and Charles McKim, of the sculptor Augustus St. Gaudens, and of the son of Frederick Law Olmsted, the landscape architect who had laid out New York's Central Park and the grounds of the Capitol. The dimensions of the plan for the public domain in the national capital, moreover, stirred the most sluggish imagination. Americans who had never set foot in Washington or studied L'Enfant's original layout were suddenly eager to see it revived and elaborated. Thus, as the details became known the project for Washington gave impetus to city planning throughout the country.

The McMillan Commission plan reinstituted the essentials of the L'Enfant plan for the city, while accepting as unchangeable such major departures as the locations of the already-constructed State Department building, the Library of Congress, and the Treasury Building—all of which cut off L'Enfant-planned vistas. Writes Green of the period:

> The return to neo-classical architecture for government buildings pleased a public tired of the vagaries of the preceding half-century—the romantic red sandstone Norman castle of the Smithsonian, the mansard-roofed Department of Agriculture . . . the State Department building, the heavy square-towered Post Office on Pennsylvania Avenue, and the ornate Italian Renaissance Library of Congress. Uniformity of style and the use of marble and pale gray granite became the rule. . . .

The City Beautiful Movement is well-represented on Capitol Hill. Union Station was designed by Burnham, and was the first Washington building to reflect the stylistic taste of the McMillan Commission. It is of Roman beaux-arts design and, as one architectural guidebook puts it, "direct from the Columbian Exposition of 1893 in Chicago." Union Station was built in 1908. A half dozen years later, Burnham co-designed the City Post Office, adjacent to the Station, in such a fashion as to assure that the newer structure harmonizes with the older without competing for the viewer's attention.[2]

Capitol Hill's greatest debt to the City Beautiful Movement, however, might well be the Old House and Old Senate Office Buildings—now called, respectively, the Cannon and Russell Buildings. Built in 1908 by the firm of Carrere and Hastings (with the former responsible for the Senate building, the latter for the House), they are very much of a piece, without being identical. Interestingly, they were attacked when they opened. The *New York Times* criticized the Russell building for its size, calling it "a building that a thousand men would feel lonesome in." Nevertheless, there has yet to be built—after four intervening attempts—a congressional office building in the same league with the Cannon and Russell buildings.

Recall that when they were built, there were only two other important public buildings on Capitol Hill—the Capitol itself, and at some remove from the Capitol's East front, the Library of Congress. The House or Senate member would walk from either wing of the Capitol to his respective office building. To his side would be the Capitol's landscaped grounds. He would cross Independence or Constitution Avenues to the nearest office-building entrance. In either case, he would climb a white stone staircase. Inside, he would walk through column-filled corridors some 20 feet high, but only after crossing through a rotunda. Even the underground passages from the Capitol end in rotundas in each building's basement.

The Cannon and Russell buildings are indeed large buildings—each built to house offices for the full membership and their staffs at that time. Each takes up an entire city block. Yet neither proclaims: "You are a little man, a superfluity."

It is 1908, and already the need for Congressional office space has overwhelmed the chance for republican architecture. The nation has changed, and never again on Capitol Hill will we hear those first words of approval: "simple," "economy in the mass of the whole structure," "moderate in size." No sensitive historian will proclaim, "*They* really knew what a republic was all about." Perhaps they did know, but circumstance had precluded the chance to tell. Each of the old office buildings, at over a half-million gross square feet, had to "speak" of other things.

They speak of greatness and the public enterprise. Forced from simplicity, still they have not forsaken nobility nor forgotten that grandeur does not proceed from size alone. And there is yet another, subtler message: a whisper from the rotundas, a message never heard in the newer Congressional office buildings. It is the message of the spherical shape: *Politics is an art*. At the base, the columns are wide apart; the art is getting the ribs to meet at the top, in just proportion.

The newer office buildings have no rotundas. They are the children of their rationalist times. When the citizen is thought a building block, public buildings become boxes. The human body is all curves, and thus the sphere seems somehow natural to us. Yet the Rayburn House and Dirksen and Hart Senate buildings are all squares and 90-degree angles. What is wide at the base is equally wide at the top. The bases do not merge at the top; there is no just resolution appropriate to each part; the distant bottoms are equidistant at their tops; a ceiling connects the sides without any narrowing of their distance. It is all hard angles. Even a pork-barrel has a more human shape.

MODERN TIMES

Four major Capitol Hill buildings have been constructed since World War II and—less important for the Hill than for

most of the "critical habitats" of American public life—
since the rise of the modernist International school. None
of these new buildings is a triumph, yet each tells us something of note about current confusions as well as the difficulties associated with building to suit the needs of the
modern Congress, which now includes 535 members,
18,000 employees—and 9,000 parking spaces. (The Library
of Congress, which began in earnest after the fire of 1814
when the Congress purchased Thomas Jefferson's library,
now has some 19 million books and several times that
number of total items in its collections.)

The effect of such demands on Congressional buildings has been predictably great. The Dirksen and Hart
Senate buildings together have more than triple the gross
square footage of the entire Capitol building (2.6 million
gross square feet to the Capitol's 719,600). The Rayburn
House building has 1.162 million gross square feet. The
new Madison Library building and the original Library of
Congress building are Capitol Hill's Mutt and Jeff. The old
building, with 666,000 gross square feet, is one-third of
[the] size of the new one (1.976 million g.s.f.).

Racing is the sport of kings, but architectural criticism
is the sport of Congressmen. In fairness to the architects of
the Capitol and to the consulting architects who collaborate on individual projects, one must note that they work
within (at least) three constraints. First, the demands for
Congressional space and facilities require large buildings.
Second, and quite properly, the height of Capitol Hill
buildings (as of all buildings in the District of Columbia) is
limited, lest any building compete visually with the Capitol's dome. Third, from the earliest plans for financing the
Capitol (when it was thought that construction might be financed by auctioning off nearby government-owned lots—
an utter flop), Congressional buildings have been favored
places to display Congress's thriftiness. Great sums do get
spent, but before the last bill is presented, panic sets in.
Facilities and ornamentation invariably are discarded, and
there is great wonder at how it all could have happened. In
an institution where each year multi-millionaire members
piously vote against increases in salaries (to the point that,
say, a U.S. Senator might dare to get paid as much as a regional sales manager of a Fortune 500 corporation), phony
displays of frugality are a tradition. Congressional buildings, like non-heir Congressmen and Senators, are easy

targets for the cheap shot. All in all, we should be relieved and delighted that Capitol Hill remains as handsome as it does. No modern building competes with the Capitol. Even the Rayburn gargantua, though it blocks some nearby views of the Capitol from the Southwest, cannot be said to *compete* visually with the Capitol. It is too perfectly ignorable. Capitol Hill has been spared the Glass Box, and such Totalitarian Modern crimes as have been visited on Southwest Washington. That is no small cause for joy.

Nevertheless, things also might have turned out better. E.J. Applewhite begins his comment on the Rayburn building with a quotation from Robert Hughes's book *The Shock of the New*: "Authoritarian architecture must be clear and regular on the outside, and let the passing eye deduce nothing of what goes on inside." Indeed, the Rayburn building is so banal that one hardly can deduce what goes on inside when one is *inside*. In a building whose principal purpose was, of course, to provide office space and committee rooms, less than a fifth of its floor space is devoted to those functions. Its corridors are dead-ends, leaving the visitor who mistakenly walks down the wrong crook of the maze no option but to retrace his steps. (If Charley ever gets off the MTA, he will never get out of the Rayburn building.)

Even when one has discounted for the demands placed on the new Congressional buildings, one cannot look at the Rayburn building without perceiving that it represents a great loss of sensibility. Greatness has become grossness. The Madison Library building is less offensive in this regard, but it repeats the error. The two dozen columns (not cylindrical, but rectangular) that bestride its main entrance induce a headache. They dwarf all who enter or pass by. For the most part, its other three sides are uninterrupted, unwindowed white marble.

The Madison building was built to hold over 12 million books and most of the staff of the Library of Congress, as well as to provide reading rooms and support services both to scholars and the public. Thus this building had to be huge. The original Library of Congress was criticized in 1898 by Russell Sturgis for "that false idea of grandeur which consists mainly in hoisting a building up . . . in order to secure for it a monstrous flight of steps which must be surmounted before the main door can be reached." Yet, ironically, something like a ''monstrous flight of steps'' to go with its already monstrous rectangular columns might have made the Madison building more welcoming.

The newest building on Capitol Hill is the Hart Senate Building, which opened late in 1982. Its exterior presents a grid of rectangular marble boxes. Inside, Le Corbusier's idea of ''streets in the air'' is faithfully executed.

The most remarked-upon feature of the building is its nine-story atrium, which rises at a 90-degree angle from the building's lobby to a skylight-roof with a grid pattern. The building was designed to house the personal staffs of fifty Senators; each Senator has a personal office sixteen feet high. Many of the Senate suites are duplexes, and many of the suites have rooms that overlook the atrium. This makes it possible to see from numerous positions inside the building the goings-on inside the staff rooms of Senators' offices. Yet, as Capitol architect George M. White points out, few staffers seem to have taken great pains to assure their privacy, and some of the vertical blinds have even been unscrewed and pushed into a quasi-permanent open position.[3]

Compared to its squatty neighbor, the Dirksen Building, the new Hart Building has refreshing aspects. The atrium at least provides a sense of space, and as one walks from the Dirksen into the new building one feels as though the person who has been sitting on one's head has finally climbed off.

Yet there is something wrong, and I would go so far as to say radically wrong, with the Hart Building. Simply put, it is not a public building, except in the most meaningless sense—that taxpayers paid for it. Because of last minute budget cuts, the building's ornamental pasties were never stuck on, so the buildings is barer than planned—*utterly* devoid of ornament. More important, the centerpiece of the nine-story atrium was not paid for, thus not delivered, and now a private fund is established to raise money for the art work. It is not, of course, a statue of Philip A. Hart, the Senator for whom the building is named. Rather, the centerpiece of the Philip A. Hart Senate Building is to be a multi-story mobile by Alexander Calder. This will perfect the Hart Building's fundamental flaw: Once the mobile arrives, the Hart Building will be *exactly* like a corporate office building, right down to the artistic embellishment that has nothing to do with the functions of those who labor there.

This is a genuine misfortune, for the Hart Building might have turned Capitol Hill building back toward the Capitol. The atrium is itself a breakthrough, and makes Hart the first Hill building in years that conveys a sense of space without making the visitor feel out of place. But it would have had to depart from its grid patterns. It would have to have had spaces fit for memorials to the men and women who spend their lives in such buildings and elevate our public life by their exertions. Instead, there is not a single crevice in the Hart Building in which a statue would not appear out of place.

Perhaps, indeed probably, Congress would have refused to pay for it (boxes are cheaper), and surely one cannot blame the architects for preferring professional respectability to an attempt that might have made them pariahs. But what does it say of our times, indeed, of the Senate, that at a cost of $150 million we produce as a Senatorial work environment an utterly non-public building, perfect for Lend-Lease to IBM, the University of Kansas, or lawyers in several similar buildings on K Street?

THE TRIUMPH OF THE CAPITOL

Yet let us not lament too much lost opportunities, nor judge too harshly those who labored under constraints we are not privy to know. Let us rather rejoice that atop the natural pedestal that is America's greatest public space, there sits America's greatest public building. It is as good, as grand, as inspiring as any of the columned marchers in that first procession might have hoped.

In the end, after all the offices are filled, the corridors built columned or plain, in marble or granite or brick or Sheetrock, a public building succeeds or fails to the extent that it conveys a message that upholds the greatness of the governmental enterprise by which a free people somehow, remarkably, continue to govern themselves—against all odds, and all the smart money of history. This the Capitol conveys. And thus it succeeds in its purpose. It is one of a handful of the world's greatest buildings.

NOTES

1. E.J. Applewhite, *Washington Itself* (New York: Knopf, 1981).

2. In the 1970's, a renovation of Union Station's main waiting room and concourse into a National Visitors Center was begun, and enormous sums were spent before the project faltered. The results were horrific. With the train-arrival area moved to a new building in the rear, the result was a hall only Albert Speer could love. Thus the architectural message of the Visitors Center was: All you who enter here are dwarves. For reasons financial and aesthetic, the renovation has ceased and there are now plans to repair the damage.

3. In time, all of the Hart offices will be filled with modular furniture. I am prejudiced on this point. Modular furniture seems to me to encourage a bureaucratic atmosphere in Senate offices (and everywhere, actually) that is worse than the evils of the huge carrier-deck desks and overcrowding that modular furniture is supposed to eliminate by providing everyone his or her "personal space." Senator Inouye complained in a Rules Committee hearing that the space dividers are made of "some crummy thing that looks like a dart board." Actually, they are not unlike the crummy things that divide the middling-level employees of every insurance company in America. The danger is that in a half dozen years the working environment of half the Senate's personal staffs will be no different from that of most federal employees: a bureaucratic slum. This is a feeling the Russell Building never conveys, even after three-quarters of a century, and vastly overcrowded, as it has been in recent years. The Dirksen Building, its ceilings too low to fit the great expanses of its hallways, its marble floors all out of place with its cheesily-painted halls, was a building born to age ungracefully.

14

The City Council Chamber: From Distance to Intimacy

CHARLES T. GOODSELL

While the term "public space" ordinarily brings to mind outdoor squares, streets, and monuments, it can also refer to the interiors of public buildings. Indeed, interior spaces may be more significant in affecting citizens and expressing political ideas, because it is in enclosed public rooms such as lobbies and auditoriums that citizens are fully embraced by the physical environment. It is here that important public rituals and deliberations take place, and where we normally find the most concentrated architectural statements of official values and ideas.

The design of American city council chambers—the rooms in which municipal governing bodies formally convene—are therefore extremely relevant to our understanding of changes in urban political culture. These spaces reflect the political ideals of the age in which they were built, and continue to affect the attitudes and behavior of today's officials and citizens. The history of changes in chamber design is one chapter—an extremely important and usually ignored chapter—in American city politics.

From The Public Interest, *Winter 1984, pp. 116–131. Copyright* © *1984 by National Affairs, Inc.*

The links between architecture and politics are subtle and indirect, of course. Unless they are totalitarian, political regimes do not dictate architectural styles; architects, not politicians, design buildings, and usually in response to reigning architectural tastes. But architects and their styles are also influenced by the same cultural ideas that affect, and are affected by, political leaders. This double movement of influence is especially apparent in the design of interior public chambers, where government officials become actively involved in planning the rooms where they will be on public display.

The history of city council chambers may be divided into three periods: the Traditional Era (1800–1930), the Mid-Century Era (1930–1960), and the Contemporary Era (1960–present). Moving through them, a general trend becomes clear: As the political distance between the governors and the governed has been reduced, a new "intimate" political relationship has been expressed in, and perhaps encouraged by, the design of city council chambers.

THE TRADITIONAL ERA

During the Traditional Era (1800 to 1930), American city council chambers openly asserted public authority. Seen through today's eyes, their design seems to demand citizen obedience and place deliberate distance between governors and the governed. This is done without subtlety or deception; everyone knows where the locus of power is. The design appears to insist that, while those in authority may be elected representatives of the people (or a privileged portion thereof), they occupy a clearly superior relationship to the people. Emphasis is on ruling rather than serving or responding.

Three architectural devices were used to express this idea, devices sometimes employed in combination and sometimes separately: the gallery or balcony, the grand staircase, and the use of authoritative objects and decoration.

In the early years of the Republic the upper-level gallery was often the only space in deliberative chambers open to public visitors. In this way citizens could observe what was transpiring below without having access to the

FIGURE 1. *Board of Aldermen Chamber, St. Louis, Mo. (1890–1904)*

chamber's floor. The elevation difference between main floor and gallery helped to avoid distractions and interruptions by agitated onlookers. At the same time, this physical distance symbolized in spatial terms the distinctions between governors and governed, representatives and represented.

This design feature is found in many state legislatures and in the House and Senate chambers of the U.S. Capitol. Early city halls also used it: The New York city hall, the oldest in the nation which is currently in use (erected 1803–1812), relegated the public to an upper gallery in the Common Council chamber. Interestingly enough, this was not so in the Board of Estimate chamber in the same building, in which a more specialized and less democratic body convened.

In the monumental French Renaissance revival city hall in St. Louis (1890–1904), the public enters the Board of Aldermen chamber on a balcony raised 15 feet above the floor and reached independently through a connecting atrium (Figure 1). A similarly strict segregation was evident in the Baltimore city hall (1867–1875) until its restoration and modification in 1977. In most chambers constructed after 1930 a gallery either does not exist or is used only for audience overflow; after the Traditional Era the public was placed on the same horizontal plane with those in authority.

A second pertinent architectural device is the grand staircase, leading up from an inner lobby or rotunda to the entrance portal of the council chamber above. On the stairway, the visitor—whether allowed on the floor of the chamber or not—is prepared to enter this civic sanctuary by ascending many steps through a massive space and alongside ornate decoration, with the chamber entryway ahead the focus of visual attention throughout the climb. Again, verticality symbolizes status differentiation; the humble citizen is not initially at the heights of power and must undergo an upward journey to reach them. The grand staircase is characteristic of both French Renaissance and Beaux Arts classical public buildings, and is exemplified in the grand foyers of the Paris Opera House and Library of Congress in Washington. Illustrative of American city halls is the second-story chamber of Wilmington's Old Town Hall (1798–1799), which is reached by two open runs of stairs that converge at a landing. From there, a final staircase rises to the chamber door. A good twentieth century example of the grand staircase is found in the city hall of Newark (1902–1906), whose Great Rotunda is dominated by a double-curved stairway of 38 steps that leads to a chamber door 123 feet away from the building's main entrance. An even more dramatic example is in the towering Oakland city hall (1911–1914), where the grand staircase rises 50 steps over three landings to the chamber door (Figure 2). The visual angle upward from main entrance to chamber door is 20 degrees along an axis 99 feet in length. At the second landing the staircase bifurcates to reveal a giant brass tablet reading:

> *The People of Oakland*
> *Erected this edifice as the seat of municipal government—A Monument Dedicated to Civic Loyalty and to the just and equal administration of those ordinances which make for social and political betterment in community life.*

Discussion of the grand staircase would be incomplete without a mention of the most magnificent classical city hall in America, that in San Francisco (1913–1915). In a

FIGURE 2. *Entrance to City Council Chamber, Oakland, Ca. (1911–1914)*

mammoth rotunda reaching 184 feet from floor to dome (the setting for President Harding's funeral in 1932), the grand staircase rises majestically to a giant chamber portal. Executed in Beaux Arts style, this entryway bears an overhead entablature with sculptured figures and deep-cut letters stating "The Board of Supervisors of City and County of San Francisco."

The third architectural characteristic of Traditional council chambers is the detailing within the rooms. Furniture, artifacts, and decoration were such that they imparted the majesty of authority. Good examples are found in the city halls of Baltimore, Philadelphia (1871–1901), and Pittsburgh (1915–1917). Here central podia are massive, high, and executed in dark-stained, carved wood, sometimes in combination with marble. The podium in Philadelphia, for example, has four levels of writing surface, the highest 6.5 feet from the floor. The President of the Council presides from a throne-like chair placed on a platform four feet high; in addition his seat is recessed in the wall for visual emphasis. At the President's right stands an ornate mace, whose globe is surmounted by a silver eagle. Below the President's feet rests a foot-long black granite block, carved from the rocks of Devil's Den as a relic of the Battle of Gettysburg.

Council members in these chambers typically sit at individual desks, similar to those occupied by members of the U.S. Senate. These desks are made of dark, carved wood, their ornateness and physical separation from each other conferring individual status on each member of the council. These desks are often arranged in a shallow arc facing the central podium and council president. The area surrounding the desks and podium is invariably surrounded by a balustrade, rail, or suspended rope. In Philadelphia this protected official zone is demarcated by a brass rail three feet high, broken only by pivoting gates.

Inner surfaces of the rooms are richly decorated. In the beautifully-restored Baltimore chamber, whose overall dimensions form a 40 foot cube, the walls bear fluted pilasters painted in scagliola (imitation marble) and topped with golden capitals (Figure 3). Ten-foot windows are shuttered, draped, and festooned; below them is dark wainscoting lining the walls, above an indented cornice. The ceiling is rectangular and vaulted with a deeply coffered inset at the center.

Of particular importance in these rooms is the backdrop, the vertical surface behind the podium. It is here that the eye of the citizen naturally rests during the proceedings. As a result, this wall space is especially useful for symbolic displays. In Pittsburgh, for example, an enormous gold eagle rests on a raised shelf between a pair of

FIGURE 3. *City Council Chamber, Baltimore, Md. (1867–1875, restored 1977)*

crossed American flags. To the left stand city and bicenten-
nial flags, to the right state and county banners. Setting off
these objects from behind is nine-foot wainscoting with inlaid figuring. This wood surface is repeated in the podium's front face, whose centerpiece inlay states ''City of
Pittsburgh'' and depicts an eagle and a gear.

THE MID-CENTURY ERA

City council chambers built or renovated between 1930 and
1960 are very different from those of the Traditional Era.
Two distinct and contrasting tendencies prevailed during
this period, and each reduced the psychological distance
between governors and governed. In some chambers, architectural symbols emphasized democratic accountability
rather than unilateral rule; in others, a relative absence of
ornamentation suggests functional, minimal government,
and downplays the officials' superior status.

There are many ''democratic'' council chambers, including those in St. Paul, Minnesota (1930–1931), Houston
(1938–1939), Alexandria, Virginia (1871–1873, remodeled

1945), Minneapolis (1887–1906, remodeled in the 1920s and 1950s), San Antonio (1888–1891, remodeled in 1927 and the early 1960s), and Peoria, Illinois (1899, remodeled 1950, partially restored 1975). These chambers reduce the distance between officials and citizens, first of all by their spatial arrangement. They are reached either by ground-floor lobbies or enclosed stairwells or elevators, obviating the need for a humbling ascension of a grand staircase. Within the chambers, citizens are seated (usually on pew-like benches) on the main floor rather than in a gallery. This arrangement requires that considerable floorspace be devoted to audience seating; hence, in Mid-Century chambers the square footage of the public zone usually exceeds that of the official zone, contrary to the Traditional pattern. Although the overall (usually rectangular) dimensions of the rooms are about the same as in the Traditional Era, ceiling height is lowered from as much as 35–40 feet to an average of 18–25. This reduces the cubic volume of the room considerably and makes it less imposing.

The furniture and its arrangement are also very different. Instead of individual desks for each council member, an integrated row of desks or a common table or dais is used. This presents the council as a corporate entity rather than as a group of delegates or representatives. In a change of fundamental symbolic and behavioral significance, the seated council members no longer face a presiding officer with their backs to the audience, but instead face the citizens. Following this "great turnabout," the presiding official sits at the dais center as a chairman rather than sitting at a removed podium. In short, the council and its leadership become corporately accountable to the public before them, not to each other.

There are many interesting variations on this theme. Sometimes the dais is straight or shaped in a shallow arc, as is the case in Alexandria, presenting the council as a unified body. Other daises are U-shaped, as in Houston, facilitating eye contact and dialogue between council members (Figure 4). The V-shaped dais, illustrated by San Antonio's, focuses attention on the presiding official seated at the apex, in this instance the mayor. In Minneapolis, where the mayor has little power but political parties are strong, council members sit at opposing rows of desks with one party on each side. In St. Paul the notion of pub-

FIGURE 4. *City Council Room, Houston, Tex. (1938–1939)*

lic accountability is especially vivid because the council is placed in the center of the chamber so that the public faces the council from two opposite directions.

Other items of furniture also express democratic themes. Professional city managers and their assistants are generally placed at removed and subordinated desks. In Alexandria, the "administration" table is directly in front of the dais but 6 inches below it. Furniture for department heads is placed even more remotely from the center of power and tends to be utilitarian in design. The press is given rather simple tables as well, but in keeping with the journalists' perceived importance in comparison to the bureaucracy, they are usually closer to the dais than the city's own staff. For those formally addressing the council, the public lectern or witness table is generally at the side of the room, near or at the boundary between official and public zones. Some can be quite ornate, such as St. Paul's 128 x 26 inch witness table, executed in Madagascar ebony and golden padouk inlaid with peanut-grained Hungarian ash.

Wall decoration also tends to have democratic content. Backdrops carry symbols of local meaning, such as city seals and murals, rather than flags and eagles. Alexandria's backdrop is a 10 x 12.8 foot lithograph of the city as it appeared in 1863, an object that visually dominates the room. Civic slogans expressing democratic themes are sometimes found on walls; for example, the doors of the WPA-era chamber in Houston are framed by the words "Justice," "Counsel," "Freedom," "Equality," and "The People Are The City." The walls of other chambers carry the voting tally board, which registers members' votes in green, red, and amber lights for all to see.

Yet these Mid-Century rooms are by no means egalitarian. Authority is still expressed, even if it has become publicly accountable. Officials are placed on raised platforms 6 to 18 inches high. The front faces of the daises are often quite high and imposing; in San Antonio the dais rises 3.6 feet above the platform and 4.6 feet above the main floor level, elevating the audience-mayor line of sight to 6 degrees above the horizontal. Physical barriers still exist: In Houston, a solid rail 3.4 feet high separates the dais from the press area, and another three-foot wall segregates the press from the audience. The height of chairs clearly demonstrates a pecking order: In Minneapolis the Council President's chair is 3.2 feet high, the Aldermen's 3 feet, the City Clerk and Attorney's 2.9 feet, the Council's aides' 2.5 feet, and reporters' 2.3 feet.

The contrasting Mid-Century style is the plainly utilitarian room as represented in Annapolis, Maryland (1768, extended 1867, remodeled 1934), Berkeley, California (1908–1909, renovated about 1950), Sacramento, California (1908–1911, renovated 1959), Des Moines (1910–1911), renovated about 1970), and Albuquerque, New Mexico (1964). Portions of the Annapolis city hall are probably the oldest structure still in use in America, although the 1934 council space bears no relation to that distant past. The buildings in Berkeley, Sacramento, and Des Moines are splendid Beaux Arts city halls whose classical exteriors, because of extensive remodeling, are no longer matched by distinctive interiors. Albuquerque's chamber illustrates the plainly functional room originally designed in this manner.

The utilitarian chamber is spatially organized like its democratic counterpart, but has simpler decor and furnishings (Figure 5). Bare walls and movable furniture make the rooms appear relatively empty as well as drab. Walls

FIGURE 5. *City Council Chambers, Berkeley, Ca. (1908–1909, renovated 1959)*

are plain plaster or covered with sound-absorbing cork; ceilings consist of acoustical tile and recessed fluorescent lights. With the exception of Annapolis, which displays several historical artifacts, chamber walls are dominated by such useful objects as clocks, calendars, and zoning maps. Even backdrops are made little use of in terms of visual messages; whereas in Annapolis a seal is exhibited and in Berkeley in 1960s-style mural, Sacramento merely has a precinct map, Des Moines a glass door, and Albuquerque a wooden partition.

Objects visible around the room all have obvious functional uses: bulletin boards, projection screens, coat racks, drinking fountains. Steel cabinets containing amplifying, broadcasting, and recording equipment are in plain view. In the newer chambers, such as Albuquerque's, television klieg lights are suspended prominently from the ceiling. Because of the very spareness of the furnishings one notices such things as waste baskets, ash trays, telephones, and plastic water pitchers.

The furniture itself is plain and functional. In Annapolis the audience sits on folding iron chairs, and in Berkeley on unpadded wooden chairs. Albuquerque provides plastic shell seats mounted on latitudinal rails. The daises in these chambers are made of plain wood, or are covered with Formica or similar material, without ornamentation. All officials, including the presiding officer, sit in plain wooden or simply-upholstered chairs; these are usually of uniform type with all backs the same height. As a result, the people occupying them appear to be quite ordinary, not remote or superior.

THE CONTEMPORARY ERA

Plainness has prevailed in much interior civic design since the middle of this century, but some contemporary efforts in civic architecture—such as the new city halls that win prizes and are featured in the architectural magazines— have decisively turned away from this stark functionalism. Once again it is fashionable for chamber design to be symbolically provocative.

In the Contemporary period (since 1960), a number of distinctive design practices have been used to reduce further the psychological distance between citizens and rulers, and to establish a certain intimacy in the chamber. Traditional city halls devoted large volumes of interior space to public use, such as lobbies and council chambers, and relatively little to workspace use in the form of offices, conference rooms, and equipment space. With the growth of modern bureaucracy it has been necessary to expand greatly the space given over to office operations. Solely on economic grounds, then, architects have reduced the proportion of ritual space in public buildings. Modern city council chambers are relatively small compared to those of 75 years ago, in area square footage as well as in cubic space. For example, the chamber of Philadelphia's nineteenth-century city hall (1871–1901) contains 5,652 square feet (including galleries), while Boston's new city hall (1962–1968) contains a mere 3,398. This factor alone has greatly contributed to bringing officials and citizens physically close together.

In an effort to play up the importance of the council as a part of city government, some architects place it in a separate structure. This is sometimes done by constructing a low building connected to a high-rise city hall, as in

Wilmington, Delaware (1976), Anaheim, California (1980), and Arlington, Texas (1981). The more drastic approach is to place the council building near to, but entirely separate from, the city hall; this may be seen in Phoenix (1963), Fairfield, California (1970), and Mesa, Arizona (1980). Here the council occupies its own legislative "temple" and is thus granted considerable respect. This spatial segregation may be regarded as echoing to some extent the gallery or grand staircase in Traditional council chambers; but whereas these earlier designs separated the citizen from the council, this one separates the council from the government. As a result, citizens attending council meetings are encouraged to think of the body as "their" organ of city government, an entity quite distinct from the alien and impersonal city bureaucracy.

A sense of citizen-council intimacy is furthered in many contemporary chambers by the configuration of the inner space itself. Long rectangular rooms, which place audience and officials far apart along a central axis, have been abandoned in favor of wide, square, or round chambers. At times the two geometric figures of square and circle are used in conjunction, as when a round, depressed seating area (or "well") is placed within a square room. This is the arrangement in Santa Rosa, California (1969) and Fort Worth, Texas (1969–1971) (Figure 6). Another design type is the perfectly round room, as illustrated in Phoenix, Wilmington, and Long Beach (1974–1977). The effect of these circular spaces is to suggest that all occupants—citizens and officials alike—have something in common. No corners exist to suggest remoteness, no separate sides to denote a distinction between "we" and "they." Since seating in these circular chambers is itself always circular, all persons, including the council, look to a common point, the center of the circle. In Fort Worth and Santa Rosa this is where those addressing the council stand, placing them in a rather uncomfortable position (informally called "the pit" in Fort Worth).

Walls, ceilings, and floors no longer consist of flat planes, but of interestingly-configured surfaces. It is not an exaggeration to describe these as forming a sculpted outer shell that holds the chamber space. In some rooms, such as those of Fairfield and Tempe, Arizona (1971), the area behind the council is angled in a rough "funnel" shape. This projects sound outward to the audience, but

FIGURE 6. *City Council Meeting Room (''The Pit''), Fort Worth, Tex. (1969–1971)*

also focuses audience attention on the council members. Another device is to slope the chamber walls inward a few degrees; this provides a greater sense of intimate enclosure than do sheer vertical walls. Floors are also sculpted, not only by incorporating depressed wells as described above, but by banking tiers of audience seats in the style of a theater. This increases the observer's field of vision, and when the banking is steep, it reinforces the intimacy of the room's embrace—one ''slides into'' the space. Sometimes canopies are dropped just above the dais to give it scale and accentuation, and decorative coffers or light fixtures at the center of the ceiling draw attention to the public lectern. Wilmington's fascinating chamber combines all these devices: a round room with inward-sloping walls, banked seating, and a wheel-like coffered ceiling with black oculus at the center. Within this space people do not just gather together, they are brought together.

In Contemporary chambers, audience and officials sit much nearer to each other than in earlier chambers. Aside from the smaller areas and volumes and non-rectangular floorplans, intimacy is achieved by simply placing the dais and first row of audience seating closer to each other. Whereas this distance is 38–41 feet in older chambers in Pittsburgh, Peoria, Philadelphia, and San Francisco, it is 21–26 feet in Dallas (1972–1977), Phoenix, Long Beach, and Wilmington.

Elevation differentials have also been changed. The daises, platforms, and chairs occupied by officials are now lower; in fact, daises are sometimes down on the main floor itself and are no higher than a comfortable writing surface (30 inches). Audience seating may also be banked, so that citizens are elevated above officials, rather than the other way around. In Boston the audience's line of sight from the back row of seating to the presiding officer's head is depressed 6 degrees from the horizontal; in Dallas this measurement is 12 degrees, and in Long Beach it is 17. Although its consequences depend on many factors, this elevation reversal is somewhat comparable to the "great turnabout" in council seating direction that occurred in Mid-Century.

Contemporary furnishings also de-emphasize the barriers between official and public zones. Rails, ropes, or walls are dispensed with entirely; instead, the zonal boundary is marked by a low platform edge, or empty "no man's land." The barrier at Austin, Texas (1975) is a low wall broken by indented spaces, suggesting permeability; at Phoenix, a cluster of staff and press tables form the barrier; at Paradise Valley, Arizona (1974) a heavy overhead transverse beam, crossing the room just above the lectern, psychologically separates officials and audience.

In addition to spatial composition and appointments, the contemporary chamber fosters a sense of intimacy through modern communications technology. The voting machine tally board and simple public address system of Mid-Century have been replaced by high-tech sophistication. Contemporary amplificaion systems employ voice-activated, lavalier-style, two-spectrum microphones, with speakers located throughout the room. As a result, stage whispers can be heard anywhere if the microphones are not turned off. And nearly every contemporary chamber is equipped with modern audio-visual equipment, including slide and motion picture projectors mounted in permanent projection booths. Screens are often hidden behind mov-

FIGURE 7. *City Council Chamber, San Bernardino, Ca. (1972)*

able panels or descend from the ceiling by remote control. The Dallas chamber, which is full of electronic gadgetry, is also equipped for closed-circuit television.

The contemporary chamber not only allows ease of communication within itself, but in communicating with the outside world. Symbolically this may be accomplished by window walls, whose intent is to tell the world it can look in on ''open'' government. For example, two of the four walls of the sizable chamber at Walnut Creek, California (1980) are made entirely of glass. In practice, however, visual communication to the outside world is through television broadcasting. While Mid-Century chambers were equipped for radio broadcasting, the Contemporary council room is designed with television fully in mind. Raised platforms for cameras are sometimes provided, although they now have been made obsolete by the hand-held camera. Klieg lights are built into ceilings and walls, so illuminating the space that it is totally transformed: The chamber becomes, in effect, a television studio. With this fact in mind designers equip it with pleated background curtains, textured dais surfaces, and prominent logos or other visual symbols, much like the set of a television news show. One of the best illustrations of theatrical staging is at San Bernardino, California (1972) (Figure 7). There a brightly-painted city seal 19 feet in diameter forms the backdrop for a rotating circular platform that carries a circular dais and administration desk. In short, the space is no longer a deliberative chamber but a public stage.

THE ARCHITECTURE OF POLITICAL LEGITIMACY

So the city council chamber as a public space has gone from a civic sanctuary reached by a grand staircase and observed from a gallery, in which the superior authority of political leaders was unmistakably clear, to a down-to-earth arena in which officials were to be publicly accountable and socially unpretentious. Recently, the council chamber has become a psychologically unifying space in which citizens and officials seem to be on almost equal terms, mutually engaged in the work of government. The "intimacy" of the contemporary chamber now extends to the outside community through television.

One cannot help but feel ambivalent about this architectural and political trend. Urban government is more responsive and open than it was in the nineteenth century, and there is no reason why the decentralization of power should not be matched by a democratic chamber design. (One wonders if council members meeting in restored Traditional chambers today feel out of place, or perhaps inspired, in them.) But it is a mistake to depict municipal politics as the intimate participation of equals, as some contemporary chambers do. Politics is not and never will be intimate.

We should be worried when the architecture and realities of government are at odds, since the legitimacy of duly-constituted authority may be eroded by an obvious gulf between them. We should also be concerned when the forms of participation begin to substitute for honest public accountability—when, in the case of television, drama substitutes for real participation. Intimacy and theatrics should not be allowed to undermine either the authority or responsibilities of democratic government.

15

Symbolism in Architecture: Courtrooms

ALLAN GREENBERG

"All architecture proposes an effect on the human mind, not merely a service to the human frame."
—John Ruskin

Since the growth of the International Style in the 1920s, the expression of symbols appears to have lost its relevance to architecture.[1] Because symbolism is a major element in the articulation of meaning in architecture, especially in the design of public buildings, its loss must count as a significant factor in any explanation of the serious functional and esthetic shortcomings of so many modern buildings in our towns and cities.

Symbolism plays an especially important role in planning the settings for the judicial system, and the design of courtrooms and courthouses offers a provocative case study for the assessments of its crucial function in architecture. Court procedures are highly formalized and should, in their operation, both uphold and emblemize the tradition and development of our democratic system of government.

Consider courtroom design. The courtroom is the setting for the administration of justice under the law and, as such, is the heart of the courthouse. The layout of a typical criminal courtroom in the United States differs markedly from courtrooms in other countries and reflects our unique system of justice. The American judge is an impartial arbi-

From Architectural Record, *May 1979, pp. 114–116.*

ter and is therefore positioned on a raised podium in the center of the front of the room. Defense and prosecution are equal adversaries and, as such, are each provided with seats at assigned tables in the well of the courtroom facing the judge. The public are silent observers, sitting at the rear of the courtroom facing the judge. Their role is just as crucial as that of the other parties for, as silent arbiters, they influence the law through the political processes of election and legislation. The jury box is placed at the side of the room, deliberately divorced from the axial relationship of judge, counsel and public. This placement reflects the impartiality of the jurors, who must decide guilt or innocence. The witness box is located adjacent to the judge's bench facing the two parties. This provides the latter with their constitutional right to confront the opposing counsel's witnesses.

In this courtroom layout, symbolism is of paramount importance. Serious consideration of the cultural and social values embodied in the court system is, therefore, a prerequisite to the design or evaluation of any courtroom.[2] The architectural forms should be seen as a "sign system through which society tries to communicate its ideal model of a relationship between judges, prosecutors, jurors and others involved in judicial proceedings."[3] In other countries, where social organization and judicial procedures are very different from ours, these differences are often directly reflected in their courtroom designs.[4] For example, in eastern European countries the prosecutor sits on the podium next to the judge, thus leaving the defendant and his attorney alone in the center of the courtroom; in some Swiss courts, the jury sits behind the judge, who may also be a member of the jury panel; and an accused person in England does not sit at a table with counsel for the defense, but is isolated in a dock with a security officer. Seen in this light, the traditional American courtroom layout is notable for its marked orientation toward the rights of the accused.

During the past decade, three new courtroom layouts have been proposed. These are the courtroom-in-the-round, courtroom with the judge's bench in the corner, and courtroom with witness located opposite the jury.[5] In each case, proponents have claimed significant improvements for court procedure and trial participants' ability to see or hear. However, any new courtroom design should be rigorously justifiable on grounds of symbolic meaning as well. For example, the appropriateness of a courtroom-in-the-round, especially in serious criminal litigation, is open to question. The equality implied by the circular form fails to differentiate between the trial participants or to express their adversary roles.

The courtroom with the judge's bench in the corner seems to lack a clearly expressed symbolic order, and the courtroom with the witness stand facing the jury is a variation of the traditional courtroom. The witness stand is relocated so as to improve the judge's and the juror's view of the witness. Unfortunately, this move establishes a cross axis of judge-counsel and witness-jury, which has no connection with adversary proceedings and severely undercuts the sense of counsel and client confronting witnesses.

The most important functional criterion is that all the participants in the trial—judge, juror, witness, clerk, court reporter, defense and prosecuting attorney, defendant or litigant, press and public—be able adequately to see and hear everything that occurs and to feel a sense of involvement in the proceedings. This is difficult to achieve in a room of 1,200 to 2,000 square feet in which the focus of attention moves unpredictably from witness to counsel, judge or reporter. Counsel occupies different positions in the courtroom during cross-examination, summation, sentencing and bench conferences, and the jury is often out of the room. The problem is further complicated by the uncontrollable factors of poor enunciation and diction and the use of the same courtroom for trials, arraignments, calling the calendar and sentencing. We are faced with a functional problem whose complex and overlapping requirements preclude the isolation of any dominant set of organizing principles. It is necessary, therefore, systematically to test a series of compromises, none of which can fully accommodate the various needs of all the participants, until layout is developed.

In order to do this, I developed a comprehensive method to evaluate the performance of any courtroom and to compare performance of any number of courtrooms.[6] By establishing principles for good sightlines and acoustics, functional problems can be readily assessed for corrective action. A point-score system is used to compare and evaluate the performance of two or more courtrooms. However, experience in designing and evaluating courtrooms has made one point abundantly clear: *there is no one optimal functional solution*. Each courtroom's configuration and dimensions have their own set of built-in advantages and problems. For example, the main deficiency of both the traditional courtroom and the courtroom-in-the-round is that the location of the witness denies judge and some jurors a good frontal view of the witness' face. The courtroom-in-the-round actually worsens the problem for the jurors nearest the witness by increasing the angle they have to turn in order to face the witness. The traditional layout may also create problems for jurors farthest from the witness, who must lean forward to obtain good sightlines to the witness. Both problems can be corrected. In the latter case, the jury box must be moved nearer the witness, and in the former jury box can be modified.

The courtroom-in-the-round reduces distances between some participants, thereby creating a sense of intimacy, but it also increases the sight angles and physical strain.[7] The latter can be alleviated to some extent by using swivel chairs. The courtroom with the judge's bench in the corner keeps the witness between judge and jury but moves the bench into a corner and turns it almost ninety degrees so as to optimize the judge's view of witness and jury. These adjustments dramatically increase the distance between counsel tables and witnesses. The courtroom with the witness located opposite the jury optimizes the judge's, jury's and reporter's view of the witness, but limits counsel's to a profile. Counsel must also cross-examine the witness from a lectern to avoid turning his back to the jury. The latter two plans optimize sightlines without unduly increasing distances. The traditional plan provides the best relationship between public, counsel and judge.

It is clear that functional analysis yields no ultimate plan, as each type has both advantages and drawbacks. In order to find a way through this maze of ergonomic data and conflicting claims by proponents of different courtroom layouts, I suggest that the most reasonable design procedure is, *first*, to select a courtroom layout which provides a desired set of symbolic relationships; and, *second*, to optimize ergonomic relationships by detailed consideration of room dimensions and subtle placement of furniture and fixtures. Once a selection of layout has been made, it must be subjected to a rigorous program of testing, adjustment and evaluation by the architect and building committee. Drawings and scale models should be used to optimize all sightlines and distance relationships. The availability of voice amplification and acoustical engineering should ensure that no one in a courtroom misses a spoken word. Having chosen a courtroom for its symbolic attributes, serious study of the functional aspects can then maximize its advantages, and careful placement of the furniture and control of sight angles can minimize the disadvantages of any layout to the extent of virtually equalizing performance factors. It should be clearly stated that advocating a primary role for symbolism in the process of selecting courtroom layout can never be used as an excuse for failing to resolve acoustic or sightline problems in any courtroom, irrespective of size or layout.

It is also important to study the fabric of the courthouse building which houses the courtrooms, as this structure is also imbued with symbolic importance. The exterior articulation of a courthouse and the relationship of the building to its surroundings expresses our concept of the role of the law in society. Similarly, the building's internal arrangement reflects the relative importance assigned to the transactions and the roles of the various groups using the building. In order to demonstrate the range of meanings and values that can be communicated by a courthouse, one can look at the Virginia State Capitol, which originally included the State Supreme Court, designed by Thomas Jefferson in 1785. Jefferson based the design on that of a Roman Temple. His idea was to express the continuity of the classical ideals of democracy and rule of law now being realized anew in the American Republic, to strengthen the Republic's young roots by demonstrating the intellectual tradition to which it was heir, and to signal to the world the greatness to which it aspired. The organization of the Capitol's plan also has symbolic significance, as the legislative chamber and supreme courtroom were expressed as co-equal branches of the government. The building was sited in a landscaped square in Richmond and elevated on a podium to signify its unique importance

as the center of the state's legal, judicial and executive activities. At the time, it was the most elaborately designed
and important building in Virginia.

Jefferson's intention was understood by citizen and architect alike, and for the next 150 years so many state capitols and courthouses followed the classical tradition that
the United States boasted more large domes and porticos
than ancient Rome. Even High Victorian Gothic structures, such as the Connecticut State Capitol at Hartford,
are planned to express the independence of the three
branches of government.

Buildings like the United States Supreme Court in
Washington, D.C., designed by Cass Gilbert in the nine-
teen-thirties, clearly refer to Jefferson's design and use
ambitious sculptural programs, mottos and inscriptions to
amplify further the themes of law, justice and democracy.
Similar principles underlie the design of our greatest public building, the United States Capitol.

Symbolic factors were of primary importance in the
design and planning of the interior of older courthouse
buildings. The beautiful lobbies indicate—by virtue of
their size, rich material and primary importance in the
organization of the plan—that public convenience has
been an overriding factor in design. Paul Cret, at the
Hartford County Courthouse (1926–28), uses light, entering one side of the lobby, to separate courtrooms and
mark the location of the entrance to office spaces on the
opposite side. The articulation of the lobby in plan and
section, which contrasts the large-scale fenestration, murals and doorways associated with courtrooms with the
small colonnade and related offices on the opposite side,
subtly informs the user that there are one major and two
minor courtrooms on one side and office functions on
the other.

The grand public spaces and elaborate design found in
older courthouses still convey an aura of dignity and, despite current overcrowding and obsolescence, continue to
provide a sense of order, orientation and hierarchical importance of destinations. The fact that they provide more
than the bare minimum of space is a celebration of human
values, a demonstration of concern for user well-being,
and a recognition of the fact that people come to a courthouse for the resolution of serious problems and require a

setting that confers the appropriate aura of dignity on their deliberations.

Perhaps the most damning characteristic of many new courthouses is the lack of a coherent and symbolically significant relationship with the surrounding buildings and environment. The messages which these buildings communicate to the taxpaying public and attorneys, witnesses, jurors, and litigants in the courthouse are that their needs, both functional and psychological, do not warrant attention or expression.

Study of older courthouses often yields valuable data which can profitably be applied to our own work. These buildings' exteriors were monumental, yet did not overwhelm the surrounding environment. They communicated the importance of the venue where society administers laws, metes out sanctions and resolves citizens' conflicts. Entrances were clearly articulated, and architectural forms provided visual pleasure. An analysis of interior spaces in offices in old courthouses also provides a wide range of useful planning information. In this regard, we have much to learn from the Beaux-Arts-trained architects who strove to design circulation systems in public buildings so that destinations were obvious and self-evident to the user. Anything less than this constituted a serious design failure. The shapes of lobbies and foyers, windows, location of stairs and elevators, strategic placement of spacious corridors and decorative elements, were all used to suggest direction of movement, hierarchical importance of destinations, and to provide a sense of orientation at all times.

It is obvious that our idea of what constitutes the most appropriate setting for a courthouse and its various departments has changed over the last two or three decades. Some people argue that the legal process itself is the monument and that the courthouse building is a very secondary concern. This attitude confuses non-design with the need to make visitors, jurors, witnesses and litigants feel comfortable and oriented in the building. This latter, desirable goal can only be achieved, I believe, by recognizing the important role of symbolism and the expression of meaning in architectural design, and by using symbols that are comprehensible to contemporary society in order to communicate with its surroundings and the user.

The design problem is more than simply providing sufficient area and minimal standards for satisfactory operations. A more fundamental question is this: ''What kind of environment is appropriate for the particular transaction?'' The answer is inextricably involved with cultural and social issues, tradition and process. A design method that ignores these factors, and does not go beyond satisfying minimum needs, results in both the architect and the client neglecting such important considerations as orientation, expression of civic role, and the provision of amenities for the individual. The lack of recognition of the role of symbolism in the courthouse also has the secondary effect of excluding *serious* consideration for provisions both for physical comfort and for psychological comfort as well.

Today, tradition-repudiating doctrines inherent in much Modern architecture compel architects to attempt the development of new design typologies with each new building they undertake. This results in a repeated reinvention of the wheel. The denial of tradition has also led to a lack of serious guidelines for courthouse design which has resulted in poorly informed clients and architects and in situations where the display of stylistic innovation and formal novelty are confused with the development of functionally appropriate solutions and genuine innovations.

How can this deficiency be remedied? Some obvious answers spring to mind. In the past, architects used a system of building types as the basis of design. Model solutions were based on the accumulated experience of the past (traditions) and constantly revised as new experience became available. There is a crying need now for a rigorous program to evaluate, systematically, the performance of new courthouses as a means of accumulating a body of data dealing with symbolic functional, psychological and physiological aspects of design. The case-study method, which was so pivotal in developing our modern system of legal education, should now be applied to the design of courthouse facilities, as well as other building types. The development of design standards for courthouses and evaluation procedures for architects, clients, and users should be a task of our architectural schools and the profession. Without such standards and procedures, experience and knowledge related to courthouse design cannot be accumulated, assessed and transmitted. It is only in this way that the challenging task of incorporating symbolic, as well as functional, concerns can be solved and that as architects, we can rise to meet Ruskin's challenge to service both man's mind and his frame.

NOTES

1. An early version of this paper was published in *Judicature*, April 1976, pages 422–428 and May 1976, pages 484–490.

2. John W. Hazard, "Furniture Arrangements as a Symbol of Judicial Roles," 19 *ETC: A Review of General Semantics*, pages 181–188 (July 1962).

3. Robert Gutman, *People and Buildings* (Basic Books), 1972, page 229.

4. Sybille Bedford, *The Faces of Justice: A Traveller's Report* (Collins), 1961.

5. C. Theodore Larson, "Future Shock Hits the American Courthouse: Opportunities for Parameters of Design," *American Institute of Architects' Journal*, July 1975, page 38.

6. Allan Greenberg, *Courthouse Design: A Handbook for Judges and Court Administrators*. American Bar Association Commission on Standards of Judicial Administration, 1975, pages 43–52.

7. *Ibid.*, pages 64–65.

III

OPEN
SPACES

INTRODUCTION

If the most characteristic American public place is open space rather than the civic plaza, its most characteristic theorist and booster was undoubtedly Frederick Law Olmsted. While we live with his ''statements'' about our landscape every day in cities such as New York, Boston, and Chicago, Olmsted also wrote occasionally about his overarching urban vision. His 1870 essay reprinted here, ''Public Parks and the Enlargement of Towns,'' is perhaps the best summary of his motivations.

Olmsted understood that America, like all western countries, had begun a rapid urbanization in the nineteenth century that would never be reversed: rural areas were emptying out, or were so tied to cities as to become mere suburbs. He did not find this shift unwelcome, bringing as it did enlightened politics and greater opportunities (especially for women). However he did believe that urban life was unhealthy for the body and dangerous to the soul: foul air, vice, and congestion threatened ''health, virtue, and happiness.'' No rural romantic, he saw the solution in a program of city parks and tree-lined streets that would bring a bit of domesticated rurality into the city. These open spaces would provide recreation and ''gregarious, neighborly interaction'' for local residents in a setting that contrasted sharply with urban life—the park as haven, not stage for civic interaction.

In ''The Motive behind Olmsted's Park,'' Roger Starr celebrates his achievement in New York's Central Park, an achievement that many hoped to improve upon (see cartoon, pp. 262–263). Yet Starr's appreciation focuses less on Olmsted's landscaping and architectural skills than on his moral and political motivations. Olmsted, it seems, was as much concerned with the moral and political status of the new urban masses as with design, and if his attitudes strike us today as a little condescending, Starr maintains that his ''egalitarian elitism'' was moderately successful in providing a safe place where all classes and races could mix with some equality.

J.B. Jackson's ''The American Public Space,'' a mild dissent from the Olmsted park tradition, begins by tracing the rise and decline of the park as our central public space. He sees the decline of the square as a civic space already beginning in the late eighteenth century, and its replacement by both the congested urban street and the rural-like public cemetery. Olmsted and the parks movement of the nineteenth century replaced the cemetery with huge, self-consciously created rural environments for purely private enjoyment, not for social interaction. Jackson expresses greater satisfaction with the small, less-planned public spaces that have arisen since then, and he is encouraged by the rediscovery of the street as a lively public space.

William H. Whyte and his Street Life Project have been the most active American chroniclers of how these smaller open spaces work today. In these selections from his book *The Social Life of Small Urban Spaces*, he reports some results of his anthropological researches using on-sight observations and time-lapse photography in plazas and streets. He summarizes the principles so as to make them proverbs for planning urban spaces: good supply creates demand, people attract people, congestion breeds conversation, plazas need streets, etc. He also learns why so many urban spaces fail: they are secluded from the street by being placed too high, or sunk too low. Whyte concludes with principles for the indoor urban space that are not dissimilar: movable chairs, food, stores—and, as always, strong ties to the street.

Historian Neil Harris offers a short history of two kinds of public indoor space in the two concluding essays. In "Living with Lobbies" he writes that grand, opulent lobbies for hotels and office buildings were the most distinctive indoor public spaces of the nineteenth century. Their grandeur and opulence declined after World War II under the economic challenge of motels and the aesthetic challenge of modernism, but he sees a revival of sorts in the new giant hotels that were begun in the 1970s. What distinguishes these lobbies, however, is that they are illusionary places to see rather than places *to be seen in*. Harris sees a similar revival of public space in his "Spaced-Out at the Shopping Center," a short history of the mall. From the 1920s to the 1950s, American shopping centers were functional affairs that focused mainly on proximity to parking, but today they are complex, multi-story edifices that try to substitute for the street. They are too uniform—in stores, merchandise, music—to succeed fully, yet they do provide a measure of grandeur and monumentality that the suburban landscape so clearly lacks.

16

Public Parks and the Enlargement of Towns

FREDERICK LAW OLMSTED

The last ''Overland Monthly'' tells us that in California ''only an inferior class of people can be induced to live out of towns. There is something in the country which repels men. In the city alone can they nourish the juices of life.''

This of newly built and but half-equipped cities, where the people are never quite free from dread of earthquakes, and of a country in which the productions of agriculture and horticulture are more varied, and the rewards of rural enterprise larger, than in any other under civilized government! With a hundred million acres of arable and grazing land, with thousands of outcropping gold veins, with the finest forests in the world, fully half the white people live in towns, a quarter of all in one town, and this quarter pays more than half the taxes of all. ''Over the mountains the miners,'' says Mr. Bowles, ''talk of going to San Francisco as to Paradise,'' and the rural members of the Legislature declare that ''San Francisco sucks the life out of the country.''

From Frederick Law Olmsted, ''Public Parks and the Englargement of Towns,'' American Social Science Association (Cambridge, Mass.: Riverside Press, 1870), pp. 1–36.

At the same time all our great interior towns are reputed to be growing rapidly; their newspapers complain that wheat and gold fall much faster than house-rents, and especially that builders fail to meet the demand for such dwellings as are mostly sought by newcomers, who are mainly men of small means and young families, anxious to make a lodgment in the city on any terms which will give them a chance of earning a right to remain. In Chicago alone, it is said, that there are twenty thousand people seeking employment.

To this I can add, from personal observation, that if we stand, any day before noon, at the railway stations of these cities, we may notice women and girls arriving by the score, who, it will be apparent, have just run in to do a little shopping, intending to return by supper time to farms perhaps a hundred miles away.

It used to be a matter of pride with the better sort of our country people that they could raise on their own land or manufacture within their own households almost everything needed for domestic consumption. But if now you leave the rail, at whatever remote station, the very advertisements on its walls will manifest how greatly this is changed. Push out over the prairie and make your way to the house of any long-settled and prosperous farmer, and the intimacy of his family with the town will constantly appear, in dress, furniture, viands, in all the conversation. If there is a piano, they will be expecting a man from town to tune it. If the baby has outgrown its shoes, the measure is to be sent to town. If a tooth is troublesome, an appointment is to be arranged by telegraph with the dentist. The railway time-table hangs with the almanac. The housewife complains of her servants. There is no difficulty in getting them from the intelligence offices in town, such as they are; but only the poorest, who cannot find employment in the city, will come to the country, and these as soon as they have got a few dollars ahead, are crazy to get back to town. It is much the same with the men, the farmer will add; he has to run up in the morning and get some one to take ''Wolf's'' place. You will find, too, that one of his sons is in a lawyer's office, another at a commercial college, and his oldest daughter at an ''institute,'' all in town. I know several girls who travel eighty miles a day to attend school in Chicago.

If under these circumstances the occupation of the country school-master, shoemaker, and doctor, the country store-keeper, dressmaker and lawyer, is not actually gone, it must be that the business they have to do is much less relatively to the population about them than it used to be; not less in amount only, but less in importance. An inferior class of men will meet the requirements.

And how are things going here in Massachusetts? A correspondent of the "Springfield Republican" gave the other day an account of a visit lately made to two or three old agricultural neighborhoods, such as fifty years ago were the glory of New England. When he last knew them, their society was spoken of with pride, and the influence of not a few of their citizens was felt throughout the State, and indeed far beyond it. But as he found them now, they might almost be sung by Goldsmith. The meetinghouse closed, the church dilapidated; the famous old taverns, stores, shops, mills, and offices dropping to pieces and vacant, or perhaps with a mere corner occupied by day laborers; but a third as many children as formerly to be seen in the school-houses, and of these less than half of American-born parents.

Walking through such a district last summer, my eyes were gladdened by a single house with exceptional signs of thrift in fresh paint, roofs, and fences, and newly planted door-yard trees; but happening as I passed to speak to the owner, in the second sentence of our conversation he told me that he had been slicking his place up in hopes that some city gentleman would take a fancy to it for a country seat. He was getting old, had worked hard, and felt as if the time had fully come when he was entitled to take some enjoyment of what remained to him of life by retiring to the town. Nearly all his old neighbors were gone; his children had left years ago. His town-bred granddaughters were playing croquet in the front yard.

You know how it is here in Boston. Let us go on to the Old World. We read in our youth that among no other people were rural tastes so strong, and rural habits so fixed, as with those of Old England, and there is surely no other country where the rural life of the more fortunate classes compares so attractively with their town life. Yet in the "Transactions of the British Social Science Association," we find one debater asserting that there are now very few more persons living in the rural districts of England and

Wales than there were fifty years ago; another referring to "the still increasing growth of our overgrown towns and the stationary or rather retrograding numbers of our rural population;" while a third remarks that the social and educational advantages of the towns are drawing to them a large proportion of "the wealthy and independent," as well as all of the working classes not required for field labor.

When I was last in England, the change that had occurred even in ten years could be perceived by a rapid traveller. Not only had the country gentleman and especially the country gentlewoman of Irving departed wholly with all their following, but the very embers had been swept away of that manner of life upon which, so little while ago, everything in England seemed to be dependent. In all the country I found a smack of the suburbs—hampers and packages from metropolitan tradesmen, and purveyors arriving by every train, and a constant communication kept up with town by penny-post and telegraph.

In the early part of the century, the continued growth of London was talked of as something marvelous and fearful; but where ten houses were then required to accommodate new residents, there are now a hundred. The average rate at which population increases in the six principal towns is twice as great as in the country at large, including the hundreds of other flourishing towns. So also Glasgow has been growing six times faster than all Scotland; and Dublin has held its own, while Ireland as a whole has been losing ground.

Crossing to the Continent, we find Paris absorbing half of all the increase of France in population; Berlin growing twice as fast as all Prussia; Hamburg, Stettin, Stuttgart, Brussels, and a score or two of other towns, all building out into the country at a rate never before known, while many agricultural districts are actually losing population. In Russia special provision is made in the laws to regulate the gradual compensation of the nobles for their losses by the emancipation of the serfs, to prevent the depopulation of certain parts of the country, which was in danger of occurring from the eagerness of the peasantry to move into the large towns.

Going still further to the eastward, we may find a people to whom the movement has not thus far been communicated; but it is only where obscurity affords the best hope of safety from oppression, where men number their women with their horses, and where laborsaving inventions are as inventions of the enemy.

There can be no doubt then, that, in all our modern civilization, as in that of the ancients, there is a strong drift townward. But some seem to regard the class of symptoms I have referred to as those of a sort of moral epidemic, the crisis and reaction of which they constantly expect to see. They even detect already a growing disgust with the town and signs of a back-set towards rural simplicity. To avoid prolonged discussion of the question thus suggested I will refer but briefly to the intimate connection which is evident between the growth of towns and the dying out of slavery and feudal customs, of priestcraft and government by divine right, the multiplication of books, newspapers, schools, and other means of popular education and the adoption of improved methods of communication, transportation, and of various labor-saving inventions. No nation has yet begun to give up schools or newspapers, railroads or telegraphs, to restore feudal rights or advance rates of postage. King-craft and priestcraft are nowhere gaining any solid ground. On the contrary, considered as elements of human progress, the more apparent forces under which men have thus far been led to gather together in towns are yet growing; never more rapidly than at this moment. It would seem then more rational to prepare for a continued rising of the townward flood than to count upon its subsidence. Examining our own country more particularly, it is to be considered that we have been giving away our public lands under a square form of division, as if for the purpose of preventing the closer agricultural settlement which long and narrow farms would have favored, and that we have used our mineral deposits as premiums for the encouragement of wandering and of forms of enterprise, individual, desultory and sequestered in character, in distinction from those which are organized, systematized and public. This policy has had its day; the choicest lands have been taken up; the most prominent and easiest worked metallic veins have been seized, the richest placers are abandoned to Chinamen, and the only reaction that we can reasonably anticipate is one from, not toward, dispersion.

The same policy, indeed, has had the effect of giving us, for a time, great command of ready money and easy credit, and we have thus been induced to spend an immense sum—say two thousand millions—in providing ourselves with the fixtures and machinery of our railroad system. This system, while encouraging the greater dispersion of our food-producers, has tended most of all to render them, as we have seen, independent of all the old neighborhood agencies of demand and supply, manufacture and exchange, and to educate them and their children in familiarity with and dependence on the conveniences and habits of towns-people.

To touch upon another line of argument, we all recognize that the tastes and dispositions of women are more and more potent in shaping the course of civilized progress, and we may see that women are even more susceptible to this townward drift than men. Ofttimes the husband and father gives up his country occupations, taking others less attractive to him in town, out of consideration for his wife and daughters. Not long since I conveyed to a very sensible and provident man what I thought to be an offer of great preferment. I was surprised that he hesitated to accept it, until the question was referred to his wife, a bright, tidy American-born woman, who promptly said: ''If I were offered a deed of the best farm that I ever saw, on condition of going back to the country to live, I would not take it. I would rather face starvation in town.'' She had been brought up and lived the greater part of her life in one of the most convenient and agreeable farming countries in the United States.

Is it astonishing? Compare advantages in respect simply to schools, libraries, music, and the fine arts. People of the greatest wealth can hardly command as much of these in the country as the poorest work-girl is offered here in Boston at the mere cost of a walk for a short distance over a good, firm, clean pathway, lighted at night and made interesting to her by shop fronts and the variety of people passing.

It is true the poorer work-girls make little use of these special advantages, but this [is] simply because they are not yet educated up to them. When, however, they come from the country to town, are they not moving in the way of this education? In all probability, as is indicated by the report (in the ''New York Tribune'') of a recent skillful examination of the condition and habits of the poor sewing women of that city, a frantic desire to escape from the dull lives which they have seen before them in the country, a craving for recreation, especially for more companionship in yielding to playful girlish impulses, innocent in themselves, drives more young women to the town than anything else. Dr. Holmes may exaggerate the clumsiness and dreariness of New England village social parties; but go further back into the country among the outlying farms, and if you have ever had part in the working up of some of the rare occasions in which what stands for festivity is attempted, you will hardly think that the ardent desire of a young woman to escape to the town is wholly unreasonable.

The civilized woman is above all things a tidy woman. She enjoys being surrounded by bright and gay things perhaps not less than the savage, but she shrinks from draggling, smirching, fouling things and "things out of keeping" more. By the keenness with which she avoids subjecting herself to annoyances of this class, indeed, we may judge the degree in which a woman has advanced in civilization. Think what a country road and roadside, and what the back yard of a farm-house, commonly is, in winter and springtime; and what far-away farmers' gardens are in haying time, or most of them at any time. Think, again, how hard it is when you city people go into the country for a few weeks in summer, to keep your things in order, to get a thousand little things done which you regard as trifles when at home, how far you have to go, and with how much uncertainty, how much unaccustomed management you have to exercise. For the perfection and delicacy—the cleanness—with which any human want is provided for depends on the concentration of human ingenuity and skill upon that particular want. The greater the division of labor at any point, the greater the perfection with which all wants may be satisfied. Everywhere in the country the number and variety of workmen, not agricultural laborers, proportionately to the population, is lessening as the facility for reaching workmen in town is increasing. In one year we find fifty-four new divisions of trade added to the "London Directory."

Think of all these things, and you will possibly find yourself growing a little impatient of the common cant which assumes that the strong tendency of women to town life, even though it involves great privations and dangers, is a purely senseless, giddy, vain, frivolous, and degrading one.

The consideration which most influences this tendency of women in families, however, seems to be the amount of time and labor, and wear and tear of nerves and mind, which is saved to them by the organization of labor in those forms, more especially, by which the menial service of households is simplified and reduced. Consider, for instance, what is done (that in the country is not done at all or is done by each household for itself, and, if efficiently, with a wearing, constant effort of superintendence) by the butcher, baker, fishmonger, grocer, by the provision venders of all sorts, by the ice-man, dust-man, scavenger, by the postman, carrier, expressmen, and messengers, all serving you at your house when required; by the sewers, gutters, pavement, crossings, sidewalks, public conveyances, and gas and water works.

But here again there is every reason to suppose that what we see is but a foretaste of what is yet to come. Take the difference of demand upon invention in respect to cheap conveyance for example. We began experimentally with street railways twenty years ago. At present, in New York, one pair of horses serves to convey one hundred people, on an average, every day at a rate of fare about one fiftieth of the old hackney-coach rates, and the total number of fares collected annually is equal to that of the population of the United States. And yet thousands walk a number of miles every day because they cannot be seated in the cars. It is impossible to fix a limit to the amount of travel which really ample, convenient, and still cheap means of transportation for short distances would develop. Certain improvements have caused the whole number of people seeking conveyances in London to be doubled in the last five years, and yet the supply keeps nowhere near the demand.

See how rapidly we are really gaining, and what we have to expect. Two recent inventions give us the means of reducing by a third, under favorable circumstances, the cost of good McAdam roads. There have been sixteen patents issued from one office for other new forms of perfectly smooth and nearly noiseless street pavement, some of which, after two or three years' trial, promise so well as to render it certain that some improvement will soon come by which more than one of the present special annoyances of town life will be abated. An improvement in our sewer system seems near at hand also, which will add considerably to the comparative advantages of a residence in towns, and especially the more open town suburbs.

Experiments indicate that it is feasible to send heated air through a town in pipes like water, and that it may be drawn upon, and the heat which is taken measured and paid for according to quantity required. Thus may come a great saving of fuel and trouble in a very difficult department of domestic economy. No one will think of applying such a system to farm-houses.

Again, it is plain that we have scarcely begun to turn to account the advantages offered to towns-people in the electric telegraph; we really have not made a beginning with those offered in the pneumatic tube, though their substantial character has been demonstrated. By the use of these two instruments, a tradesman ten miles away on the other side of a town may be communicated with, and goods obtained from him by a housekeeper, as quickly and with as little personal inconvenience as now if he were in the next block. A single tube station for five hundred families, acoustic pipes for the transmission of orders to it from each house, with a carriers' service for local distribution of packages, is all that is needed for this purpose.

As to the economy which comes by systematizing and concentrating, by the application of a large apparatus, of processes which are otherwise conducted in a desultory way, wasteful of human strength, as by public laundries, bakeries, and kitchens, we are yet, in America, even in our larger cities, far behind many of the smaller towns of the Old World.

While in all these directions enterprise and the progress of invention are quite sure to add rapidly to the economy and convenience of town life, and thus increase its comparative attractions, in other directions every step tends to reduce the man-power required on the farms for the production of a given amount of the raw material of food. Such is the effect, for instance, of every improvement of apparatus or process in ploughing, mowing, reaping, curing, thrashing, and marketing.

Another tendency arising from the improvement of agricultural apparatus, which will be much accelerated when steam shall have been as successfully applied to tillage as already to harvesting and marketing operations, is that to the enlargement of fields and of farms. From this will follow the greater isolation of rural homesteads; for with our long-fronted farms, it will be long before we can hope to have country roads on which rapid engine-transit will be practicable, though we may be close upon it whenever firm and smooth roads can be afforded.*

It should be observed that possession of all the various advantages of the town to which we have referred, while it very certainly cannot be acquired by people living in houses a quarter or a half mile apart, does not, on the other hand, by any means involve an unhealthy density of population. Probably the advantages of civilization can be found illustrated and demonstrated under no other circumstances so completely as in some suburban neighborhoods where each family abode stands fifty or a hundred feet or more apart from all others, and at some distance from the public road. And it must be remembered, also, that man's enjoyment of rural beauty has clearly increased rather than diminished with his advance in civilization. There is no reason, except in the loss of time, the inconvenience, discomfort, and expense of our present arrangements for short travel, why suburban advantages should not be almost indefinitely extended. Let us have a cheap and enjoyable method of conveyance, and a building law like that of old Rome, and they surely will be.

As railroads are improved, all the important stations will become centres or sub-centres of towns, and all the minor stations suburbs. For most ordinary every-day purposes, especially house-keepers' purposes, these will need no very large population before they can obtain urban advantages. I have seen a settlement, the resident population of which was under three hundred, in which there was a public laundry, bath-house, barber's shop, billiard-room, beergarden, and bakery. Fresh rolls and fresh milk were supplied to families before breakfast time every morning; fair fruit and succulent vegetables were delivered at house doors not half an hour after picking; and newspapers and magazines were distributed by a carrier. I have

---

*Slow freighting over earth roads is practicable; 500 locomotives are now in regular use on common roads.

seen a town of not more than twelve hundred inhabitants, the streets and the yards, alleys, and places of which were swept every day as regularly as the house floors, and all dust removed by a public dustman.

The construction of good roads and walks, the laying of sewer, water, and gas pipes, and the supplying of sufficiently cheap, rapid, and comfortable conveyances to town centres, is all that is necessary to give any farming land in a healthy and attractive situation the value of town lots. And whoever has observed in the French agricultural colonies how much more readily and cheaply railroads, telegraph, gas, water, sewer, and nearly all other advantages of towns may be made available to the whole population than under our present helter-skelter methods of settlement, will not believe that even the occupation of a farm laborer must necessarily and finally exclude his family from a very large share of urban conveniences.

But this opens a subject of speculation, which I am not now free to pursue. It is hardly a matter of speculation, I am disposed to think, but almost of demonstration, that the larger a town becomes simply because of its advantages for commercial purposes, the greater will be the convenience available to those who live in and near it for co-operation, as well with reference to the accumulation of wealth in the higher forms,—as in seats of learning, of science, and of art,—as with reference to merely domestic economy and the emancipation of both men and women from petty, confining, and narrowing cares.

It also appears to be nearly certain that the recent rapid enlargement of towns and withdrawal of people from rural conditions of living is the result mainly of circumstances of a permanent character.

We have reason to believe, then, that towns which of late have been increasing rapidly on account of their commercial advantages, are likely to be still more attractive to population in the future; that there will in consequence soon be larger towns than any the world has yet known, and that the further progress of civilization is to depend mainly upon the influences by which men's minds and characters will be affected while living in large towns.

Now, knowing that the average length of the life of mankind in towns has been much less than in the country, and that the average amount of disease and misery and of

vice and crime has been much greater in towns, this would
be a very dark prospect for civilization, if it were not that
modern science has beyond all question determined many
of the causes of the special evils by which men are afflicted
in towns, and placed means in our hands for guarding
against them. It has shown, for example, that under ordinary circumstances, in the interior parts of large and
closely built towns, a given quantity of air contains considerably less of the elements which we require to receive
through the lungs than the air of the country or even of the
outer and more open parts of a town, and that instead of
them it carries into the lungs highly corrupt and irritating
matters, the action of which tends strongly to vitiate all
our sources of vigor—how strongly may perhaps be indicated in the shortest way by the statement that even metallic plates and statues corrode and wear away under the at-
mospheric influences which prevail in the midst of large
towns, more rapidly than in the country.

The irritation and waste of the physical powers which
result from the same cause, doubtless indirectly affect and
very seriously affect the mind and the moral strength; but
there is a general impression that a class of men are bred in
towns whose peculiarities are not perhaps adequately accounted for in this way. We may understand these better if
we consider that whenever we walk through the denser
part of a town, to merely avoid collision with those we
meet and pass upon the sidewalks, we have constantly to
watch, to foresee, and to guard against their movements.
This involves a consideration of their intentions, calculation of their strength and weakness, which is not so much
for their benefit as our own. Our minds are thus brought
into close dealings with other minds without any friendly
flowing toward them, but rather a drawing from them.
Much of the intercourse between men when engaged in
the pursuits of commerce has the same tendency—a tendency to regard others in a hard if not always hardening
way. Each detail of observation and of the process of
thought required in this kind of intercourse or contact of
minds is so slight and so common in the experience of
towns-people that they are seldom conscious of it. It certainly involves some expenditure nevertheless. People
from the country are even conscious of the effect on their
nerves and minds of the street contact—often complaining

that they feel confused by it; and if we had no relief from it at all during our waking hours, we should all be conscious of suffering from it. It is upon our opportunities of relief from it, therefore, that not only our comfort in town life, but our ability to maintain a temperate, good-natured, and healthy state of mind, depends. This is one of many ways in which it happens that men who have been brought up, as the saying is, in the streets, who have been most directly and completely affected by town influences, so generally show, along with a remarkable quickness of apprehension, a peculiarly hard sort of selfishness. Every day of their lives they have seen thousands of their fellow-men, have met them face to face, have brushed against them, and yet have had no experience of anything in common with them.

It has happened several times within the last century, when old artificial obstructions to the spreading out of a city have been removed, and especially when there has been a demolition of and rebuilding on a new ground plan of some part which had previously been noted for the frequency of certain crimes, the prevalence of certain diseases, and the shortness of life among its inhabitants, that a marked improvement in all these respects has immediately followed, and has been maintained not alone in the dark parts, but in the city as a whole.

But although it has been demonstrated by such experiments that we have it in our power to greatly lessen and counteract the two classes of evils we have had under consideration, it must be remembered that these means are made use of only with great difficulty—how great, one or two illustrations from experience will enable us perhaps better to understand.

When the business quarter of New York was burnt over, thirty years ago, there was a rare opportunity for laying out a district expressly with a view to facilitate commerce. The old plan had been arrived at in a desultory way; and so far as it had been the result of design, it had been with reference more especially to the residence of a semi-rural population. This had long since passed away; its inconvenience for commercial purposes had been experienced for many years; no one supposed from the relation of the ground to the adjacent navigable waters that it would ever be required for other than commercial purposes. Yet the difficulties of equalizing benefits and damages among the various owners of the land prevented any considerable change of the old street lines. Every working day thousands of dollars are subtracted from the profits of business, by the disadvantages thus re-established. The annual loss amounts to millions. . . .

Remedy for a bad plan, once built upon, being thus impracticable, now that we understand the matter we are surely bound, wherever it is by any means in our power, to prevent mistakes in the construction of towns. Strange to say, however, here in the New World, where great towns by the hundred are springing into existence, no care at all is taken to avoid bad plans. The most brutal pagans to whom we have sent our missionaries have never shown greater indifference to the sufferings of others than is exhibited in the plans of some of our most promising cities, for which men now living in them are responsible.

Not long since I was asked by the mayor of one of these to go before its common council and explain the advantages of certain suggested changes, including especially the widening of two roads leading out of town and as yet but partially opened and not at all built upon. After I had done so, two of the aldermen in succession came to me, and each privately said in effect: "It is quite plain that the proposition is a good one, and it ought to be adopted; the city would undoubtedly gain by it; but the people of the ward I represent have less interest in it than some others: they do not look far ahead, and they are jealous of those who would be more directly benefited than themselves; consequently I don't think that they would like it if I voted for it, and I shall not, but I hope it will be carried."

They were unwilling that even a stranger should have so poor an opinion of their own intelligence as to suppose that they did not see the advantage of the change proposed; but it was not even suggested to their minds that there might be something shameful in repudiating their obligations to serve, according to the best of their judgment, the general and permanent interests committed to them as legislators of the city.

It is evident that if we go on in this way, the progress of civilized mankind in health, virtue, and happiness will be seriously endangered.

It is practically certain that the Boston of today is the mere nucleus of the Boston that is to be. It is practically certain that it is to extend over many miles of country now thoroughly rural in character, in parts of which farmers are now laying out roads with a view to shortening the teaming distance between their wood-lots and a railway station, being governed in their courses by old property lines, which were first run simply with reference to the equitable division of heritages, and in other parts of which, perhaps, some wild speculators are having streets staked off from plans which they have formed with a rule and pencil in a broker's office, with a view chiefly to the impressions they would make when seen by other speculators on a lithographed map. And by this manner of planning, unless views of duty or of interest prevail that are not yet common, if Boston continues to grow at its present rate even for but a few generations longer, and then simply holds its own until it shall be as old as the Boston in Lincolnshire now is, more men, women, and children are to be seriously affected in health and morals than are now living on this continent.

Is this a small matter—a mere matter of taste; a sentimental speculation?

It must be within the observation of most of us that where, in the city, wheel-ways originally twenty feet wide were with great difficulty and cost enlarged to thirty, the present width is already less nearly adequate to the present business than the former was to the former business; obstructions are more frequent, movements are slower and oftener arrested, and the liability to collision is greater. The same is true of sidewalks. Trees thus have been cut down, porches, bow-windows, and other encroachments removed, but every year the walk is less sufficient for the comfortable passing of those who wish to use it.

It is certain that as the distance from the interior to the circumference of towns shall increase with the enlargement of their population, the less sufficient relatively to the service to be performed will be any given space between buildings.

In like manner every evil to which men are specially liable when living in towns, is likely to be aggravated in the future, unless means are devised and adapted in advance to prevent it.

Let us proceed, then, to the question of means, and with a seriousness in some degree befitting a question,

upon our dealing with which we know the misery or happiness of many millions of our fellow-beings will depend.

We will for the present set before our minds the two
sources of wear and corruption which we have seen to be
remediable and therefore preventible. We may admit that
commerce requires that in some parts of a town there shall
be an arrangement of buildings, and a character of streets
and of traffic in them which will establish conditions of
corruption and of irritation, physical and mental. But commerce does not require the same conditions to be maintained in all parts of a town.

Air is disinfected by sunlight and foliage. Foliage also
acts mechanically to purify the air by screening it. Opportunity and inducement to escape at frequent intervals from
the confined and vitiated air of the commercial quarter,
and to supply the lungs with air screened and purified by
trees, and recently acted upon by sunlight, together with
opportunity and inducement to escape from conditions requiring vigilance, wariness, and activity toward other
men,—if these could be supplied economically, our problem would be solved.

In the old days of walled towns all tradesmen lived under the roof of their shops, and their children and appren-
tices and servants sat together with them in the evening
about the kitchen fire. But now that the dwelling is built by
itself and there is greater room, the inmates have a parlor
to spend their evenings in; they spread carpets on the floor
to gain in quiet, and hang drapery in their windows and
papers on their walls to gain in seclusion and beauty. Now
that our towns are built without walls, and we can have all
the room that we like, is there any good reason why we
should not make some similar difference between parts
which are likely to be dwelt in, and those which will be required exclusively for commerce?

Would trees, for seclusion and shade and beauty, be
out of place, for instance, by the side of certain of our
streets? It will, perhaps, appear to you that it is hardly necessary to ask such a question, as throughout the United
States trees are commonly planted at the sides of streets.
Unfortunately they are seldom so planted as to have fairly
settled the question of the desirableness of systematically
maintaining trees under these circumstances. In the first
place, the streets are planned, wherever they are, especially alike. Trees are planted in the space assigned for

sidewalks, where at first, while they are saplings, and the vicinity is rural or suburban, they are not much in the way, but where, as they grow larger, and the vicinity becomes urban, they take up more and more space, while space is more and more required for passage. That is not all. Thousands and tens of thousands are planted every year in a manner and under conditions as nearly certain as possible either to kill them outright, or to so lessen their vitality as to prevent their natural and beautiful development, and to cause premature decrepitude. Often, too, as their lower limbs are found inconvenient, no space having been provided for trees in laying out the street, they are deformed by butcherly amputations. If by rare good fortune they are suffered to become beautiful, they still stand subject to be condemned to death at any time, as obstructions in the highway.*

What I would ask is, whether we might not with economy make special provision in some of our streets—in a twentieth or a fiftieth part, if you please, of all—for trees to remain as a permanent furniture of the city? I mean, to make a place for them in which they would have room to grow naturally and gracefully. Even if the distance between the houses should have to be made half as much again as it is required to be in our commercial streets, could not the space be afforded? Out of town space is not costly when measures to secure it are taken early. The assessments for benefit where such streets were provided for, would, in nearly all cases, defray the cost of the land required. The strips of ground reserved for the trees, six, twelve, twenty feet wide, would cost nothing for paving or flagging.

*On the border of the first street laid out in the oldest town in New England, there yet stands what has long been known as "the Town Tree," its trunk having served for generations as a publication post for official notices. "The selectmen," having last year removed the lower branches of all the younger roadside trees of the town, and thereby its chief beauty, have this year deliberately resolved that they would have this tree cut down, for no other reason, so far as appears in their official record, than that if two persons came carelessly together on the roadway side of it, one of them might chance to put his foot in the adjoining shallow street-gutter. It might cost ten dollars to deepen and bridge this gutter substantially. The call to arms for the Old French War, for the War of the Revolution, the war for the freedom of the seas, the Mexican War, and the War of the Rebellion, was first made in this town under the shade of this tree, which is an American elm, and, notwithstanding its great age, is perfectly healthy and almost as beautiful as it is venerable.

The change both of scene and of air which would be obtained by people engaged for the most part in the necessarily confined interior commercial parts of the town, on passing into a street of this character after the trees had become stately and graceful, would be worth a good deal. If such streets were made still broader in some parts, with spacious malls, the advantage would be increased. If each of them were given the proper capacity, and laid out with laterals and connections in suitable directions to serve as a convenient trunk line of communication between two large districts of the town or the business centre and the suburbs, a very great number of people might thus be placed every day under influences counteracting those with which we desire to contend.

These, however, would be merely very simple improvements upon arrangements which are in common use in every considerable town. Their advantages would be incidental to the general uses of streets as they are. But people are willing very often to seek recreations as well as receive it by the way. Provisions may indeed be made expressly for public recreations, with certainty that if convenient they will be resorted to.

We come then to the question: what accommodations for recreation can we provide which shall be so agreeable and so accessible as to be efficiently attractive to the great body of citizens, and which, while giving decided gratification, shall also cause those who resort to them for pleasure to subject themselves, for the time being, to conditions strongly counteractive to the special enervating conditions of the town?

In the study of this question all forms of recreation may, in the first place, be conveniently arranged under two general heads. One will include all of which the predominating influence is to stimulate exertion of any part or parts needing it; the other, all which cause us to receive pleasure without conscious exertion. Games chiefly of mental skill, as chess, or athletic sports, as baseball, are examples of means of recreation of the first class, which may be termed that of *exertive* recreation; music and the fine arts generally of the second or *receptive* division.

Considering the first by itself, much consideration will be needed in determining what classes of exercises may be advantageously provided for. In the Bois de Boulogne there is a race course; in the Bois de Vincennes a ground for artillery target-practice. Military parades are held in Hyde Park. A few cricket clubs are accommodated in most of the London parks, and swimming is permitted in the lakes at certain hours. In the New York Park, on the other hand, none of these exercises are provided for or permitted, except that the boys of the public schools are given the use on holidays of certain large spaces for ball playing. It is considered that the advantage to individuals which would be gained in providing for them would not compensate for the general inconvenience and expense they would cause.

I do not propose to discuss this part of the subject at present, as it is only necessary to my immediate purpose to point out that if recreations requiring spaces to be given up to the use of a comparatively small number, are not considered essential, numerous small grounds so distributed through a large town that some one of them could be easily reached by a short walk from every house, would be more desirable than a single area of great extent, however rich in landscape attractions it might be. Especially would this be the case if the numerous local grounds were connected and supplemented by a series of trunk roads or boulevards such as has already been suggested.

Proceeding to the consideration of receptive recreations, it is necessary to ask you to adopt and bear in mind a further subdivision, under two heads, according to the degree in which the average enjoyment is greater when a large congregation assembles for a purpose of receptive recreation, or when the number coming together is small and the circumstances are favorable to the exercise of personal friendliness.

The first I shall term *gregarious*; the second, *neighborly*. Remembering that the immediate matter in hand is a study of fitting accommodations, you will, I trust, see the practical necessity of this classification.

Purely gregarious recreation seems to be generally looked upon in New England society as childish and savage, because, I suppose, there is so little of what we call intellectual gratification in it. We are inclined to engage in it indirectly, furtively, and with complication. Yet there are certain forms of recreation, a large share of the attraction of which must, I think, lie in the gratification of the gregarious inclination, and which, with those who can afford to indulge in them, are so popular as to establish the importance of the requirement.

If I ask myself where I have experienced the most complete gratification of this instinct in public and out of doors, among trees, I find that it has been in the promenade of the Champs Elysées. As closely following it I should name other promenades of Europe, and our own upon the New York parks. I have studiously watched the latter for several years. I have several times seen fifty thousand people participating in them; and the more I have seen of them, the more highly have I been led to estimate their value as means of counteracting the evils of town life.

Consider that the New York Park and the Brooklyn Park are the only places in those associated cities where, in this eighteen hundred and seventieth year after Christ, you will find a body of Christians coming together, and with an evident glee in the prospect of coming together, all classes largely represented, with a common purpose, not at all intellectual, competitive with none, disposing to jealousy and spiritual or intellectual pride toward none, each individual adding by his mere presence to the pleasure of all others, all helping to the greater happiness of each. You may thus often see vast numbers of persons brought closely together, poor and rich, young and old, Jew and Gentile. I have seen a hundred thousand thus congregated, and I assure you that though there have been not a few that seemed a little dazed, as if they did not quite understand it, and were, perhaps, a little ashamed of it, I have looked studiously but vainly among them for a single face completely unsympathetic with the prevailing expression of good nature and light-heartedness.

Is it doubtful that it does men good to come together in this way in pure air and under the light of heaven, or that it must have an influence directly counteractive to that of the ordinary hard, hustling working hours of town life?

You will agree with me, I am sure, that it is not, and that opportunity, convenient, attractive opportunity, for such congregation, is a very good thing to provide for, in planning the extension of a town.

I referred especially to the Champs Elysées, because the promenade there is a very old custom, not a fashion of the day, and because I must needs admit that this most striking example is one in which no large area of ground—nothing like a park—has been appropriated for the purpose. I must acknowledge, also, that the alamedas of Spain and Portugal supply another and very interesting instance of the same fact. You will observe, however, that small local grounds, such as we have said might be the best for most exertive recreations, are not at all adapted to receptive recreations of the type described.

One thing more under this head. I have but little personal familiarity with Boston customs; but I have lived or sojourned in several other towns of New England, as well as of other parts of the country, and I have never been long in any locality, south or north, east or west, without observing a *custom* of gregarious out-of-door recreation in some miserably imperfect form, usually covered by a wretched pretext of a wholly different purpose, as perhaps, for instance, visiting a grave-yard. I am sure that it would be much better, less expensive, less harmful in all ways, more health-giving to body, mind, and soul, if it were admitted to be a distinct requirement of all human beings, and appropriately provided for.

I have next to see what opportunities are wanted to induce people to engage in what I have termed *neighborly* receptive recreations, under conditions which shall be highly counteractive to the prevailing bias to degeneration and demoralization in large towns. To make clearer what I mean, I need an illustration which I find in a familiar domestic gathering, where the prattle of the children mingles with the easy conversation of the more sedate, the bodily requirements satisfied with good cheer, fresh air, agreeable light, moderate temperature, snug shelter, and furniture and decorations adapted to please the eye, without calling for profound admiration on the one hand, or tending to fatigue or disgust on the other. The circumstances are all favorable to a pleasurable wakefulness of the mind without stimulating exertion; and the close relation of family life, the association of children, of mothers, of lovers, or those who may be lovers, stimulate and keep alive the more tender sympathies, and give play to faculties such as may be dormant in business or on the promenade; while at the same time the cares of providing in detail for all the wants of the family, guidance, instruction, reproof, and the dutiful reception of guidance, instruction, and reproof, are, as matters of conscious exertion, as far as possible laid aside.

There is an instinctive inclination to this social, neighborly, unexertive form of recreation among all of us. In one way or another it is sure to be constantly operating upon those millions on millions of men and women who are to pass their lives within a few miles of where we now stand. To what extent it shall operate so as to develop health and virtue, will, on many occasions, be simply a question of opportunity and inducement. And this question is one for the determination of which for a thousand years we here to-day are largely responsible.

Think what the ordinary state of things to many is at this beginning of the town. The public is reading just now a little book in which some of your streets of which you are not proud are described. Go into one of those red cross streets any fine evening next summer, and ask how it is with their residents? Oftentimes you will see half a dozen sitting together on the door-steps, or, all in a row, on the curb-stones, with their feet in the gutter, driven out of doors by the closeness within; mothers among them anxiously regarding their children who are dodging about at their play, among the noisy wheels on the pavement.

Again, consider how often you see young men in knots of perhaps half a dozen in lounging attitudes rudely obstructing the sidewalks, chiefly led in their little conversation by the suggestions given to their minds by what or whom they may see passing in the street, men, women, or children, whom they do not know, and for whom they have no respect or sympathy. There is nothing among them or about them which is adapted to bring into play a spark of admiration, of delicacy, manliness, or tenderness. You see them presently descend in search of physical comfort to a brilliantly lighted basement, where they find others of their sort, see, hear, smell, drink, and eat all manner of vile things.

Whether on the curb-stones or in the dram-shops, these young men are all under the influence of the same impulse which some satisfy about the tea-table with neighbors and wives and mothers and children, and all things clean and wholesome, softening and refining.

If the great city to arise here is to be laid out little by little, and chiefly to suit the views of land-owners, acting only individually, and thinking only of how what they do is to affect the value in the next week or the next year of the few lots that each may hold at the time, the opportunities of so obeying this inclination as at the same time to give the lungs a bath of pure sunny air, to give the mind a suggestion of rest from the devouring eagerness and intellectual strife of town life, will always be few to any, to many will amount to nothing.

But is it possible to make public provision for recreation of this class, essentially domestic and secluded as it is?

It is a question which can, of course, be conclusively answered only from experience. And from experience in some slight degree I shall answer it. There is one large American town, in which it may happen that a man of any class shall say to his wife, when he is going out in the morning: ''My dear, when the children come home from school, put some bread and butter and salad in a basket, and go to the spring under the chestnut-tree where we found the Johnsons last week. I will join you there as soon as I can get away from the office. We will walk to the dairyman's cottage and get some tea, and some fresh milk for the children, and take our supper by the brook-side;'' and this shall be no joke, but the most refreshing earnestness.

There will be room enough in the Brooklyn Park, when it is finished, for several thousand little family and neighborly parties to bivouac at frequent intervals through the summer, without discommoding one another, or interfering with any other purpose, to say nothing of those who can be drawn out to make a day of it, as many thousand were last year. And although the arrangements for the purpose were yet very incomplete, and but little ground was at *all* prepared for such use, besides these small parties, consisting of one or two families, there came also, in companies of from thirty to a hundred and fifty, somewhere near twenty thousand children with their parents, Sunday-school teachers, or other guides and friends, who spent the best part of a day under the trees and on the turf, in recreations of which the predominating element was of this neighborly receptive class. Often they would bring a fiddle, flute, and harp, or other music. Tables, seats, shade, turf, swings, cool spring-water, and a pleasing rural prospect, stretching off half a mile or more each way, unbroken by a carriage road or the slightest evidence of the vicinity of the town, were supplied them without charge, and bread and milk and ice-cream at moderate fixed charges. In all my life I have never seen such joyous collections of people. I have, in fact, more than once observed tears of gratitude in the eyes of poor women, as they watched their children thus enjoying themselves.

The whole cost of such neighborly festivals, even when they include excursions by rail from the distant parts of the town, does not exceed for each person, on an average, a quarter of a dollar; and when the arrangements are complete, I see no reason why thousands should not come every day where hundreds come now to use them; and if so, who can measure the value, generation after generation, of such provisions for recreation to the overwrought, much confined people of the great town that is to be?

For this purpose neither of the forms of ground we have heretofore considered are at all suitable. We want a ground to which people may easily go after their day's work is done, and where they may stroll for an hour, seeing, hearing, and feeling nothing of the bustle and jar of the streets, where they shall, in effect, find the city put far away from them. We want the greatest possible contrast with the streets and the shops and the rooms of the town which will be consistent with convenience and the preservation of good order and neatness. We want, especially, the greatest possible contrast with the restraining and confining conditions of the town, those conditions which compel us to walk circumspectly, watchfully, jealously, which compel us to look closely upon others without sympathy. Practically, what we most want is a simple, broad, open space of clean greensward, with sufficient play of surface and a sufficient number of trees about it to supply a variety of light and shade. This we want as a central feature. We want depth of wood enough about it not only for comfort in hot weather, but to completely shut out the city from our landscapes.

The word *park*, in town nomenclature, should, I think, be reserved for grounds of the character and purpose thus described.

Not only as being the most valuable of all possible forms of public places, but regarded simply as a large space which will seriously interrupt cross-town communication wherever it occurs, the question of the site and bounds of the park requires to be determined with much more deliberation and art than is often secured for any problem of distant and extended municipal interests.

A Promenade may, with great advantage, be carried along the outer part of the surrounding groves of a park; and it will do no harm if here and there a broad opening among the trees discloses its open landscapes to those upon the promenade. But recollect that the object of the latter for the time being should be to see *congregated human life* under glorious and necessarily artificial conditions, and the natural landscape is not essential to them; though there is no more beautiful picture, and none can be more pleasing incidentally to the gregarious purpose, than that of beautiful meadows, over which clusters of level-armed sheltering trees cast broad shadows, and upon which are scattered dainty cows and flocks of black-faced sheep, while men, women, and children are seen sitting here and there, forming groups in the shade, or moving in and out among the woody points and bays.

It may be inferred from what I have said, that very rugged ground, abrupt eminences, and what is technically called picturesque in distinction from merely beautiful or simply pleasing scenery, is not the most desirable for a town park. Decidedly not in my opinion. The park should, as far as possible, complement the town. Openness is the one thing you cannot get in buildings. Picturesqueness you can get. Let your buildings be as picturesque as your artists can make them. This is the beauty of a town. Consequently, the beauty of the park should be the other. It should be the beauty of the fields, the meadow, the prairie, of the green pastures, and the still waters. What we want to gain is tranquillity and rest to the mind. Mountains suggest effort. But besides this objection there are others of what I may indicate as the housekeeping class. It is impossible to give the public range over a large extent of ground of a highly picturesque character, unless under very exceptional circumstances, and sufficiently guard against the occurrence of opportunities and temptations to shabbiness, disorder, indecorum, and indecency, that will be subversive of every good purpose the park should be designed to fulfill.

Nor can I think that *in the park proper*, what is called gardenesque beauty is to be courted; still less that highly artificial and exotic form of it, which, under the name of subtropical planting, the French have lately introduced, and in suitable positions with interesting and charming results, but in following which indiscretely, the English are sacrificing the simple beauty of their simple and useful parks of the old time. Both these may have places, and very important places, but they do not belong within a park, unless as side scenes and incidents. Twenty years ago Hyde Park had a most pleasing, open, free, and inviting expression, though certainly it was too rude, too much wanting in art; but now art is vexed with long black lines of repellent iron-work, and here and there behind it bouquets of hot-house plants, between which the public pass like hospital convalescents, who have been turned into the yard to walk about while their beds are making. We should undertake nothing in a park which involves the treating of the public as prisoners or wild beasts. A great object of all that is done in a park, of *all* the art of a park, is to influence the mind of men through their imagination, and the influence of iron hurdles can never be good.

We have, perhaps, sufficiently defined the ideal of a park for a large town. It will seldom happen that this ideal can be realized fully. The next thing is to select the situation in which it can be most nearly approached without great cost; and by cost I do not mean simply cost of land or of construction, but cost of inconvenience and cost of keeping in order, which is a very much more serious matter, and should have a great deal more study.

A park fairly well managed near a large town, will surely become a new centre of that town. With the determination of location, size, and boundaries should therefore be associated the duty of arranging new trunk routes of communication between it and the distant parts of the town existing and forecasted.

These may be either narrow informal elongations of the park, varying say from two to five hundred feet in width, and radiating irregularly from it, or if, unfortunately, the town is already laid out in the unhappy way that New York and Brooklyn, San Francisco and Chicago, are, and, I am glad to say, Boston is not, on a plan made long years ago by a man who never saw a spring carriage, and who had a conscientious dread of the Graces, then we must probably adopt formal parkways. They should be so planned and constructed as never to be noisy and seldom crowded, and so also that the straightforward movement of pleasure carriages need never be obstructed, unless at absolutely necessary crossings, by slow-going heavy vehicles used for commercial purposes. If possible, also, they should be branched or reticulated with other ways of a similar class, so that no part of the town should finally be many minutes' walk from some one of them; and they should be made interesting by a process of planting and decoration, so that in necessarily passing through them, whether in going to or from the park, or to and from business, some substantial recreative advantage may be incidentally gained. It is a common error to regard a park as something to be produced complete in itself, as a picture to be painted on canvas. It should rather be planned as one to be done in fresco, with constant consideration of exterior objects, some of them quite at a distance and even existing as yet only in the imagination of the painter.

I have thus barely indicated a few of the points from which we may perceive our duty to apply the means in our hands to ends far distant, with reference to this problem of public recreations. Large operations of construction may not soon be desirable, but I hope you will agree with me that there is little room for question, that reserves of ground for the purposes I have referred to should be fixed upon as soon as possible, before the difficulty of arranging them, which arises from private building, shall be greatly more formidable than now.

To these reserves,—though not a dollar should be spent in construction during the present generation,—the plans of private construction would necessarily, from the moment they were established be conformed.

I by no means wish to suggest that nothing should be done for the present generation; but only, that whatever happens to the present generation, it should not be allowed to go on heaping up difficulties and expenses for its successors, for want of a little comprehensive and business-like foresight and study. In all probability it will be found that much can be done even for the present generation without greatly if at all increasing taxation, as had been found in New York.

But the question now perhaps comes up: How can a community best take this work in hand?

It is a work in which private and local and special interests will be found so antagonistic one to another, in which heated prejudices are so liable to be unconsciously established, and in which those who would be disappointed in their personal greeds by whatever good scheme may be studied out, are so likely to combine and concentrate force to kill it (manufacture public opinion, as the phrase is), that the ordinary organizations for municipal business are unsuitable agencies for the purpose. It would, perhaps, be a bold thing to say that the public in its own interest, and in the interest of all of whom the present public are the trustees, should see to it that the problem is as soon as possible put clean out of its own hands, in order that it may be taken up efficiently by a small body of select men. But I will venture to say that until this in effect is done, the danger that public opinion may be led, by the application of industry, ingenuity, and business ability on the part of men whose real objects are perhaps unconsciously very close to their own pockets, to overrule the results of more comprehensive and impartial study, is much greater than in most questions of public interest.

You will not understand me as opposing or undervaluing the advantages of public discussion. What I would urge is, that park questions, and even the most elementary park questions, questions of site and outlines and approaches, are not questions to which the rule applies, that every man should look after his own interests, judge for himself what will favor his own interests, and exert his influence so as to favor them; but questions rather of that class, which in his private affairs every man of common sense is anxious, as soon as possible, to put into the hands of somebody who is able to take hold of them comprehensively as a matter of direct, grave, business responsibility.

It is upon this last point far more than upon any other that the experience of New York is instructive to other communities. I propose, therefore, to occupy your time a little while longer by a narration of those parts of this experience which bear most directly upon this point, and which will also supply certain other information which has been desired of me.

The New York legislature of 1851 passed a bill providing for a park on the east side of the island. Afterwards, the same legislature, precipitately and quite as an afterthought, passed the act under which the city took title to the site of the greater part of the present Central Park.

This final action is said to have been the result of a counter movement, started after the passage of the first bill merely to gratify a private grudge of one of the city aldermen.

When in the formation of the counter project, the question was reached, what land shall be named in the second bill, the originator turned to a map and asked: *"Now where shall I go?"* His comrade, looking over his shoulder, without a moment's reflection, put his finger down and said, *"Go there;"* the point indicated appearing to be about the middle of the island, and therefore, as it occurred to him, one which would least excite local prejudices.

The primary selection of the site was thus made in an off-hand way, by a man who had no special responsibility in the premises, and whose previous studies had not at all led him to be well informed or interested in the purposes of a park.

It would have been difficult to find another body of land of six hundred acres upon the island (unless by taking a long narrow strip upon the precipitous side of a ridge), which possessed less of what we have seen to be the most desirable characteristics of a park, or upon which more time, labor, and expense would be required to establish them.

But besides the topographical objections, when the work of providing suitable facilities for the recreation of the people upon this ground came to be practically and definitely considered, defects of outline were discerned, the incomplete remedy for which has since cost the city more than a million of dollars. The amount which intelligent study would have saved in this way if applied at the outset, might have provided for an amplification of some one of the approaches to the Park, such as, if it were now possible to be gained at a cost of two or three million dollars, I am confident would, if fairly set forth, be ordered by an almost unanimous vote of the tax-payers of the city. Public discussion at the time utterly failed to set this blundering right. Nor was public opinion then clearly dissatisfied with what was done or with those who did it.

During the following six years there was much public and private discussion of park questions; but the progress of public opinion, judged simply by the standard which it has since formed for itself, seems to have been chiefly backward.

This may be, to a considerable degree, accounted for

by the fact that many men of wealth and influence—who, through ignorance and lack of mature reflection on this subject, were unable to anticipate any personal advantage from the construction of a park—feared that it would only add to their taxes, and thus were led to form a habit of crying down any hopeful anticipations.

The argument that certain towns of the old country did obtain some advantage from their parks, could not be refuted, but it was easy to say, and it was said, that "our circumstances are very different: surrounded by broad waters on all sides, open to the sea breezes, we need no artificial breathing places; even if we did, nothing like the parks of the old cities under aristocratic government would be at all practicable here."

This assertion made such an impression as to lead many to believe that little more had better be done than to give the name of park to the ground which it was now too late to avoid taking. A leading citizen suggested that nothing more was necessary than to plough up a strip just within the boundary of the ground and plant it with young trees, and chiefly with cuttings of the poplar, which afterwards, as they came to good size, could be transplanted to the interior, and thus the Park would be furnished economically and quite well enough for the purposes it would be required to serve.

Another of distinguished professional reputation seriously urged through the public press, that the ground should be rented as a sheep-walk. In going to and from their folds the flocks would be sure to form trails which would serve the public perfectly well for foot-paths; nature would in time supply whatever else was essential to form a quite picturesque and perfectly suitable strolling ground for such as would wish to resort to it.

It was frequently alleged, and with truth, that the use made of the existing public grounds was such as to develop riotous and licentious habits. A large park, it was argued, would inevitably present larger opportunities, and would be likely to exhibit an aggravated form of the same tendencies, consequently anything like refinement of treatment would be entirely wasted.

A few passages from a leading article of the "Herald" newspaper, in the seventh year of the enterprise, will indicate what estimate its astute editor had then formed of the prevailing convictions of the public on the subject:—

> It is folly to expect in this country to have parks like those in old aristocratic countries. When we open a public park Sam will air himself in it. He will take his friends whether from Church Street, or elsewhere. He will knock down any better dressed man who remonstrates with him. He will talk and sing, and fill his share of the bench, and flirt with the nursery maids in his own coarse way. Now we ask what chance have William B. Astor and Edward Everett against this fellow citizen of theirs? Can they and he enjoy the same place? Is it not obvious that he will turn them out, and that the great Central Park will be nothing but a great beer-garden for the lowest denizens of the city, of which we shall yet pray litanies to be delivered?

In the same article it was argued that the effect of the construction of the Park would be unfavorable to the value of property in its neighborhood, except as, to a limited extent, it might be taken up by Irish and German liquor dealers as sites for dram-shops and lager beer gardens.

There were many eminent citizens, who to my personal knowledge, in the sixth, seventh, and eighth year after the passage of the act, entertained similar views to those I have quoted.

I have been asked if I supposed that "gentlemen" would ever resort to the Park, or would allow their wives and daughters to visit it? I heard a renowned lawyer argue that it was preposterous to suppose that a police force would do anything toward preserving order and decency in any broad piece of ground open to the general public of New York. And after the work began, I often heard the conviction expressed that if what was called the reckless, extravagant, inconsiderate policy of those who had the making of the Park in charge, could not be arrested, the weight of taxation and the general disgust which would be aroused among the wealthy classes would drive them from the city, and thus prove a serious injury to its prosperity.

"Why," said one, a man whom you all know by reputation, and many personally, "I should not ask for anything finer in my private grounds for the use of my own family." To whom it was replied that possibly grounds might not unwisely be prepared even more carefully when designed for the use of two hundred thousand families and their guests, than when designed for the use of one.

The constantly growing conviction that it was a rash and ill-considered undertaking, and the apprehension that a great deal would be spent upon it for no good purpose, doubtless had something to do with the choice of men, who in the sixth year were appointed by the governor of the state, commissioners to manage the work and the very extraordinary powers given them. At all events, it so happened that a majority of them were much better known from their places in the directory of banks, railroads, mining, and manufacturing enterprises, than from their previous services in politics; and their freedom to follow their own judgment and will, in respect to all the interior matters of the Park, was larger than had for a long time been given to any body of men charged with a public duty of similar importance.

I suppose that few of them knew or cared more about the subject of their duties at the time of their appointment, than most other active business men. They probably embodied very fairly the average opinion of the public, as to the way in which it was desirable that the work should be managed. If, then, it is asked, how did they come to adopt and resolutely pursue a course so very different from that which the public opinion seemed to expect of them, I think that the answer must be found in the fact that they had not wanted or asked the appointment; that it was made absolutely free from any condition or obligation to serve a party, a faction, or a person; that owing to the extraordinary powers given them, their sense of responsibility in the matter was of an uncommonly simple and direct character, and led them with the trained skill of business men to go straight to the question:—

"Here is a piece of property put into our hands. By what policy can we turn it to the best account for our stockholders?"

It has happened that instead of being turned out about the time they had got to know something about their special business, these commissioners have been allowed to remain in office to this time—a period of twelve years.

As to their method of work, it was as like as possible to that of a board of directors of a commercial corporation. They quite set at defiance the ordinary ideas of propriety applied to public servants, by holding their sessions with closed doors, their clerk being directed merely to supply the newspapers with reports of their acts. They spent the whole of the first year on questions simply of policy, organization, and plan, doing no practical work, as it was said, at all.

When the business of construction was taken hold of, they refused to occupy themselves personally with questions of the class which in New York usually take up nine-tenths of the time and mind of all public servants, who have it in their power to arrange contracts and determine appointments, promotions, and discharges. All of these they turned over to the heads of the executive operations.

Now, when these deviations from usage were conjoined with the adoption of a policy of construction for which the public was entirely unprepared, and to which the largest tax-payers of the city were strongly opposed, when also those who had a variety of private axes to grind, found themselves and their influence, and their friends' influence, made nothing of by the commissioners, you may be sure that public opinion was manufactured against them at a great rate. The Mayor denounced them in his messages; the Common Council and other departments of the city government refused to cooperate with them, and were frequently induced to put obstructions in their way; they were threatened with impeachment and indictment; some of the city newspapers attacked them for a time in every issue; they were caricatured and lampooned; their session was once broken up by a mob, their business was five times examined (once or twice at great expense, lawyers, accountants, engineers, and other experts being employed for the purpose) by legislative investigating committees. Thus for a time public opinion, through nearly all the channels open to it, apparently set against them like a torrent.

No men less strong, and no men less confident in their strength than these men—by virtue in part of personal character, in part of the extraordinary powers vested in them by the legislature, and in part by the accident of certain anomalous political circumstances—happened to be, could have carried through a policy and a method which commanded so little immediate public favor. As it was, nothing but personal character, the common impression that after all they were honest, saved them. By barely a sabre's length they kept ahead of their pursuers, and of this you may still see evidence here and there in the park, chiefly where something left to stop a gap for the time being has been suffered to produce lasting defects. At one time nearly four thousand laborers were employed; and for a year at one point, work went on night and day in order to put it as quickly as possible beyond the reach of those who were bent on stopping it. Necessarily, under such circumstances, the rule obtains: "Look out for the main chance; we may save the horses, we must save the guns;" and if now you do not find everything in perfect parade order, the guns, at all events, were saved.

To fully understand the significance of the result so far, it must be considered that the Park is to this day, at some points, incomplete; that from the centre of population to the midst of the Park the distance is still four miles; that there is no steam transit; that other means of communication are indirect and excessively uncomfortable, or too expensive. For practical every-day purposes to the great mass of the people, the Park might as well be a hundred miles away. There are hundreds of thousands who have never seen it, more hundreds of thousands who have seen it only on a Sunday or holiday. The children of the city to whom it should be of the greatest use, can only get to it on holidays or in vacations, and then must pay car-fare both ways.

It must be remembered, also, that the Park is not planned for such use as is now made of it, but with regard to the future use, when it will be in the centre of a population of two millions hemmed in by water at a short distance on all sides; and that much of the work done upon it is, for this reason, as yet quite barren of results.

The question of the relative value of what is called off-hand common sense, and of special, deliberate, business-like study, must be settled in the case of the Central Park, by a comparison of benefit with cost. During the last four years over thirty million visits have been made to the Park by actual count, and many have passed uncounted. From fifty to eighty thousand persons on foot, thirty thousand in carriages, and four to five thousand on horseback, have often entered it in a day.

Among the frequent visitors, I have found all those who, a few years ago, believed it impossible that there should ever be a park in this republican country,—and especially in New York of all places in this country,—which would be a suitable place of resort for "gentlemen." They, their wives and daughters, frequent the Park more than they do the opera or the church.

There are many men of wealth who resort to the Park habitually and regularly, as much so as business men to their places of business. Of course, there is a reason for it, and a reason based upon their experience.

As to the effect on public health, there is no question that it is already great. The testimony of the older physicians of the city will be found unanimous on this point. Says one: "Where I formerly ordered patients of a certain class to give up their business altogether and go out of town, I now often advise simply moderation, and prescribe a ride in the Park before going to their offices, and again a drive with their families before dinner. By simply adopting this course as a habit, men who have been breaking down frequently recover tone rapidly, and are able to retain an active and controlling influence in an important business, from which they would have otherwise been forced to retire. I direct schoolgirls, under certain circumstances, to be taken wholly, or in part, from their studies, and sent to spend several hours a day rambling on foot in the Park."

The lives of women and children too poor to be sent to the country, can now be saved in thousands of instances, by making them go to the Park. During a hot day in July last, I counted at one time in the Park eighteen separate groups, consisting of mothers with their children, most of whom were under school age, taking picnic dinners which they had brought from home with them. The practice is increasing under medical advice, especially when summer complaint is rife.

The much greater rapidity with which patients convalesce, and may be returned with safety to their ordinary occupations after severe illness, when they can be sent to the Park for a few hours a day, is beginning to be understood. The addition thus made to the productive labor of the city is not unimportant.

The Park, moreover, has had a very marked effect in making the city attractive to visitors, and in thus increasing its trade, and causing many who have made fortunes elsewhere to take up their residence and become tax-payers in it,—a much greater effect in this way, beyond all question, than all the colleges, schools, libraries, museums, and art-galleries which the city possesses. It has also induced many foreigners who have grown rich in the country, and who would otherwise have gone to Europe to enjoy their wealth, to settle permanently in the city.

And what has become of the great Bugaboo? This is what the "Herald" of later date answers:—

> "When one is inclined to despair of the country, let him go to the Central Park on a Saturday, and spend a few hours there in looking at the people, not at those who come in gorgeous carriages, but at those who arrive on foot, or in those exceedingly democratic conveyances, the street-cars; and if, when the sun begins to sink behind the trees, he does not arise and go homeward with a happy swelling heart," and so on, the effusion winding up thus: "We regret to say that the more brilliant becomes the display of vehicles and toilettes, the more shameful is the display of bad manners on the part of the extremely fine-looking people who ride in carriages and wear the fine dresses. We must add that the pedestrians always behave well."

Here we touch a fact of more value to social science than any other in the history of the Park; but to fully set it before you would take an evening by itself. The difficulty of preventing ruffianism and disorder in a park to be frequented indiscriminately by such a population as that of New York, was from the first regarded as the greatest of all those which the commission had to meet, and the means of overcoming it cost more study than all other things.

It is, perhaps, too soon to judge of the value of the expedients resorted to, but there are as yet a great many parents who are willing to trust their school-girl daughters to ramble without special protection in the Park, as they would almost nowhere else in New York. One is no more likely to see ruffianism or indecencies in the Park than in the churches, and the arrests for offenses of all classes, including the most venial, which arise simply from the ignorance of country people, have amounted to but twenty in the million of the number of visitors, and of these, an exceedingly small proportion have been of that class which was so confidently expected to take possession of the Park and make it a place unsafe and unfit for decent people.

There is a good deal of delicate work on the Park, some of it placed there by private liberality—much that a girl with a parasol, or a boy throwing a pebble, could render valueless in a minute. Except in one or two cases where the ruling policy of the management has been departed from,—cases which prove the rule,—not the slightest injury from wantonness, carelessness, or ruffianism has occurred.

Jeremy Bentham, in treating of "The Means of Preventing Crimes," remarks that any innocent amusement that the human heart can invent is useful under a double point of view: first, for the pleasure itself which results from it; second, from its tendency to weaken the dangerous inclinations which man derives from his nature.

No one who has closely observed the conduct of the people who visit the Park, can doubt that it exercises a distinctly harmonizing and refining influence upon the most unfortunate and most lawless classes of the city,—an influence favorable to courtesy, self-control, and temperance.

At three or four points in the midst of the Park, beer, wine, and cider are sold with other refreshments to visitors, not at bars, but served at tables where men sit in company with women. Whatever harm may have resulted, it has apparently had the good effect of preventing the establishment of drinking places on the borders of the Park, these not having increased in number since it was opened, as it was originally supposed they would.

I have never seen or heard of a man or woman the worse for liquor taken at the Park, except in a few instances where visitors had brought it with them, and in which it had been drunk secretly and unsocially. The present arrangements for refreshments I should say are makeshift and most discordant with the design.

Every Sunday in summer from thirty to forty thousand persons, on an average, enter the Park on foot, the number on a very fine day being sometimes nearly a hundred thousand. While most of the grog-shops of the city were effectually closed by the police under the Excise Law on Sunday, the number of visitors to the Park was considerably larger than before. There was no similar increase at the churches.

Shortly after the Park first became attractive, and before any serious attempt was made to interfere with the Sunday liquor trade, the head-keeper told me that he saw among the visitors the proprietor of one of the largest "saloons'' in the city. He accosted him and expressed some surprise; the man replied, ''I came to see what the devil you'd got here that took off so many of my Sunday customers.''

I believe it may be justly inferred that the Park stands in competition with grog-shops and worse places, and not with the churches and Sunday-schools.

Land immediately about the Park, the frontage on it being seven miles in length, instead of taking the course anticipated by those opposed to the policy of the Commission, has advanced in value at the rate of two hundred per cent per annum.

The cost of forming the Park, owing to the necessity of overcoming the special difficulties of the locality by extraordinary expedients, has been very great ($5,000,000); but the interest on it would even now be fully met by a toll of three cents on visitors coming on foot, and six cents on all others; and it should be remembered that nearly every visitor in coming from a distance voluntarily pays much more than this for the privilege.

It is universally admitted, however, that the cost, including that of the original off-hand common-sense blunders, has been long since much more than compensated by the additional capital drawn to the city through the influence of the Park.

A few facts will show you what the change in public opinion has been. When the Commissioners began their work, six hundred acres of ground was thought by many of the friends of the enterprise to be too much, by none too little for all park purposes. Since the Park has come into use, the amount of land laid out and reserved for parks in the two principal cities on the bay of New York, has been increased to more than three times that amount, the total reserve for parks alone now being about two thousand acres, and the public demand is now for more, not less. Twelve years ago there was almost no pleasure-driving in New York. There are now, at least, ten thousand horses kept for pleasure-driving. Twelve years ago there were no roadways adapted to light carriages. There are now fourteen miles of rural drive within the parks complete and in use, and often crowded, and ground has been reserved in

the two cities and their suburbs for fifty miles of parkways, averaging, with their planted borders and inter-
spaces, at least one hundred and fifty feet wide.*

The land-owners had been trying for years to agree
upon a new plan of roads for the upper part of Manhattan
Island. A special commission of their own number had
been appointed at their solicitation, but had utterly failed
to harmonize conflicting interests. A year or two after the
Park was opened, they went again to the Legislature and
asked that the work might be put upon the Park Commissioners, which was done, giving them absolute control of
the matter, and under them it has been arranged in a manner, which appears to be generally satisfactory, and has
caused an enormous advance of the property of all those
interested.

At the petition of the people of the adjoining counties,
the field of the Commissioners' operations has been extended over their territory, and their scheme of trunk-ways
for pleasure-driving, riding, and walking has thus already
been carried far out into what are still perfectly rural districts.

On the west side of the harbor there are other commissioners forming plans for extending a similar system thirty
or forty miles back into the country, and the Legislature of
New Jersey has a bill before it for laying out another park
of seven hundred acres.

I could enforce the chief lesson of this history from
other examples at home and abroad. I could show you that
where parks have been laid out and managed in a temporary, off-hand, common-sense way, it has proved a penny-
wise, pound-foolish way, injurious to the property in their
neighborhood. I could show you more particularly how
the experience of New York, on the other hand, has been
repeated over the river in Brooklyn.

But I have already held you too long. I hope that I have
fully satisfied you that this problem of public recreation
grounds is one which, from its necessary relation to the

---

*The completion of a few miles of these will much relieve the drives of
the park, which, on many accounts, should never be wider than ordinary public requirements imperatively demand.

larger problem of the future growth of your honored city, should at once be made a subject of responsibility of a very definite, very exacting, and, consequently, very generous character. In no other way can it be adequately dealt with.

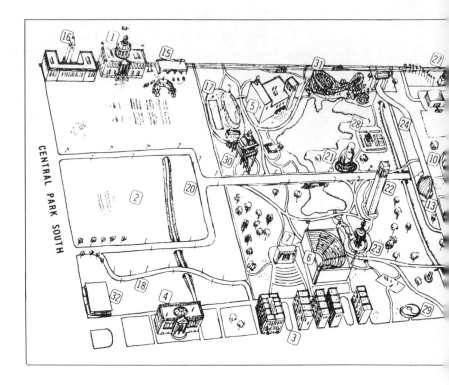

"IMPROVEMENTS" SUGGESTED FOR CENTRAL PARK SINCE 1900

1. Exposition Building, 1903.
2. Drill ground, 1904.
3. Selling off lower park for building lots, 1904; proposed for west side of Fifth Avenue by Mayor La Guardia in 1930's.
4. Building for National Academy of Design, 1909.
5. Opera House, 1910.
6. Outdoor theatre seating 50,000, 1911; opera amphitheatre proposed 1933.
7. Marionette theatre, 1912; proposed again 1964 and 1965.
8. Relocation of Central Park West streetcar tracks, 1917.
9. Trenches in North Meadow as war display, 1918.
10. Large stadium, 1919.
11. Airplane field, 1919.
12. Sunken oriental garden, Memorial Hall for war trophies and sports amphitheatre, 1920.
13. Music stand and road connecting drives to be called Mitchel Memorial, 1920.
14. Underground parking lot for 30,000 cars, 1921; proposed many times since.

Ken Fitzgerald, in Central Park: A History and a Guide *by Henry Hope Reed and Sophia Duckworth. © 1967, Henry Hope Reed.*

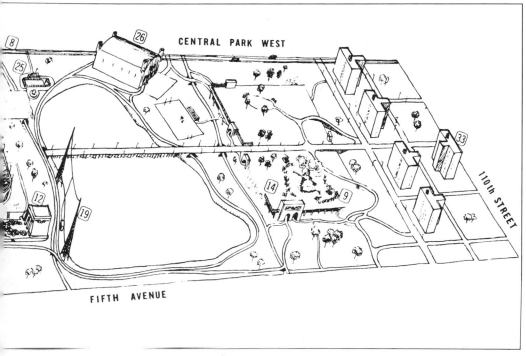

Suggested "Improvements" to Central Park Since 1900 as Seen by Ken Fitzgerald. Based on Information Gathered by Alan Becker.

Greensward Foundation.

15. Police garage, 1921.
16. Music and Art Center, 1922.
17. Swimming pool, circus and running track, 1923.
18. Filling in of Pond for new driveway, 1923.
19. Radio towers for city radio station, 1923.
20. Central roadway to relieve city's traffic congestion, 1923.
21. Statue of Buddha, 1925.
22. Carillon tower, 1925.
23. Fountain of the Seasons, 1929.
24. Promenade connecting Metropolitan and Natural History Museums, 1930.
25. Recreation building and swimming pool, 1935.
26. Armory and stables, 1940.
27. Plaza of South America, 8 acres, 1941.
28. Recreation Center for the Elderly, 1955.
29. Garden for the Blind, 1955.
30. El Station as monument to Elevated Railroad, 1955.
31. Amusement Center, 1955.
32. Huntington Hartford Outdoor Café, 1960.
33. Housing Project, 106th to 110th Streets, 1964.

17

The Motive Behind Olmsted's Park

ROGER STARR

Frederick Law Olmsted is one of those historical figures who seems less familiar the more one reads about him. At first we take him for granted as the designer of his parks, those great masterpieces of public art. Then, as we learn more about him, we wonder what prepared him to build them, and how he conceived their purpose in relation to his own experiences and training, and more especially to the cities into which they were placed.

A DISCONTINUOUS CAREER

Most of Olmsted's work as a park builder came after the 1860s, by which time landscape architecture had already become something of a profession. Yet nothing in the life of this great urban park builder suggests adequate preparation for such undertakings. M.M. Graff, one of the shrewder of his present-day admirers, managed to sustain in the midst of her admiration a sharp sense of his professional deficiencies. "Horticulture," she wrote in a pamphlet about Central Park, "is a profession in which no unqualified person ever hesitates to meddle. Olmsted was no

From The Public Interest, *Winter 1984, pp. 66–76. Copyright © 1984 by National Affairs, Inc.*

exception. Central Park still suffers from the effects of his ignorance of the nature and habits of plant material.''[1]

If Olmsted was not a gardener or landscape architect—though that is how he later described himself in submitting park proposals to cities other than New York—neither was he an engineer. Nevertheless, the engineering achievements of Central Park (and even more impressively, of Boston parks) were substantial. They included an effective drainage plan for the southern end of the park, which had formerly been swampy and useless for pedestrian traverse; the depressing of the four roads that the Central Park Commission was required to cut across the park in order to join the east and west sides of Manhattan; and the successful separation of the different kinds of intra-park traffic—pedestrian, vehicular, and equestrian—so they could see each other without interfering with each other. And, not least, there was the management of rock and removed fill: The scooped-out material from some changes in natural configuration was used to elevate the terrain at others.

What Olmsted demonstrated was not the engineering skills and discipline required to design all of the above, but judgment in selecting the most promising designs of others (and the ability to direct, manage, co-ordinate, and protect their work even when the political pressure of the Central Park Commission became unreasonable or niggling). And if he was neither a landscape architect nor an engineer, likewise he was no designer of buildings. (Many of his admirers insist on considering him one, perhaps because of the way in which he managed to keep people in his shadow—for example, Calvert Vaux, his extremely talented junior partner who actually designed the buildings, and Jacob Maul, who conceived and executed their fascinating details.)

Olmsted came to Central Park, and through Central Park to his preeminence as a park builder, almost by accident. Although the final plans had not yet been selected, work on Central Park had begun, and the superintendent's position was vacant. At the suggestion of a friend, Olmsted applied, even though by today's standards he was woefully underqualified. His only real credential was as a writer on parks, and this itself was limited to passages he had written in travel books about Europe. As to his other qualifications, he had twice tried and failed as a "scientific farmer," once in New England, once on Staten Island. His career as a publisher ended in bankruptcy. And his travel books on the American South were a disappointment to his editor, Henry Raymond. (By this time, Olmsted had concluded that slavery was irreconcilable with the future of America, harmful both to slave and master, and was turning his attention more directly to the conditions necessary to produce a just, democratic society.)

But he was appointed, and from this position he submitted, along with Calvert Vaux, the famous "Greensward Plan" for the completion of the park. This was the winning plan of the design contest (though it would later cause a certain amount of friction between Olmsted and Egbert Viele, the park engineer, whose own plan had been passed over).

Olmsted never really finished the work in Central Park; he left, exhausted by his constant battles with the Commission, and in particular with Andrew Green, its chief financial officer and a fiscal niggler who allowed neither political allegiance, personal sympathy, nor a sense of the park's ultimate importance to support any expense for which he could not find a bookkeeping justification. Olmsted's next assignment was as radical a break with his past as the park superintendency had been: He directed the U.S. Sanitary Commission, a sort of battlefield Red Cross, during the first two years of the Civil War. He left abruptly, on the edge of a nervous breakdown, and moved to California, where he ran a mine (without notable financial success).

THE MOTIVES OF A MORALIST

This chronicle of discontinuous careers, failures, or, at best, partial successes stands in sharp contrast to the achievements of Frederick Olmsted as the modern world perceives them. But there is no doubt that he left a uniquely impressive mark on American cities. He was not simply an executive (the terms "administrator" and "expert in public administration" come to mind, but simply do not fit), and neither was he merely a designer who was trying to promote an aesthetic vision. What distinguished

Olmsted's work was the motive behind it: It expressed his determination to bring a constructive and fruitful order to human life among the lower classes in emerging industrial cities of the second half of the nineteenth century. Central Park was not only intended as a source of joy and relaxation for the middle and upper classes, to whom it offered a rural experience within the city; it was also to be an instrument, perhaps the crucial instrument, in the imposition of moral order on the city's disorganized poor. It expressed not merely a topographical or an architectural or horticultural vision, but a vision of the constituent institutions of a good society.

In 1882, Olmsted wrote a pamphlet describing his ordeals in Central Park, calling it "The Spoils of the Park," and labeling himself in its subtitle as a "wholly unpractical man." The description is both half-right and completely wrong. Though he strove mightily to be a social philosopher, he could not restrain himself from practical activities; though he immersed himself in practical work, he could not convey to the political people for whom he worked the moral and political significance of what he was doing. Starting his park work at a time when the injustice of chattel slavery seemed reflected in the injustice of wage slavery and the conditions of life in the industrial city, Olmsted was likely to describe his object as an effort to make the vision of democracy real. The "new birth of freedom," which Lincoln spoke of in 1863, was by itself an empty abstraction for Olmsted, without the means to inspire moral order. He saw the solution to social problems in public works, not private words.

Most of those who actually frequented Central Park were thrilled by its appearance, and assumed that what animated Olmsted was the tension between a garden-like arrangement of nature and a cunning representation of nature in the wild. Certainly this was the goal of his collaborators—Vaux, Maul, and Ignaz Pilat—whom Mrs. Graff credits with saving Olmsted from the full consequences of his uninformed horticultural enthusiasms. But Olmsted was not preoccupied with aesthetics in 1857, but rather with the fear common in reformist and religious circles (and sharpened by the Draft Riots of 1863) that the emerging city would inflict disorder on its residents, infect them with contagious diseases, separate them from the institutions that inspire order (such as churches and guilds), and leave them without the means or the inspiration to overcome the consequent social disorganization.

It was Olmsted's strange mixture of motives that enabled him to accept technological improvements as both a cause of and a remedy for the growing social confusion of the time. High skill would make the very existence of the park possible, given its unpromising surroundings; and an understanding of social needs would shape its land use so that it could perform its rehabilitative *and* aesthetic functions. High technology, he recognized, particularly in sanitary engineering and water supply improvements, was already increasing life expectancy. And this technology would necessarily arise in the city, not in rural surroundings. For that reason the city was, at least potentially, the nursery of the social improvements required in the face of the breakdown of the strong family influences and local, parochial institutions one associates with rural and village life. But to be that nursery, the city would have to be reshaped.

IMPROVING THE HEALTH OF THE NEW URBAN MASSES

The first necessity was to reduce the human density of the most crowded cities. In his and Vaux's proposals for what is now Prospect Park, Olmsted pointed out to the Brooklyn officials that in London, with an average population density of 50,000 people per square mile in 1860, life expectancy was 26 years, while in Liverpool, with its much greater population density of 140,000 per square mile, life expectancy was only 17 years. It is obvious today that high densities produce social problems, as well as the higher morbidity that results from contagious infections. The building of a park tends, if anything, to raise the density of the population in the rest of the city, but as Olmsted pointed out to the Brooklyn officials, it also reduces the threats to both physical and social health.

He wrote at length of the problems caused by density: the lack of sunlight, for example, that is imposed on narrow streets by lining them with six story buildings. In the park, the resident of such a neighborhood would have a chance, for part of the day or week, to enjoy the benefits of the sun of which he was otherwise deprived. The park also would, in Olmsted's words, counter the morbid effects of a certain gas (not identified precisely but clearly meant to be carbon dioxide) produced by concentrated human respiration. It is certainly true that trees absorb carbon dioxide and nitrogen and exhale oxygen, but the effect of a park in purifying the air must be greatly attenuated, especially if the noxious gases are produced by other human polluters.

More important is the possibility of improving the physical health of the city dwellers through the physical exercise connected with parks. Obviously Olmsted planned for certain types of exercise in Central Park, but it must be remembered that at the time he and Vaux prepared the Greensward Plan, competitive athletics, so familiar today, were practically unknown. Women were not expected to engage in them (and were dressed so as to make serious exercise impossible). Men's competitive games like hockey, football, tennis, and basketball had not even been invented. And for both sexes, the need for physical exercise was less than what it has become since the development of machines that lighten the burden of physical work and self-propelled locomotion. One of the interesting features of the Olmsted parks, however, is that they have proved themselves quite adaptable to the demand for space for vigorous exercise. (The spaces that have since been reserved for competitive athletics had originally been intended for military training and parading.) Some Olmsted purists resent the intrusion of physical and competitive exercise on a large scale in the parks, because these exercises reduced the area available for less violent movement, and seem to them inconsistent with the spirit of Olmsted's day. But that reaction is based on a misunderstanding of what Olmsted really expected the parks to accomplish.

"SPEECHLESSNESS" AND MORAL REGENERATION

In an early report on Prospect Park, it is clear that he expected that park to produce a moral change in those who would frequent it. He claims that the ''addition of health, strength, and morality'' that comes from a park is both good in an absolute sense and good materially, since it im-

proves the economic productivity of the city's economy by
regenerating human energy following the draining daily
toil.

The park, he writes, by "diverting the imagination,"
present new stimulants to the senses that are both agreeable in themselves and a welcome relief from the urban objects people encounter day in, day out. The park, he says,
must provide scenery that contrasts as vividly as possible
with what is to be seen in the rest of the town. Further, the
park must provide an opportunity for "people to come together for the single purpose of enjoyment unembarrassed
by the limitations with which they are surrounded at
home, or in the pursuit of their daily avocations, or of such
amusements as are elsewhere offered."

As to the first of these two requirements, Olmsted is
apparently contrasting nature and man. The contrast, in
this case, seems to fall far short of the romantic naturalist
view that "only man is vile." Yet, without Olmsted actually saying so, it is clear that he saw the urban man of his
time as in an imperfect state, one in which material values
counted for too much, spiritual values for too little. Nature
does not provide the outline of a better moral order, but
simply a small slice of order itself. At this juncture, Olmsted parts company with the more formally-trained horti-
culturists. They claim, as we gather from Mrs. Graff's remarks, that natural order is betrayed or parodied by a park
designer who insists on cluttering the park landscape with
exotic plants that could not naturally grow there. In Central Park, for example, Olmsted planted trees that he had
admired in Europe or even in Panama. To the unschooled
observer, their incongruity is not noticeable. To the trained
horticulturist, however, the result is not orderly but fanciful, just as Calvert Vaux's Belvedere Castle, in the middle
of the park—which conjoins Gothic, Moorish, Romanesque, and Norman elements in a structure that is as seductive as a toy store, but as disorderly as a dream—
seemed fanciful to trained architects.

Probably, though, Olmsted wanted the rural elements
not to emphasize the natural orderliness of the non-
human world, but for another purpose altogether. Like
many other Americans who were worrying about the practical problem of keeping young people in the city from a
life of vice and destruction, Olmsted wanted the rural con-

trast of the park to suggest that nature was more moral, or less immoral, than man, particularly urban man. It was a widespread belief in the nineteenth century that sending slum children to the country would improve their souls (as we can learn in Professor Paul Boyer's pioneering book, *Urban Masses and American Moral Order*), and this view remains credible to many people today. The faith in the moral regenerative capacity of farms and parks was partly based on the realistic observation that a critical mass of children would not be assembled there, so mob psychology would not overcome individual conscience.

Another part of the faith in rural surroundings was surely rooted in the notion that nature is benign, a misconception that continues to afflict some sentimentalists. Most people now know better. They recognize that the non-human world is a battleground for survival, and that if it can be said to set forth any example of morality, it does so only by providing an escape from those human vices connected with speech: hypocrisy, lying, group hatred, envy. It is a long list. What the park offers is a relief from the constant buzz of the city, and the stony messages implicit in its buildings. The park offers speechlessness.

Olmsted expressed this view tangentially in a letter to the commissioners in January 1859. Under the heading "Motive of the Park," he writes:

> [The park] should present an aspect of spaciousness and tranquility with variety and intricacy of arrangement, thereby affording the most agreeable contrast to the confinement, bustle, and monotonous street-division of the city. . . . At present, in the lower Park especially, except in those places where the work of improvement is already well advanced, its aspect is one of mere undignified ruggedness. But this is due almost entirely to the absence of soil and foliage. When these are supplied, as they will be in a few years, that peculiar picturesqueness of effect, which can only be obtained in a high degree where rocky masses exist as a basis of operations, will become strikingly obvious. Grass and shrubbery can be formed anywhere, but great rocks, and those salient forms of earth-surface which are only found in nature where rock exists, can never be imitated on a large scale with perfect success. Although, therefore, it will require a heavy expenditure to make the Park complete, the final artistic effect will be much finer than could possibly be obtained upon a tract of the richest and most easily worked soil, the natural outlines of which were tame and prosaic.

The word "tranquility" suggests not merely silence but peace, the absence of contention. He was trying to tell the commissioners not to stint on the engineering costs of the park if they expected it to fulfil the functions so necessary to an orderly city: to make the restless multitudes confront the silence and permanence of rock, and perhaps modify their restless misbehavior as a result. It is perhaps fanciful, but irresistible, to suggest that Olmsted was trying to achieve in the park the three-dimensional essence of Sunday London that Wordsworth captured from Westminster Bridge. The park designer, like the poet, saw in the silent speechlessness of stone and buildings a moral orderliness that the weekday city outside the park could not provide. The park would bring about the same kind of urban structure that so impressed Wordsworth only when "the very houses seemed asleep and all that mighty heart was lying still."

AN EGALITARIAN ELITIST?

And yet that was only part of the reason behind the park. Olmsted probably saw even greater promise in the prospective commingling of social classes, which could be promoted by the proper design of the park, just as he dreamed of a democracy in which all would share the ideals of a genuine aristocracy. Olmsted might be called an egalitarian elitist. Like many Americans who did not attend Yale or Harvard, or did not spring from the Adams family tree, he probably overvalued the uplifting effect of hearing college lectures or breaking bread with descendants of the first families. As a practical man, he was also quite well aware of the fact that new arrivals in a still nascent society do not draw an understanding of its mores from the air. It is the elites who have the responsibility for transmitting those mores through the city's informal educators: teachers, policemen, tradesmen, clergy. He imagined that the required mores would be transmitted in a park setting to those who most needed the instruction.

Olmsted expresses his hope for accomplishing this commingling-by-design in the same report to the commission. One of the features of his Greensward Plan was the special adaptation he made of the "Parade Ground" that was required under the terms of the Commission's mandate. Greensward added some space to the Parade Ground, and Olmsted illuminated his and Vaux's intentions in these words: "Ordinarily it [the Parade Ground] will be like a great country green or open common, a place where children may run about and play until they are tired, in nobody's way, and without danger of being run over or injured if they fall.''

The rather sly replacement of the mandated Parade Ground by an "Open Common" is simply further evidence for a view of Olmsted's purposes that was put forth with clarity by Charles Beveridge and David Schuyler in their notes to the third volume of Olmsted's papers.[2] They quote from letters written by him to James T. Fields, editor of the *Atlantic Monthly*, and Henry Bellows, who wrote for that magazine. While some newspapers, notably the *New York Herald*, were mocking the notion that different social classes could enjoy the same park at the same time, Olmsted wrote Fields: ''I think it is good time, too, for showing how strongly experience in the park argues against certain political and social fallacies [i.e., the impossibility of social commingling] commonly entertained & how far it thus far justifies the highest hopes which have been entertained of its moral influence.''

Olmsted was strengthened in his conviction by a letter from the Mayor of Birmingham, England, about that city's Aston Park. Mayor Thomas Lloyd wrote:

> . . . I have great pleasure in stating that I consider [Aston Park] to have afforded decided evidence of the uselessness of corrective measures in any matter where the amusements of the people are concerned. We have had, as you are aware, nearly 300,000 people in the past half year, and they have walked about, played games, and on several occasions danced by daylight and have taken refreshment, including beer and spirits (if asked for) without restriction, and there has been only occasion for the interference of the Police (and it is not very often that we have them at the Park) on two occasions of very trifling importance.

Olmsted's letter to Fields resulted in an article by Bellows, who, after visiting the unfinished park, was quite swept away by the social vision that ''engraft[ed] the energy, foresight, and liberality of concentrated power on democratic ideas, and [kept] all that adorned and improved the past while abandoning what has impaired and disgraced it.''

A MIXED SUCCESS

In fact, as everybody must know, Central Park was immensely successful, but not really in the way, and for all the reasons, that Olmsted imagined. In the first years after

its construction, it was so far away from the sections of the
city occupied by those who most needed its uplifting influence that it remained rather a playground for the city's
original aristocracy. That clientele changed over the years,
but only because the city kept producing new elites, new
aristocracies, who came to live in row houses on the side
streets to the east and west of the park. It is true that as the
elevated trains were built on Columbus and Third and Second Avenues, tenement houses for low income families
followed. Some of their children did use the park, but
many preferred to play on the streets; and those who did
come to the park were not generally motivated to absorb
morality from the children of the rich. They were more
likely to take footballs from them.

Later, as the cost of domestic help rose and transportation to the suburbs improved, many of the families who
had originally occupied the row houses nearest the park
moved from the city. Their former one-family homes became rooming houses for the very poor. The northern edge
of the park became Spanish Harlem, and then, as the His-
panics moved to the east, their place was taken in part by
American blacks. Vandalism became a more serious problem than before; some of the handsomest small structures
in the park were destroyed, and in the areas that were still
safe, crowds were attracted by a band shell and a skating
rink with artificial ice. In neither case did the architecture
harmonize with what Vaux and Olmsted had originally
designed.

Now, a new, non-white middle class is beginning to
emerge, and the safer central sections of the park are providing these people with many recreational opportunities.
As the architectural preservation movement attracts more
patrons and adherents, restoration work on the buildings,
notably the Belvedere, has made magnificent progress.
But it seems unlikely that the park has been able to do
much to establish moral order among the urban masses.
Its service to the old and new elites has been invaluable; it
has provided other, less affluent people with invaluable
open space, where baseball, soccer, and touch football are
played (even to the dismay of some who believe they understand the purity of Olmsted's intentions). The problem
of the urban masses and moral order is probably as serious
today in New York as it was in the last century. And while

it is regrettable that the park did not make good on one of Olmsted's main reasons for its construction, there certainly remains much to rejoice in.

NOTES

1. M.M. Graff, *The Men Who Made Central Park* (New York: Greensward Foundation, 1982), p. 35.
2. Charles E. Beveridge and David Schuyler, eds., *The Papers of Frederick Law Olmsted,* volume 3 (Baltimore: Johns Hopkins University Press, 1983), p. 273, footnote 14.

18

The American Public Space

J. B. JACKSON

Those of us old enough to remember what America was like a half century ago have lived through a significant but largely unnoticed development in our landscape. By that I mean not the growth of our cities but a development that came about largely as a consequence of that growth: the great increase in the number and variety of public places all over the nation.

A public place is commonly defined as a place (or space) created and maintained by public authority, accessible to all citizens for their use and enjoyment. This tells us nothing about the different ways in which we use and enjoy them, nor about the different types of public involved, but we have only to look about us to see that they are often outside the center of town and even in the open country. Many have an educational purpose: historic zones, outdoor museums, botanical gardens. And more and more spaces are being designed to give us a brief experience of nature: hiking trails and wilderness areas and beaches, for example. When we include among the newer public spaces the parking lot, the trash disposal area, and the highway, it is evident that the public is being well provided for, not

From The Public Interest, *Winter 1984, pp. 52–65. Copyright © 1984 by National Affairs, Inc.*

only as far as places for enjoyment are concerned, but for their use as well.

Implicit in the word "public" is the presence of other people. We know better than to resent that presence; they have as much right to be there as we have. Just the same, it is characteristic of many modern public spaces that contact between persons is likely to be brief and noncommittal. Indeed, when the public is too numerous we are made uncomfortable. We did not come here for what an earlier generation called "togetherness," we came for an individual, private experience—a sequence of emotions, perceptions, sensations, of value to ourselves. This is not to say that we are unfriendly, merely that we do not necessarily associate every public place with social intercourse. We assume, in fact, that there are special places appropriate for that. Yet when we look for them today we find they are few.

CIVIC SPACE

Much has changed in America since the time when *every* public space was intended to be the setting for some collective, civic action. I think it can be said that beginning in the eighteenth century every public space—every piece of land controlled by the authorities—was meant to serve a public institution rather than to serve the public as an aggregate of individuals. In the newer planned towns of New England an area of public land was set aside for the support of the local church and its preacher, though not for public use. Section 16 in the townships created by the National Land Survey of 1785—the only designated public space in the township—was to support a local school. Hence its name: school section, still a feature of the western landscape. Communities more urban in character recognized the need for public spaces that the public could use, but only for the benefit of the community at large. The newly created towns of the late-eighteenth and early-nineteenth century almost invariably contained well-defined public places for the market, the drill field, the wharf, the "established" church, as well as places for a college or academy, and of course for public celebrations and public assembly. A civic function characterized them all; people were present in them to perform some public service or play some public role.

Public is a word without mystery: It derives from the Latin *populus*, and means belonging to or characteristic of the people. A public space is a people's space. But "people" as a word is less obvious. With us it simply means humanity, or a random sample of humanity, but until well into the nineteenth century it meant a specific group: sometimes the population of nation or a town, sometimes the lowest element in that population, but always an identifiable category. Thus a common phrase in England was "the nobility, the gentry, and the public." People in this sense implied an organization and a territory; and as an organization it had an organizing or form-giving authority.

Perhaps it can be said that, as a noun, "public" implied the population, or the people, while as an adjective it referred to the authorities. Thus a public building in the eighteenth century was not a place accessible to all, for their use and enjoyment, but was the working or meeting place of the authorities.

This strictly political meaning of the word helps us interpret the kind of public place or square found in most of the new towns and cities in colonial and post-colonial America. The invaluable collections of town plans in three books by John Reps show in some detail how early planners and promoters emphasized the importance of public places.[1] Each community, each town was given a grid plan or a variation on a grid, and though many of them were little more than a cluster of square blocks, invariably there was a symmetrical array of (proposed) public buildings on a piece of public land—courthouse, market, jail, etc.

It is interesting to see how faithful colonial and frontier America was to the early Renaissance practice of according more dignity to the building than to the square in front of it. Our own perception, of course, is the opposite: In our love of open spaces we see the building as "facing" the square, the square as the focal point in the urban composition. The eighteenth-century belief was that the square, however large and imposing, derived its dignity from its association with the building, and was in fact merely the place where the inhabitants gathered to pay homage to the authorities within. Many town maps indicate proposed smaller squares, inserted into what would eventually be built-up residential areas. These were undoubtedly meant to be surrounded and dignified by public buildings, as William Penn had proposed for the four minor squares in his plan for Philadelphia. It was only in the nineteenth century that these small squares were seen and treated as parks, and this change from concentrating on the public building to concentrating on the public space would eventually produce public places bearing little or no aesthetic relationship to their urban surroundings.

Few of these neo-classical towns ever grew to resemble their paper prototypes. Many grew in an entirely unpredicted way: into monolithic compositions of identical blocks, as in Chicago, which are ideally suited to the purposes of the real estate speculator. Others did not grow at all. But their plans are no less interesting for that. They are diagrams, provincial and greatly simplified, of what Americans wanted in the way of towns: a rational, egalitarian, political ordering of spaces and structures, a sharp division between public and private, so that spaces for recreation or non-political, non-civic functions were left to the private sector to provide as best it could. The only truly public, or people's, space was the large central public square where all qualified citizens came together: a vast architectural roofless room, a stage, where all acted out their familiar assigned roles. And this, I think, is what really distinguished the traditional public space from our contemporary public space. Two centuries ago, despite the Revolution, it was still widely believed that we were *already* citizens (to the extent that we could qualify) when we appeared in public. We knew our role, our rank and place, and the structured space surrounding us merely served to confirm our status. (Much as in certain denominations we are members of the community of Christians from the moment of baptism; our subsequent participation in certain rites within the church simply *confirms* our permanent religious status.) But now we believe the contrary—that we *become* citizens by certain experiences, private as well as public. Our variety of new specialized public spaces are by way of being places where we prepare ourselves—physically, socially, and even vocationally—for the role of citizen.

DECLINE OF THE SQUARE

There are still many among us who hold that our public spaces should perform the same civilizing, political role. Nevertheless, as the nineteenth century progressed it be-

came evident that the public square was losing prestige.
During the Revolution the centers of popular excitement
had been Faneuil Hall, Independence Hall, and the New
York Common. But when political oratory and political
demonstrations went out of fashion, the public began to
frequent the busier streets, the tree-lined promenades,
and the waterfront. Other developments gave the centrifu-
gal movement further impetus. Middle-class families felt
the attraction of the suburbs or of the independent home-
stead. Newcomers, many from overseas, had no sentiment
for the established customs, and in newer parts of town
evangelical churches competed with the established
church in the center. The coming of the railroad and the
factory and the mill shifted leisure time activities to the
less built-up outskirts of town; and finally the public
buildings themselves ceased to be the locus of real power,
and gradually became office buildings for the bureaucracy.
In almost every American town the traits Sam Bass Warner
has identified with mid-nineteenth century Philadelphia
became more and more prevalent:

> The effect of three decades of a building boom . . . was a city with-
> out squares of shops and public buildings, a city without gathering
> places which might have assisted in focusing the daily activities of
> neighborhoods. Instead of subcenters the process of building had
> created acres and acres of amorphous tracts—the architectural hall-
> mark of the nineteenth and twentieth century American big city.
> . . . Whatever community life there was to flourish from now on
> would have to flourish despite the physical form of the city, not be-
> cause of it.[2]

Though the older towns and cities of the East retained
their tradition of central park spaces, towns laid out in the
Midwest and throughout the Great Plains were predomi-
nately grid plans of uniform blocks. Some of them, judging from Reps's *Cities of the American West*, provided for one
or two "public squares" or "public grounds," yet few of
these were centrally located and it is hard to find any of
them associated with a public building. In many cases the
larger spaces set aside for parks were soon subdivided into
building lots. No doubt the reluctance to plan for public
spaces in the potentially valuable downtown can be ascribed to the proprietor's eagerness to make money in
downtown real estate. But by cutting straight through the
average small American town and establishing its station
and freightyards near main street, the railroad trans-

formed the traditional center in ways that the railroad in Europe was never allowed to do: There the station was exiled to the outskirts. Thus the American town very early in the game developed a substitute social center (for men only) around the station and freightyards—a combination skidrow, wholesale district, and horse transportation complex that seems to have offered a variety of illicit and lower class attractions, as well as being a center for news. But this was a poor substitute for the traditional urban space where citizens could forgather and talk, a place described by the anthropologist R. Baumann ''as special, isolated from others and enjoyed for its own sake, because talking there may be enjoyed for its own sake and not as part of another activity or for some special instrumental purpose.'' And so strong was the urge to have such places easily accessible yet detached from the workaday world that the American urban public, or a fraction of it, soon discovered a new and agreeable space on the outskirts of town—a favorite spot for relaxation and sociability. That was the cemetery.

THE RECREATIONAL CEMETERY

The story of the development of the so-called rural cemetery in America is familiar to anyone who knows our urban history. It began in 1831 with the designing of Mt. Auburn Cemetery in Cambridge, Massachusetts, as a picturesque landscape of wooded hills, winding roads with paths, and rustic compositions of lawn and stream with pleasant views over the Charles, all in the style of the landscaped gardens fashionable in England at that time. This new type of cemetery immediately became a popular goal of excursions from the city. To quote Norman Newton's account, Mt. Auburn ''soon became very popular as a quiet place in which to escape the bustle and clangor of the city—for strolling, for solitude, and even for family picnics. Following its success other cemeteries of the same type began to spring up.''[3]

These rural cemeteries, usually located within easy reach of the city, attracted thousands of pleasure-seeking visitors, both before the presence of graves and tombstones, and after. Downing estimated that more than 50,000 persons visited Greenwood Cemetery in Brooklyn in the course of nine months in 1848. They came on foot and in carriages. Guidebooks in hand, they admired the monuments and the artistic planting and the views. They wandered along the lanes and paths, and rested on the expanses of lawn, sketched, ate lunch, and even practiced a little shooting. They had discovered a kind of recreation that the city had never offered.

The generally-accepted explanation for the popularity of the rural or picturesque cemetery is that it satisfied the new romantic love of nature. No doubt this had something to do with the enthusiasm, but the existence of widespread nature romanticism among working class Americans—or indeed among working class Europeans—has yet to be established. What evidence we have is largely literary, and like our contemporary environmentalism, nature romanticism seems to have been essentially a middle-class movement. In the writings of A.J. Downing, one of the most influential exponents of romanticism in architecture and landscape architecture, there are frequent suggestions that a taste for the romantic was peculiar to persons of refinement and wealth. In fact we now know enough about the fashion to recognize that a carefully-designed and well-executed picturesque landscape park called for considerable skill. It was not a "natural" space, it was (in the hands of the artist-designer) a highly structured space, a "painterly" composition whose rules and techniques were inspired by established landscape painters. It was Olmsted who best understood the canons of the picturesque and who applied them on a grandiose scale in Central Park and Prospect Park. To the average urban working-class American, relaxing in a rural cemetery, the appeal of the new landscape was quite different from that of Downing's well-to-do patrons. He was less aware of the subtleties of romantic composition, or even of the possibility of a direct contact with nature, than of the apparent *lack* of structure. The informal landscape offered the delights of spontaneous contact with other people in a setting that in no way prescribed a certain dress code or a certain code of manners. It was a public space of a novel kind: full of surprises, where emotions and pleasures were fresh and easily shared. It was not simply another artificial space; it was an *environment*, a place for new, primarily social, experiences. It represented the rejection of structure, the rejection of classical urbanism with its historical allusions, and the rejection of architectural public space.

As further evidence that nature romanticism had little or nothing to do with the acceptance of the rural cemetery, we might consider another, less familiar example of the popular American preference for unstructured public places: the camp meetings or revivals, the evangelical gatherings which were numerous in rural and frontier communities through the first half of the nineteenth century. Each of them attracted hundreds of men and women and children, black as well as white, and each lasted several nights and days. Almost always they had a forest background. Yet despite the wilderness setting and the prevailing emotionalism, it would be hard to find any trace of nature awareness in the proceedings, nor in their religious experiences. On the contrary: The forest seemed to free men and women from *any* environmental influences. Again, it was the lack of structure, the lack of behavioral design that produced the exhilaration.

OLMSTED'S ISOLATED ART-WORKS

The park movement did not evolve out of the Great Revival, but out of the rural cemetery. It was a remarkable instance of how quickly and effectively Americans can respond to a humanitarian need—in this case the need for agreeable, healthy, and beautiful places where the urban population could enjoy itself and (of course) have contact with nature. In 1851 the New York legislature authorized the city to acquire some 840 acres for a public park. Seven years later Frederick Law Olmsted had won the design competition and work had begun on Central Park.

Ten years after that, despite the intervening war, there was not a major American city without a rural park, or the prospect of one, and many of those parks had been designed by Olmsted and his associates. Though at the beginning there were expressions of disapproval—the park would be taken over by rowdies, it was too large, it lacked the more formal qualities of the European royal parks—it was not long before parks in general were accepted as invaluable from the point of view of health, of innocent recreation, and as antidotes for the crowded and filthy city slums. Innumerable rural parks were created in smaller towns, and in the new towns of the West. It would be impossible to identify the number of college campuses, courthouses and institutional landscape designs, to say nothing of the landscaped cemeteries, that helped beautify communities throughout the country. Few of these spaces were designed by professionals. Most were the work of local amateur gardeners, and the transformation of many New England commons into neat little parks was frequently done by local women's organizations. For the most part these smaller, unpublicized parks were of no great artistic worth. They had their small lakes, their bandstands, their pretzel paths, and a monotony of elms or cottonwoods, but it must be said that they kept alive the civic tradition of public spaces at a time when the great Olmsted parks were fighting it. In those provincial parks political orators addressed the voters, band concerts were given, ethnic pageants were organized, and patriotic flowerbeds were admired. In the 1890s Frank Waugh, the landscape architect, described the typical western park as containing "race tracks, baseball grounds, camp meeting stands, carp ponds, fountains or fences."

It was this indiscriminate mixture of uses that horrified the readers of *Garden and Forest*, the organ of the Olmsted school of landscape design. For by the end of the century there had developed a very self-assured set of standards for the design of rural parks, and the most fundamental rule was that the "primary purpose of a rural park within reach of a great city is to furnish that rest and refreshment of mind and body which come from the tranquilizing influence of contact with natural scenery." This implied two restrictions: First, no building of any kind was to be erected in the park, nor (in the words of Olmsted's son John) "formal gardens, statuary, conservatories, botanical or zoological gardens, concert groves, electric fountains or the like; also popular athletic grounds, parade grounds, ball grounds for boys and facilities for boating and bathing." These installations were not themselves objectionable, and could well have been harmonized with "contact with nature." But the park was *not* nature, or a "natural environment." It was *scenery*, a whole landscape where the visitor could wander for hours over meadows and through woods and next to lakes and streams. For such was Olmsted's ideal: The park as a three-dimensional work of art. This in turn meant that the park should be visibly isolated from the surrounding city, enclosed by an impenetrable wall of greenery, so that the outside urban world would never impinge on the ''rural'' landscape, or on the experience of those visitors seeking rest and ''refreshment of mind and body.''

OXYGEN AND VIRTUE

On aesthetic as well as on demographic grounds, there were reasons for this uncompromising isolation. But remoteness also promoted what Downing, Olmsted, and others had always considered the true role of the rural park: the physical and moral regeneration of the individual visitor. From the very beginning of the park movement there had been frequent references to the elevating influence that the rural park would have. ''No one who has closely observed the conduct of the people who visit the park,'' Olmsted wrote, ''can doubt it exercises a distinctly harmonizing and refining influence upon the most unfortunate and lawless classes of the icty—an influence favorable to courtesy, self-control and temperance.'' To supplement this influence, Olmsted created a special park police force to control misconduct, including walking on the grass. But he also relied on the force of example to give the poor ''an education to refinement and taste and the mental and moral capital of gentlemen.'' This was to come from observing and emulating the manners and behavior of upper-class visitors to the park. As Thomas Bender notes, ''Olmsted's generation saw no difficulty in recommending that Central Park, their symbol of the democratic community, be surrounded by elegant private villas that would exert an elevating influence upon the masses who visited the park.''[4]

The early vision of the rural park and its function survived intact for no more than fifty years. One of its original objectives had been the improvement of the health of city dwellers. But medical science soon proved that this was not simply a matter of fresh air and contact with nature; it was a matter of training, and the park was the appropriate place for such training. ''Foul air prompts vice,'' said a New York physician, ''and oxygen to virtue as surely as the sunlight paints the flowers of our garden. . . . The varied opportunities of a park would educate [the slum child] and his family in the enjoyment of open-air pleasures. Deprived of these, he and his are educated into the ways of disease and vice by the character of their surroundings.''

In the 1880s the well-organized playground movement, which had started by providing small playgrounds in the slums, demanded access to the park, and at much the same time a public eager for places to play various outdoor games brought pressure on the city to provide appropriate space. ''It was easier to persuade the city fathers to make use of existing parks than to purchase additional land for recreation. . . . In some cases the introduction of recreational facilities was achieved with intelligence and in conformity with the original park design. In other instances the results were detrimental to the former park purpose.''[5]

At the time of Olmsted's death in 1903 the park had largely ceased to be an environment in which the individual could enjoy solitary contact with nature, and had become an environment dedicated to guidance in recreation, health, citizenship, and nature knowledge. It was often crowded with cultural and recreational facilities, group activities, and increasingly populated by professional recreationists, playground supervisors, and leadership counselors. Even the definition of the park underwent drastic revision: It is now described in official documents as an open space, containing public facilities and with the appearance of a natural landscape. It is merely one element in a nation-wide ecosystem.

THE LANDSCAPE OF DIVERSITY

In retrospect, how unpredictable and how extraordinary was the change over a period of less than a century in the American concept of public spaces! The neo-classical square, in part surrounded by public buildings, and located in the heart of the city, had been the symbol of political status, recognized by all. In the 1860s, however, the rural park began to replace it in the public perception, and the rural park not only rejected any contact with architecture and formal urbanism, but was located as far as possible from workaday activities, as if to say: Here is the true center, the place where nature established the laws.

But perhaps the most dramatic contrast between the two public spaces was in their respective definitions of community. The neo-classical square implied a body of people, politically and socially homogeneous, inhabiting a well-defined political territory with clear-cut class divisions. The visitors to the rural park came singly, each in pursuit of an individual contact with nature, a private experience. The ideal romantic community was the garden suburb, where reverence for the environment was the only common bond, and anything like an urban or political center was discouraged. Where can such a center be seen in Olmsted's design for Riverside, the Chicago suburb? It is a pleasant tangle of curving roads and lanes where all residences are isolated by greenery. Community did not mean homogeneity or uniformity, it meant diversity, and nothing was more gratifying to Olmsted than to see a diverse public in Central Park. Again and again he described ''the persons brought closely together, poor and rich, young and old, Jew and Gentile.'' But this was a diversity of *individuals*. When the various recreational activities invaded the park in the 1880s, what ensued was a diversity of *groups*: age groups, ethnic groups, sports groups, neighborhood groups. That was quite another kind of diversity, and the spaces occupied by these groups, if only temporarily, constituted so many public places in the strictest sense: places where like-minded people came together to share an identity.

The emergence of these hitherto non-existent groups was probably the greatest contribution of the rural park. Long after the old-fashioned solitary pursuit of the contact with nature had vanished from the scene, these miniature societies with special identities continued to flourish and to acquire increasing public recognition over the years. Eventually they expanded beyond the park, and I think it was the automobile that encouraged this dispersal.

Though it is common practice to blame the automobile for having destroyed many territorial communities—particularly rural ones—the car has made it possible for us to come together over great distances and in a shorter length of time than ever before, and this in turn has made possible the creation of many new and different public spaces throughout the landscape. Without the automobile countless recreational areas, monuments, national parks, to say nothing of remoter sections of our cities, would never have become part of those experiences which Americans always pursue. Quite aside from what they teach us, they serve as way-stations, as it were, in our American, essentially Protestant, pilgrimage of self-perfection through endless education.

We do well to encourage the creation of all such spaces combining recreation with knowledge of nature and of our past. Their popularity is their best reason for existing. Yet many of us are aware that another, no less important public space, the one where we seek out and enjoy the company and stimulation of others, has been much neglected. We have outgrown the classical monumental square with its political overtones. We now seldom congregate as citizens, and when we do, it is more to protest than to celebrate our collective identity. We have learned from experience that such oversize public spaces—and I would certainly include the Olmsted style park with its oversize natural landscapes—eventually can be subverted by the authorities and used to indoctrinate us with some establishment philosophy: the Wonders of Nature, the Wonders of Art, the Wonders of Physical Fitness, or the supreme Wonders of the Commissars looking down at us from their podium. Small, more intimate, less structured spaces are what we now prefer. ''This loss of the natural impulse to monumentality,'' John Summerson observed, ''should not be a matter of regret. It is a perfectly natural reflection of the change which is taking place in the whole character of western culture. All those things which suggested and supported monumentality are in dissolution. The corporate or social importance of religion was one of them. The sense of the dominance of a class—of the exclusive possession of certain privileges by certain groups—was another.''[6]

To these things supporting monumentality in the past must be added the concept of a monolithic Public, the concept of a homogeneous People. For the public now is a composition of constantly shifting, overlapping groups—ethnic groups, social groups, age groups, special interest groups—and each of them, at one time or another, needs its own space, distinct from the surrounding urban fabric, where its own special social forms, its own special language and set of relations, can flourish, a space which confers a brief visibility on the group. We have too few of these spaces today, too few resembling the Prado in the North End of Boston, or the ad hoc open air social spaces which often evolve in urban ethnic or racial neighborhoods and do so much to maintain a sense of local identity and custom. With great taste and infinite goodwill, landscape architects have designed many mini-parks to relieve the monotony of our towns and cities. But the Olmsted tradition persists, and what we all too often have are overelaborate spaces with the inevitable display of vegetation, the inevitable ingenious fountain, and the inevitable emphasis on individual isolation. Yet contact with other people, not contact with nature, is what most of us are really after.

A RETURN TO THE STREET

Despite our current admiration for the formal square as a feature of the urban scene, despite our attempts to introduce it in our residential areas and shopping centers and in urban renewal projects, the time is approaching, I suspect, when we will turn our attention elsewhere. There are in fact many signs that the street, or a given fragment of the street, will be the true public space of the future.

If in fact this is the case, we will be reverting, unconsciously of course, to a medieval urban concept which long preceded the Renaissance concept of the public square. In the Middle Ages it was the street—tortuous, dirty, crowded—and not the public space identified with the church or castle or market, that was the center of economic and social life. The street was the place of work, the place of buying and selling, the place of meeting and negotiating, and the scene of the important religious and civic ceremonies and processions.

But its most significant trait was its blending of domestic and public life, its interplay of two distinct kinds of space. The narrow, overcrowded buildings bordering it spilled over into the street and transformed it into a place of workshops, kitchens, and merchandising, into a place of leisure and sociability, and confrontation of every kind. It was this confusion of functions, the confusion of two different realms of law and custom, that made the medieval

street a kind of city within a city, and the scene of innovations in policing, maintenance, and social reform. Until
the eighteenth century the street was actually something
far more extensive than the travelled space between the
houses. It was the matrix of a community, always alive to
threats of intrusion, jealous of privileges and customs, and
conscious of its own unique character.

For many economic, social, and aesthetic reasons, we
are now beginning to think of the street and its relation to
its inhabitants in a way that recalls the medieval concept.
Robert Gutman wrote:

> The revival of interest in the urban street has been accompanied by
> a wholly new emphasis in the view of the street's primary social
> function. Put simply, what sets the contemporary idea apart from
> previous definitions is the conviction that the street should be de-
> signed and managed for the benefit of its residents. . . . These im-
> pulses to make the street work, to make it into a community, some
> of which are specific to the situation of the city today, have gained
> strength because . . . the residents of urban streets until recently
> regarded themselves as a relatively homogeneous population. This
> important point is often overlooked. We are concerned about the
> street community in large part because for the very first time in the
> history of cities the simple virtues and joys of urban life have been
> diminished for all social groups; and we connect this reduction in
> our level of satisfaction and safety with the breakdown of the com-
> munity.[7]

Not every street can be defined as an essential spatial
element in a community. The majority will continue to be
public utilities. But insofar as certain streets will be seen as
public places, as being closely related to their immediate
built environment, they will be playing the social role we
have long associated with the traditional public square: the
place where we exhibit our permanent identity as members of the community. The learning experience, the experience of contact with new sensations, new people, new
ideas belongs elsewhere. The street as the public space of a
community, modest in size, simple in structure, will serve
a strictly traditional purpose. It will be where, in the words
of Paul Weiss, we recognize and abide by ''a mosaic of accepted customs, conventions, habitual ways of evaluating,
responding, and acting . . . men must, to be perfected, become social beings. They must act to make the structure of
the group an integral part of themselves and a desirable
link with others.''

NOTES

1. John Reps, *The Making of Urban America* (Princeton: Princeton University Press, 1965), *Tidewater Towns* (Williamsburg VA: The Colonial Williamsburg Foundation, 1972), *Cities of the American West* (Princeton: Princeton University Press, 1979).

2. Sam Bass Warner Jr., *Private City* (Philadelphia: University of Pennsylvania Press, 1968), p. 55.

3. Norman Newton, *Design on the Land* (Cambridge MA: Harvard University Press, 1971), p. 268.

4. Thomas Bender, *Toward an Urban Vision* (Lexington KY: University Press of Kentucky, 1975), p. 179.

5. George Butler, ''Change in the City Parks,'' *Landscape 8* (Winter 1958–59).

6. John N. Summerson, *Heavenly Mansions* (New York: Norton Library, 1963).

7. Robert Gutman, ''The Street Generation,'' in *On Streets*, Stanford Anderson, ed. (Cambridge MA: MIT Press, 1978).

19

The Social Life of Small Urban Spaces

WILLIAM H. WHYTE

INTRODUCTION

This book is about city spaces, why some work for people, and some do not, and what the practical lessons may be. It is a by-product of first-hand observation.

In 1970, I formed a small research group. The Street Life Project, and began looking at city spaces. At that time, direct observation had long been used for the study of people in far-off lands. It had not been used to any great extent in the U.S. city. There was much concern over urban crowding, but most of the research on the issue was done somewhere other than where it supposedly occurred. The most notable studies were of crowded animals, or of students and members of institutions responding to experimental situations—often valuable research, to be sure, but somewhat vicarious.

The Street Life Project began its study by looking at New York City parks and playgrounds and such informal recreation areas as city blocks. One of the first things that

From William H. Whyte, The Social Life of Small Urban Spaces *(Washington, D.C.: The Conservation Foundation, 1980), pp. 10–23, 54–59, 76–81.*

struck us was the *lack* of crowding in many of these areas. A few were jammed, but more were nearer empty than full, often in neighborhoods that ranked very high in density of people. Sheer space, obviously, was not of itself attracting children. Many streets were.

It is often assumed that children play in the street because they lack playground space. But many children play in the streets because they like to. One of the best play areas we came across was a block on 101st Street in East Harlem. It had its problems, but it worked. The street itself was the play area. Adjoining stoops and fire escapes provided prime viewing across the street and were highly functional for mothers and older people. There were other factors at work, too, and, had we been more prescient, we could have saved ourselves a lot of time spent later looking at plazas. Though we did not know it then, this block had within it all the basic elements of a successful urban place.

As our studies took us nearer the center of New York, the imbalance in space use was even more apparent. Most of the crowding could be traced to a series of choke points—subway stations, in particular. In total, these spaces are only a fraction of downtown, but the number of people using them is so high, the experience so abysmal, that it colors our perception of the city around, out of all proportion to the space involved. The fact that there may be lots of empty space somewhere else little mitigates the discomfort. And there is a strong carry-over effect.

This affects researchers, too. We see what we expect to see, and have been so conditioned to see crowded spaces in center city that it is often difficult to see empty ones. But when we looked, there they were.

The amount of space, furthermore, was increasing. Since 1961, New York City has been giving incentive bonuses to builders who provided plazas. For each square foot of plaza, builders could add 10 square feet of commercial floor space over and above the amount normally permitted by zoning. So they did—without exception. Every new office building provided a plaza or comparable space: in total, by 1972, some 20 acres of the world's most expensive open space.

We discovered that some plazas, especially at lunchtime, attracted a lot of people. One, the plaza of the Seagram Building, was the place that helped give the city the

idea for the plaza bonus. Built in 1958, this austerely elegant area had not been planned as a people's plaza, but
that is what it became. On a good day, there would be a
hundred and fifty people sitting, sunbathing, picnicking,
and shmoozing—idly gossiping, talking "nothing talk."
People also liked 77 Water Street, known as "swingers'
plaza" because of the young crowd that populated it.

But on most plazas, we didn't see many people. The
plazas weren't used for much except walking across. In the
middle of the lunch hour on a beautiful, sunny day the
number of people sitting on plaza average four per 1,000
square feet of space—an extraordinarily low figure for so
dense a center. The tightest-knit CBD (central business district) anywhere contained a surprising amount of open
space that was relatively empty and unused.

If places like Seagram's and 77 Water Street could work
so well, why not the others? The city was being had. For
the millions of dollars of extra space it was handing out to
builders, it had every right to demand much better plazas
in return.

I put the question to the chairman of the City Planning
Commission, Donald Elliott. As a matter of fact, I en-
trapped him into spending a weekend looking at time-
lapse films of plaza use and nonuse. He felt that tougher
zoning was in order. If we could find out why the good
plazas worked and the bad ones didn't, and come up with
hard guidelines, we could have the basis of a new code.
Since we could expect the proposals to be strongly contested, it would be important to document the case to a
fare-thee-well.

We set to work. We began studying a cross-section of
spaces—in all, 16 plazas, 3 small parks, and a number of
odds and ends. I will pass over the false starts, the dead
ends, and the floundering arounds, save to note that there
were a lot and that the research was nowhere as tidy and
sequential as it can seem in the telling. Let me also note
that the findings should have been staggeringly obvious to
us had we thought of them in the first place. But we
didn't. Opposite propositions were often what seemed obvious. We arrived at our eventual findings by a succession
of busted hypotheses.

The research continued for some three years. I like to
cite the figure because it sounds impressive. But it is calen-

dar time. For all practical purposes, at the end of six months we had completed our basic research and arrived at our recommendations. The City, alas, had other concerns on its mind, and we found that communicating the findings was to take more time than arriving at them. We logged many hours in church basements and meeting rooms giving film and slide presentations to community groups, architects, planners, businessmen, developers, and real-estate people. We continued our research; we had to keep our findings up-to-date, for now we were disciplined by adversaries. But at length the City Planning Commission incorporated our recommendations in a proposed new open-space zoning code, and in May 1975 it was adopted by the city's Board of Estimate. As a consequence, there has been a salutary improvement in the design of new spaces and the rejuvenation of old ones.

But zoning is certainly not the ideal way to achieve the better design of spaces. It ought to be done for its own sake. For economics alone, it makes sense. An enormous expenditure of design expertise, and of travertine and steel, went into the creation of the many really bum office-building plazas around the country. To what end? As this manual will detail, it is far easier, simpler to create spaces that work for people than those that do not—and a tremendous difference it can make to the life of a city.

THE LIFE OF PLAZAS

We started by studying how people use plazas. We mounted time lapse cameras overlooking the plazas and recorded daily patterns. We talked to people to find where they came from, where they worked, how frequently they used the place and what they thought of it. But, mostly, we watched people to see what they did.

Most of the people who use plazas, we found, are young office workers from nearby buildings. There may be relatively few patrons from the plaza's own building; as some secretaries confide, they'd just as soon put a little distance between themselves and the boss. But commuter distances are usually short; for most plazas, the effective market radius is about three blocks. Small parks, like Paley and Greenacre in New York, tend to have more assorted patrons throughout the day—upper-income older people,

people coming from a distance. But office workers still predominate, the bulk from nearby.

This uncomplicated demography underscores an elemental point about good urban spaces: supply creates demand. A good new space builds a new constituency. It stimulates people into new habits—al fresco lunches—and provides new paths to and from work, new places to pause. It does all this very quickly. In Chicago's Loop, there were no such amenities not so long ago. Now, the plaza of the First National Bank has thoroughly changed the midday way of life for thousands of people. A success like this in no way surfeits demand for spaces; it indicates how great the unrealized potential is.

The best-used plazas are sociable places, with a higher proportion of couples than you find in less-used places, more people in groups, more people meeting people, or exchanging goodbyes. At five of the most-used plazas in New York, the proportion of people in groups run about 45 percent; in five of the least used, 32 percent. A high proportion of people in groups is an index of selectivity. When people go to a place in twos or threes or rendezvous there, it is most often because they have decided to. Nor are these sociable places less congenial to the individual. In absolute numbers, they attract more individuals than do less-used spaces. If you are alone, a lively place can be the best place to be.

The most-used places also tend to have a higher than average proportion of women. The male-female ratio of a plaza basically reflects the composition of the work force, which varies from area to area—in midtown New York it runs about 60 percent male, 40 percent female. Women are more discriminating than men as to where they will sit, more sensitive to annoyances, and women spend more time casting the various possibilities. If a plaza has a markedly lower than average proportion of women, something is wrong. Where there is a higher than average proportion of women, the plaza is probably a good one and has been chosen as such.

The rhythms of plaza life are much alike from place to place. In the morning hours, patronage will be sporadic. A hot-dog vendor setting up his cart at the corner, elderly pedestrians pausing for a rest, a delivery messenger or two, a shoeshine man, some tourists, perhaps an odd type, like a scavenger woman with shopping bags. If there is any construction work in the vicinity, hard hats will appear shortly after 11:00 A.M. with beer cans and sandwiches. Things will start to liven up. Around noon, the main clientele begins to arrive. Soon, activity will be near peak and will stay there until a little before 2:00 P.M. Some 80 percent of the total hours of use will be concentrated in these two hours. In mid and late afternoon, use is again sporadic. If there's a special event, such as a jazz concert, the flow going home will be tapped, with people staying as late as 6:00 or 6:30 P.M. Ordinarily, however, plazas go dead by 6:00 and stay that way until the next morning.

During peak hours the number of people on a plaza will vary considerably according to seasons and weather. The way people distribute themselves over the space, however, will be fairly consistent, with some sectors getting heavy use day in and day out, others much less. In our sightings we find it easy to map every person, but the patterns are regular enough that you could count the number in only one sector, then multiply by a given factor, and come within a percent or so of the total number of people at the plaza.

Off-peak use often gives the best clues to people's preferences. When a place is jammed, a person sits where he can. This may or may not be where he most wants to. After the main crowd has left, the choices can be significant. Some parts of the plaza become quite empty; others continue to be used. At Seagram's, a rear ledge under the trees is moderately, but steadily, occupied when other ledges are empty; it seems the most uncrowded of places, but on a cumulative basis it is the best-used part of Seagram's.

Men show a tendency to take the front-row seats, and, if there is a kind of gate, men will be the guardians of it. Women tend to favor places slightly secluded. If there are double-sided benches parallel to a street, the inner side will usually have a high proportion of women; the outer, of men.

Of the men up front, the most conspicuous are girl watchers. They work at it, and so demonstratively as to suggest that their chief interest may not really be the girls so much as the show of watching them. Generally, the watchers line up quite close together, in groups of three to five. If they are construction workers, they will be very demonstrative, much given to whistling, laughing, direct salutations. This is also true of most girl watchers in New York's financial area. In midtown, they are more inhibited, playing it coolly, with a good bit of sniggering and smirking, as if the girls were not measuring up. It is all machismo, however, whether uptown or downtown. Not once have we ever seen a girl watcher pick up a girl, or attempt to.

Few others will either. Plazas are not ideal places for striking up acquaintances, and even on the most sociable of them, there is not much mingling. When strangers are in proximity, the nearest thing to an exchange is what Erving Goffman has called civil inattention. If there are, say, two smashing blondes on a ledge, the men nearby will usually put on an elaborate show of disregard. Watch closely, however, and you will see them give themselves away with covert glances, involuntary primping of the hair, tugs at the earlobe.

Lovers are to be found on plazas. But not where you would expect them. When we first started interviewing, people told us we'd find lovers in the rear places (pot smokers, too). But they weren't usually there. They would be out front. The most fervent embracing we've recorded on film has usually taken place in the most visible of locations, with the couple oblivious of the crowd.

Certain locations become rendezvous points for coteries of various kinds. For a while, the south wall of Chase plaza was a gathering point for camera bugs, the kind who like to buy new lenses and talk about them. Patterns of this sort may last no more than a season—or persist for years. Some time ago, one particular spot became a gathering place for raffish younger people; since then, there have been many changeovers in personnel, but it is still a gathering place for raffish younger people.

What attracts people most, it would appear, is other people. If I belabor the point, it is because many urban spaces are being designed as though the opposite were true, and that what people liked best were the places they stay away from. People often do talk along such lines; this is why their responses to questionnaires can be so misleading. How many people would say they like to sit in the middle of a crowd? Instead, they speak of getting away from it all, and use terms like "escape," "oasis," "retreat." What people *do*, however, reveals a different priority.

This was first brought home to us in a study of street conversations. When people stop to have a conversation, we wondered, how far away do they move from the main pedestrian flow? We were especially interested in finding out how much of the normally unused buffer space next to buildings would be used. So we set up time-lapse cameras overlooking several key street corners and began plotting the location of all conversations lasting a minute or longer.

People didn't move out of the main pedestrian flow. They stayed in it or moved into it, and the great bulk of the conversations were smack in the center of the flow—the 100 percent location, to use the real-estate term. The same gravitation characterized "traveling conversations"—the kind in which two men move about, alternating the roles of straight man and principal talker. There is a lot of apparent motion. But if you plot the orbits, you will find they are usually centered around the 100 percent spot.

Just why people behave like this, we have never been able to determine. It is understandable that conversations should originate within the main flow. Conversations are incident to pedestrian journeys; where there are the most people, the likelihood of a meeting or a leave-taking is highest. What is less explainable is people's inclination to remain in the main flow, blocking traffic, being jostled by it. This does not seem to be a matter of inertia but of choice—instinctive, perhaps, but by no means illogical. In the center of the crowd you have the maximum choice—to break off, to continue—much as you have in the center of a cocktail party, itself a moving conversation growing ever denser and denser.

People also sit in the mainstream. At the Seagram plaza, the main pedestrian paths are on diagonals from the building entrance to the corners of the steps. These are natural junction and transfer points and there is usually a lot of activity at them. They are also a favored place for sitting and picnicking. Sometimes there will be so many people that pedestrians have to step carefully to negotiate the steps. The pedestrians rarely complain. While some will detour around the blockage, most will thread their way through it.

Standing patterns are similar. When people stop to talk on a plaza, they usually do so in the middle of the traffic stream. They also show an inclination to station themselves near objects, such as a flagpole or a statue. They like well-defined places, such as steps, or the border of a pool. What they rarely choose is the middle of a large space.

There are a number of explanations. The preference for pillars might be ascribed to some primeval instinct: you have a full view of all comers but your rear is covered. But this doesn't explain the inclination men have for lining up at the curb. Typically, they face inwards, toward the sidewalk, with their backs exposed to the dangers of the street.

Foot movements are consistent, too. They seem to be a sort of silent language. Often, in a shmoozing group no one will be saying anything. Men stand bound in amiable silence, surveying the passing scene. Then, slowly, rhythmically, one of the men rocks up and down: first on the ball of the foot, then back on the heel. He stops. Another man starts the same movement. Sometimes there are reciprocal gestures. One man makes a half turn to the right. Then, after a rhythmic interval, another responds with a half turn to the left. Some kind of communication seems to be taking place here, but I've never broken the code.

Whatever they may mean, people's movements are one of the great spectacles of a plaza. You do not see this in architectural photographs, which typically are empty of life and are taken from a perspective few people share. It is a quite misleading one. At eye level the scene comes alive with movement and color—people walking quickly, walking slowly, skipping up steps, weaving in and out on crossing patterns, accelerating and retarding to match the moves of the others. There is a beauty that is beguiling to watch, and one senses that the players are quite aware of it themselves. You see this, too, in the way they arrange themselves on steps and ledges. They often do so with a grace that they, too, must sense. With its brown-gray monochrome, Seagram's is the best of settings—especially in the rain, when an umbrella or two spots color in the right places, like Corot's red dots.

How peculiar are such patterns to New York? Our working assumption was that behavior in other cities would probably differ little, and subsequent comparisons have proved our assumption correct. The important variable is city size. As I will discuss in more detail, in smaller cities, densities tend to be lower, pedestrians move at a slower pace, and there is less of the social activity characteristic of high-traffic areas. In most other respects, pedestrian patterns are similar.

Observers in other countries have also noted the tendency to self-congestion. In his study of pedestrians in Copenhagen, architect Jan Gehl mapped bunching patterns almost identical to those observable here. Matthew Ciolek studied an Australian shopping center, with similar results. ''Contrary to 'common sense' expectations.'' Ciolek notes, ''the great majority of people were found to select their sites for social interaction right on or very close to the traffic lines intersecting the plaza. Relatively few people formed their gatherings away from the spaces used for navigation.''

The strongest similarities are found among the world's largest cities. People in them tend to behave more like their counterparts in other world cities than like fellow nationals in smaller cities. Big-city people walk faster, for one thing, and they self-congest. After we had completed our New York study, we made a brief comparison study of Tokyo and found the proclivity to stop and talk in the middle of department-store doorways, busy corners, and the like, is just as strong in that city as in New York. For all the cultural differences, sitting patterns in parks and plazas are much the same, too. Similarly, shmoozing patterns in Milan's Galleria are remarkably like those in New York's garment center. Modest conclusion: given the basic elements of a center city—such as high pedestrian volumes, and concentration and mixture of activities—people in one place tend to act much like people in another. . . .

THE STREET

Now we come to the key space for a plaza. It is not on the plaza. It is the street. The other amenities we have been discussing are indeed important: sitting space, sun, trees, water, food. But they can be added. The relationship to the street is integral, and it is far and away the critical design factor.

A good plaza starts at the street corner. If it's a busy corner, it has a brisk social life of its own. People will not just be waiting there for the light to change. Some will be fixed in conversation; others, in some phase of a prolonged goodbye. If there's a vendor at the corner, people will cluster around him, and there will be considerable two-way traffic back and forth between plaza and corner.

The activity on the corner is a great show and one of the best ways to make the most of it is, simply, not to wall it off. A front-row position is prime space; if it is sittable, it draws the most people. Too often, however, it is not sittable and sometimes by an excruciatingly small margin. Railings atop ledges will do it. At the General Motors Building on Fifth Avenue in New York City, for example, the front ledge faces one of the best of urban scenes. The ledge would be eminently sittable if only there weren't a railing atop it, placed exactly five and three-quarter inches in. Another two inches and you could sit comfortably. Canted ledges offer similar difficulties, especially in conjunction with prickly shrubbery.

Another key feature of the street is retailing—stores, windows with displays, signs to attract your attention, doorways, people going in and out of them. Big new office buildings have been eliminating stores. What they have been replacing them with is a frontage of plate glass through which you can behold bank officers sitting at desks. One of these stretches is dull enough. Block after block of them creates overpowering dullness. The Avenue of the Americas in New York has so many storeless plazas that the few remaining stretches of vulgar streetscape are now downright appealing.

As a condition of an open-space bonus, developers should be required to devote at least 50 percent of the ground-floor frontage to retail and food uses, and the new New York City zoning so stipulates. Market pressures, fortunately, are now working to the same end. At the time of our study, banks were outbidding stores for ground-level space. Since then, the banks have been cutting back, and economics have been tipping things to stores. But it does not hurt to have a requirement.

The area where the street and plaza or open space meet is a key to success or failure. Ideally, the transition should be such that it's hard to tell where one ends and the other begins. New York's Paley Park is the best of examples. The sidewalk in front is an integral part of the park. An arborlike foliage of trees extends over the sidewalk. There are urns of flowers at the curb and, on either side of the steps, curved sitting ledges. In this foyer, you can usually find somebody waiting for someone else—it is a convenient rendezvous point—people sitting on the ledges, and, in the middle of the entrance, several people in conversations.

Passersby are users of Paley, too. About half will turn and look in. Of these, about half will smile. I haven't calculated a smile index, but this vicarious, secondary enjoyment is extremely important—the sight of the park, the knowledge that it is there, becomes part of the image we have of a much wider area. (If one had to make a cost-benefit study, I think it would show that secondary use provides as much, if not more, benefit than the primary use. If one could put a monetary value on a minute of visual enjoyment and multiply that by instances day after day, year after year, one would obtain a rather stupendous sum.)

The park stimulates impulse use. Many people will do a double take as they pass by, pause, move a few steps, then, with a slight acceleration, go on up the steps. Children do it more vigorously, the very young ones usually pointing at the park and tugging at their mothers to go on in, many of the older ones breaking into a run just as they approach the steps, then skipping a step or two.

Watch these flows and you will appreciate how very important steps can be. The steps at Paley are so low and easy that one is almost pulled to them. They add a nice ambiguity to your movement. You can stand and watch, move up a foot, another, and, then, without having made a conscious decision, find yourself in the park. The steps at Greenacre Park and at Seagram's plaza are similarly low and inviting.

A slight elevation, then, can be beckoning. Go a foot or so higher, however, and usage will fall off sharply. There is no set cut-off level—it is as much psychological as physical—but it does seem bound up with how much of a choice the steps require. One plaza that people could be expected to use, but don't, is only a foot or so higher than two comparable ones nearby. It seems much higher. The steps are constricted in width, sharply defined by railings, and their pitch is brisk. No ambiguity here; no dawdling; no drifting up.

Sightlines are important. If people do not see a space, they will not use it. In the center of Kansas City is a park just high enough above eye level that most passersby do not realize it is there. As a result, it's lost. Similarly lost is a small, sunny plaza in Seattle. It would be excellent and likely quite popular for sitting—if people could see it from the street, which they cannot.

Unless there is a compelling reason, an open space shouldn't be sunk. With two or three notable exceptions, sunken plazas are dead spaces. You find few people in them; if there are stores, there are apt to be dummy window displays to mask the vacancies. Unless the plaza is on the way to the subway, why go down into it? Once there, you feel rather as if you were at the bottom of a well. People look at you. You don't look at them.

One of the best students of spaces I know is the dancer Marilyn Woods. With her troupe, she has staged stunning "celebrations" of public places across the country. These celebrations are an intensification of the natural choreography of a place. The best places, not too surprisingly, make for the best performances, the most appreciative audiences. (Seagram's and Cincinnati's Fountain Square are at the top of the list.) Significantly, the only places where her celebrations didn't work were sunken plazas. They felt dead, Woods recalls, as if a wall had been put between the dancers and the audience.

What about Rockefeller Plaza? It is a very successful place, and it has a sunken plaza in the middle. So it has. Those who cite it, however, are usually unaware of how it works. The plaza is a great urban space, but the lower plaza is only one part, and it is not where most of the people are. They are in the tiers of an amphitheater. The people in the lower plaza provide the show. In winter, there is skating; in summer, an open-air cafe and frequent concerts. The great bulk of the people—usually about 80 percent—are up above: at the railings along the street, along the mezzanine level just below, or on the broad walkway heading down from Fifth Avenue.

What gets copied? Some cities have dug near facsimiles of Rockefeller Center's lower plaza, in one case to the exact dimensions of the skating rink. What they haven't copied is the surrounding space. They wind up having a stage without a theater, a hole without the doughnut. And they wonder what went wrong.

The plaza of the First National Bank of Chicago is also quite sunken—some 18 feet below street level. And it is the most popular plaza in the country, with well over 1,000 people at lunchtime on a nice day. It is successful because just about everything has been done to make it successful—there is plenty of sitting space, a splendid outdoor cafe, a fountain, murals by Chagall, and usually music and entertainment of some kind at lunchtime.

The First National Bank plaza has an excellent relationship to the street. The sidewalks are part of its space, and there is a strong secondary use by the thousands who pass by. Many pause to look at what's going on. Some will drift down a few steps, then a few more. Again, an amphitheater—with several tiers of people looking at people who are looking at people who are looking at the show. . . .

INDOOR SPACES

As an alternative to plazas, builders have been turning to indoor spaces. There are many variants: atriums, galleries, courtyards, through-block arcades, indoor parks, covered pedestrian areas of one shape or another. Some are dreadful. In return for extra floors, the developers provided spaces and welshed on the amenities. But some spaces have been very successful indeed, and there is enough of a record to indicate that the denominators are much the same as with outdoor spaces. Here, briefly, are the principal needs:

1. *Sitting*. Movable chairs are best for indoor parks. Most of the popular places have had excellent experience with them; some places, like Citicorp, have been adding to the numbers. In all cases the total amount of sitting space has met or exceeded the minimum recommended for outdoor spaces—one linear foot for every 30 square feet of open space. There is a tendency, however, to overlook the potentials of ledges and planters. Too many are by inadvertence lower or higher than need be.
2. *Food*. Every successful indoor space provides food. The basic combination is snack bars and chairs and tables. Some places feature cafe operations as well.
3. *Retailing*. Shops are important for liveliness and the additional pedestrian flows they attract. Developers, who

can often do better renting the space for banks or offices, are not always keen on including shops. They should be required to.

4. *Toilets.* If incentive zoning achieved nothing else, an increase in public toilets would justify it. Thanks to beneficient pressure, new indoor parks in New York are providing a pair or more, unisex-style as on airplanes. These facilities are modest, but their existence could have a considerable effect on the shopping patterns of many people, older ones especially.

One benefit of an indoor space is the through-block circulation it can provide for pedestrians. Planners believe this important, and developers have been allowed a lot of additional floor space in return for it. But walking space is about all that some developers have provided, and it has proved no bargain. Unless there are attractions within, people don't use walkways very much, even in rainy or cold weather. The street is a lot more interesting. At New York's Olympic Towers, which is taller by several million dollars' worth of extra space for providing a through-block passage, the number of people traversing the passage is about 400 per hour at peak. On the Fifth Avenue sidewalk that parallels the passage, the flow is about 4,000 per hour.

Not so paradoxically, the walk-through function of a space is greatly enhanced if something is going on within it. Even if one does not tarry to sit or get a snack, just seeing the activity makes a walk more interesting. Conceivably, there could be conflict between uses. Planners tend to fret over this and, to ensure adequate separation, they specify wide walkways—in New York 20 feet at the minimum. But this is more than enough. As at plazas, the places people like best for sitting are those next to the main pedestrian flow, and for many conversations the very middle of the flow. Walkers like the proximity, too. It makes navigation more challenging. At places where there is a multiplicity of flows, as at the IDS Center in Minneapolis, one often gets blocked by people just standing or talking, while there are others in crossing patterns or collision courses up ahead. The processional experience is all the better for the busyness.

In an important respect, public spaces that are inside differ from public spaces that are outside. They're not as public. The look of a building, its entrances, the guards do have a filtering effect and the cross section of the public that uses the space within is somewhat skewed—with more higher-income people, fewer lower-income people, and, presumably, fewer undesirables. This, of course, is just what the building management and shop owners want. But there is a question of equity posed. Should the public underwrite such spaces? In a critique of the Citicorp Building, Suzanne Stephens argues in *Progressive Architecture* that it should not. The suburban shopping mall, she notes, is frankly an enclave and "owes its popularity to what it keeps out as well as what it offers within. Whether this isolationism should occur in 'public spaces' created through the city's incentive zoning measures should be addressed at the city planning level. . . . Open space amenities are moving from the true public domain, the street, to inner sanctums where public and private domains blur. Thus this public space is becoming increasingly privatized."

This is very much the case with most megastructures. They are exclusionary by design, and, as I will argue later, they are wrongly so. But buildings with indoor spaces can be quite hospitable if they are designed to be so, even rather large ones. The Crystal Court of the IDS Center is the best indoor space in the country, and it is used by a very wide mix of people. In mid-morning, the majority of the people sitting and talking are older people, and many of them are obviously of limited means.

Inevitably, any internal space is bound to have a screening effect; its amenities, the merchandise lines offered, the level of the entertainment—all these help determine the people who will choose to come, and it is not necessarily a bad thing if a good many of the people are educated and well-off. But there should be other kinds of people, too, and, if there are not, the place is not truly public. Or urban.

The big problem is the street. Internal spaces with shops can dilute the attractions of the street outside, and the more successful they are, the greater the problem. How many more indoor spaces it might take to tip the scale is difficult to determine, but it is a matter the planning commissions should think very hard about. More immediate is the question of the internal space's relation to the street. If the space is underwritten by incentive zoning, it should not merely provide access to the public, it should invite it.

A good internal space should not be blocked off by bland walls. It should be visible from the street; the street and its surroundings should be highly visible from it; and between the two, physically and psychologically, the connections should be easy and inviting. The Crystal Court of the IDS Building is a splendid example. It is transparent. You are in the center of Minneapolis, no mistake. You see it. There is the street and the neighboring buildings, and what most catches the eye are the flows of people through doorways and walkways. It is an easy place to get in and out of.

Most places are not. Typically, building entrances are overengineered affairs centered around a set of so-called revolving doors. The doors do not of themselves revolve; you revolve them. From a standing start, this requires considerable foot-pounds of energy. As does opening the swinging doors at the sides—which you are not supposed to use anyway. These doors are for emergency use. So there is frequently a sign saying PLEASE USE REVOLVING DOOR mounted on a pedestal blocking the center of the emergency door. Sometimes, for good measure, there is a second set of doors 15 or 20 feet inside the first.

All this is necessary, engineers say, for climate control and for an air seal to prevent stack-effect drafts in the elevator shafts. Maybe so. But on occasion revolving doors are folded to an open position. If you watch the entrances then, you will notice that the building still stands and no great drafts ensue. Watch the entrances long enough, and there is something else you will notice. The one time they function well is when they are very crowded.

I first noticed this phenomenon at Place Ville Marie in Montreal. I was clocking the flow through the main concourse entrance, a set of eight swinging doors. At 8:45 A.M., when the flow was 6,000 people an hour, there was a good bit of congestion, with many people lined up one behind another. Ten minutes later the flow was up to a peak rate of 8,000 people an hour (outside Tokyo, the heaviest I've ever clocked). Oddly, there was little congestion. People were moving faster and more easily, with little queuing.

The reason lies in the impulse for the open door. Some people are natural door openers. Most are not. Where there is a choice, they will follow someone who is opening a door. Sometimes they will queue up two or three deep rather than open a door themselves. Even where there are many doors, most of the time the bulk of the traffic will be self-channeled through one or two of them. As the crowd swells, however, an additional door will be opened, then another. The pace quickens. The headway between people shortens. In transportation planning, it is axiomatic that there should be a comfortable headway between people. In doorway situations, the opposite is true. If the interval between people shortens to 1.2 seconds or less, the doors don't get a chance to close. All or most of the doors will be open, and, instead of bunching at one or two of them, people will distribute themselves through the whole entrance.

One way to provide a good entrance, then, is to have big enough crowds. But there is another possibility. Why not leave a door open?

This novel approach has been followed for the entrance of an indoor park. As part of the new Philip Morris building, architect Ulrich Franzen has designed an attractive space that the Whitney Museum will operate as a kind of sculpture garden. An entrance that invited people in was felt to be very important. Before the energy shortage an air door would have been the answer, and had been so specified in the zoning code for covered pedestrian areas. But this was out of the question now. So, at the other end of the scale, was the usual revolving-door barricade.

To check the potentials of an open door, I did a simple study of heavily used entrances. I filmed rush-hour flows with a digital stop watch recorded on the film, and then calculated how many people used which parts of the entrance. Happily, the weather was mild, and at several of the entrances one or two doors would be wedged open. As at Place Ville Marie, it was to the open door that most people went. This does not mean that the other doors were redundant; even if one doesn't choose to use them, having the choice to do so lessens one's sense of crowding. But for sheer efficiency, it became clear, a small space kept open is better than a wider space that is closed. At the main concourse entry to the RCA building, two open doors at one side of an eight-door entrance accounted for two thirds of the people passing through during the morning rush hour. At Grand Central Station, most of those using the nine-door entrance at 42nd Street traversed open doors, and at any given time three doors accounted for the bulk of the traffic. The doors at Grand Central are old, in disrepair, and the glass is rarely cleaned. But they do work well.

Franzen's design for the entrance to the Philip Morris indoor park incorporates these simple findings. Visually, the entrance will be a stretch of glass 20 feet wide. At the center it will have a pair of automatic sliding doors. In good weather and at peak-use times, the doors will be kept open to provide a clear, six-foot entry. This should be enough for the likely peak flows. For overflows, and people who like to open doors, there will be an option of swinging doors at either side. In bad weather, the sliding doors will open automatically when people approach. In effect, there will be an ever-open door. It is to be hoped there will be many more.

20

Living with Lobbies

NEIL HARRIS

In an era of political corruption and influence-peddling, the word lobby, as noun or verb, usually refers to those representatives of special interests who attempt to win the blessings of legislators. Dictionaries, however, particularly those with historical interests, spend much more space on the word's architectural status; originally a covered walk in a monastery, or a passage which could be used as an anteroom, the lobby has also denoted, at various times, apartments under a ship's quarterdeck, a small enclosure for cattle, and an entrance hall in which members of Parliament met constituents, a usage which led to its modern political meaning.

As an architectural setting, however, the lobby was relatively unimportant until the 19th century and the growth of modern hotels, office buildings, theaters and apartment houses. As urban centers developed special institutions for amusement, lodging and work, a new need appeared: to shelter briefly, for purposes of convenience, movement or communication, promiscuous assemblages of people.

Physical demands were supplemented, in the United States, by ideological constraints. Taught to suspect great demonstrations of private wealth, Americans found a convenient site for collective fantasies in the public rooms of commercial establishments like hotels. Forbidden palaces

From The New Republic, *May 8, 1976, pp. 19–22. Reprinted by permission of* The New Republic, © *1976, The New Republic, Inc.*

and castles, republican Americans enjoyed the opulence of fancy carpets, crystal chandeliers and elaborate furniture through the kindness of their local publicans, whose huge establishments astonished foreign visitors and gladdened the heart of every loyal patriot.

Moreover, because most American towns and cities neglected to provide easily accessible and well-maintained sanitary facilities, lobbies (along with restaurants and department stores) became havens for the frantic and the footsore, their toilets and washrooms providing oases of comfort. Lobbies, of course, served many other functions as well: they were centers for display, arenas for assignation, spots to gain information and directions, and small shopping centers convenient for the purchase of cigars, toiletries and postcards.

Hotel lobbies were particularly rich in their capacity to sustain social encounters. Film-makers and novelists gloried in their profusion of furniture, foliage and hidden corners, from which the house detective, the jilted lover, or a hated business rival might emerge at any moment. In the dozens of chairs which usually lined any well-appointed lobby sat the loungers, including pickpockets, the unemployed and those simply waiting to meet friends or business acquaintances. The moral tone of the lobby was tolerant enough although, as Sam Spade told his friend Luke in *The Maltese Falcon*, cheap gunmen with suspicious bulges in their jackets didn't help much. With few settings that encouraged sauntering or quiet contemplation, Americans welcomed lobbies. The obvious services they performed disguised one of their true functions: a place one could go to rest and pretend to be waiting for something to begin, rather than, as so often happened, waiting for something to end.

The role of the lobby as refuge was explored by many novelists, among them by Theodore Dreiser in *Sister Carrie*. Dreiser used the lobby to signal Hurstwood's decline. The former restauranteur "knew hotels well enough to know that any decent-looking individual was welcome to a chair in the lobby." But taking that chair was a "painful thing to him. To think he should come to this! He had heard loungers about hotels called chair-warmers. He had called them that himself in his day. But here he was, despite the possibility of meeting someone who knew him, shielding himself from cold and the weariness of the streets in a hotel lobby.''

Lobbies also supported more hopeful social encounters. Dreiser, again, this time in *An American Tragedy*, employed the Green-Davidson Hotel to initiate Clyde Griffiths into a taste for worldly luxury. The lobby was ''more arresting, quite, than anything he had seen before. It was all so lavish. Under his feet was a checkered black-and-white marble floor. Above him a coppered and stained and gilded ceiling. And supporting this, a veritable forest of black marble columns,'' which surrounded ''lamps, statuary, rugs, palms, chairs, divans, têtes-à-têtes—a prodigal display.''

Lobbies, in effect, became stage sets, permitting a theatricality of manner that would have been out of place anywhere else. Making a return visit to the United States Henry James caught the appeal of the ''hotel spirit'' to the display-conscious social climbers who moved through the public rooms of the old Waldorf-Astoria in a golden haze of clatter and publicity. It was the concentration, the accumulation, the intensity of the hotel world that absorbed James, its capacity to include almost everyone and to break down every barrier but two: the appearance of respectability and the filled wallet. ''Protected at those two points the promiscuity carries, through the rest of the range, everything before it,'' parading ''through halls and saloons in which art and history, in masquerading dress, muffled almost to suffocation as in the gold brocade of their pretended majesties and their conciliatory graces, stood smirking on its passage with the last cynicism of hypocrisy.''

Such stage sets were naturally placed in the hands of free-spending decorators. The expense of the rugs, the antiquity of lamps and tables, the ornateness of grills and cuspidors, all formed part of every hotel or apartment house's pride. The Book Cadillac Hotel in Detroit, opened in 1924, chose a Venetian motif for its main lobby; lavish promotional literature described its walls ''of beautiful colored Brèche Violette marble trimmed with white Alabama,'' and the bronze railings rested on black walnut beams which protected balcony promenaders. A ceiling of intricately designed gold leaf panels, emblazoned with the arms of Cadillac, the founder of Detroit, oversaw a selection of furniture which included several pieces "taken from Sarah Bernhardt's drawing room," as well as imported old Sèvres vases. Even the telephone booths and candy cases were made of walnut with marble bases, to carry out the motif chosen by the hotel's proud management. The Los Angeles Biltmore selected Spanish Renaissance for its theme: beamed ceilings, murals and painted panels, heroic antique lanterns, a giant Long Gallery and a magnificent staircase adorned in its public areas. The Book Cadillac and the Biltmore were matched in their splendors by hundreds of other hotels in every American city, fighting for patronage, as the Albert Pick Company put it in 1928, "through appeals to love of luxury and beauty." George B. Post & Sons, designers of the Statler Hotels in Boston and Buffalo, New York's Hotel Roosevelt and Seattle's Hotel Olympic; Schulze and Weaver, who planned the Los Angeles and Miami Biltmores, the Roney Plaza in Miami Beach, the Hotels Pierre, Lexington and Waldorf-Astoria; Weeks and Day, architects of San Francisco's Mark Hopkins and Sir Francis Drake, were among the major contributors to this outpouring of ostentation. And to this must be added, of course, the work of cinema designers like Rapp & Rapp, John Eberson, Thomas Lamb and Walter Ahlschlager, whose lobbies made the gaudiest hotel interiors seem reticent by comparison.

Because the lobby established the personality of the building it introduced, managers did not begrudge its expense. And they understood the apparent deceits. In the case of theaters, it was legitimate, wrote Harold Rambusch in 1930, for the showman to hold sway at the entrance as well as the stage. "Even a very elaborate entrance and foyer has a certain effect after the excitement of the street. Lobbies may well be full of gold, mirrors and posters." The office building lobby, argued a designer of the 1920s, was meant to suggest "the prosperous conditions of the various business concerns housed in the building." And for apartment house dwellers, according to Lois Wagner in 1956, the elaborate lobby acted "to confirm the good fortune of the tenants who have secured leases to what may be an overpriced warren, and to create, by association, an aura of prosperity to dazzle their guests."

In the late '20s and early '30s many lobbies were created in a somewhat more restrained opulence than their predecessors. The greater austerity of *art moderne* relied on rich materials rather than a profusion of objects. Sleeker (and easier to keep clean), these lobbies used lighting more effectively to create the prosperous hush appropriate to expensive structures. But the crisis of the depression and the pressures of post-war rebuilding interrupted this tradition of lobby luxury. Builders exploited the new savings possible by making lobbies simpler, smaller and more utilitarian. Glass walls summoned the outdoors to the aid of illusion, blurred the boundaries between building interiors and exteriors and so achieved a spaciousness possible, at one time, only in large rooms with high ceilings. The furniture diminished in elaborateness, and gradually also the lobby's borderline role began to grow vaguely disturbing.

The trend appeared first in apartment houses and theaters, for new hotel construction did not really get under way until the 1950s. Apartment house owners grew concerned about security. With labor costs rising it was difficult to maintain the previously ubiquitous liveried doormen. Buzzers and room telephones began to take their place, but they were stationed in ante-rooms, cut off from the lobby itself. Why spend money on furnishings that thieves could rip off with effortless ease? Those locked in the building could gaze out at potentially threatening passers-by, or better yet stay safely in their own apartments. Lobbies grew smaller and in some instances practically disappeared. Movie theaters, particularly those featuring the new European art films, tended to be simpler and to treat the large decorated spaces of the older palaces as embarrassments. And motels, which mushroomed in the 1950s and for a time threatened to end all hotel construction, went even further. Where possible the swimming pool, open only to registered guests, substituted entirely for the lobby's recreational pleasures. The chief exceptions here were the lavish resort hotels being constructed in places like Las Vegas and Miami Beach. In these gilded El Dorados, restraint was a cardinal sin.

Although some critics argued, in the 1950s, that the anonymity of modern buildings dressed in their glass and metal façades might lead to lobby extravagance as part of the search for personality, this did not happen. Instead, as security became a greater problem, the lobby's spatial

shrinkage was accompanied by the disappearance of its social functions. A necessary pass-through, the lobby could
be dominated by some large art work (metal sculpture,
hard to damage or to move, became increasingly popular),
or by plantings. The foliage softens the hard-edged look of
marble and metal, and can be maintained on contract.

Thus in Chicago, a stroll through newer office buildings like the Standard Oil and Sears towers reveals clini-
cally clean and smooth lobbies, with little to distract business people from making their appointed rounds. Simple
fixtures and Alexander Calder's Universe dominate Sears'
understated entrance. The shopping arcade is on a lower
floor. Closed-circuit television cameras, aids to security
guards, complete the sense of wandering through alien
territory. Television cameras are also a feature of many
apartment house lobbies. Where doormen can still be
maintained, apartment houses attempt a show of ele-
gance, but increasingly these lobbies are bare, quiet and
vacant.

The only lobbies that retain some of their older features
and have not been converted totally into danger zones are
hotel lobbies. But here, sad damage has been done. In the
large urban hotels of the 1920s, while much of the ground
and lobby floors was devoted to stores, the great central
spaces were planned for the convenience of guests and visitors. Milwaukee's Hotel Schroeder (by Holabird & Roche),
had a lobby of 53 by 86 feet, with practically all of the furniture ''placed between the four large columns in the center of the room, leaving a passage around the columns to
be used as a circulation space, insuring comfort and ease
where people are sitting.'' Three steps away was a lounge,
almost as large, with tables, lamps, couches and other ac-
cessories.

Would that hotels continue to be so solicitous! In the
1950s and 1960s the lounges practically disappeared, and
the lobbies were defaced by concessions and partitions.
Although impressive spaces remain in some older urban
and resort hotels—Chicago's Palmer House retains its
grand stairway and 138-foot lobby—many hotels carved
bars and cocktail lounges out of public areas, and new hotels, unhampered by legacies of generosity, could be still
more efficient in their planning.

Within the last 10 years, however, a burst of hotel planning has attempted to recapture, and even expand upon, these lost glories. Two diverging paths have been chosen. One is exemplified by Chicago's new Ritz Carlton, opened just a few months ago. The Ritz, seeking to inherit the *grande luxe* tradition, has spent a fortune to reinstate the lobby floor, and make it a center for promenading, eating and drinking. Once again the materials are rich and costly and the long Promenade is impressive; moreover, the views, from its 12th floor location, are dramatic and enticing. Just as its advertisements try to evoke memories of Cesar Ritz and Escoffier, the hotel identifies itself with the era of palm courts, crystal chandeliers and chamber groups playing for well-dressed diners and drinkers.

But the Ritz lobby is not completely satisfying, partly because the secure eclectic vision of the older hotels has been so weakened. It believes in luxury, but without stylistic conviction. The marble and the carpets don't really suit the furniture; in the main lobby, as opposed to the Promenade, seating is inconspicuously placed in side sections rather than amply and invitingly in the center. Bars and restaurants, as well as the large central fountains and plantings, organize a traffic flow which is effectively shielded from wandering pedestrians by an elevator trip. The stage-set quality that absorbed Henry James is quickly apparent, but the Marshall Field showcases, which are scattered about every few feet, remind guests of the commercial urgency of the enterprise.

But if retailing intrudes, the Ritz lobby is rich, capacious and even occasionally reassuring in its old fashioned opulence. A very different model, in the lobby revival, has been developed by John Portman, and applied in Chicago, San Francisco, Knoxville and several other cities. And it has just been elaborated in its first home, Atlanta, by three huge new hotels which have either opened or are about to open. The Portman lobbies, and those which embody their principles, are special kinds of places. Enormous, dwarfing spaces, large enough to contain (as in Atlanta's Peachtree Plaza) an artificial lake and extensive plantings, they dazzle visitors, but they no longer function quite as lobbies once did. The layered tiers of floors, the activity and the multiple views are exciting but often dizzying; few nooks and corners permit quiet conversation or restful observation except, of course, for the bars and restaurants which exact a price for the privilege.

These new lobbies are not ceremonial stage sets or retreats for the tired and the expectant. They are closer to movie screens, illusionistic amusement parks whose glitter encourages activity, not repose, and speed in place of stateliness. No longer ante-rooms or border areas, these lobbies are the climaxes, the sum totals, the holy of holies of their respective buildings. They may soon need lobbies of their own. Miniature cities, with extensive shopping areas, avenues and occasionally even recreated historic sites, they exemplify the closed landscapes that are increasingly being substituted for the wide open visions that used to form the American dream of space. Once American towns and cities differentiated themselves from Europe by their limitless, ungirdled vistas, the absence of defining walls, moats and battlements; their attenuated streets stretched out to the infinite. "Instead of looking inward to a hermit realm of refuge," Fred Somkin argued in *Unquiet Eagle*, our ante-bellum towns "scanned the horizon with an exaggerated ambition bordering on the fantastic."

Now, befitting an older civilization, the lobby's function has become illusionistic: to reassure the anxious that it does, in fact, contain limits—doors, walls, roof—and yet can include every variety of nature, only more intensely than the outdoors itself. The glass elevators and revolving roof-top restaurants, both of which fit the conventions of distant spectatorship, allow these limits to be explored and experienced; once visitors have discovered them they can revel in tours through the park and jungle of the lobby floor, punctuated by glances up at the enclosed heaven.

The success of these new interiors is partly a function of changing travel experiences. Railroads mixed ceremony in their stations, with endless horizons on their tracks. But airlines join informality and rapid movement, at the airport, with enclosed transcendence of earth-bound limits, in their flights. The combination of enclosure and transcendence differentiates the new lobbies from the old. Border spaces once bridged public and private functions, their fulsome decoration serving as tributes to hidden resources of wealth and generosity. Their extravagance was a form of public flattery that humored masses of people into appropriate public behavior. The newer spaces disperse rather than concentrate social encounters, filtering not spotlighting meetings. No longer objectifying the social setting, the lobby overruns it, surmounts the environment by its own enclosure. Thus, like so many contemporary arrangements, the new lobby preserves the illusion of individualism by relying on secure controls. Vulgar and pompous the old lobbies were, but their elaborate decoration spoke more obviously of manipulation. Less has indeed become more.

21

Spaced-Out at the Shopping Center

NEIL HARRIS

The year 1976 is an anniversary for all kinds of things besides American independence. It marks, for example, the 20th anniversary of the Southdale Shopping Center near Minneapolis, the work of Victor Gruen & Associates. Southdale has a special place in the history of the American shopping center; it marked the debut of the large, enclosed mall, and set a pattern which has been extensively imitated and adapted in the last two decades. The regional shopping center is now so ubiquitous, that it is surprising how short a history it actually possesses. All the more reason then, to survey its varieties and social implications, as they become more apparent.

Early shopping centers, like so many modern innovations, developed in California during the 1920s and '30s. Living in the first set of urban communities built entirely around the automobile, Californians quickly discovered the advantages of placing groups of stores around or within parking areas. Similar arrangements soon appeared in other parts of the country. Richard Neutra designed a small shopping center for Lexington, Kentucky; New Jersey had the Big Bear Shopping Centers, built around giant groceries, with parking space for up to 1000 cars.

From The New Republic, *December 13, 1975, pp. 23–26. Reprinted by permission of* The New Republic, © *1975, The New Republic, Inc.*

In the '30s also, chain and department stores, both vital to the future centers, began to adapt their businesses to the increasingly affluent suburbs and the ever mobile automobile. Until then, retail location in large American cities had been generally a function of existing transportation lines. But as automobile usage spread, downtown location became more problematic. "The automobile emancipated the consumer but not the merchant," the *Architectural Forum* noted in 1949, and well before then firms like Macy's and Sears Roebuck had begun building in the suburbs or on the peripheries of metropolitan centers.

It was the union of department stores with the older ideal of grouping easily accessible smaller stores that produced the first regional centers. This was supplemented, of course, by the explosion of highway construction during the Eisenhower era. The years from the early '50s to the late '60s were the golden era of shopping center construction. By the end of the '60s more than 10,000 shopping centers of every size and shape had been built. The huge shift of wealth and population to the suburbs guaranteed their profits. Large department stores—like Hudson's in Detroit and Dayton's in Minneapolis—were eager to get a piece of this action. Instead of simply opening up more branches, department stores began to organize their own centers, hire architects and developers, and get mortgages from life insurance companies, whose huge supply of capital enabled them to influence the suburban landscape as powerfully as their huge downtown skyscrapers shaped the center cities.

By the middle '50s also, developers began to realize the crucial role of design planning. The department stores were the magnets, their drawing power and placement making or breaking the profits of their smaller neighbors. The straight lines of the early malls, like John Graham's Northgate in Seattle, began to yield to more informal treatments. In Chicago, whose suburbs offer a veritable encyclopedia of shopping center forms, Old Orchard in Skokie, and later Oakbrook, opened in 1962, contained several department stores and carefully landscaped courtyards, with flower beds, streams, ponds, bridges, fountains and seating areas. The rambling, informal lines of these centers, and the series of differently sized quadrangles, produced a village-like atmosphere, the large size (sometimes more than one million square feet) deliberately underplayed. At

Mondawmin Shopping Center, in Baltimore, developer James Rouse used two levels to produce what contemporary critics found to be an intimate, casual setting, something like "a charming market town." By the late '50s two-level centers were increasingly popular; they cut down on the forbiddingly long walks between stores, a feature of older malls.

If the rambling, garden-like centers of the late '50s and early '60s were profitable and inviting to shoppers, the Southdale model was the wave of the future. Gruen concentrated his buildings in a two-level mall, and in his enclosed, air-conditioned structure he placed sculpture, trees, benches, so arranging the various spaces to give the impression of downtown bustle. Serenity and village charm were not Southdale's goals; instead, it sought a replication of downtown energy, exploiting the concentration that two enclosed levels, each open to the sight of the other, permitted.

Precedents existed. Glass-covered arcades like Milan's Galleria and London's Burlington Arcade were familiar to European-born designers like Gruen. A few American cities—Cleveland and Providence among them—also possessed important arcades. But even more exemplary were the courtyards and light wells of American commercial buildings constructed at the turn of the century. Department stores, for example, had courts that were cathedral-like in their boast of space, sometimes topped by stained glass domes. Aware of being surrounded by hundreds of other shoppers, customers made their way in an atmosphere of bustle and activity.

This kind of collective drama was what Southdale and many of its successors sought. Shopping centers, Gruen wrote in 1960, "can provide the need, place and opportunity for participation in modern community life that the ancient Greek Agora, the Medieval Market Place and our own Town Squares provided in the past." The new open spaces, he continued, "must represent an essentially urban environment, be busy and colorful, exciting and stimulating, full of variety and interest."

Thus two levels quickly became standard for most centers along with ramps, escalators, broad staircases and two-level parking lots. Ramps were particularly useful for women shoppers (the vast majority of customers), who could move strollers and high heeled shoes easily up and down the undulating inclines, and catch a maximum view of other shoppers and store fronts. Even more than the verticality, it was the enclosed character of the new malls that delights their users. Southdale was covered because of cold winters and hot summers, but areas with mild climates also sought temperature control. Marvin Richman, of Chicago's Urban Investment and Development Company, points out that the continued profitability of open centers like Oakbrook does not diminish the zeal of tenants to move into covered centers. "It is unlikely we will see any more of the large open centers constructed," he concludes.

If that is what customers want, that is what they will get. Little at the shopping centers is left to chance. Along with Disneyland they were early experimenters in the separation of pedestrian and vehicular movement, and the isolation of service activities from customers. Ingenious devices handled crowded parking lots, security problems and the normal difficulties of congestion. Logos were adopted and incorporated into shopping bags, maps and guard uniforms. Graphics and lighting experts facilitated shopping convenience. But nothing was given away, and efforts made only where they could show. Seen from the outside, from its vast acreage of parking lots, the typical shopping center looks like a pile of blocks. The elemental shapes of the center don't blend into the landscape—for there is no landscape to blend into—but they are not easily separable from it either. The streets are inside, so there is little reason to control facades which abut highways and parked cars.

But if clarity and concern are absent from the outside, the manipulation and self-consciousness become clear once the complex has been entered. Piped-in music, pavements designed to cushion noise, forced ventilation, controlled lighting, all screen the customer from distraction and aid his sense of location. The malls and arcades that lead to the main courts, writes an analyst and designer of shopping centers, Louis Redstone, "should strive for an intimate character and subdued atmosphere. The purpose is to have the shopper's eye attracted to the store displays." To encourage "shopping interest," when upper galleries are separated by large spaces, connecting bridges should promise convenient access and "give tempting views of the lower floor." Everything that goes into the center is organized to enhance the shopping act. "The typical shopper," according to one designer, "makes no thoughtful judgments concerning good or bad graphics, architecture or space design. He feels good or uncomfortable concerning buying or not buying, staying or leaving." Thus most shopping centers don't aim for good design as such; they seek an environment that will pull people in, keep them there, and encourage them to return.

If the end is unambiguous, the setting is not. The desire for variety coexists with an insistence on order; the marvel of discipline and control yields impulse buying; the natural environment is destroyed in order to produce a re-planted landscape; indoors and outdoors are blurred through climate control and conceit of street lamps, trees and occasionally, aviaries and zoos.

There are legal as well as environmental ambivalencies. In the past 15 years shopping center owners have had to fight a series of challenges that focus specifically on the public/private, or inside/outside character of their properties. The rights of freedom of speech and assembly, of picketing and distributing pamphlets, are not totally clear. The latest Supreme Court decision split 5–4, in determining that, in fact, shopping centers were not public thoroughfares but could limit activities normally permitted in public spaces. But it is probably not the last word.

The shopping center itself exemplifies how strongly boundary problems influence contemporary design and social life. One thrust of modern technology has been to permit and even to encourage acts which were once public and collective to be broken down into more private compartments. The automobile, which took the traveler out of a shared setting and allowed him to move either by himself or with selected companions, has spearheaded these changes, aided by the telephone, radio and television. The potential for social violence, the threat of crime and the nature of racial tensions have also served to limit the number of public occasions for casual mingling.

Compartmentalization, however, has inevitably produced reactions. The hunger for great, enclosed spaces that can provide dramatic settings for collective acts can be detected in the many new sports arenas, the Portman hotel interiors, the atriums and courtyards of a number of recent city skyscrapers. Substitutes for streets, which are now so pervasively associated with danger and dirt, nodes of concentration in a sprawl that does not quite satisfy the urban memories of the displaced, the shopping centers permit suburbanites to shop, eat, attend films, exhibitions, lectures, even orchestra concerts and plays.

The designers offer several options. If some suburbanites seek to recall urban glitter and excitement, planners can oblige. Real limitations exist, of course. While all cities are attempts to control chaos, their control is frequently disguised because of the lengthy period of imposition. In the shopping center, artificiality is more obvious because nothing is any older than anything else. There is nothing worn, nothing used; even the flower beds stay fresh. But when the developer aims unambiguously at an urban mood—as in Woodfield Mall, near Chicago, or Eastridge in San Jose—he produces, with hard materials and bright colors, exciting, dynamic interplays of light, texture and movement; great hanging mobiles, huge open plazas, balconies, ramps and stairways cutting with sharp angles across the empty spaces. From dozens of vantage points the shopper can gaze across what seem to be limitless vistas, depressing when they are empty, but exhilarating when they are filled with active people, a landscape in perpetual movement, assertive and ever changing.

Even cities need to recall what they once were, or are still trying to become. Many have built their own shopping centers, in an effort to retrieve the downtown. Chicago's new Water Tower Place, beginning its slow unfolding this month, has carried the vertical possibilities of center design to new extremes. The shopping center, that supports a 22-story hotel and 40 floors of expensive condominiums, has seven levels. Seen from the outside its marble, windowless walls (which conceal the service corridors) could be housing a warehouse or convention hall. The street is as irrelevant to it as the suburban parking lots are to their centers. Inside, however, after customers arrive by escalators at the mezzanine, they will encounter a seven story courtyard, bulging at the middle floors, crossed by three glass-enclosed elevators. Powerful lights will pick out the prismatic colors of the glass, increasing the sense of movement within the center; five other small courts, two and three-story, will be scattered through the rest of this quintessentially urban setting.

The glitter and extravagance of Water Tower Place's atrium recall another period of Chicago design, the era of John Root and his partner, Daniel Burnham. Root provided, in the Rookery, the Masonic Temple, the Chicago Hotel, the Mills Building in San Francisco, Kansas City's Board of Trade and the Society for Savings in Cleveland, a series of unforgettable light courts in glass and iron, surrounding delicately banistered staircases and filigreed elevator wells. Passage upward in those elevators, unlike the closed cabs of today, was an exhilarating adventure, playing lights and shadows against one another. ''Through the constant interplay of dualities,'' writes Donald Hoffmann, Root's biographer, ''of solid and void, structure and space, stasis and kinesis, opacity and transparency, darkness and light,'' the architect achieved a vital resolution. With its totally artificial lighting and very different materials it is not yet clear that Water Tower Place can approach the achievement of 19th-century masters like Root. But the effort to try to recapture the lost glories of courtyard, stairway and elevator is a welcome one.

Water Tower Place and Woodfield, centers that are urban in spirit or place, form only one among many varieties. The developers of Water Tower Place have just opened another shopping center, this one in Aurora, Illinois. It maintains the conventions of size and enclosure, its retail space projected at well over one million square feet; but its very different approach to large space gives it another kind of personality. The Fox Valley Center is almost as large as Woodfield but much less urban in feeling: its use of wood and tile—in flooring, fixtures, railings and columns—the subdued earth colors, the controlled scale of its courts and its lighting system, prevent this center from unleashing a sense of overpowering size or energy. The vast distances are disguised, and the center courts divided into two unequal parts, each a studied contrast to the other. Each department store has its own plaza, but they are or appear to be more intimate than their cubic footage suggests. The shopper can still detect the several levels, and come upon large, dramatic openings, but the wood and the foliage screen and break up the stark vistas, faintly echoing the village-like qualities of the older, open centers like Oakbrook.

Not that the ''rural'' centers are any ''softer,'' to apply Robert Sommer's term, any more flexible or responsive to individual needs. These are, on the whole, hard environments, their seating and traffic patterns clearly established and permanently fixed. The shopping itself can be disappointing. Because small, individually-owned businesses do not generally have the capital to relocate here, chain stores and franchises dominate. One shopping center repeats the outlets found in another. The music, the fixtures, the forced air can all be dreadful. At certain times of day there is an inertness, a deadness about the centers which no city space ever quite descends to. They are dominated by homogeneous groups—housewives, older people or teenagers—and thus lack the human variety of the street scene. And finally there is that single-minded devotion to the profit motive, the supervisory spirit which has outraged those critics who prefer to associate architectural innovation with more disinterested planning, and who find closed interiors to be oppressive.

But there is little evidence that many customers object to the total definition of the shopping center. There may indeed be relief at the lack of ambiguity, the limits on choice which the environment poses. All the attractions are controlled. One walks from the car to the center, and then tours the shops. Everyone seems there for a reason. Social transactions are simplified and dignified by the spatial drama of the great courts. Aware of the amphibious quality of contemporary American life, the merging of one function or activity into another, the studied informality to so many personal inter-changes, developers have created integrated spaces with multiple uses that can handle anything from the most trivial errand to an evening on the town.

It is their capacity for visual surprise and contrast, and their impressive displays of technical virtuosity, that make the shopping centers stand out. The last architectural form that serviced American dreams so effectively were the movie palaces of the interwar years, and they relied on decorative detail and costly materials. Architectural fantasy today employs space and lighting rather than electric stylistic quotation. Engineering technologies permit the shopping center to expand the achievement of their true ancestors, the great railroad stations, span a void in metal and glass, and use the proportions to honor the activity within. Space and light have always been luxurious, and few have exploited them as cleverly as the center designers. Conspicuous spatial consumption brings monumental status. In joining modern pleasure in large, unadorned surfaces to an older, baroque theatricality, the best of these buying machines remind us, once again, that the commercial spirit has nurtured much of our most interesting American design.

IV

PUBLIC
ART

INTRODUCTION

When we travel to Europe and stand in its public spaces, we are most struck by the swirl of activity they contain. But when we return, chances are that our memories, like our photographs, will be shaped to a greater degree by the public art those places contain: statues and columns, fountains and mosaics. Even in a great American public space like the Washington Mall we tend to forget the unbroken views and the wall of classical facades, and remember the Washington Monument and the Lincoln and Jefferson Memorials.

Yet it must be admitted that art, and especially modern art, rests uncomfortably in the American public space today; democratic politics and a democratic culture do not seem to produce a shared sense of what democratic public art should look like. The enormous controversy over the siting and, at this writing, planned removal of Richard Serra's *Tilted Arc* from Manhattan's Foley Square in the mid-1980s was just one example of the growing public dissatisfaction with the art being placed in parks and squares by contemporary artists, and paid for with public funds.

Perhaps the most provocative contribution to the highly charged debate over contemporary public art was Douglas Stalker's and Clark Glymour's "The Malignant Object: Thoughts on Public Sculpture," reproduced here with several dissenting opinions and the authors' retort. Stalker and Glymour make a strong claim: public art has become a form of public pornography. By this they mean that citizens, by being forced to finance art that they find deeply offensive and must constantly view in the public domain, suffer the same kind of harm caused by the ubiquitous display of pornography. Until contemporary artists are able to produce work that is "iconographic" rather than "iconoclastic," Stalker and Glymour feel public art programs should be halted.

This view is strongly rejected by Wolf Von Eckardt and Edward Levine, who charge Stalker and Glymour with Philistinism and "know-nothingism." A more mixed response comes from John Beardsley, who agrees that these charges once had some validity, but that public art programs have been reformed sufficiently to allow agreed standards to emerge through greater public participation;

he feels that less offensive, more popular works should now be built. Ronald Lee Fleming suggests how such public participation has been institutionalized in several cities, leading to the siting of small-scale, representational works that have received public support.

But sculptures are rare in America's parks and squares, and hardly define our sense of public place. Sadly, what defines it more clearly in the minds of most New York City residents is another kind of public ''art'': graffiti. While it may be debatable whether graffiti is art or simply a crime, Nathan Glazer writes in ''On Subway Graffiti in New York'' that it clearly makes subway riders feel unsafe—as though neither they nor the police can maintain control over this important public space. Glazer reviews the possible responses to the problem (most of which have been tried or seriously considered) and finds that no easy solution presents itself. Like so many other elements in American urban life today, the public ''art'' of graffiti will shape our public places as it pleases, without political direction.

22

The Malignant Object: Thoughts on Public Sculpture

DOUGLAS STALKER
and CLARK GLYMOUR

Millions of dollars are spent in this country on public sculpture—on sculpture that is created for the explicit purpose of public viewing, placed in public settings, and constructed generally by contemporary artists without any intention of commemorating or representing people or events associated with the site. The objects in question may be clothespins, boulders, or tortuous steel shapes. The money may sometimes come from private sources, but much of it comes from public treasuries.

One of the clearest and most general attempts to provide a justification for financing and placing these objects in public spaces is given by Janet Kardon, who is the Director of Philadelphia's Institute of Contemporary Art. "Public art," Ms. Kardon writes, "is not a style or a movement, but a compound social service based on the premise that public well-being is enhanced by the presence of large scale art works in public spaces." Large scale art works executed, to be sure, not to public taste but to the taste of the

From The Public Interest, *Winter 1982, pp. 3–21. Copyright © 1982 by National Affairs, Inc.*

avant-garde art community. Elsewhere, she writes: ''Public art is not a style, art movement or public service, but a compound event, based on the premise that our lives are enhanced by good art and that good art means work by advanced artists thrust into the public domain.''[1] The justification here is moral rather than aesthetic, phrased in terms of well-being rather than those of beauty. Public art is good for us. Her thesis is put simply and with clarity; it is perhaps the same thesis as that put forward by many writers who claim that public art ''enhances the quality of life'' or ''humanizes the urban environment,'' even ''speaks to the spirit.''

Our view is that much public sculpture, and public art generally as it is created nowadays in the United States, provides at best trivial benefits to the public, but does provide substantial and identifiable harm. This is so for a variety of reasons having to do with the character of contemporary artistic enterprises and with prevalent features of our society as well. We will discuss these issues in due course, but for now we want to make our view as clear as we can.

There is abundant evidence, albeit circumstantial, pointing directly to the conclusion that many pieces of contemporary public sculpture, perhaps the majority, are not much enjoyed by the public at large—even though the public firmly believes in a general way that art is a very good thing. In short, the outright aesthetic benefits are few and thin. Perhaps the public is wrong in its distaste or indifference, perhaps members of the public *ought* to take (in some moral sense, if you like) more pleasure in these objects thrust upon them, but these questions are wholly beside the point. Government, at whatever level, only has a legitimate interest in publicly displaying contemporary art in so far as that display provides *aesthetic* benefits to the citizenry. Many artists, critics and art administrators think otherwise, and claim for contemporary public sculpture, and for contemporary art more generally, various intellectual, pedagogical, or economic virtues which are appropriate for the state to foster. By and large the objects in question have no such virtues, so even if governments did wish to foster them, they could not properly or efficiently do so by placing contemporary sculpture in public environs. Further, there are identifiable harms caused by public contemporary art. These harms are akin in structure, though perhaps not in degree, to the harms often said to be caused by the public display of pornography. After considering the arguments developed subsequently, we hope the reader will conclude that this last contention is not so outrageous at it may seem to be at the outset. Thus, our argument runs, public contemporary sculpture does little or nothing to enhance the quality of life generally, and governments have no intrinsic interest in promoting it. Whatever legitimacy there is to government support of such displays derives from the tradition of serving the special interests of a very limited group of citizens—those served, for example, by museums of contemporary art. But this justification is overwhelmed by the fact that publicly displayed contemporary sculpture causes significant offense and harm, and does so in a way that intrudes repeatedly into people's normal living routines.

Doubtless some people will misread our argument and take it to be an attack on contemporary art *per se*. Our reasoning in no way depends on whether contemporary art is in general good or bad, or on whether particular pieces are or are not good art. It depends only on the facts (or what we claim to be facts) that much of the public derives minimal aesthetic pleasure from such contemporary art as is publicly displayed, that a significant segment of the public is offended and harmed by such displays, and that governments have, in these circumstances, no legitimate interest in furthering *public* art. Accordingly, this view is in no way a denigration of contemporary art; it is, however, a denigration of certain accounts of the value of that art, specifically those which find in the works of various artists, or schools of artists, vital lessons which the public desperately needs to learn.

PUBLIC OPINION OF PUBLIC SCULPTURE

Contemporary public art is public *contemporary* art, and there is considerable evidence that the communities into which it is ''thrust'' do not revere it, like it, or (sometimes) even tolerate it. Examples abound, and we offer only a few that are representative.

In October 1980 a piece of public statuary was unveiled in Wilmington, Delaware. The piece was executed by Richard Stankiewicz, known for his "junk" art of the 1950's. The unveiling was received with cat-calls and denunciations from much of the public audience. In Pittsburgh, there has been popular, organized resistance to a proposal to build a piece of modern cement sculpture on a vacant lot on the North Side of the city. The people of the North Side, a middle-class working community, want a fountain, not a piece of modern sculpture. (It may or may not be relevant that the sculptor is not a resident of the community, but lives in the Squirrel Hill district of Pittsburgh, a predominantly affluent and academic neighborhood.)

Alexander Calder and Claes Oldenburg have each left a work in the city of Chicago. One rarely hears anything good said of them by Chicagoans who dwell outside of the Art Institute of Chicago. Away from the shadows and in the sunshine of the Letter-to-the-Editor columns, there is dismay at Calder's "Flamingo" and Oldenburg's "Batcolumn." But the public dislike for these works hardly compares with the crescendo of distaste for a recent exercise in "Rag Art" at Chicago's Federal Building. A typical response to the exhibition bears quoting:

> Q. Please tell me how to complain about those unsightly canvas rags that have been wrapped around the pillars of the John C. Luzinski Federal Building. Those rags are a disgrace. While you're at it, what's all that scrap metal doing strewn around? Many blind people go in and out of the building, and it's a wonder no one trips over this garbage.
>
> F. G., Franklin Park[2]

The *Chicago Sun-Times* kindly informed the resident of Franklin Park that "the rags and scrap metal are objets d'art," which would have to be tolerated through December of 1978. And so into the winter of that year pedestrians in the Second City had to suffer the assaults of both the elements and the artistes.

In 1977, Carl Andre, the well-know "minimal" artist, executed a public sculpture for the city of Hartford, Connecticut for $87,000. Andre's "Stone Field Sculpture" consists of 36 boulders deposited in rows on a lawn. Mr. Andre has assured us privately that "Stone Field Sculpture" seems to have settled rather nicely into Hartford, and that there is no real public outrage directed at it. His assurance notwithstanding, the *Hartford Courant* was filled with articles like these in the summer and fall of 1977: "Criticisms of Park Art Doesn't Rock Sculptor''; ''Sculpture Foes Shaping Plans''; ''Rock Opponents Tighten Stand.'' Taking note of this public indignation and even joining it, the city fathers considered refusing payment but were advised by attorneys that the contract with Andre was valid and binding. Works by Sugarman, Ginnevar, di Suvero, and other sculptors have created even more intense controversy in other cities, not simply because the public objected to paying for the works, but because significant segments did not want the objects publicly displayed in the settings into which they had been, or were to be, thrust. (These cases, and many more, are recorded apologetically in Donald W. Thalacker's book, *The Place of Art in the World of Architecture*.)

The public distaste for today's public sculpture often goes well beyond mere words. The common responses include petitions, assemblies, litigation, and, occasionally, direct action. Enraged by what is thrust at them, the public often takes up a kind of vigilantism against contemporary public sculpture, and in community after community spontaneous bands of Aesthetic Avengers form, armed with hammers, chisels, and spray-paint cans. Jody Pinto's ''Heart Chambers for Gertrude and Angelo,'' erected on the University of Pennsylvania campus for Ms. Kardon's own Institute of Contemporary Art, was turned into rubble overnight. Barnett Newman's ''Broken Obelisk'' was rapidly defaced when it was put on display in 1967. Removed to Houston, Texas, it is now placed in a pool away from errant paint. Claes Oldenburg's ''Lipstick'' was so thoroughly defaced at Yale that the sculptor retrieved it. Of course, for any object there is some thug or madman willing or eager to destroy what he can of it, but the defacement of some pieces of public sculpture seems to enjoy a measure of community support or at least tolerance.

The examples could be continued into tedium. On the whole, the public does not like today's public art. Of course, some people do actually take pleasure in ''Batcolumn'' or in the twisted, painted tubes and rusted shards that can be found in almost every large American city. But the vast majority, convinced that art is a good thing, still takes no pleasure in the actual pieces of public art themselves. An expensive piece of contemporary sculpture has a life cycle of a predictable kind, a cycle frequently noted by others. Received with joy by a small coterie of aesthetes and with indignation by a sizable element of the community, the sculpture soon becomes an indifferent object, noticed chiefly by visitors. If it is very elaborate or very expensive, the local citizenry may try to take whatever minimal aesthetic pleasure they can from the thing; typically, after all, they paid a bundle for it. In time the aesthetes move on, no longer interested in a piece that is derrière-garde. But the public must remain.

Impressionistic evidence is rightfully mistrusted, and those who advocate public sculpture might well demand more precise evidence as to the extent and intensity of public dislike or indifference for contemporary public sculpture. But the plain fact is that there is little non-impressionistic evidence to be had, one way or the other. Remarkably, although considerable sums are spent on public sculpture in this country by government and by corporations, virtually nothing is spent to find out whether or not the public likes particular objects or dislikes them, how intense such feelings are, or, most importantly, what proportion of the affected public would prefer that the space be put to some other use.

Louis Harris's polling organization has taken three extensive opinion surveys since 1973 dealing with attitudes towards art and its accessibility. None of these opinion surveys address questions dealing with the reception of public sculpture. The 1973 survey asks for responses to a number of items about "visual pollution," but no opportunity was given for respondents to indicate whether or not they found leaning girders or canvas rags to be a form of visual pollution. For any serious purpose in evaluating the impact of public art, the Harris surveys are quite useless. The only attempt at a useful survey on the impact of contemporary public sculpture is reported by Margaret Robinette, who conducted a survey during 1972 and 1973.[3] Though her pilot study does address the reception of contemporary public sculpture, it is without value as evidence regarding the issues raised here. The sampling procedure almost certainly produced a biased sample, the questions did not ask respondents to consider the sculpture against a range of alternatives, and even so the results cannot be unequivocally interpreted as evidence of public pleasure in contemporary public art. Indeed, the results provide internal evidence that many of the respondents did not fully understand the import of some of the most important questions put to them. In lieu of better studies of the same kind, we have the impressionistic evidence of letters to the editors of newspapers, of recorded public controversies, of organized public opposition to particular pieces of contemporary public art. There is no *prima facie* reason to doubt that this opposition is generally sincere, fairly widespread, and sometimes even thoughtful.

MONUMENTS TO THE MUNDANE

What basis can there be, then, for the claim that contemporary public sculpture enhances public well-being? The most obvious value of an aesthetic object—the aesthetic pleasure in seeing it and touching it and living with it—is apparently not present in today's public sculpture. By and large, the members of the public feel no pleasure, or very little, in seeing and touching and having such things. What else can be said in Ms. Kardon's defense? Perhaps that people become accustomed to public sculpture. After a piece has been in place for a while, the outrage, the shouts, the complaints cease. Children play on the thing if it can be played on. Old people may sit by it. This is a sorry defense, in which people's adaptability, and their impotence to control their environs, is used against them. People will, in fact, make what they can of *almost anything*, no matter how atrocious or harmful, if they have no choice. They will adapt to burned out tenements, to garbage in the streets, to death on the sidewalks. However horrible, tasteless, pointless, or insipid an object may be, if children can make a plaything of it they will. Bless them, not the artists.

Today's public sculpture, like the rest of contemporary art, is often defended for its intellectual value, for what the piece says or expresses, rather than for what it looks like. If this is to be any serious defense at all, it must be shown that typical pieces—or at least *some* pieces—of contemporary public sculpture are saying something serious and interesting, and doing so in a way that makes what is being expressed especially accessible to the public. None of these requirements is met—and moreover these requirements are *obviously* not met—by today's public sculpture.

Attempts to articulate the thought expressed by various pieces are, virtually without exception, trivial or fatuous or circular. Consider some remarks in *Newsweek* in defense and interpretation of a notable piece of public art: "Claes Oldenburg's work—his 'Batcolumn' in Chicago, for example—is formally strong as well as ironic. Oldenburg's silly subjects state a truth often overlooked: inside those self-important glass boxes, people are really thinking hard about such things as baseball bats or clothespins." We have no evidence that this is not the very thought that occurs to people when they see Oldenburg's column—but we doubt it. But even if it were, it is a patently trivial thought, and if the object is justified by the expression rather than the sensation, would not a small sign have been in better taste? The author continues, "Among other things, a work like Athena Tacha's 'Streams' in Oberlin, Ohio, reminds people, through its uneven steps, of what it means to walk."[4] Tacha's work is at least pleasing to our eyes, but we have not yet been reminded of what it "means" to walk. But if uneven steps will do the trick, the meaning can be found in any city park, forest path, or homebuilt staircase. Why do we need monuments to the mundane? Why should the public pay for what it can get for free?

It is impossible, and in any case too painful, to examine the range of pretentious, vapid claims made by professional art critics for the intellectual content of contemporary sculpture. Much of it reads like the prose of ambitious students of a Schaumm's Outline on "Wittgenstein Made Simple" or "Beginning Phenomenology," or "Quantum Mechanics Made Simple." It is not serious. An example or two will have to suffice.

The late critic and sculptor Robert Smithson has written about the Park Place Group of sculptors, which includes Mark di Suvero, who has done a number of public sculptures (including "Moto Viget" in Grand Rapids, Michigan, and "Under Sky/One Family," Baltimore) in the leaning girder style. Smithson claims that the members of the Group "research a cosmos modeled after Einstein. . . . Through direct observation, rather than explanation, many of these artists have developed ways to treat the theory of sets, vectorial geometry, topology and crystal structure." Smithson also claims that these and other modern sculptors celebrate "entropy" or "energy-drain."[5] Taken literally, this is somewhere between unlikely and silly. What is a "cosmos modeled after Einstein"? A cosmos modeled after some solution to the field equations of general relativity? Which solution, of the infinity of them, and why that one? Do these sculptors really know *anything* about relativity? Perhaps. Perhaps di Suvero and company really do have some deep understanding of quantum theory, general relativity, and transfinite cardinals, but even that unlikely contingency will not justify the imposition of their art upon the public. There is no interesting lesson about these subjects which the citizen can be expected to draw from simple geometrical shapes cast together in a public place. That is simply the fact of the matter, and it guts any attempt to found the benefits of public art upon the thin and far fetched theories of certain art critics. For what is undeniable about nearly every critical account of the message of one or another school of contemporary art is that the message—whether it is about physics or philosophy—is *esoteric*, and cannot be garnered from any amount of gazing at, climbing on, or even vandalizing of the object.

MORE FAILED JUSTIFICATIONS

Inevitably, today's public sculpture is justified in a kind of circular way: The very fact that the public dislikes it, or even violently abhors it, is taken to warrant its presentation. Thus Jody Pinto, rather typically, remarked after her sculpture at the University of Pennsylvania was destroyed that "Tons of letters were written to the *Daily Pennsylvanian*, both pro and con, which is wonderful. If art can stimulate that kind of discussion and really make people think, then it's accomplished probably more than most artists could even hope for."[6] Thus the justification for public art is that it causes people to think about why they do not like it, or about the propriety of having destroyed it. That is indeed a virtue, one supposes, but a virtue shared quite as much by every calamity.

There is also the common suggestion that, like travel, contemporary art in public places is broadening. It introduces the public to the fact that there are other and different tastes and sensitivities, alternative and unconventional standards of beauty. It makes people *tolerant*. In fact, there is no case at all that public sculpture makes people tolerant of anything that matters. Today's public sculpture may well make people tolerant of public sculpture, for the simple reason that if the object is too large, too strong, or too well fortified, they have no choice. Does it make people tolerant of, or sensitive to, the aesthetic expectations of other cultures or times? One doubts that it does, and surely not as well as an exhibition of Chinese calligraphy, or American ghetto art, or Tibetan dance, or the treasures of King Tut.

It is sometimes urged, rather opaquely, that there are significant economic benefits to be derived from public art. The case is seldom developed in any detailed fashion, and there is good reason to doubt that public support of permanent or quasi-permanent public art structures can lean very much on such considerations. These are some of the reasons.

First, the presence of public sculpture in booming areas is not evidence that the art itself makes significant contributions to the economies of Winston-Salem, or Charlotte, or Seattle. The effect is most likely in the other direction. (The same holds, of course, for the performing arts. As Dick Netzer remarks, ''It is hard to believe that the presence of the Charlotte Symphony has much, if anything, to do with that area's booming economy.''[7])

Second, while art may provide economic benefits for a few centers where the variety, or quality, or number of objects and events is markedly better than in surrounding areas, it cannot have much economic effect when more widely and, from the point of view of public patronage, more justly distributed. People may very well go to St. Louis to view its arch, but how many now go to Oberlin, Ohio, to see Tacha's ''Streams'' or to Chicago to see ''Batcolumn''?

Third, those who point to the alleged economic benefits of public art almost always neglect to consider opportunity costs: Would the money spent on public art have produced greater economic benefits if it had been invested in capital equipment or in subsidies for business or for public transit or in amusement parks? And, finally, even in those circumstances where the availability of cultural amenities provides or would provide significant economic benefits, there is no evidence that public sculpture of the sort bedecking our cities and towns contributes very significantly to that benefit. The forms of artistic culture which attract people and their money may very well be, as it seems to us, chiefly those of museums, music, and theatre.

Ms. Kardon's claims for the benefits of public art are unjustified and unjustifiable, and they can only result from a failure to be candid about the social conditions of contemporary art. Contemporary art has a small audience composed of some of the very rich who can afford to buy it and some of the not-so-very rich who go to galleries and museums to see it. The audience for this art takes pleasure in it for any of several not very complex reasons: because of the aesthetic appeal of a particular object, because of an interest in a segment of cultural history, because of the notoriety of its creator, because they find it an amusing joke (on other people), or perhaps, simply because they have been led to believe that they *ought* to enjoy it.

The aesthetic pleasures of contemporary art are not shared generally or widely, and the citizenry who must pay for and daily observe a public sculpture can take no pleasure in a joke played on others; for if Mr. Andre's "Stone Field Sculpture" is a joke, it is a joke played on the citizens of Hartford themselves. Some people, attending to the histories of past art that has proved to be great art, might be more tolerant about the untoward reactions to "Stone Field Sculpture" and its equivalents. Monet and Renoir caused quite a stir in their time, and the public did not take much pleasure in their works. Yet many of these same paintings have proved in time to be good, even great, art. Indeed, believing that this is a recurring and prevalent course of events with novel art in any form and time, it might seem prudent to take a different view of adverse reactions to our revolutionary and experimental works of public sculpture. This would be a mistake, for the appeal to art history wholly misses the point at issue: It is not for government to promote new conceptions or realizations of art. In short, the ultimate aesthetic quality of the works is not in question; their public display is.

THE PROPRIETY OF GOVERNMENT SUPPORT

If today's public sculpture is not much enjoyed for its aesthetic qualities, and if it carries no effective and important message which will enlighten the public, how does it improve the quality of life? How are citizens made better off by its presence? Advocates may dig in their heels and claim that those exposed to such pieces just *are* better off, whether they know it or not, for seeing and living with the things. But an inarticulable and unidentifiable benefit is no benefit at all, only special pleading.

Government at various levels may be legitimately concerned to promote the public welfare, but it cannot be legitimately concerned to promote activities with no demonstrable or even very plausible connection with the well-being of the citizenry. The argument for public art fails entirely if it is based on considerations of direct general welfare. What remains to be said in defense of public sculpture is only a kind of analogy. Governments at various levels support museums, even museums wholly or partly given over to contemporary art, and such support is ordinarily thought to be entirely proper. The public at large is thought to benefit by having art collections available, and a small segment of the public does benefit from active and repeated use of such collections. Why, it might reasonably be asked, is public sculpture any different? Granted that only a small segment of the population actively enjoys the things, why should not the government support that interest while providing to others the benefits of availability in case they change their minds or their tastes? The answer brings us to another conclusion: The objects of contemporary public sculpture are not benign or indifferent.

Public sculpture presents *moral* issues which outstrip related questions, such as those associated with the social justice or injustice of public funding of the arts, exactly because the works of public art are indeed thrust upon the public. They are unavoidable; if one goes about one's normal routine in Pittsburgh or Denver or New York or Grand Rapids one *will* see public sculpture, willy-nilly, like it or not. The moral questions associated with the public display of large pieces of contemporary art are rather like the moral issues surrounding the public display of pornography. The analogy between public contemporary art and public pornography is revealing, and we will pursue it, not because we believe that the harms caused by public contemporary art are the same harms as those caused by public pornography, but because the different harms in the two cases arise in similar ways, and belong to similar categories.

PUBLIC SCULPTURE, PUBLIC PORNOGRAPHY

The public display of pornography is widely claimed to cause several kinds of harm in several ways. In the first place, merely seeing pornographic depictions of events offends many people who do the seeing. The offensiveness of these displays to such people is at least partly aesthetic—it involves their immediate repugnance at what they perceive. (It is in that way different from the repugnance which is expressed by evangelical prudes at anyone, anywhere, gazing upon pornographic displays, no matter how much pleasure the gazer may find.) There are philosophers, such as Joel Feinberg, who treat offenses of this kind as something other than harms, but we see no real basis for sustaining such a distinction.[8] An offense given is a harm done, however minor and relatively unimportant a harm it may be.

Second, the public display of pornography is claimed to have a kind of reflective effect on some people. On reflection, if one is a woman, one is *humiliated* by the depiction of women as simply and rightfully objects of lust who are nothing more than sexual slaves. Third, the public display of pornography is claimed to have indirect effects which do substantial harm: It is alleged to promote sex crimes, for example, and to cause or to sustain the repression of women and discrimination against them. More clearly, the public display of pornography violates the interests of those who value modesty, who are offended by pornographic displays, and who wish society not to develop in such a way that immodesty and pornography are ubiquitous. The public display of pornography can be reasonably expected to contribute to the further erosion of taboos against immodesty and public sexuality in various forms, and thus to cause the evolution of society in such a way that is inimical to the interests of those who prefer a society whose members confine their eroticism to private circumstances. There are rather familiar objections to public pornography, and anyone who has thought or talked much of the subject has met versions of them. Most have a valid analogue in public art.

A good deal of today's public sculpture offends the public eye. It offends twice: once because it is simply unsightly, as with garbage, auto salvage yards, and scrap heaps; and again because it is unsightly *art*. It is offensive to be presented with rags and scrap metal, but perhaps equally offensive to be told that an unsightly mess must be respected as art. What the gentleman from Franklin Park felt in downtown Chicago may perhaps not be fairly characterized as revulsion, but he was surely offended by the art objects, quite as genuinely as are those who must pass by drive-in theaters exhibiting pornographic films.

There is a relative harm of the second kind, a reflective harm which is a kind of insult or humiliation. Viewing public sculpture and finding it ugly or silly or simply commonplace, the common person brings his own eye and mind into direct conflict with the judgment of the aesthetic and political authorities. He can only draw one of three conclusions. Either his own judgment is hopelessly flawed, so that he is a complete aesthetic incompetent; or else that of the authorities is flawed in like fashion; or, finally, he and his fellow citizens have been made the butt of a joke by the artist, his associates, and his admirers. The second conclusion is not widely held, though it is a logical possibility, and is doubtless sometimes true. In the first case, the citizen can only be humiliated by an object which, try as he will, he cannot find the beauty of; in the third case, he can only be insulted and righteously indignant at those who have erected an object which is an expression of contempt for the public. Both to the timid and to the self-confident, the object acts with malice. We are not sure that the harm associated with the humiliation and insult given by public sculpture is altogether less intense than the humiliation some people feel at public pornography. And the harm is repeated and repeated and repeated. The citizen can only escape by moving his domicile or work or normal activities, or by cultivating indifference.

In a third way, as well, the erection of public sculpture of the contemporary kind harms the interests of citizens who find it offensive: It begets more of the same. It does so directly by means of artistic influence, through mechanisms familiar to everyone. It does so indirectly by influencing the sense of beauty in the youthful, and thus causing them to welcome more of the same. Everyone has an interest in society developing in such a way that his own aesthetic sensibilities are not everywhere outraged; for much of the citizenry, most works of today's public sculpture act against that interest.

THE ICONOCLAST AT LARGE

The harm done by public sculpture to the interests of the public is real harm, less vivid and perhaps less important than some other social harms, but real enough. To those harms we have noted, we must add the general harm, in the case of publicly financed public sculpture, of having to finance an object from which no benefit is derived, and the special exquisiteness of having to finance one's own humiliation. We should also note that the forms of resistance to public sculpture are rather like the forms of resistance to public pornography: People write letters, hold rallies, circulate petitions, sue, and deface. In short, the analogy between public contemporary art and public pornography should not be lightly dismissed, for it is sound. This is not to say that there are no occasions when a public sculpture, even a contemporary public sculpture, is by intent or by chance so executed that it catches the public taste, pleases many, and offends few. Undoubtedly, there are such happy events, but the impressionistic evidence we find, at any rate, is that they are extremely rare.

If it is a banal observation that today's public art violates public tastes, a less banal contention is that this is not a benign or indifferent conflict, but one that is genuinely inimical to the public interest. The explanation of the banality is straightforward, but it serves to remind us why, unless either avant-garde art or public interests change dramatically, the harms are inevitable. Much of the business of contemporary artists has been to locate a tacit constraint on the prevalent sense of what is artful, a limitation on the sense of beauty, and to deliberately execute an object that violates that constraint yet somehow still retains an aesthetic appeal. Done brilliantly, the results can be admirable, and the retention of a fragment of what pleases old sensibilities, in combination with new forms, can lead to new and original aesthetic values. But such art cannot be iconographic in traditional and, to many, out-moded ways. This does not mean that it must discard representation and realism in favor of non-objectivity and abstraction. Rather, impertinent or irrelevant iconography and realism can be one way for art to be iconoclastic.

Two of George Segal's public sculptures illustrate the point. Both his "The Steelmakers" and "The Restaurant" represent ordinary scenes in realistic ways: in the first case two steelworkers laboring at an open hearth, and in the second case three people arranged around a restaurant façade. The steelworkers seem obviously pertinent and relevant to their place and purpose, which is serving as a monument to the main industry of Youngstown, Ohio. The restaurant figures, however, seem plainly ill-suited and ill-placed outside the Federal Building in Buffalo, New York. The latter does not, nor does other iconoclastic work, realize and celebrate and exemplify a common tradition and shared political, cultural, and aesthetic heritage. That is what public sculpture is expected to do, and what iconoclastic art can never do. Put otherwise, contemporary art is essentially experimental art. It is not valued by those who care about it because its objects are new and exquisite applications of enduring and precise requirements and constraints. It is valued at least largely for its very novelty. The public has no wish to be made guinea-aesthetes.

THE QUESTION OF ART POLICY

The harm done by the public display of contemporary sculpture far outweighs the benefits such displays afford to a certain segment of the public, chiefly the benefit of seeing the sculpture without having to visit a museum or art park. Though some would think otherwise, this state of affairs does not even really present a question of regulating activities which give offense: We regulate dress, noise, architecture, advertising displays, smoking in public places, and so on, because such things can give general offense or do harm, and the harms are taken to outweigh the benefits to the offender. In the case of public sculpture, publicly supported, it is only a question of not *subsidizing* an activity that gives offense and does harm. Consider an apt but unpleasant analogy. It is widely thought to be outrageous that, fully knowing the harms done by smoking, the government continues to subsidize the growing of tobacco, thereby helping to harm many seriously while providing benefits of a less vital kind for a few. The government has no *intrinsic* interest in the growing of tobacco, and it can offer no other just considerations than those involved in the balancing of benefits and harms. In structure, it is quite the same with today's public art: The government has no intrinsic interest in the promulgation of contemporary art, and it can only justify its subsidies by an appeal to a balance of benefits and harms to the citizenry. The most relevant difference, of course, is that the harms of public sculpture are less serious and less well-established than those of tobacco use. In the case of public art, privately supported, different issues will naturally arise, chiefly those of the appropriate and proper uses of private property, and of the resolution of the conflicts that arise when actual or proposed uses are inimical to the interests of those who do not own the property. The only consequence of our argument is a *caveat* about the resolution of such conflict: Based on the fact that what is to be constructed is *art*, government should not give extra weight to the claims of owners who would also be public exhibitors.

It is one thing to recognize a harm, quite another to understand how to incorporate that recognition within public policy. Lawrence Alloway, who recognizes the public distaste for today's public sculpture, but who does not take account of the harm to the public, claims that public sculpture will be defaced if it can be.[9] Consequently, he proposes that a public sculpture should be invulnerable or inaccessible. One might as soon conclude that it should be well-policed. In the present order of things, in which public art is indeed thrust upon the public without any direct requirement that the public favor the object, Alloway's recommendation is no more than an injunction to overcome the public antipathy by physical means, and to take from the people even the desperate recourse of Aesthetic Vengeance.

There are other remedies. Zoning is a common solution to the problem of public displays or advertisements of pornography. It is possible to apply the same solution to public sculpture—indeed, one might say that the solution is already in force in upstate New York, where two hundred acres near the town of Lewiston have been set aside as "Artpark," a place for contemporary sculptors to display their wares to the public should it care to see them. One might also say that the solution is already in force elsewhere, but not strictly enough, for galleries and museums congregate in a common area in many cities.

Alloway also appears to endorse the direct involvement of the public in the selection of public sculpture, so that after solicitation of proposals, the public can determine by preferential voting which pieces of sculpture are to be executed. Something like this procedure was used, as Alloway notes, for selecting sculpture for the West Side of New York City. But Alloway's proposal seems to use entirely half-hearted and tacitly paternalistic. The public has no *a priori* interest in the erection of sculpture on public sites, as against playgrounds or fountains or unadorned parks or monuments. There is no justification for the presentation to the public of a body of proposals for sculpture exclusive of other alternatives. In the great majority of cases, we believe any fair public plebiscite would have turned against *any* contemporary sculpture, and in favor of more benign objects: swings and slides and trees.

We do not offer a particular mechanism for representing public tastes and preferences in decisions about public aesthetics, and we scarcely believe that there is a single correct procedure. What we do insist is that public preference not be discounted by government agencies and that special pleadings on behalf of the art community be recognized for what they are.

THE PLACE OF REASON

By and large, the art community has addressed the issues we have raised only obliquely and disingenuously—as problems of salesmanship. This stance often shows up in articles that appear in art magazines whose audience is primarily the artistic community. In content if not in style, these discussions of public distaste for contemporary public sculpture are very much akin to discussions of "market resistance" in industrial trade magazines. An unmistakable instance of this focus on salesmanship is a recent suggestion that the friends of public sculpture should try to develop a tradition of contemporary public pieces in a community by introducing first one, then another, and then yet other and even more contemporary works.[10] In brief order, this sort of sculpture will, by its very numbers, come to dominate public areas and perhaps seem to the public familiar, expected, and appropriate. This seems nothing more than the standard corporate strategy of market proliferation to secure increased sales, indeed to dominate the marketplace for a certain type of product, be it cigarettes or breakfast cereals.

Big time art is an industry that has moved out of the cottage, an industry that has an articulate and influential lobby at many levels of government. That industry has captured a piece of the public purse, quite as surely as have the tobacco farmers and dairymen, and thereby has obtained a substantial and diverse subsidy. Like some purloined letter, the most hidden part of that subsidy lies out in the open: It is the cost to those who must regularly view contemporary public sculpture and endure whatever harm it occasions them. If large scale sculptures were required to be housed behind walls, or away from the course of daily routine, the real costs of these pieces would be more evident. Instead, public display transforms internal costs into external ones which are diffused, subjective, and not easily measured.

Artists, critics, and art administrators may find this argument to be simply an endorsement of philistinism, but that is a grievous confusion. Philistines are people too, and, whether or not one shares their tastes, the moral point of view requires that their interests be considered. If art is serious then aesthetic values must interact with moral values and aesthetic reactions must also help determine moral obligations. The artistic community generally is constitutionally allergic to close argument and clear statement, preferring allusion and non-sequitur. But any serious discussion about art and social obligation cannot be so self-indulgent, and that is why we have found Ms. Kardon's statements so welcome. If there is a serious defense of the view that today's public art enhances public well-being, it is not enough to presuppose it, allude to it, imply it, or suggest it. Give it.

NOTES

1. See the introduction to the booklet *Urban Encounters: A Map of Public Art in Philadelphia, 1959–1979* (Philadelphia: Falcon Press, 1980); also the introduction to the brochure for the exhibition "Urban Encounters: Art Architecture Audience," Institute of Contemporary Art, University of Pennsylvania, March 19–April 30, 1980.

2. "Action Time" column, *The Chicago Sun-Times*, November 6, 1978. For a complaint about "Flamingo" and "Batcolumn," see the "Action/reaction" column, *The Chicago Sun-Times*, November 10, 1978.

3. The Harris surveys are *Americans and the Arts: A Survey of Public Opinion, Americans and the Arts 1975*, and *Americans and the Arts*, available from the American Council for the Arts. Margaret Robinette's survey is presented in her book *Outdoor Sculpture: Object and Environment* (New York: Watson-Guptill Publications, 1976).

4. "Sculpture Out in the Open," *Newsweek*, August 8, 1980, p. 71.

5. Nancy Holt, ed., *The Writings of Robert Smithson* (New York: New York University Press, 1979) pp. 9, 17, 18.

6. " 'I Don't Think of Myself As a Stevedore,' " an interview by Maralyn Polak in *Today Magazine*, February 1, 1981, p. 8.

7. Dick Netzer, *The Subsidized Muse* (Cambridge: Cambridge University Press, 1978) p. 161.

8. Joel Feinberg, *Social Philosophy* (Englewood Cliffs, New Jersey: Prentice-Hall, 1973) pp. 41–45.

9. "The Public Sculpture Problem" in Lawrence Alloway's collection *Topics in American Art Since 1945* (New York: W.W. Norton & Company, 1975) pp. 245–250.

10. Kate Linker, "Public Sculpture II: Provisions For Paradise," *Artforum*, Summer 1981, pp. 38–39.

DISSENT AND REPLY

The Malignant Objectors

WOLF VON ECKARDT

Heaven knows, it is high time our breathless modern avant-garde looked back. It would realize that nobody much is following, let alone bringing up the rear. But Stalker and Glymour's argument, I am afraid, is not going to cause modern artists, and the small but vocal industry of critics, curators, and dealers which sustains them, to pause and reflect. On the contrary, such intolerant and ignorant generalizations will only widen the unfortunate gap in our society between elitist culture and popular culture, between artists and "the people." Besides, intolerant and ignorant catering to the baser, iconoclastic instincts of the common man can only lead to censorship and bad art, such as *völkische Kunst* and socialist realism.

At their best, Stalker and Glymour warm over William Morris's hundred year-old gospel about "art made by the people, and for the people, as a happiness to the maker and the user." Like Stalker and Glymour, Morris deplored the art of his time with more indignation than discernment. He saw it as "defacements of our big towns," "unutterable rubbish," and "burdensome and degrading." He, too, did not want art to be "slave of the rich, and the token of enduring slavery of the poor." He rambled about the wickedness of art for art's sake.

Morris, of course, saved England's arts and crafts from death by industrialization. He inspired the German Werkbund and Bauhaus, which set out to save art by marrying it with technology. (The marriage is still uneasily struggling along.) But Morris also provoked some critics to conclude that any art that was not "by the people and for the

From The Public Interest, *Winter 1982, pp. 22–36. Copyright © 1982 by National Affairs, Inc.*

people" was "degenerate." Around the turn of this century, the idea gained currency that a "healthy society" ought to rid itself of such garbage as Wagner's music and Rossetti's poems. Stalker and Glymour may like *Die Goetterdaemmerung*, but obviously share this disastrous sentiment when it comes to Calder, Oldenburg, or di Suvero. They write with implied approval about "Aesthetic Avengers armed with hammers, chisels, and spray cans." In the past, this sentiment has led to the high breasted bronze maidens and bull-necked stone men of totalitarian art. So much for "art made by the people and for the people."

At this point, Stalker and Glymour will probably retreat a little and reiterate that they only resent the public *paying* for art it does not like. Like it or not, in civilized society art is considered necessary as both an instrument and an object of culture. Necessities must be paid for. It is just as absurd to make such payment subject to a plebiscite on the art works as it would be to make public support of higher education subject to plebiscite on the curriculum. Would Messrs. Stalker and Glymour like to have their classrooms closed because some people did not like or did not understand the philosophy they teach? Art, like philosophy, cannot be judged by a popularity contest. Not even Miss America is chosen by plebiscite. No democracy can function without its experts. Experts, or professionals, are the gears that keep democracy in motion. The people, also known as the masses, and sometimes known as the mob, are no more, but also no less, than the driving force.

What the argument comes down to, then, is whether the experts and informed citizens who select public art and the procedures they follow for doing so are fair. Stalker and Glymour do not address this question, except to imply that Janet Kardon of the Philadelphia Institute of Contemporary Art and the ("degenerate"?) "small coteries of aesthetes" commit all those "substantial and identifiable harms" that get Stalker and Glymour so upset. The fact is that, thanks largely to the "Guiding Principles for Federal Architecture" which Senator Daniel P. Moynihan wrote when he was an Assistant Secretary of Labor in the Kennedy Administration, the methods for selecting public art for public buildings are as painstaking and sensible as anyone could wish who is interested in art rather than ideology. Municipalities and states follow similarly enlightened procedures.

This is not to say that the art works these panels select or commission necessarily represent a golden age. Ours is more likely an age of rusting steel. There is, indeed, a possibility that the shock of the new is getting old, and that the eternal avant-garde is lost in its abstractions, avant of nothing and nobody. But these are problems of the art and architecture of our time—of an epoch not yet come to terms with itself. They cannot intelligently be discussed within Stalker's and Glymour's rubbery framework of boys-in-the-backroom generalities.

Why, for instance, should the creator of a public sculpture have ''any intention of representing people or events associated with the site''? That marvellous obelisk on Washington's Mall, to cite just one example, represents nobody and nothing associated with the Potomac swamps. Should we, the people, therefore not have paid for it?

Some citizens thought so. In 1854, a band of them gathered at midnight, locked up the watchman, and then defaced a block of the marble shaft and threw it into the river. The following year, the same group sabotaged the fund raising drive by seizing the property of the Memorial Society. The citizens (Aesthetic Avengers?) were known as Know Nothings. The Washington Monument was built despite them and has become a symbol of America's identity.

A society can resist its Know Nothings. It can yield to them. But it cannot reason with them.

Nor can we ask our art selection panels to give us an art that is different from the best our time and its artists produce. We must cure the measles (if indeed we have them) rather than scratch the rash. Stalker and Glymour do not even want to scratch. They do not want *any* (their emphasis) modern sculpture. They want ''swings and slides and trees.'' They want to declare the artistic and intellectual bankruptcy of America. That is worse than Know Nothingism. That is a cop-out.

A former Representative from Michigan was not as easily discouraged. Some years ago, he told the House that his city, Grand Rapids, as it redeveloped its downtown business district ''purchased what is called 'a Calder.' ''

"At the time I did not know what a Calder was," he continued. "I doubt if many people here do today. It was somewhat shocking to a lot of our people out home. I must say that I did not really understand, and I do not today, what Mr. Calder was trying to tell us. But I can assure the Members that that Calder in the center of the city, in an urban redevelopment area, has really helped to regenerate a city . . . . The federal arts and humanities program was a participant and it was a good investment both locally and federally . . . . The response has been overwhelming."

The Congressman's name is Gerald R. Ford.

Wolf Von Eckardt is architecture and design critic at Time *magazine.*

Paradigms in Public Sculpture

JOHN BEARDSLEY

The history of contemporary public sculpture is too short for paradigms. It has been a scant fifteen years since the government began supporting—through the National Endowment for the Arts, the General Services Administration, the Department of Transportation and the Veterans' Administration—the placement of artworks in public spaces. Those years have seen failures to be sure but it has been the avowed purpose of agencies such as the National Endowment for the Arts to support art in public places in a spirit of experimentation, in the hope that the occasional failures and more frequent successes would lead eventually to the emergence of useful criteria for the incorporation of art into public buildings, parks, and plazas. Messrs. Stalker and Glymour are blowing the whistle, just as it seems those criteria might be appearing.

"Government," Messrs. Stalker and Glymour begin, "at whatever level, only has a legitimate interest in publicly displaying contemporary art in so far as that display provides *aesthetic benefits* to the citizenry." This is the premise of contemporary art in public places programs. They operate on the assumption that if panels of critics, curators, collectors, and residents of the sponsoring communities are convened to select artists for public commissions, the results will be artworks conceived with a sensitivity to the character and needs of those communities, by artists acknowledged by art professionals to be highly capable. The results, in short, should have aesthetic merit.

That Messrs. Stalker and Glymour think they do not should be of no particular interest to anyone. That they compare them to pornography should merely elicit some amusement. But that they draw the largely unsubstantiated conclusion that much of the American public agrees with them should raise many an eyebrow. In support of their contention, they quote a few letters to the editor; one can find equally as many letters to support an opposing view. All these many letters prove is that we lack universally accepted standards of merit. In a society as pluralistic as ours, this seems inevitable. We have a population that is simply too heterogeneous, too disparate in its moral and social values, and too various in its levels of aesthetic sophistication ever to agree on standards of aesthetic quality. We might best just make peace with this fact. If we cannot, and it appears Messrs. Stalker and Glymour cannot, then we must rely on other validations.

So Messrs. Stalker and Glymour abandon their assertion that "aesthetic benefits" are the only criteria, and insist that "ultimate *aesthetic quality* of the works is not in question; their *public display* is." They go on to formulate quite conventional (but not thereby inherently invalid) criteria for public display. Reluctantly admitting that Segal's *The Steelmakers* might be an acceptable piece of public sculpture, they find it "obviously pertinent and relevant for [its] place and purpose." They find it fits the traditional criteria: [to] realize and celebrate and exemplify a common tradition and shared political, cultural, and aesthetic heritage." But as I have argued elsewhere (*Artforum*, Summer 1981), traditional notions of public art were suspect, even in their nineteenth-century heyday. One need only bring to mind the predominantly north-facing Confederate generals-on-horseback of Richmond's Monument Avenue, who perpetually confront the south-facing Union generals of Washington's traffic islands, to realize that political, cultural, and even aesthetic values are a function of their time and place, and not necessarily shared at all.

If we cannot make peace with a divergence in aesthetic opinion, and, if as it seems, it is futile to strive endlessly for representations of shared political and moral values, what then are we to do? Shall we give up entirely, as Messrs. Stalker and Glymour would have us do? Happily, there are those who do not think so, who are engaged in an effort to evolve a public art that *is* "pertinent and relevant" and that *does* "enhance the public well-being." Extra-aesthetic content is one means, as exemplified by *The Steelmakers*. Segal's use of the narrative subject memorialized Youngstown's dying steel industry. Extra-aesthetic function is another. For example, Dan Flavin recently completed relighting several gloomy subterranean platforms at New York's Grand Central Station with installations of cheerful white, pink, and yellow neon. Robert Morris reclaimed an abandoned gravel pit in King County, Washington, converting it into a grassy, terraced amphitheatre with views of the nearby Kent Valley and Cascade Mountains. Joseph Kinnebrew designed for Grand Rapids, Michigan, an architectonic structure that permits spawning salmon and trout to migrate upstream beyond a dam that had previously blocked their passage, while providing viewers with a platform from which to observe the spectacle of the rushing water and the leaping fish.

There are other, somewhat more involved means of insuring that art enhances the public well-being. The County Board of Arlington, Virginia, has commissioned sculptor Nancy Holt to design a park for the intensively developed commercial district of Roslyn. Holt is working with county engineers and landscape architects on the overall plans for a park that will include earthen forms of her design together with sculptural elements. Significantly, she is working through the conventional planning process, which includes public hearings, competitive bidding, and other standard procedures, so that her work will not be an imposition on the landscape, but a product of Arlington's planned growth. Seattle is experimenting with similar procedures. There, the Arts Commission appoints an artist to work with architects, engineers, landscape architects, and community residents on the design of public works such as bridges and power stations. Each facility is completed with an artwork that has emerged from the public planning process and is carefully integrated with its surroundings.

Perhaps these projects will in time become the paradigms for successful public sculpture. Ideally, we should be allowed art for art's sake. But if in the public arena that seems too problematic, as it does for the faint-hearted Messrs. Stalker and Glymour, then let us also have art for utility's sake, or as a function of intelligent public planning. Meanwhile, let us encourage the government to pursue its nascent art in public places programs. I contend that there is an enlarging audience and growing enthusiasm for these programs, particularly those that support community-initiated projects.

Although it is not made clear by Messrs. Stalker and Glymour, there is a significant distinction between federally sponsored artworks, such as those commissioned by the General Services Administration, and those that are sponsored at the community level and merely supported by the government. The National Endowment for the Arts' "Art in Public Places" program operates on the later model; it supports projects in which both site and artist are selected on the local level. These are not artworks that are unthinkingly imposed on their host communities. Between 1967 and 1980, the Endowment supported 312 projects in 46 of the 50 states. Sponsoring communities ranged in size from tiny Hanna, Wyoming, to New York City. The Endowment grants totaled $5,541,000 for artworks that cost a total of $17,139,000. That is, over twice the total of the Endowment grants was raised at the local level, in both large and small amounts. These figures support my contention that there is a significant constituency for art in public places. Where such a constituency exists, the government has a legitimate right to support it.

John Beardsley is a curator of the Corcoran Gallery of Art, Washington, D.C., and author of several books on contemporary art.

The Meaning of Place

RONALD LEE FLEMING

Professors Stalker and Glymour have performed a useful service with their tightly reasoned (if whimsically malicious) assault on modern public sculpture. They slice through many of the fatuous rationalizations that hang like unwieldy halos over certain abstractions on the cityscape. They grapple with these objects, find them meaningless, and are prepared to cast them out as a public nuisance or at the very least put them in special pornographic districts—little Storyvilles of public sculpture—where abstract lumps of Korten can consort together with their special interest groups in the Art World. They contend that such work, promoted by a small network of critics, offends a hard core of public sensibilities. They would require public art to "realize, celebrate, and exemplify a common tradition and shared political, cultural, and aesthetic heritage," and since most contemporary public sculpture does not meet this standard, they argue against public funding for such art.

Unfortunately, they do not define a process for getting what they want, and one fears that their argument provides an excuse for the demolition of publicly sponsored art programs like those in the NEA and GSA, rather than support for a more balanced situation in which public sculpture would both express the artist's personal vision and also, as the best public sculpture always has, strengthen a sense of place. Interestingly, they never discuss the *context* of much public sculpture: where it is specifically, in what city, where in a city, and what it is doing there. Would they ban government from commissioning sculpture because we have erected several generations of concrete, glass, and steel abstractions? Unfortunately, modern public sculpture often successfully complements such structures, and all too accurately expresses certain aspects of our contemporary life, public and private. It can be slick and brutal, multifaceted and anonymous, even elegant and cruel. We may find that reality repugnant, but we cannot forbid the art to express that reality.

But there is a more positive tack to take toward public sculpture: We should help it to express a more holistic and humane view of our culture. Having spent some years now at the grass roots trying to implement public art projects which create, enrich, reveal, or reinforce place-meaning, I do not want the funds to go away just because some public sculpture continues to express our collective angst and confusion, or merely the ego of the artist. Rather, I would propose that we make some adjustments in the process of commissioning public art. I believe that if we allow the community to become involved in the process of determining what kind of art is suited for *this* place at *this* time, the results will be benign, though perhaps still novel or iconoclastic. The problem is how to help artists more effectively relate to a given context, so that their work reflects and strengthens the meaning of the cityscape and thus helps us to lay claim to it.

I do not believe the Stalker/Glymour contention that the government has no intrinsic interest in promoting "new concepts or realizations of art." Just as government supports innovations in science, it should support innovation in art. But we need a balanced view of public art that acknowledges that the pendulum of a legitimate taste may swing back toward art that has accessible meaning, just as opinion among architects is moving away from the abstractions of the International Style. This does not mean that there should not be public display of some artistic expressions which have meanings which are difficult to fathom; after all, one characteristic of art is its capacity to say different things to different people, with an ambiguity that some artists obviously go out of their way to nurture. We should encourage ambiguity by a density of meaning rather than the absence of it—and it is absence of meaning that seems to characterize some of the art that the authors properly skewer.

But this is not true of George Segal's sculpture (referred to in the article) of the two steelworkers in front of the Youngstown City Hall. The sculpture commemorates two workers who were in fact nominated by co-workers. It tells you that steel was and is made in Youngstown. The local people supported this sculpture. The steelworkers' union helped move parts of a donated blast furnace, which serves as a backdrop for the life-size figures. Local efforts were matched by NEA funds. Segal himself said that it was the first time in over twenty years that so many other people's attitudes and decisions had been involved in his work.

In Buffalo, Segal's "The Restaurant" did not include the same involvement. GSA, the funding agency which covered the entire cost, has almost invariably been content to let the artist do his or her thing. Donald Thalacker, GSA's arts administrator, does not consider the relevance of context, or "place-making" potential, in his book on GSA art projects. Significantly, the enthusiastic response to Segal's Youngstown piece is believed to have contributed to the doubling of the Ohio state legislature's arts funding for 1980.

The Segal-Youngstown approach is not the only valid approach to public sculpture, but I have found in my work in various communities that when local people are involved in trying to determine just what should be there, and for what purpose, they do want more than swings, slides, and trees. Nor is their involvement a philistine rejection of the individuality and vision of the artist. But we should recognize that public sculpture often involves and should involve more than the vision of the single isolated artist, enticed from his studio into the public square by a major commission, and working in the same isolation on a public piece that he works in on his private pieces. Public sculpture can involve—and many of the works that delight us do involve—not only the great artist but a variety of artists, craftsmen, artisans, builders, and the community. It is this kind of ensemble, over time, that makes the places we treasure in many cities, and the idiosyncratic and individual work may or may not be a part of it. It is this kind of joint process that helps build a positive association between a community and a place, that engenders a sense of proprietorship—"this is ours, and we will protect it from misuse and graffiti"—and that strengthens public support for a more carefully constructed and more fully expressive built environment.

Can the process of creating public sculpture lead to such results, as well as to the awesome object in the sterile field? I think it can, and I have some suggestions. For example, more of our public commissions should involve a number of artists and craftsmen, rather than allocating the whole of a substantial commission on a single artist. Such an approach can end up more respectful of the distinctive fabric of a place.

A number of towns with which our organization, the Townscape Institute, has consulted wanted to use small-scale representational public art pieces to create a sort of thematic trail connecting a college campus to main street or the railroad to downtown. A wonderful idea. But these innovative approaches, which were connected to the existing townscape, were not understood by NEA Art in Public Places review panel members, who favored the creation of a single object by one regionally prominent artist.

We should encourage collaboration among artists, local people, and other design professionals (architects, landscape architects, urban designers, artisans). Artisans today are, for the most part, divorced from the building arts, and as individuals have no way of incorporating their work—stained glass windows, wood carving, metal work, ceramic tile, weaving—into contemporary structures. Arts funding could encourage attention to the aspects of buildings that are the work of artisans and provide support to help move arts and crafts out of the gallery. We could fund a reference guide to artists and artisans, whose work could be incorporated into major office buildings and subsidized housing, for example. Often, it is simply a matter of explaining to developers what can be done and showing them the economic benefits per square foot of space that includes hardware, panelling, or floor surfaces designed by artists and artisans.

Our planning process for public art should at the least include a check-list in writing to ensure that the physical, social, and cultural context of a community has been thoroughly examined before the art is commissioned. Understanding the local mind-set and how art might relate to it should be planning activities which are eligible for funding. They are not, under the existing Art in Public Places program, although that agency does fund consultants who may consider such things.

We have ourselves proposed that in each case, before commissioning a work of public art, we develop an "environmental profile" of an area. Who lives there? Who has lived there? What economic activities take place and took place there? What historic events are associated with the place? What are the existing amenities, and how do people respond to what is there now? What did the place once look like? How do people use the space now? How do their present habits suggest they might use the space if retailored in this or that way? One cannot—and certainly should not—draw up such a profile in isolation: It needs the participation of local public officials, storekeepers, historians, developers, and residents, and feedback from all of them. It should include a clear statement of the design constraints as well as the available arts resources and traditions. Then, local people and the artist together should develop in a workshop session some basic artistic concepts and themes. In the case of George Segal's ''The Steelworkers,'' it can be a means of fusing the distinctive vision and style of the artists with the saga of the community. Ultimately, every process requires an endpoint, a decision, and that might mean settling for the glamour of a great contemporary name in art, and ending up with another ''Batcolumn.''

But the process of compiling the environmental profile becomes a tool for encouraging interaction among different groups as well as a means of generating a body of information that an individual artist or community member would probably have difficulty acquiring on his own. The profile should not be viewed as a constraint on the artist's creativity, but rather as a mechanism for challenging him to respond to the context of a given environment and to understand what that context connotes. It should help the artist tap into the energy that is already invested in place-meaning, as well as document for the sponsoring agency the sentiments of the community. The modest expense of such an effort might avoid the more exorbitant cost of stalemate, outright failure, or lingering community resentment which has characterized quite a number of public art projects.

This process could address the concern of Professors Stalker and Glymour for the moral basis of public art. I find this moral basis in the capacity of public art to connect people with their history, their culture, their place, and to do this in novel and iconoclastic ways with a set of associations that affect many (never all) viewers and users. Public art tells us we are connected to a place, and leads us to a sense of proprietorship of it. It is only by making these meanings more accessible to more people that we can restore a vision of place as something of public value. This mental linkage of people to place, reinforced or recreated by public sculpture, becomes the basis of an ethic. It can be the basis for treating the built environment more respectfully and responsibly. Working as he did in the natural environment, Aldo Leopold recognized this connection between ethic and image earlier in this century when he wrote:

> An ethic presupposes the existence of some mental image of land as a biotic mechanism. We can be ethical only in relation to something we can see, feel, understand, love, or otherwise have faith in.

Public art responsive to place can become one basis for an ethic of the built environment.

Ronald Lee Fleming is coauthor of Placemakers: Public Art That Tells You Where You Are. *He is the founding chairman of the Cambridge Arts Council and is President of the Townscape Institute.*

Artists in Society

EDWARD LEVINE

In *The Malignant Object* we find a rather casually researched attack, ostensibly against some forms of public sculpture, but tacitly against "modern art." It does not seem productive to engage in a refutation of the view set forth in the article. The problems with the article are partly due to ignorance of the discipline. It is sufficient to say that there are statements made without supporting data on one hand, or without careful or adequate definitions on the other. For example, how do we know that the public has a distaste for public sculpture? What does it mean for art to "say something interesting or serious"? What are the criteria for these adjectives beyond the "tastes" of the authors? How does one determine or define the "public interest" or the benefits to the public? How does one talk about the significance of contributions to a discipline if one is not thoroughly familiar with the language of that discipline, its history, and its critical issues? Why are not the questions about public sculpture also raised in relationship to public architecture or public design?

The issue which deserves further comment is the value of the artistic attitude in a democratic society and the responsibility of artistic consciousness to the public and society. "If art is serious then aesthetic values must interact with moral values and aesthetic reactions must also help determine moral obligations." I agree with the authors that aesthetic values must interact with all values but not in the way implied by the authors—that art or public art should reflect or support those values. If art were to interact with social or moral values in the terms of the authors, then art would become at best social criticism or at worst illustration. Both of these activities have their importance, but neither is central to artistic activity, nor are they involved in the overriding values art has for a society.

The activity of art can be defined as that which interrogates the values and assumptions of a culture. The particular realm of the visual artist is that of perception and the investigation of visibility itself. The social situation in which the artist is placed or in which the artist places himself affords a perspective which permits a probing of the values that a society holds as well as its prevalent intellectual assumptions.

In part, this aspect of artistic activity is acknowledged by the authors, who look at the modern artist's work as an attempt "to locate the tacit constraints on the prevalent sense of what is artful, a limitation on the sense of beauty . . ." Whatever "beauty" is, it is not a real issue for the artist. A search for beauty would merely be a form of indulgence. It may be a result of art but not its goal. What is intentional is a refusal to accept the restraints of the culture and even of the discipline. Or, put another way, these restraints become the source of further investigation and form the basis of new perspectives which uncover the limitations of the older views. All art, then, is by nature experimental, not just "modern art." As an activity it is constantly crossing the boundaries which tend to limit where it may go or what it may question. In fact, it is an activity which puts everything in the interrogative mode. We should not assume that it must arrive at one answer. It is sufficient to suggest that there may be other alternatives or viewpoints which may expand or even alter what we conceive as the irrefutable grounds of our beliefs and knowledge.

Because the artist has the freedom to investigate these assumptions and question these values, we become aware of how they limit or circumscribe what may be known or experienced. This is, at the same time, a very dangerous position for the artist to take. First, it may lead to an increasing alienation of the artist from society. Second, it may lead the artist to excesses and to a polemical art. Third, it places the artist in an adversary role in relationship to the values and norms of society. This position often leads some members of a society to seek limits to or to destroy the artist's freedom. The freedom for which the artistic activity stands is in tension with the more conservative activities a society must take to protect itself and preserve its stability. On the one hand we find the artist who searches for new order, who is restless with the status quo; and on the other side we find the natural bent of a society to maintain itself and maintain its authority. Out of this confrontation we can expect the inevitable desire to limit artistic activity that is manifested in the attitudes of the authors. (Plato was insightful about art—he wanted to limit the role of the poet in his society.)

The interrogation and confrontation the artist has with public values usually does not take place directly. It is the result of the activity of art itself which may be called its existential character. It grows out of the nature of the artist's activity as a personal search, a seeking for the not-known. What is at stake is the individual's attempt to assert the value of personal sensibility against the corporate and communal sensibility of the society. Art can only be serious when this sensibility is asserted, where the artist, by claiming the right of his sensibility, at the same time makes a tacit claim for the values of each individual's sensibility. Art then makes a statement about subjectivity.

But this does not mean a cult of aestheticism or a denigration of the objectives, only that both must exist for a society to remain vital and whole. One sensibility attends more to quantifications while the other attends more toward the particularity of experience and its tactility. We should avoid seeing this relationship as dichotomous, when in actuality it is complementary, each activity forming a base for the other sensibility to exist. Art makes no claims for being anything of value to the larger society. Its existence is a witness to another aspect of being which the society can choose to accept or ignore. Art has no public policy. Rather, the public has a policy toward art. Art's lack of public posture is its strength. Once it makes demands on society, it may lose its perspective and a central aspect of its freedom. On the other hand, it is interesting to note how society continues to make demands on art, as we see the authors attempting to do.

There is a sense in which artists are not prepared for working within the public domain. The work of most artists within this arena is actually art made public, which we can distinguish from public art, in which the artist's intention was to take into account the restraints of both the environment and the people who use a particular location. Artists have, for the most part, been isolated in their studios both as a result of the nature of their activity and the social situation in which they find themselves. When they are asked to do a "public" work, they often find it difficult to deal with the politics of the situation. Here I am using "politics" in the best sense of the word, to mean the values and issues of the public and the nation. But what the authors fail to recognize in their argument is that the artist is asked to play a certain public role by the public's representatives. He or she makes a contribution of the work which is then judged by the society. There is no moral or ethical question to be directed to the artist about the work in the public domain, only an aesthetic one.

There is no issue about the imperiousness of the process since the sculpture placed in a public context comes about through public policy administered by the public's representatives screening public art. Questions about the judiciousness of this policy should not be cloaked in the grammar of ethics or morality of art, but in the context appropriate to public policy regarding art. Art is not a moral issue. The actual moral issue concerns the tactics and processes used by those who desire to limit access to art. There is no *a priori* right and wrong. There is certainly an issue about the rights of the individual versus the rights of the society. But such issues must be worked out through dialogue. They cannot be resolved if one party is eliminated.

The support of the arts, whether public or private, is neither defensible nor indefensible. This support, or lack of it, has very little to do with art as an act of inquiry or discovery. There is an interesting symmetry here. The authors raise questions about art and value as a social experience. On the other hand, artists are continually raising questions about the values and ideas of society. The symmetry is broken, however, when one party refuses to permit the possibility of sharing one of the few public experiences which has the potential to transcend the isolation of our subjectivity through its affirmation. Because art acknowledges the primacy of individual sensibility, one wonders how the elimination of one of its primary manifestations can strengthen the public good. How incongruous to claim the authority to make judgment for the public which would preclude each person's opportunity to strengthen and assert his or her own aesthetic sensibility through personal response.

Edward Levine is Professor at the Minneapolis College of Art and Design.

A Reply

DOUGLAS STALKER and CLARK GLYMOUR

Mr. Fleming takes our argument seriously, and accordingly discusses how one might accommodate contemporary sculpture and the public interest. We welcome his remarks and find a good deal of merit in them. Unfortunately, our three other commentators leave us disappointed and dismayed, and for three main reasons.

First, they rarely address the argument in our paper. For example, Professor Levine doesn't think it a view worth refuting and Mr. Beardsley reads our analogy with public pornography as nothing more than a minor amusement: They substitute disdain for coherent objection. Second, these commentators repeatedly misrepresent our claims. For example, Mr. Von Eckardt thinks that choosing what is taught in a public university has some bearing on our point. It does not, for we are concerned with determining what to display in a public place and our classrooms are not public in anything like that sense. Again, Mr. Von Eckardt sees our paper as an attack on contemporary art and a defense of some other type of art. This is a misreading that we explicitly cautioned against; if the truth be known, one of us actually admires many of the pieces we have discussed. Third, a good portion of these comments—far too large a portion—amount to invective and *ad hominem* argument. Mr. Von Eckardt, for instance, compares us to Know-Nothings, while Mr. Beardsley thinks we are merely ''faint-hearted'' in the face of today's public sculpture, Professor Levine charges us with ignorance of art, but utterly fails to indicate what knowledge would dispel our case. Neglecting these irrelevancies, we will examine briefly a few points from each of these three replies.

Mr. Von Eckardt makes two main points, and both are in error because they disregard the interests of people who are affected by public sculpture. His first point is that public policies in accord with our argument would lead to the public display of bad art. How so? These policies would consider the interests of all of the affected public, including the Philistines. Of course, such consideration might lead to the display of art deemed bad by the art community, but this does not show anything is wrong with these policies or the argument with which they are in accord. That argument is about a matter of public concern, the use of public spaces, be it for sculpture, parks, prisons, or parking lots. In a matter of public concern, it seems patently immoral to simply disregard the interests of members of the public in question. Mr. Von Eckardt's second point is that nothing is amiss with the current practice of spending tax dollars for today's public sculpture. The government has guidelines for doing this, and the guidelines are followed by panels of experts which select works of contemporary art. Mr. Von Eckardt thinks this is as fair as can be. But there is abundant circumstantial evidence that much of the public does not like the works selected, and, as we argued, these works produce identifiable harms to the public. The mere citation of bureaucratic procedures is insufficient to make any case that they afford protection against the harms we allege, or even involve recognition of such harms.

Mr. Beardsley thinks that a good deal of the public really does want contemporary sculpture in its public places. With regard to our claim to the contrary, he implies that our evidence is confined to letters in newspapers. Yet our evidence is in fact drawn from a wide variety of sources which, in the absence of valid sociometric results, merit serious consideration. To show that the public (at least much of it) wants today's public sculpture, Mr. Beardsley cites figures on how much local governments appropriated for these works between 1967 and 1980. Such figures show little, if anything, about how much the public wants contemporary art in its public areas. They do show something about the way tax dollars are spent. To put the point simply, we do not believe that many of these expenditures were the result of direct referendums. Since the question is one of the moral justification for an area of public expense, the question is only begged by pointing out that it is a large public expense.

Professor Levine attempts to show that today's public sculpture is good for us. Quite simply, he claims this art does something that needs doing in public—it raises "questions about the values and ideas of society." Professor Levine says nothing to substantiate such claims. He says nothing to *show* that today's public sculpture typically raises provocative and important questions in an accessible fashion; he never considers whether today's sculpture raises these questions better than an editorial or a sermon, or whether raising these questions outweighs the dislike and harm we argue much of today's public sculpture occasions. It is a typical litany within the art community that today's public art enhances public well-being, and Mr. Levine is just following in this dismaying tradition without addressing the real issues in any substantial way. Our very point is that such claims can only be taken seriously if these elementary issues are addressed in a thorough and plausible way.

23

On Subway Graffiti in New York

NATHAN GLAZER

For six years or so one of the more astonishing sights of New York has been the graffiti on the subway trains. The work "graffiti" scarcely suggests, to those who have not seen them, the enormous graphics which decorate the sides of subway cars—murals which march relentlessly over doors and windows, and which may incorporate successive cars to provide the graffiti maker a larger surface on which to paint. They are multicolored, and very difficult to read, but they all, in one way or another, simply represent names. There are no "messages"—no words aside from names, or rather simplified and reduced names, nicknames, or indeed professional names, often with a number attached. (One will not see an Alfredo, Norman, or Patrick, but Taki 137, Kid 56, Nean.) There are no political messages or references to sex—the two chief topics of traditional graffiti. Nor are there any personal messages, or cries of distress, or offers of aid. There are just large billboard-type presentations of the names of the graffiti-makers, in an elaborate script which, with its typical balloon shapes, covers as much surface as possible.

If that were all, then the view that this is art-as-personal-expression, that graffiti are controlled productions reflecting a canon of aesthetic criteria that is beyond mid-

From The Public Interest, Winter 1979, pp. 3–11. Copyright © 1979 by National Affairs, Inc.

dle-class understanding or appreciation, and to be welcomed and savored rather than suppressed, might made
sense. Alas, there is more. The insides of the cars are also
marked-up—generally with letters or shapes or scrawls
like letters, made with thick black markers, and repeated
everywhere there is space for the marks to be made, and
many places where there is not. Thus the maps and signs
inside the car are obscured, and the windows are also obscured so that passengers cannot see what station they
have arrived at. The subway rider—whose blank de-
meanor, expressing an effort simply to pass through and
survive what may be the shabbiest, noisiest, and generally
most unpleasant mass-transportation experience in the developed world, has often been remarked upon—now has
to suffer the knowledge that his subway car has recently
seen the passage through it of the graffiti ''artists'' (as they
call themselves and have come to be called by those, including the police, who know them best). He is assaulted
continuously, not only by the evidence that every subway
car has been vandalized, but by the inescapable knowledge that the environment he must endure for an hour or
more a day is uncontrolled and uncontrollable, and that
anyone can invade it to do whatever damage and mischief
the mind suggests.

I have not interviewed the subway riders; but I am one
myself, and while I do not find myself consciously making
the connection between the graffiti-makers and the criminals who occasionally rob, rape, assault, and murder passengers, the sense that all are part of one world of uncontrollable predators seems inescapable. Even if the
graffitists are the least dangerous of these, their ever-
present markings serve to persuade the passenger that, indeed, the subway is a dangerous place—a mode of transportation to be used only when one has no alternative.

Of course the *sense* of a dangerous place is different
from the *reality* of a dangerous place. The thoughtful head
of the transit police, Sanford Garelik, will point out—and
has statistics to prove—that the subway is less dangerous
than the streets. It is well-patrolled, and the occasional
sensational crime is no index to the everyday experience of
the passenger. Yet the cars in which persons unknown to
the passengers have at their leisure marked-up interiors,
and obscured maps, informational signs, and windows,

serve as a permanent reminder to the passenger that the authorities are incapable of controlling doers of mischief. One can see earlier graffiti underneath a fresh coat of paint that itself is beginning to be covered by new graffiti that mock, as it were, the hapless effort to obscure their predecessors. Thus the signs of official failure are everywhere. And the mind goes on, and makes a link between the graffiti and the broken signs—behind broken glass—that are supposed to tell passengers where the train is going, the damaged doors that only open halfway, and the other visible signs of damage in so many cars.

The graffiti artists, who have been celebrated by Norman Mailer and others, are to the subway rider, I would hazard, part of the story of "crime in the subway," which contributes to the decline of subway ridership, which in turn of course contributes to increasing the danger because of the paucity of passengers. (Official signs in stations warn passengers that between 8 P.M. and 4 A.M. they should congregate in the front cars of the trains, to give what protection numbers may provide against the marauders whose presence must always be assumed.) If this linkage is a common one, then the issue of controlling graffiti is not only one of protecting public property, reducing the damage of defacement, and maintaining the maps and signs the subway rider must depend on, but it is also one of reducing the ever-present sense of fear, of making the subway appear a less dangerous and unpleasant place to the possible user. And so one asks: Why can't graffiti be controlled?

A LITANY OF PROPOSALS

Interestingly enough, as Chief Garelik points out, this is one crime whose perpetrator is known by the mere fact of the crime itself. The graffiti artist leaves his mark, his name, or a variant of it. Most of these names and marks are known to the police. Chief Garelik will show the visitor an astonishing "mug book," consisting of color photographs of the work of each graffitist, accompanied by a name and address. Almost every graffiti artist becomes known. Indeed, the police have invited graffiti artists up to police headquarters and engaged in "bull sessions" with them to try to figure out the best course of action. Nor is the number of graffiti artists so great—from one perspective—as to present too diffuse a target for police action. There are, at any given time, only 500 or so. They begin at about age 11, the mean age is 14, and they begin to graduate from graffiti after age 16—by then it is presumably "kid stuff." Or perhaps penalties rise as graffitists stop being considered juveniles. Young ones begin by marking the inside of cars, and later advance to the grand murals. There are aesthetic traditions. There are also rules, more or less observed, such as: One does not paint on another's graffiti.

Commonly, paints are stolen. The number of spray-paint cans required to embellish the side of a subway car is prodigious and it is hardly likely that young teenagers would have the money. In any case, the police assure the visitor that most paint is stolen. Moreover, Chief Garelik emphasizes—against the chic position that graffiti are art and fun—that the graffiti artists do graduate to more serious crime. The police studied the careers of 15-year-old graffiti artists apprehended in 1974: Three years later, 40 percent had been arrested for more serious crimes—burglary and robbery. Graffiti may be self-expression, but they are not only self-expression. For almost half the graffiti artists there is evidence that graffiti-making is part of an ordinary criminal career.

But if the police know most of them, and there are only 500, then why can't graffiti be controlled? One can go through the litany of proposals—only to end up baffled.

The first suggestion: Arrest them, punish them, make them clean up the graffiti. Indeed, for a while the police were arresting them (or giving out summonses) in very substantial numbers. There were 1,674 arrests in 1973; 1,658 in 1974; 1,208 in 1975; 853 in 1976; 414 in 1977; and 259 in the first half of 1978. As one can see, the arrests dropped radically after 1975, but not because graffiti artists could not be caught—rather because the effort seemed futile. The police began to concentrate on the more determined graffitists and to uncover more serious crimes with which to charge them. For after all, what could one do after arrest that could deter graffitists from going back to graffiti? Put them in juvenile-detention centers? What judge would do that when there were young muggers, assaulters, and rapists to be dealt with, who were far more menacing to their fellow-citizens—and who themselves could not be accommodated in the various overcrowded institutions for juveniles?

But even if juvenile graffitists were not punished by detention, could they not be required to clean up graffiti? This was popular with some judges for a while, but it turned out that it was expensive to provide guidance and supervision (the cleaning usually had to be done on weekends, requiring overtime payment for those who taught and supervised the work), and the police believe that its main effect was to teach the graffitists the technical knowledge necessary to produce graffiti that effectively resist removal.

Could one, so to speak, "harden the target" by securing the yards in which the cars are stored, and where, as is evident from observing the graffiti, much of the work is done? (The large murals extend below the surface of the subway platform, and clearly must be done while the cars stand on sidings and the whole surface is accessible.) Chief Garelik points out that there are 6,000 cars, that one car-yard alone is 600 acres in extent, that many cars cannot be accommodated in the yards and stand in middle tracks, that there are 150 miles of lay-up track, and finally, that wire fences can be cut.

Is there a "technological fix"—a surface that resists graffiti and from which it can be easily washed off? Perhaps, but so far nothing has worked, though certainly the shiny surfaces of new cars put into service make it somewhat harder to apply dense graffiti to them. In time, however, the new surfacing wears off and will take paint. The more serious problem here is the fact that once graffiti gets on a car, it must be taken off immediately so as not to encourage other graffitists. This is the practice in Boston where, as in other cities, the mass-transit system does not have graffiti. But the New York system, so much huger, does not have enough maintenance men, and so the policy of immediately eliminating graffiti cannot be implemented.

One could give graffiti artists summer jobs, as a way of providing them with something else to do, and indeed the police have been instrumental in finding summer jobs for 175 of the young people involved. Well, it is worth a try. But one wonders whether most jobs available for unskilled youths would match the excitement of painting graffiti onto silent subway cars in deserted yards, watching for the police, stealing the paints, organizing the expeditions.

There are more imaginative proposals, such as hiring them to paint the cars in the first place. But one can imagine the technical problems involved in handing over such good (and well-paid) jobs to 11- to 16-year-olds.

One proposal after another has been considered, evaluated, tried. The police have not given up—far from it. Their favored approach, if it could be financed, would be intensive work, on a one-to-one basis, by youth workers (students in psychology and sociology), a "big brother" program that would involve young graffitists in other activities and introduce them to young adults who would help find other outlets for their energies. But one wonders whether the youth workers might not be converted by the graffiti artists, who do not believe they are doing anything wrong. They do see their graffiti as art and self-expression (and create albums in which fellow graffiti artists reproduce miniatures of their designs—the police have a few of these, which are quite beautiful examples of urban, vernacular art). They are not at this point in their lives engaged in the uglier crimes that are so common in New York. What arguments would the youth workers, who might themselves reflect the culture that has given approval to making graffiti (as to smoking marijuana, and other formally illegal activities), be able to present to convince the young graffiti artists to give up their work? What could they provide them in its place?

There have been some efforts to divert the energies of the young graffiti artists from the sides of subway cars to canvases. Some of the graffitists produce canvases for sale, with the assistance of the adults who work with them. Some have gone on to art school—have indeed gained fellowships because adults working with them saw talents that could be developed. But it is hard to imagine this kind of thing making much of an impact on the problem, though it may be a solution for a dozen or two a year. Indeed, these very opportunities might be attractive enough to serve as an incentive for others to try to develop and demonstrate their talents by working on subway cars!

As one learns more about the graffiti artists, realizes that most of them are known to the police, that their more serious crimes (if they move on to them) will take place after they have given up graffiti, and that among all the things urban youth gangs may specialize in this is not the worst—then, one's anger at the graffiti makers declines. One begins to accept graffiti as just one of those things that one has to live with in New York. But this tolerance should not lead us to forget the 3-million subway riders per day who do not have the opportunity to study the graffiti problem, who are daily assaulted by it, and who find it yet another of the awful indignities visited upon them by a city apparently out of control and incapable of humane management. Even if graffiti, understood properly, might be seen as among the more engaging of the annoyances of New York, I am convinced this is not the way the average subway rider will ever see them, and that they contribute to his sense of a menacing and uncontrollable city. The control of graffiti would thus be no minor contribution to the effort to change the city's image and reality.

SYSTEMATIC DETERRENCE?

But how? Chief Garelik suggests some food for thought. Why are there so few graffiti on trucks, he asks. Trucks provide great surfaces, without windows or doors. If one motive for making graffiti—as the kids tell us—is seeing one's name being sped through the four contiguous boroughs, and the thrill of the thought that one's name will be seen by people unknown, then trucks should offer an attractive opportunity. But truck drivers beat up the kids they find trying to deface their trucks! And there are no graffiti on trucks.

Why are there no graffiti on commuter railroad trains? Their car yards are as accessible as those in which subway cars are stored, and their trains run through low-income areas. Perhaps it is because the graffiti artists and their friends don't ride the commuter lines and don't care to advertise their skill and daring in unknown places. But Chief Garelik has a simpler answer: The maintenance men for those lines use buckshot. "They do?" I asked incredulously. Well, that is what the kids believe. Either there was such an experience, or rumor of it, and that seems enough to protect the commuter cars. Certainly here is a hint of something that might work. In fact, early in the graffiti plague, there was a proposal to use guard dogs in the subway yards. It might have been impractical for various reasons. But it might have worked, too. In any event, there was such an uproar at the prospect of juveniles being bitten or mauled that the idea was abandoned.

So it is possible, perhaps, to deter graffitists. But it is not possible to deter them through the regular juvenile-justice system, in which a weary judge, confronted by many difficult and intractable problems, can think of nothing better than asking Johnny to promise he won't do it again. Punishment at the scene of the crime seems to deter marvelously: being beaten up by a truck driver or facing a burst of buckshot if you are caught. The dogs also might have worked.

In other words, there are methods to deter graffiti artists. But are there any ways to institutionalize these methods in an orderly, rule-bound, and humane system of law enforcement? It is not possible to tell the transit police, "Don't bring the kids in, just beat them up." We would not want the transit police to do so, and the transit authorities would not want to encourage such uncontrolled and uncontrollable behavior: A transit police force of 3,000 members must be governed by rule and order rather than informal sanctions, informally applied. And rule and order mean that the graffiti artists are brought into a system of juvenile justice which has more important crimes to deal with, and in which punishment, if any, will be minimal.

Is it possible to apply deterrence in a systematic way in a large bureaucratic system? It should be. Chief Garelik points out that a natural experiment, comparing the treatment of those who avoid paying tokens in two boroughs, suggests that deterrence does reduce illegal acts. In one borough, for some reason, those given summonses for trying to get into the subway without paying a fare were fined on the average 99 cents; in the other, during a comparable period, they were fined on the average $10.45. In the first borough, 20 percent of those caught were repeat offenders; in the second, only 3 percent. Obviously there are other plausible differences between the two boroughs that would have to be taken into account to explain why fare-avoiders in one are so much more commonly repeaters than in the other. But it is not unreasonable to take as a first possibility that in one borough this act is more severely punished.

Undoubtedly there is some form of deterrence that would reduce graffiti-writing. Some graffiti artists, we are told, inform on others when threatened by a term in a tough detention center. (Whether the police could deliver on such a threat is another matter.) Would a few days in the detention center have more effective results than a few weekend sentences to erase graffiti? What would be the problems in trying to test such an approach? In trying to institute it?

NEW APPROACHES

Aside from deterrence approaches, there are what we might call "education" or "therapy" approaches. Trained juvenile officers, social workers, counselors, or other youth workers would work with the apprehended graffiti artist, either directly or by finding some social agency with which he would be required to maintain contact. Such programs have been begun on an experimental basis. Chief Garelik favors such approaches, has gotten some grants to institute them, and needs more such grants. It is certainly premature to evaluate these new programs, though certain considerations immediately come to mind. Unlike the case with some other crimes, it is difficult to enlist a youth's conscience or sense of right and wrong to combat his desire to make graffiti. There will be problems as well in getting youth workers to discourage graffiti-writing, both because it does not offend their sensibilities, and because they may view it as a comparatively insignificant offense. Nevertheless, these new programs constitute one of the few approaches that is available, and, in light of the proven ineffectiveness of other approaches, are certainly worth trying.

Graffiti raise the odd problem of a crime that is, compared to others, relatively trivial but whose aggregate effects on the environment of millions of people are massive. In the New York situation especially, it contributes to a prevailing sense of the incapacity of government, the uncontrollability of youthful criminal behavior, and a resultant uneasiness and fear. Minor infractions aggregate into something that reaches and affects every subway passenger. But six years of efforts have seen no solution. Graffiti of the New York style came out of nowhere, and strangely enough do not afflict other mass-public-transportation systems, except for that of Philadelphia. Maybe graffiti will go away just as unexpectedly, before we find a solution. But in the meantime, 500 youths are contributing one more element to the complex of apparently unmanageable problems amidst which New Yorkers live.

V

CITY
AND
PLANNING

INTRODUCTION

The essays in this final section turn from theoretical, historical, and critical inquiries to examine the possibility of planning and creating American public spaces today. The background for such speculations is sketched out sharply in Charles W. Moore's well-known essay, "You Have to Pay for the Public Life." Writing in the mid-1960s, Moore takes up the question of monumentality in American architecture (a recurring theme in this volume) and finds that, in California at least, monumentality is becoming more difficult to achieve as private concerns have gained hegemony over public ones in planning and architectural thinking. "The public life," as he calls it, requires a private sacrifice to the public realm, and Americans seem less willing to make it; instead, they have created bits of public life within the framework of private architecture and design. Writing before the age of the large shopping mall, he points to theaters, restaurants, and especially to Disneyland as models of the new public space. The spaces may be public, he writes, but they are utterly lacking in political character, and one pays for them, not through taxes, but at the gate. The last hope he sees for publicly funded spaces are freeways.

One finds a different perspective from New York in the 1980s. Still a city crowded by pedestrians, New York continues to offer the possibility of a shared public life, but that promise is rarely fulfilled because, as Nathan Glazer writes in "Paris—the View from New York," New York just does not "work" the way a great European city like Paris may be said to. In comparing the two cities Glazer de-emphasizes the obvious differences in order to focus on the ethos of planning in Paris, where he finds a professional civic service, an interest in planning at the highest levels of government, and more consensus in the approaches to preservation and contextual building among all political figures. None of these conditions exists in New York. Consequently, New York politics focusses more on "soft" social services and other budgetary matters, less on "hard" urban infrastructure, and the physical public environment is allowed to deteriorate, or left to private interests.

Joseph B. Rose's "Landmarks Preservation in New York" is a case study in how difficult public planning is in the United States, and especially in New York. He shows how an originally non-controversial goal—the preservation of historical landmarks—became a fairly radical and controversial policy due to administrative decentralization, interest-group politics, court intervention, and ideology. By separating preservation from other worthy planning goals and treating it inflexibly, New Yorkers have made it more difficult to plan their city.

Much of the blame for our planning disorders is often placed on the American architectural profession itself, and consequently on the schools of architecture that train it. Is it possible to train architects to pay more attention to the public space? Robert Gutman's "Educating Architects: Pedagogy and the Pendulum" provides the historical background for approaching this question. Gutman finds that, although architecture is one of our fastest growing and increasingly prestigious professions, there is an underlying discontent in the architecture schools as they become more distanced from this professional success. He traces the eclipse of engineering and urban planning in the schools, and the narrowed focus on aesthetic design that has accompanied the "studio method" of teaching, and argues that training has become too narrow. Gutman suggests that the studio method be rethought and perhaps reorganized so as to reincorporate some of the older professional concerns with construction, the human use of buildings, and public policy.

Jaquelin Robertson, former director of the Office of Midtown Planning in New York City, now dean of the University of Virginia School of Architecture, offers some personal reflections on why architectural education must make urban design central to its concerns. In "The Current Crisis of Disorder" he complains about the increasing physical bleakness of American cities over the past forty years, and claims the architectural profession has encouraged this trend by ignoring urban design, or turning it into a powerless specialty in the schools. We have an architecture of parts, not of the whole, he writes, which may be inevitable in a democratic culture with no innate sense of hierarchy and order. However, he is heartened by recent

public and professional interest in older buildings, in preservation, and architectural contextualism; Americans are
rediscovering the pleasures of the street. This is a hopeful
sign, but it is not yet planning for the whole. He then list
some of the issues—parking, landscaping, public art, citizen participation—that architecture schools must face if
they are to train students to build public cities again.

24

You Have to Pay for the Public Life

CHARLES W. MOORE

Any discussion of monumental architecture in its urban setting should proceed from a definition of (or, if you prefer, an airing of prejudice about) what constitutes "monumental," and what "urban" means to us. The two adjectives are closely related: both of them involve the individual's giving up something, space or money or prominence or concern, to the public realm.

Monumentality, I take it, has to do with monuments. And a monument is an object whose function is to mark a *place*, either at that place's boundary or at its heart. There are, of course, private monuments, over such places as the graves of the obscure, but to merit our attention here, and to be of any interest to most of the people who view it, a monument must mark a place of more than private importance or interest. The act of marking is then a public act, and the act of recognition an expectable public act among the members of the society which possesses the place. Monumentality, considered this way, is not a product of compositional techniques (such as symmetry about several axes), of flamboyance of form, or even of conspicuous consumption of space, time, or money. It is, rather, a function

Reprinted from Perspecta 9/10: The Yale Architectural Journal, *1965, pp. 57–97.*

of the society's taking possession of or agreeing upon extraordinarily important places on the earth's surface, and of the society's celebrating their pre-eminence.

A version of this agreement and this celebration was developed by José Ortega y Gasset, in *The Revolt of the Masses*, into a definition of urbanity itself. "The *urbs* or *polis*," he says, "starts by being an empty space, the *forum*, the *agora*, and all the rest is just a means of fixing that empty space, of limiting its outlines. . . . The square, thanks to the walls which enclose it, is a portion of the countryside which turns its back on the rest, eliminates the rest, and sets up in opposition to it."

Ortega y Gasset's product is the city, the urban unit based upon the Mediterranean open square, a politically as well as physically *comprehensible* unit that people used to be willing to die for. The process of achieving an urban focus is the same as that of achieving monumentality: it starts with the selection, by some inhabitants, of a place which is to be of particular importance, and continues when they invest that place with attributes of importance, such as edges or some kind of marker. This process, the establishing of cities and the marking of important places, constitutes most of the physical part of establishing civilization. Charles Eames has made the point that the crux of this civilizing process is the giving up by individuals of something in order that the public realm may be enhanced. In the city, that is to say, urban and monumental places, indeed urbanity and monumentality themselves, can occur only when something is given over by people to the public.

Planners have a way of starting every speech by articulating their (private) discovery that the public body's chief concern is *people*. The speech then says unrelatedly that it's too bad the sprawling metropolis is so formless. It might well be that if the shibboleth about people were turned inside out, if planning efforts went toward enlarging people's concerns—and sacrifices—for the *public* realm, that the urban scene would more closely approach the planners' vision, and that the pleasures of the people would be better served.

The most evident thing about Los Angeles, especially, and the other new cities of the West is that in the terms of any of the traditions we have inherited, hardly anybody gives anything to the public realm. Instead, it is not at all clear what the public realm consists of, or even, for the time being, who needs it. What is clear is that civic amenities of the sort architects think of as "monumental," which were highly regarded earlier in the century, are of much less concern today. A frivolous but pointed example is the small city of Atascadero, which lies in a particularly handsome coastal valley between Los Angeles and San Francisco. It was first developed in the '20s as a real-estate venture with heavy cultural overtones and extensive architectural amplification. Extraordinarily ambitious "monumental" architecture popped up all over the townsite. Buildings of a vague Italian Romanesque persuasion with a classic revival touch, symmetrical about several axes, faced onto wide malls punctuated or terminated by Canovesque sculpture groups. The effect was undeniably grand, if a bit surreal, exploiting wide grassy vistas among the dense California oaks. But there wasn't much of a town until the '40s. Then, on the major mall, an elaborately sunken panel of irrigated green, there cropped up a peninsula of fill surmounted by a gas station. Later, there came another, and more recently an elevated freeway has continued the destruction of the grand design. All this has happened during the very period in which Philadelphians, with staggering energy and expense, have been achieving in their Center City long malls north from Independence Hall and west from a point just off their City Hall, grand vistas at every scale, an architectural expression overwhelmingly serene, all urban desiderata which the Atascaderans did not especially want or need, and have been blithely liquidating. Doesn't this liquidation constitute some sort of crime against the public? Before we start proceedings, we should consider what the public realm is, or rather, what it might be in California now and during the decades ahead, so that the "monumentality" and the "urbanity" that we seek may be appropriate as functions of our own society and not of some other one.

In California cities, as in new cities all over the country (and in California just about all cities are new cities), the pattern of buildings on the land is as standard as it is explosive. Everywhere near population centers, new little houses surrounded by incipient lawns appear. They could be said to be at the edge of the city, except that there is no real edge, thanks to the speed of growth, the leapfrogging of rural areas, and the long commercial fingers that follow the highways out farther than the houses have yet reached. Meanwhile, in areas not much older, houses are pulled down as soon as zoning regulations allow, to be replaced with apartments whose only amenity is a location handily near a garage in the basement.

The new houses are separate and private, it has been pointed out: islands, alongside which are moored the automobiles that take the inhabitants off to other places. It might be more useful and more accurate to note that the houses and the automobiles are very much alike, and that each is very like the mobile homes which share both their characteristics. All are fairly new, and their future is short; all are quite standard, but have allowed their buyers the agonies of choice, demonstrating enough differences so that they can readily be identified during the period of ownership, and so that the sense of privacy is complete, in the car as well as in the house. This is privacy with at least psychic mobility. The houses are not tied down to any *place* much more than the trailer homes are, or the automobiles. They are adrift in the suburban sea, not so mobile as the cars, but just as unattached. They are less islands alongside which the cars are moored than little yachts, dwarfed by the great chrome-trimmed dinghys that seek their lee.

This is, after all, a floating world in which a floating population can island-hop with impunity; one need almost never go ashore. There are the drive-in banks, the drive-in movies, the drive-in shoe repair. There is even, in Marin County, Frank Lloyd Wright's drive-in Civic Center, a structure of major biographical and perhaps historical importance, about whose forms a great deal of surprisingly respectful comment has already appeared in the press. Here, for a county filling up with adjacent and increasingly indistinguishable suburban communities, quite without a major center, was going to be *the* center for civic activities, the public realm, one would have supposed, for which a number of public-spirited leaders in the community had fought long and hard. It might have been, to continue our figure, a sort of dock to which our floating populace might come, monumental in that it marked a special place which *was* somewhere and which, for its importance, was civic if not urban. But instead of a dock for floating suburbanites, it is just another ship, much larger than most, to be sure, and presently beached (wedged, in fact) between two hills. It demands little of the people who float by, and gives them little back. It allows them to penetrate its interior from a point on its underside next to the delivery entrance, but further relations are discouraged, and lingering is most often the result of inability to find the exit.

A monster of equivalent rootlessness heaves into view from the freeway entrance to California's one established anchored city, San Francisco. The immense new Federal Building just being completed by John Carl Warnecke and a host of associated architects, stands aloof from the city's skyline, out of scale with it, unrelated to anything in the topography, no part even of the grandiose civic center nearby. Slick details, giant fountains, and all, it draws back from the street and just stands there. It is one of the West's largest filing cabinets, and it is unfair, of course, to expect from it any attributes of the public realm. Indeed, if San Francisco, one gathers, had not grudgingly stepped aside for it, some distant bureaucrats would spitefully have removed it to Oakland. So much for the Federal Heart of the city.

Even in the few years of Yankee California's existence, this kind of placelessness has not always been characteristic. During the '20s and into the '30s, with what was doubtless an enormous assist from the Hollywood vision in the days of its greatest splendor, an architectural image of California developed which was exotic but specific, derivative but exhilaratingly free. It had something to do with Helen Hunt Jackson's *Ramona*, with the benign climate, with the splendor of the sites and their floral luxuriance, with the general availability of wood and stucco, and with the assurance supplied by Hollywood that appearances *did* matter, along with the assumption (for which Hollywood was not necessary but to which it gave a boost) that we, the inheritors of a hundred traditions, had our pick. What came of this was an architecture that owed something to Spain, very little to the people who were introducing the International Style, and a great deal to the movie camera's moving eye. It seemed perfectly appropriate to the energetic citizens of Santa Barbara, for instance, that after their city had been devastated by an earthquake, it should rise

again Spanish. The railroad round house appeared to become a bull ring, the movie house a castle. Everywhere in
the town, the act of recalling another quite imaginary civilization created a new and powerful public realm.

Out of this public act came one of the most extraordinary buildings in the United States, probably the most
richly complex and extensively rewarding stew of spatial
and sculptural excitements west of Le Corbusier's Carpen-
ter Visual Arts Center: the Santa Barbara County Court
House. It was completed in 1929. William Mooser was the
architect, and the inspiration, say the guidebooks, was
Spanish. But nothing in Spain was ever like this. Instead of
setting itself off against the landscape, in Mediterranean
fashion, this assemblage of huge white forms opens itself
up to it. The landscape is a big and dramatic one in Santa
Barbara, where the coastal plain is narrow, the ocean close
at hand, and the mountains behind unusually high and
startlingly near. The Court House takes it all in: it piles
around one end of a large open park, whose major forms
are sunk into the ground, thus allowing the giant arch, the
main feature among the dozens of features visible from the
street side, to lead not into the building but through it and
immediately out the other side, so that the building mini-
mizes its enclosure function and asserts itself as backdrop—a stage set, if you will—with the power to transform
the giant landscape. It is almost too easy to make a comparison with Le Corbusier's new Harvard building, similarly pierced (in Cambridge, in 1963, by a make-believe
freeway ramp) and similarly composed of an immensely
rich but strongly ordered concatenation of sculptural
forms. At Harvard they are twisted enough and powerful
enough to dislocate all the polite false Georgian buildings
around, to wrench them loose and set them whirling.
Fewer structures are set whirling by the Court House, but
a full complement of phantoms is raised up out of the lush
landscape.

The Santa Barbara County Court House did so much
about sweeping the whole landscape up and in that one
might expect the really large-scale projects of the '60s to
catch even more of the grandeur of the place. Whole new
college campuses, for instance, which are springing magi-
cally out of fields across the state, surely present unparal-
leled chances to order a public realm, to invest a place of

public importance with the physical attributes of that importance. Yet, by any standards, the clearest and strongest campus to be found in the state is still the old campus at Stanford (designed in Boston by Shepley, Rutan, and Coolidge, and built in the years just after 1887). The buildings in the old campus are H.H. Richardson warmed over (and cooled off again in the long passage from the architects' Boston kitchens); the gaudy mosaic façade of the chapel, the centerpiece of the composition, is an affront to the soft yellow stone surfaces around. But the play of the fabled local sunshine with the long arcades, the endlessly surprising development of interior spaces from big to small to big again, the excitement of a sensible framework that is strong; and supple enough to include the most disparate academic activities—all combine to make this a complete and memorable place. Even though the surrounding countryside is not swept into the picture, as at Santa Barbara, at least there is an orchestration of spaces varied and complete enough to evoke a complex public use. It is a place, however, that dates from the previous century, and this is a survey of our own times, times that have multiplied opportunities for spatial and functional orchestrations like the ones at Stanford and Santa Barbara. What, then, do we have?

Foothill College in Los Altos, by Ernest J. Kump and Masten and Hurd, comes first to mind, because it has won every prize in sight, and because it is a beguiling place. It sits strong on a pleasant rolling site, on which prodigies of bulldozing have created earthworks worthy of a Vauban, though a bit dulled by a foreground of parking lot. Its nicely detailed buildings share the charm of the best Bay Region domestic architecture, topped by memorable shingle roofs, which have added the glories of old Newport and older Japan to the idiom of the Bay, without ever losing control. Yet I am bound to report that this sensitive and disciplined complex is simply not in the same league as the older campus or the Court House. There is no heightening of importance, no beginnings, even, of the establishment of a *place* singled out for special public importance and illuminated by that recognition—a place, for instance, important enough for an academic procession to occur. The old Stanford campus may not culminate in anything of special beauty or worth, but it works at culminating. Foothill, rather, with great charm, dissipates itself and loses its powers. Sasaki and Walker's landscaping senses well this urge to dissipate, and devotes itself to filling with impenetrable bosques the places where the spaces might have been. Equalitarian, it is: every tree and every building is as important as the next.

And so the public realm is made scarcely distinguishable from the private; the college's fortress base of earth does not anchor it, and it floats, as free as the houses in the suburban seas around.

The same firm's newer campus, for Cabrillo College near Santa Cruz, is far less beguiling and floats even more free. The buildings, carefully and sophisticatedly detailed, stick close to the idiom established when California was young and places were Places, but the idiom does not stretch to cover the requirements, and the act of multiplying varying sizes of hipped-roof buildings surrounded by porches only serves to confirm the rigidity of a whole campus made of a single verandaed form. A window is a simple thing, and not new. In the cool climate of coastal northern California, the sunshine it can admit is pleasant if there is not a wide veranda in front to reduce north, east, south, and west to shady equality. The citizens of old Monterey built porches like these in the cool fog, lived behind them, and died like flies from tuberculosis; presumably medical science and the mechanical engineer will save us this time.

Meanwhile, the attempt to stuff the functions of a whole college into this rigid domestic idiom puts Cabrillo in strong contrast with the old Stanford campus, where the spaces evoke a wide variety of uses; here everything is not only equalitarian but equal. Impeccable details and all, it makes nothing special, it adds nothing to the public realm.

During the years of California's growth, as its cities have appeared, the extravagances of the landscape and of the settlers upon it have suggested to many that straight opulence might create centers of the public realm. Three city halls, especially, clamor for our attention: The San Francisco City Hall probably heads the list for sheer expensive grandeur. The expensiveness was, one gathers, as much a political as a physical phenomenon, but the grandeur is a manifestation of the highly developed Beaux-Arts compositional skills of architects Bakewell and Brown.

These great skills, though, have been curiously ineffectual in commending themselves to public concern. It is a curious experience, for instance, to stand in the towering space under the aggressively magnificent dome and to notice that hardly anyone looks up. And the development of the extensive and very formal civic center outside has had remarkably little effect on the growth of the downtown area, which has remained resolutely separate from all this architectural assertion. Surely a part of the failure to achieve an important public place here rests with the entirely abstract nature of the Beaux-Arts' earlier International Style. It takes a major master, like Sir Edwin Lutyens at New Delhi, to lift this idiom out of the abstract and to give some point to its being somewhere. The San Francisco City Hall demonstrates skill but no such mastery, so the city is not specifically enriched by this building's being here; it could be anywhere.

Or almost anywhere. It could not easily be in Gilroy. A small garlic farming community north of Salinas, Gilroy relied on a similar, if more relaxed, show of opulence in the building of its own City Hall in 1905. An elaborateness of vaguely Flemish antecedent served the town's desires; a truly remarkable array of whirls and volutes was concentrated here to signal the center of the public realm. But, alas, this concentration has not kept its hold on the public mind much more effectively than San Francisco's City Hall has, and now this fancy pile is leading a precarious life as temporary headquarters for the town's Chamber of Commerce and police station.

The citizens of Los Angeles adopted a slightly different route to achieve importance for their City Hall. In their wide horizontal sprawl of a city, they went *up* as far as seemed practical, and organized their statutes so no other buildings could go higher. But economic pressure has mounted, and now commercial structures bulk larger on the skyline than the City Hall. The Angelenos' vertical gesture should get some credit, in any case, for being a gesture, an attempt to make a center for a city which otherwise had none. As a formal gesture, it has even had some little hold on the public mind, although its popular image now involves a familiar tower rising in the smoggy background, while a freeway interchange fills the sharp foreground. Investing it with life, and relating the life behind its windows to the life of the city, may never have been possible; such investment, of course, has never happened.

It is interesting, if not useful, to consider where one would go in Los Angeles to have an effective revolution of the Latin American sort: presumably, that place would be the heart of the city. If one took over some public square, some urban open space in Los Angeles, who would know? A march on City Hall would be equally inconclusive. The heart of the city would have to be sought elsewhere. The only hope would seem to be to take over the freeways, or to emplane for New York to organize sedition on Madison Avenue; word would quickly enough get back.

Thus the opulence and the effort involved in the San Francisco, Gilroy, and Los Angeles City Halls all seem to come to very little in the public mind, lacking as they all do any activity which elicits public participation or is somewhat related to public participation. Whatever the nature of the welfare state, these public buildings seem to offer far less to the passer-by than such typical—and remarkable— California institutions as the Nut Tree, a roadside restaurant on the highway from Sacramento to San Francisco, which offers in the middle of a bucolic area such comforts as a miniature railroad, an airport, an extensive toy shop, highly sophisticated gifts and notions, a small bar serving imported beers and cheeses, a heartily elegant—and expensive—restaurant, exhibitions of paintings and crafts, and even an aviary—all of them surrounded and presented with graphic design of consummate sophistication and great flair. This is entirely a commercial venture, but judging from the crowds, it offers the traveler a gift of great importance. It is an offering of urbanity, of sophistication and chic, a kind of foretaste, for those bound west, of the urban joys of San Francisco.

In the days before television, moving picture theaters afforded one of the clearest and easiest ways for people to participate in the National Dream. In California, especially southern California, where movies came from and where the climate allowed forecourts for theaters to be largely out of doors, some of the most image-filled places for the public to congregate, some of the most important parts of what at least seemed to be the public realm, were these theaters. The Fox in Santa Barbara invites our inspection on many of the same grounds as the Santa Barbara County

Court House. The idiom is a movieland Spanish (again, like nothing in Spain), the architectural opportunity a double one: First, to make of the immense auditorium, set a block back from the theater's entrance on the main street, one of the city's noblest bastions, with high white walls sprouting turrets and balconies and follies. Only the grandest of the princes of the other hemisphere could have afforded walls this size to stick their balconies onto; second, and more importantly for the city, to make partly roofed and partly open the block-long passageway from the box office to the ticket taker, thus providing the opportunity to extend the sidewalks of the city, still outdoors, past gardens and along a tiled esplanade, where soft lights play at night, and where by day the sun filters down among the leaves. Santa Barbara's sidewalks are ordinary enough, but in the mind's eye they merge with the passage to the Fox Theater and other commercial arcades and patios off State Street to form a public realm filled with architectural nuance and, even more importantly, filled with the public.

Another such public monument, which should not soon be forgotten, although it has been left isolated by Los Angeles' swiftly changing patterns, is Grauman's Chinese Theater, on Hollywood Boulevard, which seems more astonishingly grand today than it did in the days when millions in their neighborhood theaters watched movie stars immortalizing bits of its wet concrete with their hands and feet.

More recent years have their monuments as well. Indeed, by almost any conceivable method of evaluation that does not exclude the public, Disneyland must be regarded as the most important single piece of construction in the West in the past several decades. The assumption inevitably made by people who have not yet been there—that it is some sort of physical extension of Mickey Mouse—is wildly inaccurate. Instead, singlehanded, it is engaged in replacing many of those elements of the public realm which have vanished in the featureless private floating world of southern California, whose only edge is the ocean, and whose center is otherwise undiscoverable (unless by our revolution test it turns out to be on Manhattan Island). Curiously, for a public place, Disneyland is not free. You buy tickets at the gate. But then, Versailles cost someone a great deal of money, too. Now, as then, you have to pay for the public life.

Disneyland, it appears, is enormously important and successful just because it recreates all the chances to respond to a *public* environment, which Los Angeles particularly does not any longer have. It allows play-acting, both to be watched and to be participated in, in a public sphere. In as unlikely a place as could be conceived, just off the Santa Ana Freeway, a little over an hour from the Los Angeles City Hall, in an unchartable sea of suburbia, Disney has created a place, indeed a whole public world, full of sequential occurrences, of big and little drama, of hierarchies of importance and excitement, with opportunities to respond at the speed of rocketing bobsleds (or rocketing rockets, for all that) or of horse-drawn street cars. An American Main Street of about 1910 is the principal theme, against which play fairy-tale fantasies, frontier adventure situations, jungles, and the world of tomorrow. And all this diversity, with unerring sensitivity, is keyed to the kind of participation without embarrassment which apparently at this point in our history we crave. (This is not the point, nor am I the appropriate critic, to analyze our society's notions of entertainment, but certainly a civilization whose clearest recent image of feminine desirability involves scantily dressed and extravagantly formed young ladies—occasionally with fur ears—who disport themselves with wildest abandon in gaudily make-believe bordellos, while they perforce maintain the deportment of vestal virgins—certainly a civilization which seeks this sort of image is in need of pretty special entertainment.) No raw edges spoil the picture at Disneyland; everything is as immaculate as in the musical comedy villages that Hollywood has provided for our viewing pleasure for the last three generations. Nice-looking, handsomely costumed young people sweep away the gum wrappers almost before they fall to the spotless pavement. Everything works, the way it doesn't seem to any more in the world outside. As I write this, Berkeley, which was the proud recipient not long ago of a set of fountains in the middle of its main street, where interurbans once had run and cars since had parked, has announced that the fountains are soon being turned off for good, since the chief public use developed for them so far as been to put detergent in them, and the city cannot afford constantly to clean the pipes. Life is not like that in Disneyland; it is much more real: fountains play, waterfalls splash, tiny bulbs light the trees at night, and everything is clean.

The skill demonstrated here in recalling with thrilling accuracy all sorts of other times and places is of course one which has been developing in Hollywood through this century. Disney's experts are breathtakingly precise when they recall the gingerbread of a turn-of-the-century Main Street or a side-wheeler Mississippi River steamboat, even while they remove the grime and mess, and reduce the scale to the tricky zone between delicacy and make-believe. Curiously, the Mickey Mouse-Snow White sort of thing, which is most memorably Disney's and which figures heavily in an area called Fantasyland, is not nearly so successful as the rest, since it perforce drops all the way over into the world of make-believe. Other occurrences stretch credulity, but somehow avoid snapping it. The single most exciting experience in the place, surely, is that which involves taking a cable car (as above a ski slope) in Fantasyland, soaring above its make-believe castles, then ducking through a large papier-maché mountain called the Matterhorn, which turns out to be hollow and full of bobsleds darting about in astonishingly vertical directions. Thence one swings out above Tomorrowland. Now nobody thinks that that mountain is the Matterhorn or even a mountain, or that those bobsleds are loose upon its slopes—slopes being on the outsides of mountains. Yet the experience of being in that space is a real one, and an immensely exciting one, like looking at a Piranesi prison or escalating in the London Underground.

Of course Disneyland, in spite of the skill and variety of its enchantments, does not offer the full range of public experience. The political experience, for instance, is not manifested here, and the place would not pass our revolution test. Yet there is a variety of forms and activities great enough to ensure an excellent chance that the individual visitor will find something to identify with. A strong contrast is the poverty or absurdity of single images offered up by architects, presumably as part of an elaborate (and expensive) in-group professional joke. The brown-derby-shaped Brown Derbies of an earlier generation, which at least were recognizable by the general public, have given way to such phenomena as the new Coachella Valley Savings and Loan in Palm Springs which rises out of vacant lots to repeat Niemeyer's Palace of the Dawn, in Brasilia. Across the street from this, a similar institution pays similar in-group tribute to Ronchamp. The most conspicuous entry in this category of searches after monumentality, though, is architect Edward Durrell Stone's revisitation of Mussolini's Third Rome in Beverly Hills. This one has plants growing out of each aerial arch. Apparently there was a plethora of these arches, for they crop up again along Wilshire Boulevard, as far away as Westwood Village, without, however, contributing much continuity to that thoroughfare.

Methods of seeking "character" for buildings in northern California are mostly much less theatrical, and adhere more strictly to a single pattern, an outgrowth of the redwood Bay Region Style in the direction of the standard universal American motel, employing stucco walls, aluminum windows, wooden shakes, and casual, if not cavalier, attitudes toward form. A case in point is a recent competition conducted by Los Gatos, a small and pleasant residential city near San Jose, for its city hall and civic center, to be located on a block near the center of the town, which backs onto a wooded hill and boasts some magnificent trees. Most of the entries were less concerned with responding to the site than with attempting to create a local character from long blocks roofed with widely overhung gables, and roofs covered with thick wood shakes, usually verandaed, and smothered in shrubbery—where there were no parking lots. It really isn't fair to describe this newer shagginess by invoking the Bay Region Style, an appellation devised to describe wooden houses of chaste simplicity, clarity, and economy of means. It is better, perhaps, to cast the blame across the seas and christen the idiom, as an Arizonan of my acquaintance has, "Califuji." The winner of the Los Gatos competition, I hasten to point out, was not at all of this persuasion. The scheme, by Stickney and Hall, is a completely simple and smoothly functioning set of flat-roofed blocks placed around a central space built on the top of the council chamber. The group of buildings fronts on the main street—the buildings relating to each other and to parking—and opens up, thanks to the plaza above the council chamber, to the wooded hill behind.

New monumental buildings in northern California, which sometimes bear firm recollection of the residential Bay Region Style, have achieved varying degrees of architectural and critical success. John Carl Warnecke's post office and book store adjoining the old campus at Stanford University uses its materials, masonry walls, and Mediterranean red tile roofs as a point of departure to make, with two large, steep overhanging roofs, a form almost strong enough to take its place beside the old campus. A finely detailed colonnade roofed with hyperbolic paraboloids (presumably the approved late twentieth-century successor to the arcuated colonnade) tucks rather redundantly under the great tile overhang, and fails to measure up to the rest. The care taken in framing its concrete members is, however, heartening assurance that the arts of construction have not yet died out.

At the University of California Student Union, in Berkeley, Vernon De Mars has sought to induce an active public response by devising (in a manner that closely parallels Disney's) astonishing juxtapositions of fragments which, individually, are often exquisitely designed but are left to fend for themselves in a hubbub meant to recall, within a planned environment, the chaos of the city. The forms, like Disney's, sometimes unabashedly recall another time or place: a steel trellis surmounting the major block of the building is said to owe allegiance to Bernard Maybeck's wooden ones of an earlier generation, which generally bore vines; the spaces around the building are by way of appreciation of the Piazza di San Marco; and the carefully developed street furnishings recall Scandinavia. But the scope offered for this collection of occurrences is by no means Disney's, so that the chance to recreate the moods of the city is severely restricted, and Student Union has just one mood: it is cheerful, unremittingly cheerful. Mostly, this is fine, but on the occasions when a soberer tone is wanted, something is missing: from the Student Union there is no aerial tramway direct to Tomorrowland, no Disneyland chance to create still another world.

Whatever is missing, however, this collector's approach to enlivening the public realm demonstrates certain advantages over the single-mindedness of, say, the San Francisco City Hall or some of the soberer classroom blocks that stand about on the Berkeley campus. The simplicity and the anonymity of these high blocks, mostly tile-roofed, set on knolls in groves of oaks and giant eucalypti, are in the spirit of the Bay area, are praiseworthy, and have often been praised. But success eludes most of them, probably because they set out to recall the area's last two lively idioms, but seldom with enough conviction to rise above the perfunctory. The two local idioms they seek to recall were lively ones, and look lively still.

The first, a high-spirited explosion of classical or other borrowed forms, which break apart to leave voids in astonishing places, so as to create lofty spaces and dark shadows, has left a major monument on the campus, the Hearst Mining Building of 1907. John Galen Howard was its architect, but in it the magnificent mad hand of Bernard Maybeck, the local culture hero, is evident. The second local idiom, in whose development William W. Wurster has been the central figure, usually comes out best at small scale, since the carefully understated, spare, almost anonymous efficiency of a well-understood carpenters' constructional system is most clearly in evidence there. "No matter how much it costs," Mrs. Wurster points out about her husband's work—and the best of the rest of the vernacular—"it will never show." The new large buildings on the Berkeley campus of the University of California, where they succeed, succeed because they share either in the exuberance of the first local idiom or in the naturalness of the second. When they fail, they fail from dispiritedly attempting continuity with the first local idiom (their great tile roofs lifted up and out of sight) or from seeking to cash in on the apparent casualness of the second local idiom, without noting that that is a casualness born of an intimate understanding of a constructional system and a way of life.

Not only the University but all of California and the West now face an architectural crisis different in many ways from the problems of the rest of the country. The Boston architects of the nineteenth-century railroad tycoon Leland Stanford had their own clear notions, social and architectural, of the nature of hierarchy, and they manifested them with great success in the old Stanford campus. But twentieth-century California has been equalitarian. As its population grows phenomenally, the people who comprise it, rich and poor, come from all sorts of places and owe no allegiance to any establishment of the sort that exercises at least some control of money and taste in areas less burgeoning. While California was largely rural, this equalitarianism lent special delights to living here. In southern California, from a combination of white-walled story-book Spanish and white-walled International Style, there developed, through Gill and Schindler and Neutra and *Arts and Architecture* magazine, and thanks to the climate and the landscape, a way of building large numbers of private houses of a charm and comfort never before possible anywhere on such a scale. This development was surpassed only in northern California, where, if the climate was a bit moodier, the views of bays and forests were better, and there were architects, first of the generation of Bernard Maybeck, then of the generation of William Wurster, Gardner Dailey, and Hervey Parke Clark, who were willing and eminently able to make the most of the opportunities, to develop a domestic architecture not only esteemed by architects but almost universally accepted and enjoyed by the people for whom it was made. This is the domestic architecture we can call (though the architects who made it don't much like the appellation) the Bay Region Style.

When California was rural, a golden never-never land with plenty of room, with open fields for the public realm, with magnificent scenery for a sharable image, and with Hollywood's grandiose offerings for a publicly sharable experience, nothing could have been more natural than this emphasis on provision for domestic life, nothing more understandable than the gradual atrophying of concern for a public realm that people go to and use. The public weal was being extensively considered in projects built hundreds of miles from Los Angeles and San Francisco to provide those cities with water and electric power; but the kind of monumentality that occurs when the Establishment requires buildings more important than other buildings, in places of special importance, when skilled architects give physical form to this requirement, and when human use and the public imagination confirm this importance, never occurred. It never occurred because the Establishment didn't exist, and because there was no need for it. California during the first four decades of the twentieth century was being developed mostly at a domestic scale, and very well, too; it seemed quite proper that man's impact on the land should be of this cozy, equalitarian, and very pleasant sort.

The process, however, is continuing in 1964, and by now it brings worry. The domestic arrangements of the earlier decades are being reproduced endlessly, no longer in the places that laid some claim to public attention—places like Bel Air, Berkeley, and Sausalito for the view; San Francisco and San Diego for the bay; Hollywood for a very special activity; and Santa Barbara for high mountains coming close to the sea—but in the no-places in between, such as Hayward, Daly City, Inglewood, Manchester, and other municipal fictions even less memorable. The character and the sense of special place that came to the first communities for free, from the oak trees around them and the yellow hills and the mountains and the sea, do not similarly serve the later comers, or anyone: the oak trees go and the yellow hills vanish, the smaller mountains are flattened and even portions of the sea are filled in, all to be covered in a most equalitarian way with endless houses. Even the movie studios are being covered up.

It occurs to some, as the gray domestic waves of this suburban sea fill in the valleys and the bays, and lap at and erode the hills, that something should be done, and that the something should be urban and monumental. The Bay Region Style, for all its domestic triumphs, offers no architectural framework for making a special celebration; the characteristic Wurster reticence, which has served so well in helping to create the continuous domestic fabric of the Bay cities, is too deeply ingrained to allow that. In southern California a latterday straightforwardness born mostly of a habit of commercial expediency militates against architectural celebration of a particular place. But even more basic than the absence of a viable architectural idiom for making public centers is the absence of any Establishment ready to shoulder the responsibility for, to take a proprietary interest in, the public realm. So what, as we started out by asking, might we have instead, for an architectural framework and for an opportunity?

The hope exists that the first best chance for differentiation in these floating gray suburbs will come from our developing an interest in and techniques for a much more accurate definition than we seek presently of what the problems really are. If all places and problems are similar (as we might suspect from our endlessly repetitive new cities), then the whole act of marking something special is spurious and futile. If, on the other hand, there are valid bases for differentiating one place from another and one building from another, and if the differentiation is not now made because our techniques for defining a problem are too crude, then the use by architects of other tools already available, among them the tools of mathematics and of operations research, might offer help. We should be able to expect that our developing industrial plant, controlled by electronic devices of incredible sensitivity and complexity, should be able to give us a much wider, rather than a more restricted, range of products. Just so we might expect, as architects, that by using the techniques available to us, from computer and operations research methods to our own underused analytical capacities, in order to discover more accurately and completely than we do now the particularities, even the peculiarities, of the problems we are assigned, we might achieve a much wider, fuller, more differentiated and specific range of solutions than we do now. We would, then, at least have a method. Given the chance, we might rescue the dreary suburban sea from the sameness forced upon it as much by the blindness of our analytical tools and our tendency as architects to generalize on an insufficient base, as by the social and economic restrictions thrust upon us. . . .

There is no need and no time to wait for a not-yet-existent Establishment to build us the traditional kind of monuments or for a disaster gripping enough to wake the public conscience to the vanishing Places of the public realm we got for free. Most effectively, we might, as architects, first seek to develop a vocabulary of forms responsive to the marvelously complex and varied functions of our society, instead of continuing to impose the vague generalizations with which we presently add to the grayness of the suburban sea. Then, we might start sorting out for our special attention those things for which the public has to pay, from which might derive the public life. These things would not be the city halls and equestrian statues of another place and time, but had better be something far bigger and better, and of far more public use. They might, for instance, be freeways: freeways are not for individual people, like living rooms are and like confused planners would have you believe the whole city ought to be; they are for the public use, a part of the public realm; and if the fidgety structures beside them and the deserts for parking—or for nothing—under them don't yet make sense, it is surely because there has so far been too little provision for and contribution to and understanding of the public realm, not too much. The freeways could be the real monuments of the future, the places set aside for special celebration by people able to experience space and light and motion and relationships to other people and things at a speed that so far only this century has allowed. Here are structures big enough and strong enough, once they are regarded as a part of the city, to re-excite the public imagination about the city. This is no shame to be covered by suburban bushes or quarantined behind cyclone fences. It is the marker for a place set in motion, transforming itself to another place. The exciting prospects, not surprisingly, show up best at Disneyland. There, on the inside of the Matterhorn from the aerial tramway over the bobsled run on the inside of the plastic mountain, is a vision of a place marked out for the public life, of a kind of rocketing monumentality, more dynamic, bigger, and, who knows? even more useful to people and the public than any the world has seen yet.

25

Paris—the View from New York

NATHAN GLAZER

In the two weeks after my return from a year in Paris, the *New York Times* reported that there were some serious derailments on the New York City subway, trains were slowed in the August heat to prevent further derailments, and lines were closed for emergency repairs. There was a mass attack by young hoodlums on people attending a Central Park concert by Diana Ross, and an invasion of the Tavern on the Green to rob the well-to-do patrons of that landmark restaurant. There was an electrical blackout and great damage to electric generating facilities caused by a water main break in the garment district. There was the opening—yet again—of a bid for bus shelters, still not constructed after four or five years of controversy over improper political influence. (The bus patrons of New York City still wait in rain and snow or under a hot sun.) While New York was spared the horrors of another mid-summer garbage strike, I recalled that when I lived in New York a few years before, in a high-bourgeois area very much like my Paris neighborhood, the streets were regularly lined with masses of garbage in bursting plastic bags and an array of garbage cans of all types and sizes.

From The Public Interest, *Winter 1984, pp. 31–51. Copyright © 1984 by National Affairs, Inc.*

One could not help reciting the contrasts with the city I had just left. The Paris metro operates efficiently and quietly on rubber wheels. The construction that one runs into everywhere is not to repair decaying and dangerous rails and ties, but to extend and modernize the system, and to lay down new tracks. The streets of Paris are often turned up, just like the streets of New York; but in almost every case it is not to repair damage and breakdown, but to replace old facilities with new. Perhaps it is only a matter of luck—but one does not recall summer electrical blackouts in Paris (of course it is true there are fewer air conditioners, and thus no need for an enormous surge of power in the summer). Bus shelters are found almost everywhere in Paris, and have been for many years. Their sides are filled with useful maps and information—the routes of all the buses that stop there, in detail and spread in summary on a large-scale map of the system, maps of lines that operate nights, maps of the nearby neighborhood and where one can buy *carnets* (the books of tickets with magnetic strips good for all subways and buses, including suburban lines in the city). In contrast to the patron of the New York City buses, the Paris patron waits in comfort, with benches and protection from rain and sun, and he boards showing his monthly orange card (90 percent of the riders seem to use them). The occasional rider who must pay in coins or bills is accommodated by the bus driver. The garbage is put in uniform, covered gray and orange containers issued by the city of Paris, and built so that their tops fit into the trucks that collected garbage every morning of every day—indeed, one does not see filled containers past 8:00 a.m. Paris's squares and small parks are clean and flowers raised in the city botanical gardens are regularly put out in ravishing displays.

THE CITY THAT "WORKS"

Paris is a "city that works," and while explaining why would take more information than I could acquire in a year as a resident not involved in any formal study of the city, one must lay out the contrasts and ponder the problem. Why does Paris work as well as it does? I speak now of the ordinary facilities based on municipal public investment and services—transportation, garbage collection, utilities, parks, and open spaces. I will leave out crime and police services, because it is taken for granted, and understood, that American crime rates are peculiarly high, and that the lack of safety in New York and other American cites can scarcely be ascribed to inadequacies of policing as such. Further, as a capital, Paris can call on many more police, of more varied types, then New York can. The relative difference in crime and the sense of safety must be attributed to social factors for which, one assumes, no public administration can be held responsible. (It is possible that more important in affecting differences in crime rates are differences in powers of the police and in the operation of the courts. But I will take the difference in level of crime and sense of safety as a given, and consider other areas of difference.)

Let us begin with a few elements that cannot explain the differences between Paris and New York. Paris is big—as big as New York, if we consider the two agglomerations. They are roughly (depending on how we define their borders) of comparable size, wealth, and stage of economic development. It is true that the *city* of Paris, the city of the twenty *arrondissements*, within the lines traced by its nineteenth-century walls and now by the peripheral freeway that rings the city, is considerably smaller than the political entity of New York City—2.3 million people, compared to New York's seven million. This historic and political Paris, from the point of view of the function it serves and the image held of it in the metropolitan area, is roughly equivalent to Manhattan. When I speak of Paris, I will be speaking of this city, rather than the region, a city that comprises 20 percent of its regional population, against the more than half that New York City comprises of its metropolitan area. I am considering the central city, as we call it in the United States. To compare Paris with New York is, then, from the point of view of scale of the metropolitan region, and scale and functions of the inner city, not unreasonable, and indeed is often done. The Paris metropolitan district contains a population almost as large as New York's, producing as many workers requiring trips into a central business district, as much garbage, as many automobiles, as much need for public spaces, and so on, as New York. The differences are not differences of orders of magnitude.

There are differences, nonetheless. Paris closes down

in August, as New York does not. Paris's climate does not call for air conditioning or snow removal—which is undoubtedly a help to city and private finances. Paris sharply limits the height of buildings, and so its central business district is spread over a larger area—a help for transportation. Paris's river is less an obstacle to traffic than New York's is. One can list other differences—and yet if one considers why Paris does so much better in creating the environment of a very large city and world capital than New York does, one cannot resort to any major difference in scale or wealth or geography.

There once was another explanation of why Paris did better, one that will not hold much any more, if it held two decades ago: Paris is now a city almost as ethnically and racially mixed as New York. One will be surprised in the subways at the number of blacks, North Africans, and Asians. The population ofthe city of Paris is now one-fifth foreign (I speak of formal political status). But that understates its heterogeneity. There are many French citizens who are considered "foreign" because of race, accent, religion, name. And there are native "minorities" within Paris. After the municipal elections of 1982, *Le Monde* carried a front-page story on the Jewish vote. Apparently 10 percent of the voters of Paris (the city) are Jewish: One must conclude that if the average Frenchman's view of France as a homogeneous country still marks off France strongly from the United States, and Paris from New York, the reality of racial, cultural, religious, and linguistic diversity brings Paris much closer to New York.

PROFESSIONAL EXPERTISE: "THEY TRY HARDER"

One needs some explanation: it is not the scale of the two cities, is no longer the difference in social composition, and is not particular advantages of climate and physical features. In 1978, a group of American urban experts, all based in New York, attended a conference in Paris with their French counterparts (or as close as one could come to French counterparts) to discuss the problem of Paris and New York. An interesting idea, and it begins to bring us closer to the unique characteristics that make Paris work so much better than New York. It turned out the American experts talked a good deal about Paris (as well as New

York), while the French experts talked only about Paris—perhaps they were too polite. The title of the deliberations has a distinctly New York air—*Survival Strategies: Paris and New York*.[1] The French would never have dreamed of such a title. Their problem with Paris has been how to prevent it from threatening the survival of other French cities: *Paris and the French Desert*, as the title of a famous book pronounced.

The simple comparison of those who attended the conference underlines some of the key differences between the two cities. The Americans were Edward J. Logue, Eli Ginzberg, Ada Louise Huxtable, Mitchell Sviridoff, Raquel Ramati, Franklin A. Thomas, Edward A. Costikyan, Eleanor Holmes Norton, and John P. Keith, President of the Regional Plan Association of New York. They are people who have been in and out of government, but not one is making a regular career as a professionally-trained person following his profession *in* government. The American participants included, as I count, only *one* professional planner. The French experts were mostly professional planners or administrators working on plans as civil servants. The Americans included a majority of people who work on social problems—minorities, race, unemployment. (They could have included a crime expert as well: The chairman of the New York City Planning Commission made his reputation in this field.) There were no equivalents on the French side.

The Americans deal with social problems, the French with physical problems. And understandably so: They have fewer social problems than we do. Trying to make use of their expertise on social problems (especially race), the Americans needled their French counterparts, suggesting in various ways that the French were ignoring issues and problems that would bring them the same degree of pain that plagues the American city. Edward Logue wrote:

> Most serious American urbanists believe that race, or rather the consequences of racial discrimination, is the central urban problem of our society, and they are not confident they have the answers. . . . The French have a very different concept of their race problem. The number and percentage of blacks and Arabs is comparatively small. . . . Since the phenomenon of a nonwhite sector of the work force is of relatively recent origin, they do not yet see it in its generational aspects. I believe our French friends thought we were just not well-informed when we pressed them on their race problem.

For our part, we piously hoped we had laid a foundation for greater concern.

This issue came up again and again. After all, the Americans could clearly tell the French nothing about the *physical* planning of a world city; they *could* tell them about social problems. The French did not seem very interested. (Five years later, they would have been more interested.) The French did not tell the Americans what they thought of New York City; they simply described how they plan for Paris and the Paris region, how their ideas about planning have changed. The Americans were impressed. As Logue wrote: ''there is no question that we found ourselves exposed to a program and *city* administrative arrangement which was clear about its values, its priorities, its resources, and its powers. This is something one can say about very few American cities and certainly not New York.'' And after describing the disaster that has struck American cities, and noting that ''no riot has or will equal the devastation which has created the bombed-out areas of Central Brooklyn and the South Bronx,'' Logue concluded: ''It is from this perspective that I look upon our French experiences. It is carefully considered. It is implemented. After a while they decide it is wrong. Carefully, professionally, they propose a new policy very different from the old one. It is adopted. It is financed. It is being implemented.

''They try harder. I like that.''

SHARED COMMITMENTS IN A DECENTRALIZED SYSTEM

As well he might. But just how they manage to do this is still something of a mystery. Clearly one must think of differences in government and administration to explain some of what we see. I have suggested, for example, that the Americans at this conference were men and women of varied skills, without governmental responsibilities, who may move in and out of government, and may occasionally hold positions of major significance, while the French delegation consisted of permanent civil servants of defined specialties and roles. One senses that this difference is important: If one had tried to find French equivalents to the American urban experts, one could find very few (one could find urban critics, but not as many who had also been major administrators and played key roles in government). If one tried to find American equivalents to the French participants, one would have to reach much further down the chain of administrative command. Our top administrators are politicians, or are politically appointed. The American civil servant who has a particular function has much less authority and much less experience at the highest levels of government than does his French equivalent. So should we begin by considering that France is a more highly-centralized country, with a powerful permanent civil service that produces a more coherent and less hobbled form of government than we have in the United States?

Perhaps. And yet experience in France modifies considerably the old picture of a highly centralized state, in which all power flows from the center through the appointed prefects, and in which local mayors and elected councils are, for good or ill, without power. Reading the newspapers, and the more sophisticated accounts, one finds that the notion of a centralized state that rides roughshod over local and partial interests, and implements the ideas of a central body of planners, is somewhat out of date. It may be the way things once happened, but now the reality is different: There are 38,000 communes in France, more local governments than exist in the United States. They maintain a good deal of autonomy. It is not easy to knock their heads together, or to reorganize them. Their formal powers may be small, but the mayor is often active in a national party, may be a deputy or even a minister, and thus has informal routes to represent his commune and its interests. A most interesting account of the building of the French new towns—one of those monumental projects that has proceeded at a rate that dizzies the American mind, moving from conception and plan to execution at a pace and on a scale for which we have no parallel—reveals how much attention must be given to the views of local communes. Local governments must be accommodated, and maintain their power in the new town. The part of the left-controlled commune that falls within the new town will build government-assisted low-cost housing, while the part of the right-controlled commune that falls within the new town will make its choice for privately-owned housing.

The scale and speed of execution are especially impressive. The first government document supporting the new towns policies came in 1965, large scale construction began in 1970, and by the late 1970s 20,000 new housing units and 1,500 jobs a year were being added to the new towns. The comparison with England's New Towns policies is revealing. In England, despite its apparently longer and stronger traditions of strong local government, the New Towns did ride roughshod over local government, since they were created as government corporations with wider powers than the French bodies had, and could act independently of local authorities.[2]

Clearly Paris has a somewhat different status. There are indeed 1,300 local governments in the Paris region that the major public planning authorities must consider, but Paris proper is only one commune, and was without any strong countervailing powers against central government until a 1975 law gave it a mayor. The first mayor of Paris was, and still is, Jacques Chirac, a contender for national power against both former President Valéry Giscard d'Estaing, and present President François Mitterrand. Until the middle 1970s, the national government, operating through its prefects and ministries and many other bodies, dominated the development of Paris. Its powers are considerably reduced now. Indeed, President Mitterrand's plans for a great international exposition to celebrate the 200th anniversary of the French Revolution were dropped in spring 1983, after considerable planning, because of Mayor Chirac's resistance to the exposition's cost. (The matter is more complicated: Perhaps President Mitterrand, at a time of economic crisis, was also concerned with cost, but he had made it clear that the exposition would not go forward without the cooperation of the local authorities.[3]) The fact is that the great works of Paris today do go forward not simply because central government rules with no countervailing power—or at least, when one reviews the complex administrative arrangements that govern Paris and the Paris region, they do not give one that impression.

But these conflicts suggest one possible answer to the question of why Paris works: It works because people at the highest level of government—kings and emperors in the past, a President and a mayor who hopes to be President now—took an immediate and personal interest in

Paris, made key decisions, and exercised their power to make Paris great, but also to make it work. Paris is of interest to the highest levels of government—and has been for at least 130 years, since Napoleon III and his Prefect Baron Haussmann took over the rebuilding of a largely medieval city that was marked by a few great monuments. Haussmann was denounced in his time as Robert Moses was in ours (and is still denounced by many, but by a declining number). Napoleon III took the initiative to rebuild Paris as a "modern" city, and appointed Haussmann. Note two features: the interest of the Emperor, who himself laid out some of the great avenues to be cut through Paris, which were to serve, among other functions, as access to the new railway stations; and the fact that he could call upon a regular civil servant of the Corps of Prefects, George Eugène Haussmann, who had the energy and skill to carry out the huge public works. Haussmann in turn could call on other regular public servants, government engineers, members of the Corps des Ponts et Chaussés, Adolphe Alphand and Eugène Belgrand, to carry out the great works of cutting avenues through the city, providing it with water and sewers, and with parks.

THE FRENCH PLANNING TRADITION

Paris is still, to an amazing degree, Haussmann's Paris. He served as Prefect of the Seine from 1853 to 1870, and the shape of the city, its great avenues, its parks, and its monumental underground works, are still in large measure those laid out or begun under him and continued by the Third Republic.

One authority asserted in 1971, while Paris was undergoing vast rebuilding, that 60 percent of the buildings and streets of Paris were built in Haussmann's time—certainly an exaggeration.[4] But it is true that the only major addition to Paris's equipment and facilities until World War II was the Metro. Its pattern of open spaces is still, in large part, Haussmannian. Paris as a city of trees and greenery is dominated by the great avenues, even more than by the modest parks Haussmann and his associates were able to lay out—though all the substantial parks of Paris (Monceau, de Montsouris, des Buttes-Chaumont) were laid out in his administration. (The other large open spaces of

Paris—the Esplanade of the Invalides, the Tuileries and the Champ-de-Mars—are the heritage of Louis XIV and Louis XV.)

Haussmann's work may still have left Paris deficient in open space by some international standard, but what it has is primarily due to that phenomenal burst of city shaping between 1850 and 1870. And the great avenues, which leveled so much of medieval Paris, served not only as roadways, but also gave Paris a *sense* of openness and greenery.

The design, laid out for the city by public servants under the authority of the chief of state, has had remarkable staying power, has accommodated the building of systems of public transportation unknown in the time of the designers, and has even been able to survive the devastating impact of the automobile. Certainly this is an amazing feat of city planning, even more amazing because it cannot be attributed to any preternatural insight or genius.[5] Rather, both in the past and today, two elements seem to mark the planning and building of Paris and its government: Interest and involvement at the highest levels of government, and a permanent and high-level civil service. But these alone can also be a recipe for disaster. One must add a third element: The ongoing tradition of French planning and building, derived from the royal works of the seventeenth and eighteenth centuries. This tradition grew up in the course of building palaces and gardens, rather than cities, but its principles were then adapted to cities. And until the last three decades, these principles of planning have retained their hold on all the powers responsible for Paris, and in some measure still do.

The trademarks of the French garden and urban planning tradition are formalism, symmetry, long vistas, and the grand scale. Nature is sharply disciplined: Avenues of trees are set out in straight lines, roads cut through forest or medieval city straight as an arrow, artificial pools and canals are edged in straight courses of stone set in geometrically regular forms. It is a far cry from the American or English idea of a proper approach to nature, devoid of romanticism, grave and sober. It has not attracted those with democratic and romantic instincts, yet the French remained committed to it through five monarchs, two emperors, and five Republics.

Napoleon III had been taken by the very different style of English gardens, and they influenced the planting and design of the Bois de Boulogne and the Bois de Vincennes, and of the smaller parks within Paris, which were laid out in imitation of the romantic vision of organic nature, rather than in the formal lines of French gardens. But the great avenues ran straight as an arrow, framing vistas and important buildings, and on a monumental scale. In time, the sidewalks were cut back to accommodate automobiles, and rows of trees were cut down. And yet Paris remains still so green! It is a phenomenon of planning. Of course, the losses distress the observers and lovers of Paris, yet even the complaints attest to Paris's superiority: Only 27.5 percent of Paris's 1,300 kilometers of streets, complained Bernard LaFay in 1975, are planted. That "only" seizes the eye, and produces a sigh in the breast of the New Yorker. Paris, it seems, has only 1.4 square meters of park per inhabitant—compared to 5.5 for New York, 9 for Rome and London, 25 for Vienna, 50 for Washington—but it makes a marvelous display with those modest meters.

PRESIDENTS AND THEIR PROJECTS

Though battered—as what would not be?—by the inroads of modernism in planning and architecture, and the drastic impact of modern technology, the official interest at the highest levels, committed and able civil servants, and a 300-year-old tradition of formal design, still shape the design of Paris, and have prevented the worst from happening.

It is the first that still strikes the visitor as being uniquely French, and certainly quite far from American experience. Much of the history of Paris in the past 20 years has been determined by the French presidents, inheritors of a tradition of centralized power which has always concerned itself with the city. It is President Mitterrand himself, we read in the newspapers, who has selected the winner of the international competition for a great complex of structures to house two ministries and a center of communications to be built at La Défense. This major complex will complete a monumental axis that has been under construction for 300 years, and runs from the Louvre, through the Tuileries and the Champs Élysées, through the Arc de Triomphe. In the French context, it is taken for granted that one will have to take account of how the monumental complex will look when viewed through the Arc de Triomphe. It is also President Mitterrand who chooses the winner of the international competition for a new opera house at La Bastille. And it is he who determined that an international competition should be held for the last open space in Paris that can accommodate a park, at La Villette in the northwest.

How many of these decisions are *his*, and how many those of his advisors, it would be hard to tell—one must await memoirs. And yet he takes the responsibility, and personally makes the decision (guided, it is true, by advisory bodies of architects and planners). And much of the recent history of Paris can be told in terms of his predecessors' actions. Thus it was President Pompidou who determined that Paris should be brought into the automobile age, called for freeways on the Left and Right Banks, and approved the introduction of high towers into Paris. It was he who determined that a great center of contemporary art should be built on the cleared area of the Plateau Beaubourg, and refused to stop the destruction of Les Halles. It was his successor, President Giscard d'Estaing, who stopped the building of freeways and towers, determined that the proposed tall international trade center on a part of the Les Halles site should be replaced with a park, determined that the Gare d'Orsay should be a museum of the nineteenth century, and that the great unused structure at La Villette, designed to serve the *abattoirs* of the area, should be an enormous museum of science and technology.

Paris has had a mayor since 1976, and President Mitterrand does not have as wide a stretch of power as did his predecessors. He must share his power over Paris with Mayor Chirac, who has national ambitions and who also builds *his* reputation on the beautification of Paris. But Mitterrand too will leave his mark in Paris. One learns that the competition for the public park around the enormous new museum at La Villette was instituted by President Mitterrand because he did not like the decision made by his predecessor—or perhaps because he wanted to set his stamp on one of the great enterprises that would be completed under his *septennat*, as the French called the seven-year presidential term. La Villette was an area of slaughterhouses, and stands in a working class district. It is the last major space available for a park in Paris. Certainly one understands that the president of the left would not want the only major park created in Paris since the time of Baron Haussmann to be built to the design chosen by the president of the right.

Pompidou, Giscard d'Estaing, and Mitterrand, under a democratic and bounded state, with incredibly more complex administrative arrangements, seem to follow in the line of Louis XIV and Louis XV, Napoleon I and Napoleon III, in taking a direct interest in Paris and its grand design. Of course one interest is in making Paris the greatest city in the world. Another is to glorify themselves. But these grand personal motives are also combined with the ambition to make Paris work.

This must be a key to the matter. Can one imagine President Reagan deciding on the design of the new Asian and African wing of the Smithsonian, or Mayor Koch on the design of the new convention center of New York?[6] In Paris, one cannot imagine otherwise. The Presidents celebrate themselves through great works, and the Mayor of Paris establishes his reputation on the beautification of the city, on making it work. This is not to deny that France is a welfare state and that more than great works of urban design are necessary to a president or a mayor. But their achievements and satisfactions are also found in areas that, in this country, we leave to commissions, to bureaucrats, to private funding.

We do have some parallels. Governor Nelson Rockefeller set his personal stamp on the design of Albany, alas. But he was considered an exception in this respect, and perhaps it was his private fortune and the private Rockefeller role and experience that led him to undertake the extravagant and awful Albany Mall. It turned out that either the level of design available, or the taste of those making choices, had undergone an unimaginable decline between the time of Rockefeller Center and the Albany Mall, or the Albany campus of the State University of New York. In contrast, the involvement of French emperors and presidents was not exceptional—it was expected. But the personal involvement of the head of state operated within a tradition of design which helped to avoid the worst, at least within historic Paris.

The tradition itself, upheld by architects, planners, the public, and bureaucrats, would reassert itself if choices strayed too far. Thus it is now accepted that Pompidou, with freeways and skyscrapers inside Paris, was imposing solutions and designs that contradicted 300 years of development in Paris: There was a roar of protest from architects, urbanists, and other Parisians against the destruction of the wonderful iron and glass sheds of Les Halles, against the destruction that would be caused to the complex patterning of the banks of the Seine by a Left Bank freeway. Giscard d'Estaing stopped these projects, and reversed the course. Of course presidents, like other democratically-elected leaders, are responsive to public opinion; my point is that they do not abdicate, that they operate within a long tradition in which they are expected to make choices and decisions. And they have at hand administrative structures that can implement decisions, and a tradition of urban design that, with whatever aberrations, seems to weigh on and affect all the participants, leading to results that the world admires.

WHO SPENDS WHAT—AND HOW

Is there a simpler answer? Money is part of the story. Yet just how to analyze what is spent on Paris is extremely difficult. As a national capital, one thinks, a great deal of money is poured into Paris. It has long been believed that Paris is favored over provincial cities in facilities. The government and citizens of Paris no longer think so. Its new, very expensive metro extensions are matched by new metros in Lyons and Lille. Its new museums are matched—on a lesser scale—by elegant new museums in the major provincial cities. Studying a recently-published book comparing the government and finances of Paris, London, and New York, one is struck by the similarity of problems and questions, but further by the difficulty of asserting in any clear and unambiguous way that the national government in France spends proportionately more on Paris than our federal government spends on New York. One wishes there were tables comparing how much each city raises from its own resources, how much of its budget is paid for from central government sources, and where the money goes. But it would take a major research project to reduce the complexities of the budgets of these great cities to any comparative form. They have very different ways of paying for transport, police, education, social services, and major construction projects, and the differences are so great that it is hard to say unambiguously that Paris gets more than New York. One is struck by the fact that a great deal of information is presented in this French work on the New York City budget, very little on the Paris budget or budgets. Is this availability of comprehensible information on the financial condition of New York City owing to the recent New York City financial crisis and the number of oversight bodies and research groups that now monitor New York City government? One would think it easier to compare, not the money spent and its sources, but the output of services, as measured, for example, in the number of employees devoted to different tasks. But even that is not easy. One finds only one clear area in which Paris is much better served than New York. Paris deploys far more police: 35,000 in the Prefecture of Police (which still operates under a separate, state-appointed Prefect), for a city of 2.3 million![7] New York manages with 25,000 for a city of 7 million. Of course the Paris police also serve the great concentration of central government buildings, and perform functions (for example, issuing the documents that all Frenchmen and residents of France carry) the New York City police do not, but this can explain only a small part of the disparity.

Is there a great disparity in other areas? I have not found the evidence, but it may be so. So, indecisively, I conclude that perhaps the state in France spends more to support basic urban services in Paris than the federal government and New York State do for New York City. Perhaps Paris works better because it puts more money and people into the job of making a city work, and so its streets are paved, its mass transportation is efficient, comfortable, and clean, its garbage is collected and does not litter the streets, and its parks are well maintained. In short, all the elements that create a better ambience for urban life, and that depend on money and services, are better provided in Paris. I suspect that when all the research is done this will explain part of the reason Paris works so well.

But the issue, I think, is not simply more money—New York City's budget provides $2,500 of services for every man, woman, and child in the city, and I truly doubt that Paris provides much more than that. I suspect the answers will be in *where* the money is spent. Paris spends its money on "hard" services: the metro and the new high-speed underground, collecting the garbage, improving the streets, keeping up the parks and open spaces. New York spends a higher proportion of its on "soft" services: welfare, social services, education, criminal justice. By "hard" services I literally mean expenditures on concrete, streets, trucks, flowers, and planting. By "soft" I mean those services meant to improve people by education, advice, or correction. (Admittedly there is no absolute distinction.)

Of course, it is understandable why there should be this disparate distribution. We have more social problems, and we try to deal with them by the only methods we know. But we do not do very well with them. If we shifted some of the money from "soft" to "hard" social services we might even affect some of the social problems. We might provide more jobs for those who do not have them, improve the morale of those who must live in the unkempt and crumbling parts of the city. One hesitates to press this forward as any practical solution; municipal workers simply get too much money to permit much expansion of their numbers. Which leads to a final, unscientific observation: In Paris, parks are kept clean and garbage is collected, one notes, mostly by dark-skinned immigrants. One suspects they are not paid very much. And perhaps this permits a greater return for expenditure in those "hard" services in which unskilled immigrants can be employed. In the United States, jobs collecting the garbage are too well-remunerated to be given to immigrants. As a result, we have few doing it, and we do a worse job of it.

"BUILD THE CITY ON TOP OF THE CITY"

A tradition of urban design and a high level of public social services may not seem to have much in common, but they do. It is the public services that make the design work: replacing the trees that cannot withstand Paris's atmosphere, putting in and replacing flower beds, maintaining the small parks, redoing the small squares with their few benches, maintaining the strips of park along the Seine. But there is a design with which to work. Of course, the design is not only the result of human foresight, ingenuity, talent; it is the result of the layering of history, in which accident and organic growth alternate with grand schemes. Writing in the previously-mentioned conference report on Paris and New York, a French architect, Antoine Grumbach, demands: "Build the City on Top of the City." Do not wipe out its physical history for some presumed modern advantage; save its past, build in the interstices. Obviously this cannot be done in the huge new housing developments that have accommodated the enormous population growth of Paris outside the city, and that respond to the demand for greater living space and new facilities. They have overwhelmed the little villages for which they are named. But in Paris the errors of total demolition have been fortunately few—and have aroused sufficient opposition when they have happened.

Haussmann was denounced for the brutality of his remodeling of Paris. But now, with our interest in the preservation of a past whose techniques, talents, and orientations we can never recover, it is apparent that behind the Haussmannian avenues, with their great widths, their many rows of trees, and their vistas, medieval Paris remained. How fortunate to have had a rebuilder whose interest was in imposing grandeur and efficiency over a complex pattern, rather than wiping the slate clean, as modern urban renewers seem to have preferred, and substituting a design that produces no grandeur and only marginal and doubtful efficiency.

> It apparently never occurred to either Napoleon or Haussmann, in their most extravagant dreams of demolition, to pull down all of old Paris in order to rebuild it anew. [It did occur to Le Corbusier.] They wanted to improve the city, not destroy it. What lies beyond the new boulevards was neither the 'appalling disorder,' nor unspeakable slums, but the tightly knit, highly organic, and lively fabric of the old town, which was just as essential to the everyday life of all Parisians as were the new boulevards. After all, the upper middle class bourgeois did not live by champagne and lobster alone, but by bread, sausages, and red wine as well, and plain cotton goods, old books, and the products of artisan labor and small shopkeepers . . . these items were not to be had in the expensive new stores and cafes along the boulevard. Rents and overhead were much too high. . . . [But they] were to be found just around the corner in the narrow streets and old houses left standing behind the great streets. . . .[8]

How striking the contrast with the rebuilding of recent years which has demolished some of the old areas of Paris! Paris has its planning disasters, in which a historically-created complex of streets and houses, improvable by introducing more water and bathrooms and kitchens, was leveled for modern towers and streets. Norma Evenson describes "The Passing of the Rue Nationale," on the basis of the work of Henri Coing, and it seems a tragedy similar to that chronicled by Herbert Gans in his study of the razing of the West End of Boston (*The Urban Villagers*).

The Rue Nationale ran near the Place d'Italie in the 13th *arrondissement*, one of the "unhealthy blocks" that for decades planners had hoped to level. The story is almost too familiar to bear repeating. The complex physical texture that had developed over a century sheltered an equally complex, and unreproducible, social life. We find the same "urban village" we also find in British and American working-class districts, and the same destruction of both the physical fabric—created and shaped by individual decisions into a rich environment no planner or architect could ever duplicate—and the social fabric, equally built up out of elements that social workers cannot recreate.

> Living in close quarters made it necessary for neighbors to maintain good relations . . . neighborly relations often went far beyond the minimum. 'In case of trouble, our building becomes a real community; I really saw this when my father died, and my wife was confined. . . .' Relations among housewives became particularly intimate, with the common courtyard becoming a place of frequent encounter. Naturally, with shared toilets and water taps, with windows closely overlooking neighbors, with children playing together in the courts, frequent meetings were inevitable. . . . In spite of the bad conditions in the buildings, many residents bitterly regretted the demolitions. . . . One could frequently hear in the cafes such remarks as: 'Why tear down all this? It was beautiful before, our Rue Nationale.'[9]

One looks in sorrow at the pictures in Norma Evenson's book. In place of 48 cafes, the new plan provided for one. Ten bakeries were replaced by two, 26 butcher shops by eight, and 29 grocery stores by five.

PLANNED FORMALITY AND UNPLANNED COMPLEXITY

The design of Paris consisted of the formal new laid over the organic old. Haussmann's indifference to providing directly for the welfare of the poor may have been to their advantage: His plan destroyed fewer of their houses and environments, and his massive works provided them with jobs. The housing left behind, everyone knows, was awful: shared toilets, water taps, no bathrooms. But the solution to that was not demolition, but the prosperity that finally came to the working classes of France, and the establishment of a welfare state, in the post-World War II period. Prosperity made it as easy to improve these deficiencies with minimal destruction of the old physical and social fabric, as to demolish and build anew. The same subsidies could have been available for renovation. It is true in either case that the increasing attractiveness of Paris to those with more money eventually would have forced out many of the Parisian shops, small manufacturing plants, and working-class families. Paris was not immune to the general circumstances that affect the lives of great cities, but it was scarcely necessary for public authorities to spur the process on.

What was striking in the texture of Haussmannian Paris was the interplay between planned formality and unplanned complexity, as if the baroque city and medieval city lived together in useful symbiosis, the great spaces and the *medina* living cheek by jowl. Certainly this is what still gives Paris, even after so much rebuilding, its enormous attractiveness for walking, for living, for watching. There is nothing so attractive as medieval and organic texture once the filth has been moved out, the garbage has been collected, transportation in and out has been improved, and the inhabitants have risen from begging and penury to decently-paid work. The social side is generally the part that has to be attended to in the urban slum: It was well attended-to in postwar Paris. As a result, less public attention to the physical texture was needed—in many cases, as in that of the Rue Nationale, it got far more than it needed.

Once prosperity comes to historic cities, one becomes aware of the touches of vernacular wisdom that present-day architects find so hard to introduce, working as they must on large scales, without artisans, dependent on an elaborate subdivision of specialists and labor, using massive machinery and manufactured elements not easily adapted to specific circumstance. Consider the court that creates an inner quiet area away from the busy streets, and that is an almost universal feature in the old Paris apartment house (whether pre-Haussmann, Haussmann, or post-Haussmann). The modern apartment house, of course, cannot manage to introduce a court—it needs too great an expanse of floor for uniform treatment, too great an economy in stairs and elevators to be able to wrap an apartment house around an eccentric space. Modern building cannot commonly adapt, as the French apartment house does, to the most amazingly shaped sites—sites that nevertheless were treated with a symmetrical facade that did not break the street line, and with an inner court for many of the windows to overlook, achieving blessed relief from traffic noise.

This complex pattern offered other virtues. Fragments remain of private gardens from Paris's many convents and monasteries (or, in the more-favored, Western parts, royal and aristocratic gardens), gardens that many people could see, if not enter. Again, a delightful return from a complex history. In the heart of the great block in the 13th *arrondissement* formed by the Boulevard Port-Royal, the Rue de la Glacière, the Boulevard Arago, and the Rue de la Santé, there lies the enormous garden of an Augustinian convent, overlooked by many hundreds of windows from the huge apartment houses (many post-World War II) which form a solid edge to the block. No one walking along the streets could be aware of the pleasantness that lies within, with birds singing and flowers blooming, and dark-clad nuns occasionally walking along the paths.

From the design point of view, Paris worked—and much of it still works—because it provided a satisfying combination of the kind of city that no one can design, but only the thousands of decisions made in a history of centuries can create, and the kind of human intervention which produced a totally different effect of grandeur and control. The Haussmannian boulevards are as satisfying as the complex texture that lies behind them—though there are those who strongly prefer one to the other.

As for "open space," Parisians still complain about how little there is. But Paris puts on a grand show with its 1.4 square meters per inhabitant. How does it manage such a show? By dispensing with the large parks that do not exist and cannot be created within Paris, it does, with the modest spaces available, almost everything one would want done with green and open space. The boulevards themselves, even in their sadly reduced state to accommodate more traffic, are something like strip parks, with two or more rows of trees planted in earth, not concrete. (Alas, they are horribly soiled by dog droppings, the one element of urban disorder that Paris displays more than most other cities.) The strips along the Seine are beautifully designed and landscaped, providing sudden release from the noise and presence of the city. The larger open spaces offer the very different charms of the romantic landscape of Les Buttes-Chaumont and the park-like Monceau and Montsouris. Paris, it, seems, can create romantic gardens in very small spaces. One can descend into the gardens around the Grand Palais, or the Chaillot, and discover waterfalls, rustic bridges, and little thickets, all the elements of an Olmsted park, in the heart of the city. This is on a handkerchief-sized scale compared to Central Park or Prospect Park, but if one aim of such landscape is to provide contrast and relief from the city of stone, even these fragmentary acres do it. And of course there are the contrasting royal spaces set down in strict formality: the Tuileries, the Luxembourg. The contrasts in the residential pattern between French formality and medieval complexity are mirrored by the open spaces, with their contrast between baroque vistas and English and romantic landscapes.

DESIGN, COMMITMENT, AND RESOURCES

Beginning these scattered thoughts, I said I would leave out one element—the level of crime and civility. But safety and civility directly affect what one can do with, and in, open spaces. Parisians complain about what has happened to their city. *Insécurité* (meaning domestic, not international) was a major issue in the municipal elections of 1982. One reads advertisements everywhere for armoring one's door and introducing burglar alarms, still primitive by American standards. The rate of burglary apparently approaches American levels. Paris is not as homogeneous as it was, and the public discipline maintained when almost everyone is of the same culture—in which older people can discipline children, and youth can be shamed by a look or a word—no longer is what it was. But on one score, Paris still does well. There is public civility. The parks are well used, but one sees little vandalism or graffiti (what little exists tends to be political rather than "expressive" or destructive). Even the new apartment houses that have been springing up and changing many quarters show a concern for public planting and greenery that reflects not only taste, but also the knowledge that shrubs will not be torn up and vandalized.

But in the end one goes back to a few key elements: the history of urban design; the attention paid at the highest levels of government; perhaps the resources poured into adding to and maintaining the public equipment of the city. This is what stands out in Paris.

NOTES

1. *Survival Strategies: Paris and New York* (New Brunswick: Transaction Books, 1979). The conference was sponsored by French-American Foundation and the Council for Urban Liaison.

2. James M. Rubinstein, *The French New Towns* (Baltimore: Johns Hopkins University Press, 1978).

3. For a fuller analysis see Julia Trilling, "Paris: Architecture as Politics," *The Atlantic* (October 1983).

4. Howard Saalman, *Haussmann: Paris Transformed* (New York: George Braziller, 1971).

5. Paul Gagnon points out that the massive underground works for sewers and water permitted the installation of new utilities—gas, electricity, telephones—and their modernization with less disruption, and that in general the *initial* investment in urban equipment is higher in Paris than is common in the United States.

6. From a recent exhibit in Washington on Lafayette Square—which sits right in front of the White House, the President's front yard, so to speak—one learns that some presidents did concern themselves with its design, particularly when it was proposed to tear down the pleasant mixed rows of nineteenth-century town houses for a government office building. President Roosevelt prevented the demolition of one row for a new State Department building. President Kennedy (even more so, his wife) prevented their demolition for huge new executive office buildings, and was eventually decisive in getting an architect, John Carl Warnecke, who worked out a design that saved the town houses and placed the massive bulk of the new buildings behind them. It is my impression that this kind of intervention is exceptional.

7. See Bertrand Chardon, *Gouverner les Villes Géantes: Paris-Londres-New York* (Paris: Economica, 1983). Chardon attempts no comprehensive

comparison, but other figures of numbers of employees are of interest, though they all raise questions. Chardon indicates 150,000 employees for the city of Paris, far more (taking comparative size of population into account) than one finds in the city of New York. He reports 35,000 employees for the city (*Mairie*), 5,000 for the Department of Paris, co-extensive with the city, 45,000 for *assistance publique*, 25,000 for *"services divers"* (p. 199). Elsewhere he lists no less than 50,000 state employees who exercise functions that relate directly to Paris: in education, sanitary and social affairs, postal services, etc. (p. 131). It is because different services are provided by different levels of government that any direct comparison of the budget(s) of Paris with those of New York is not helpful. In any attempt to determine whether Paris spends more on the city than New York, one would have to take account of these services, some of which in New York are under the city, some of which, as in Paris, are central government functions (for example the post office). The task is one that requires a major research undertaking, which I have not undertaken, nor has anyone I have discovered.

8. Saalman, *Haussmann: Paris Transformed*, p. 114.

9. Norma Evenson, *Paris: A Century of Change, 1878–1978* (New Haven: Yale University Press, 1979), pp. 257–258.

26

Landmarks Preservation in New York

JOSEPH B. ROSE

No current discussion of cities can avoid addressing the issue of historic preservation. Twenty-five years ago, the solution of the "urban crisis" was said to be the demolition of cramped obsolete structures and their replacement with ordered modern towers in a pristine environment free from clutter; today, urban planners want to save older buildings as a means "to justify an increasingly dismal existence in a rapidly deteriorating urban environment."[1] What 50 years ago was the sole province of wealthy dowagers has become the latest weapon of urban reformers, who argue that:

> If preservation is not to fall into the trap of total irrelevance, we must learn to look beyond our traditional preoccupation with architecture and history, to break out of our traditional elitist intellectual and aesthetic mold, and to turn our preservation energies to a broader and more constructive social purpose.[2]

In its 1978 decision in *Penn Central v. The City of New York*, the U.S. Supreme Court used the controversy over the preservation of New York's Grand Central railroad terminal to sanction local legislation designed to promote and

From The Public Interest, *Winter 1984, pp. 132–145. Copyright* © *1984 by National Affairs, Inc.*

enforce historic preservation.[3] Since then, the preservation ethic has dominated in American cities. The subsequent record of public preservation attempts is mixed. Bold successes such as Boston's Faneuil Hall and New York's South Street Seaport remind citizens of their cultural and architectural heritage, and have proved effective tools for economic revitalization. Yet local "landmarking" activities have also caused mounting controversy. Critics claim that preservationists are too indiscriminate in their landmark designations, inflexible in the enforcement of restrictions, and blind to the public and private costs of widespread landmarking. These charges have been aimed especially at New York City's landmarking process, the vanguard of the preservation movement. An examination of New York's experiences reveals that these criticisms have some merit, and illustrates the difficulties of systematic landmarks preservation.

A LANDMARKING "BINGE"?

Extensive government involvement in historic preservation is quite new. Federal legislation dating back to 1906 and 1935 enabled the executive branch to acquire and maintain national monuments, but the first far-reaching legislation was the National Historic Preservation Act of 1966. This provided for an inventory of historic property (the National Register of Historic Places) and committed the federal government to provide incentives and grants for the preservation of those properties. Subsequent legislation, including the Tax Reform Act of 1976 and the 1981 Economic Recovery Act, has provided significant benefits to landmark properties, such as accelerated depreciation schedules and tax credits for a portion of renovation costs. The federal government has avoided offering more than preservation incentives; local governments, on the other hand, have vigorously exercised their police powers to preserve both publicly and privately owned buildings. New York City has led the way by designating far more landmark buildings and districts than any other city, and by enacting strict landmark laws which have been imitated throughout the country.

The demolition of several prominent structures (including Pennsylvania Station) prompted New York City to pass its 1965 Landmarks Preservation Act. The law created an eleven member Landmarks Preservation Commission (LPC) appointed by the mayor, with the mandate to designate and regulate individual landmarks and historic districts. The law declares that a landmark may be:

> any improvement, any part of which is thirty years old or older, which has a special character or special historical or aesthetic interest or value as part of the development, heritage, or cultural characteristics of the city, state, or nation. . . .[4]

Designation takes effect immediately after a majority vote of the Commission, but the City's Board of Estimate has 90 days to modify or repeal the designation. Though eligibility for landmark status is not narrowly defined by law, the consequences of designation are laid out very specifically. The owner of a landmarked building must keep it in ''good repair'' and cannot alter it in any way or demolish it without explicit permission from the LPC. The owner must obtain a permit for such minor changes as painting, adding a new door or sash, installing an air-conditioner, or redesigning a business sign. The LPC's denial of permission is binding, and failure to abide by these restrictions is a serious offense, punishable in some cases by imprisonment. The owner of a designated building who is denied an alteration or demolition permit can appeal on the grounds of financial hardship (defined as the inability to earn a 6 percent return of the property's assessed value), but such appeals must also be addressed to the LPC, and are rarely successful.

Because of the serious restrictions accompanying designation, and the dubious constitutional grounds of such infringements on property rights, the LPC was initially circumspect in its designation of privately owned structures. After the Supreme Court's 1978 decision against the Penn Central Corporation, however, the Commission became bolder and started to designate more buildings, including many whose owners had objected to landmark status. To date, the LPC has designated 44 historic districts (containing more than 16,000 buildings), 690 individual landmarks, and 45 interior or scenic landmarks. This energetic designation policy surpasses the actions of any other city. While some feel the Commission still has a long way to go, the ever-increasing designations have led some original supporters of preservation to refer to a "landmarking binge."

At the outset all agreed that the city needed to guarantee the survival of its unique architectural gems: federalist buildings dating back to the eighteenth century, neo-classical and romanticized Gothic structures from the early nineteenth century, and the architectural legacy of the robber barons (ornate mansions and some particularly appealing commercial towers). New York also contains superb works by the nation's most prominent architects, such as Stanford White and C.P.H. Gilbert. Historic district designation has also protected a few special neighborhoods such as Greenwich Village and Brooklyn Heights, where irresponsible individual actions could ruin the architectural unity and historic flavor of an entire area. Initially the Commission moved to designate only these sorts of widely-accepted landmarks.

Soon, however, the strict interpretation of the original mandate came under fire from those with greater aspirations; for example, Columbia University sociologist Herbert Gans attacked the Commission for trying to "preserve only the elite portion of the architectural past." Preservationists quickly embraced a broader policy, showing concern, "not only for sites with special historic association and with special architectural value, but also a concern for social history—how the average person lived."[5] It became a shibboleth of the American preservation movement that a democratic society should, according to one member of the Commission, "record and celebrate the history of the ordinary, not just the history of the very famous and the wealthy."[6] Professor Gans has even suggested that nineteenth-century tenements be preserved and inhabited in their "dilapidated stinking state" for educational purposes. Driven by this new ideology and free from any strict standards of historic or aesthetic value, the LPC began to designate an extraordinarily broad range of structures, including much of the IRT subway system, lower Manhattan's gnarled street plan, and even the abandoned and decaying Parachute Jump at Coney Island (which the Commission's chairman called "the Eiffel Tower of Brooklyn"). As early as 1972 the Citizen's Union Research Foundation reported that, "In selecting landmarks, however, the commission has looked beyond the buildings popularly regarded as landmarks to buildings highly valued by special interest groups such as historical architects and history buffs.''[7]

Preservationists have claimed with pride that, unlike European efforts that give highest priority to aesthetics, the United States primarily values historical associations. This coupling of historic preservation with democratic social history has made it difficult to disqualify *any* aged structure—including an old elevated subway track that was designated ''an excellent example of a parabolic braced-arch structure,'' despite the City Planning Commission's objections and characterization of it as a blight.

LANDMARKS POLICY v. LAND USE POLICY

A far more troubling charge is that the LPC has overstepped its role by becoming involved in land use matters that should properly be addressed by the City Planning Commission. Once it became evident that the Landmarks Commission's power went beyond saving widely-accepted architectural treasures, various community activists rushed to the LPC for assistance in neighborhood preservation and the obstruction of unwanted development. The LPC has often acquiesced in these demands. As a result, the Landmarks Commission has become involved in heated land use disputes that have divided its original constituency and have tarnished the Commission's reputation.

The most egregious example of trespass on planning and zoning matters was the LPC's 1981 designation of a large portion of Manhattan's Upper East Side as a historic district. In one vote the Commission gave blanket protection to 60 city blocks containing 1,044 buildings on some of New York's most valuable real estate, thereby freezing development in one of the city's most vital areas. Though some hailed the designation as an indication of the mayor's strong pro-preservation stance, even supporters of the designation admitted that the area contains many less-than-distinguished structures. Even Beverly Moss Spatt, a former LPC chairman known for her aggressive preservationist views, voted against the designation because she felt the Commission was ''usurping the City Planning

Commission's powers to prevent demolition, to prevent development and change'' in an area that was not ''a unified historic district in terms of architectural style or historicity.''[8] Critics contended that the Landmarks Commission, by refusing to designate the area's accepted landmarks individually, was making an inappropriate planning decision about neighborhood scale and density. Giorgio Cavaglieri, the New York State Preservation Coordinator of the American Institute of Architects, sent a scathing letter to the *New York Times* explaining that the Upper East Side's aesthetic character had more to do with zoning than with rigid design controls. Mr. Cavaglieri has not often been known to quarrel publicly with his fellow preservationists.

LPC chairman Kent Barwick dismissed these criticisms, remarking, ''It is not the attitude of this commission—nor should it be—to preclude development.''[9] Soon, however, the worst fears of the architects, real estate industry, and many alienated preservationists were realized. Only six months after the historic district designation, the LPC refused to approve construction of a slender masonry tower that was fully in keeping with the character of the neighborhood. Paul Goldberger, architecture critic for the *New York Times*, had nothing but praise for the design and its suitability in the heart of the district, ''the most promising residential project to be proposed for New York in some years . . . intelligent and sensitive . . . the facades are elegant and discreet . . . indeed this is an object lesson in architectural tact.''[10] Still, fearing that approval would signal leniency, the Commission vetoed the building, ''on the ground that it would detract from the architectural unity of its block.'' Such resolve pleased local community activists and some elements of the preservation movement, but it dismayed previous stalwarts such as the American Institute of Architects, whose New York executive director remarked in exasperation, ''We wonder what if anything the commission will approve for the area.''[11]

Nor has the Landmarks Commission been shy about exercising its powers on matters of height and density in individual cases. So many religious buildings of dubious aesthetic significance have been restricted by the Commission that an interfaith panel formed by the Committee of the Religious Leaders of the City of New York charged the

Commission with "willingly accommodating local groups in abusing the law by employing it for zoning purposes rather than for its lawful purpose of architectural preservation."[12] Some, such as the *Times*'s Goldberger, have embraced this new LPC activity on the grounds that: "There is precious little sky available in Manhattan and there is less and less of it visible every day. One of the greatest gifts the city's churches and theaters convey, then, is the open air above them."[13] But opponents insist correctly that a law designed to protect architectural treasures is inappropriate for preserving open air.

PRESERVATION BY A THOUSAND CUTS

One explanation for the LPC's aggressive behavior is the relative ease with which it implements its administrative decisions. Regulating land use in New York City has always been a hotly-contested and bitter battle. To guarantee every side a fair hearing, the city developed a regulatory process that, though unwieldy, prevents hasty decisions that ignore the concerns of affected property owners. If the City Planning Commission (CPC) wishes to impose controversial zoning restrictions, it must first obtain a three-fourths vote of the city's Board of Estimate. The weighted voting of the Board makes obtaining such a majority so difficult that critics charge that the CPC is powerless in contested cases. Even unopposed zoning regulations proposed by the CPC must go to the Board of Estimate.

No such restrictions apply to landmark designations. Not only does a designation become effective immediately after a majority vote of the LPC; it can only be overturned if the Board of Estimate votes within 90 days to repeal landmark status. Though the Planning Commission has an affirmative obligation to gain a three-fourths majority for its proposals, the Landmarks Commission need only obtain a simple majority in those rare cases when its actions come to the attention of the Board (the weighted voting allows this majority to be obtained from as few as three of the Board's eight members). Thus landmarking policy, which can be far more controversial than zoning policy, has virtually no checks and balances. The city bestowed considerable powers on the LPC after the controversial

Penn Station case; granting sweeping emergency powers to the LPC was then hailed as an enlightened commitment to the city's remaining architectural heritage. The subsequent liberal use of these powers leads one to question the prudence of giving any such agency too much freedom.

To be sure, the Landmarks Commission does allow a disgruntled owner to appeal to appeal a designation, but only *after designation takes effect*. Every defense of the LPC's activities includes a reference to the "hardship clause" for owners who can show that designation prevents them from earning a 6 percent return on their investment. The frequency with which preservationists refer to this clause does not match the few instances in which hardship pleas have been accepted by the LPC: Of the more than 16,000 designated landmarks in New York City, only five owners have ever been granted permission to demolish a building due to reasons of economic hardship. Moreover, as the recent case of the Mt. Neboh Synagogue illustrates, it is far easier to impose a landmark designation than it is to relieve an owner's hardship afterward.

The designation of the former Mt. Neboh Synagogue on West 79th Street is a telling example of preservation run amok. At a February 1982 hearing the Commission decided to postpone decisions on such notable structures as the Woolworth Building in lower Manhattan and Lever House in midtown. Instead, the LPC debated the merits of designating an abandoned six-story synagogue that was scheduled to be replaced by a 17-story apartment building. A developer, Alexander Edelman, had purchased the structure in March 1981 for $2.4 million, and expected to begin construction on a building of the same height as neighboring apartment buildings, fully in keeping with the area's zoning. However, some residents of the community formed the "Committee to Save Mt. Neboh" and asked the LPC to confer landmark status on the 55-year-old building because of its "synthesis of Byzantine and other Near-Eastern influences." Twenty-five supporters of this committee then attended the meeting of the LPC to urge designation and to cheer speakers supporting their position. Despite LPC chairman Kent Barwick's characterization of the structure as "not architecturally significant," and although no one had an alternative plan for the abandoned synagogue, the Commission voted to designate it because "it represents the important role played by the Jewish Community on the Upper West Side and proudly exhibits a unique and unusual blend of stylistic influences." Commission member Elliot Willensky defended his vote in favor of designation, saying, "We designate buildings because they mean something in time."

Several months later, the Commission decided to accept the owner's hardship pleas and finally granted the owner permission to raze the structure one year later. (By this time the owner had lost about $1 million in interest on interim financing and in increased construction costs.) The LPC made clear that it had not rescinded landmark status but merely acknowledged that the building could not yield a "reasonable return." The LPC's decision enraged the community group, which maintained that the building could be used "as either a memorial to victims of the Holocaust or as an international art center that would further the cause of world peace."

After freezing the site for a year, the Landmarks Preservation Commission washed its hands of the case and decided to permit demolition. But the Committee to Save Mt. Neboh continued its battle in the courts, using the building's landmark status as grounds for the appeals. The Committee was able to prevent demolition by obtaining injunctions and court orders from the State Supreme Court and a state appeals court. The Committee finally exhausted all avenues of appeal, and demolition was just recently permitted. But now, after years of paying staggering interest costs, the developer appears to be short of funds. So the building sits fenced off and decaying, criticized by community residents as an eyesore.

WHO BEARS THE COST?

The Landmarks Commission does not have to confront the economic effects of its decisions, which may be why it has been able to overstep its original mandate. The Commission explicitly rejects financial criteria in its designation process, instead deciding each case on broad aesthetic and historical grounds. But religious institutions, individual owners, and even the city's tax base can bear a substantial burden as a consequence of landmark designation. Besides imposing strict maintenance requirements, land-

mark status often forces an owner to forgo extremely attractive development opportunities. Such sacrifice may be
appropriate in special cases, but failure to consider private
and public expense allows the LPC to make designations
where a full calculation of overall benefit and loss would
urge restraint.

The LPC's license to impose these costs without providing compensation dates back to the Supreme Court's
Grand Central decision. The Penn Central Corporation
had asserted that the Commission's refusal to permit construction of an office tower above Grand Central Terminal
constituted a taking of private property rights without just
compensation in violation of the Fifth Amendment. The
Court disagreed, holding instead that the denial of permission was a constitutional exercise of the local government's
police power, much like a zoning ordinance. While the
New York Landmarks Commission has taken this ruling as
unrestricted permission to designate, critics such as John
Costonis, a professor of property law at New York University, have maintained that the decision has been overread,
and was addressed mainly to the particular issues in the
Grand Central case.

Other critics claim that the entire framework of the decision was inappropriate. Among this latter group was Justice Rehnquist, who wrote in his dissent that failing to distinguish between zoning and landmarking "represents the
ultimate in treating as alike things which are different."
The majority of the Court viewed landmarks designation
as a legitimate attempt to promote the public welfare "by
prohibiting particular contemplated uses of land." The
Court ruled that the particulars of the case (including an
offer by the city to allow development rights from the terminal to be transferred to adjacent sites) did not justify
concluding that the city was "forcing some people alone to
bear public burdens which, in all fairness and justice,
should be borne by the public as a whole."

Justice Rehnquist disagreed vehemently. He argued
that landmark designation differs from broadly-applied
zoning ordinances because zoning restricts all property
owners in a given area and generates common benefits,
whereas landmark designation imposes substantial costs
solely on the owner of an individual property while providing a costly amenity to the public free of charge. In the

Grand Central case the railroad was forced to sacrifice at least \$3 million a year in rent from the proposed tower. Rehnquist argued that such a penalty violated the principle of "an average reciprocity of advantage," which Justice Holmes had delineated in deciding a 1922 zoning controversy, *Pennsylvania Coal v. Mahon*. Rehnquist felt that the landmark designation had infringed on the railroad's legitimate property rights to such a degree that it constituted a taking of private property and warranted just compensation from the city government. He closed his dissent by recalling Justice Holmes's earlier admonition that, "We are in danger of forgetting that a strong public desire to improve the public condition is not enough to warrant achieving that desire by a shorter cut than the constitutional way of paying for the change."

The often severe infringement of private property rights is not the only economic sacrifice that New York's landmarks process ignores. Restricting the potential for development on valuable sites also contracts the city's tax base. First, the city forgoes increased revenues from the more intensive uses of land which might have replaced landmarked structures. Second, landmark designation can lower an existing structure's market value and thus require a reassessment and consequent lowering of real estate taxes. A recently-published book argues persuasively that tax assessors have yet to come to grips with the effects of landmark designation on property valuation.[14] The author, David Lisotkin, makes the case that many landmark properties are being overassessed, and his sophisticated analysis of assessment practices deserves careful attention. Lisotkin's main concern appears to be the removal of unfair tax burdens from already-encumbered landmarks. A further point that Lisotkin treats only indirectly, but that the six New York City case studies he presents illustrate clearly, is that landmarking privately-owned buildings is a very expensive municipal enterprise. In each case the owner of a landmarked structure appealed the building's assessment, asserting that landmark restrictions on development significantly diminished the property's value. In four of the cases the courts substantially reduced the assessments; appropriate reductions are still being considered in the other two cases. Standard assessment practices will clearly be revised over the next few years to acknowledge the effects of landmarking. When they are, the previously hidden public cost of landmarking will certainly receive much scrutiny.

Landmark designations do have accompanying costs, but this does not necessarily mean that these costs make all designations inappropriate. It simply suggests the need for cost-benefit analysis and imaginative alternatives to designation. Fairness dictates that landmarking's economic sacrifices be justly distributed throughout society rather than be inflicted selectively on individual owners. Forcing the designation process to address economic factors as well as historical and aesthetic ones may well be the way to restrain the Landmarks Commission. Requiring some form of compensation to owners deprived of development rights and adding calculations of public tax expenditures to the designation process would certainly make the LPC more cautious about what structures it is willing to designate and what steps it will take to save those it does designate.

THINKING ABOUT COMPENSATION

Any reform of the designation process must accept that, while city governments are willing to regulate to promote preservation, they have not been willing to tax or spend scarce funds for that purpose. It is politically unrealistic to expect New York City, in its beleaguered financial state, to consider doling out vast sums for historic preservation, especially when the Supreme Court has deemed it unnecessary. Hence, most proposed reforms have focused on another valuable urban currency: transferable development rights. Because landmark structures usually use only a small portion of the height and density permitted by zoning laws, allowing the unused rights to be sold for use on another site can be a means of compensating owners for designation restrictions.

New York has attempted to implement this sort of compensation, but rigid controls and labyrinthine approval processes have undermined the program's effectiveness. New York City currently permits a landmark's development rights to be transferred only to an adjacent property. This so severely limits the market for those rights that the benefit becomes virtually useless. And since the complex approval process for any transfer can begin only after designation, the landmarking decision is separated from any consideration of appropriate compensation. This eliminates the disincentive to landmark which the prospect of vast development rights transfers might otherwise provide.

A different and far more promising approach has been developed by Professor John Costonis, who has attacked the New York method.[15] He proposes the drawing of "development rights transfer districts," which would enhance the market value of transferable rights by defining a broader area in which they could be sold. Costonis calls for local landmark authorities to devise a compensation package prior to designation. Such a package would include agreed-upon transfer rights and real estate tax reduction to reflect the landmark property's reduced value. Costonis maintains that "tax losses will be more than offset by increased tax yields from the larger buildings authorized by the transfered development rights." Switching to transfer districts might also spare cities the incongruous juxtaposition of tiny landmark buildings and immense office towers.

Of course, development rights, if they are to have any value, must land somewhere, and many critics are suspicious that transfer plans might lead to serious overbuilding. It quickly becomes clear that a landmarks commission, with its small staff and limited expertise, is ill-equipped to make these far-reaching land use judgments. Therefore, the City Planning Commission should be intimately involved in the landmark designation process, not only to delineate suitable transfer districts but also to further the city's planning and zoning goals. The city assessor should state the probable public cost of a proposed landmark designation. Requiring the City Planning Commission's approval and the tax assessor's comment on any landmarking action could balance the current designation process and restore strict standards to landmark evaluation.

SAVING PRESERVATION—FROM ITSELF

Preservationists will no doubt object to this intrusion on the Landmarks Commission's designation power, but such a modification may turn out to be beneficial for preservation goals as well. By relying exclusively on landmark designation, the Commission has failed to consider less drastic incentive programs and zoning ordinances that can still achieve preservationist goals. One such program was the city's J-51 legislation which provided tax exemptions and abatements for the renovation of older buildings. Though originally enacted in 1955 to eliminate unsafe housing conditions in New York's tenements, the program was expanded to promote as well the adaptive reuse of obsolete commercial buildings. Numerous brownstones and commercial loft buildings of real, if not spectacular, architectural merit were benefited. By 1980, over 700,000 housing units had participated in the program, including 55 percent of the city's pre-World War II private multiple dwellings.[16] Almost by accident, J-51 became the most effective means to preserve great numbers of New York's older buildings. It guaranteed variety to the city's housing stock by making the preservation and renovation of obsolete buildings economically viable. (Over the past few years, however, the J-51 program has been virtually dismantled by the state legislature at the urging of community activists who consider it a public gift to private interests. Not a word in defense of J-51 has been issued by the Landmarks Commission or other preservationist groups.)

Another area that New York's preservationists have neglected is the effect of zoning decisions on urban aesthetics. Preservationists and art historians may think of upper Park Avenue's consistent cornice line as a reflection of beaux-arts design principles, but it is really the product of a previous zoning ordinance which calculated allowable height as a multiple of street width. Subsequent zoning revised the rules and now permits unsightly apartment towers to puncture what was once an elegant vista. Rather than responding with blanket landmark designation for the entire area (something the LPC cannot effectively administer), the Landmarks Commission should instead encourage the Planning Commission and Board of Estimate to create zoning ordinances more sensitive to questions of design.

New York's landmarking experience teaches that preservation authorities must remain aware of the effects of their actions. Landmarks programs blind to expense and unaware of intermediate measures will be unable to regulate themselves and will miss vital opportunities. It is ironic that New York, whose best architecture reflects ingenuity and unfettered economic exuberance, has employed a landmarks process so insensitive to urban economics, one that preserves the undistinguished structures along with the great.

NOTES

1. Robert Stipe, "Why Historic Preservation?" in *Legal Techniques for Historic Preservation* (Washington, D.C.: National Trust for Historic Preservation, 1972), pp. 1–2; cited in *Readings in Historic Preservation*, Norman Williams, Edmund H. Kellogg, and Frank B. Gilbert, eds. (New Brunswick: Center For Urban Policy Research, 1983), p. 60.

2. Ibid.

3. 438 U.S. at 104 (1978).

4. New York City Charter and Administrative Code, 8A, 207–1.0(n).

5. *Readings in Historic Preservation*, p. 57.

6. Elliot Willensky quoted in "Harlem Viaduct: Blight or Landmark?", *New York Times*, March 3, 1982.

7. John S. Pyke Jr., *Landmark Preservation* (New York: Citizen's Union Research Foundation, 1972), pp. 17–18, cited in *Readings in Historic Preservation* p. 135.

8. Beverly Moss Spatt, quoted in "Panel Creates A Historic District in Manhattan's East 60's and 70's," *New York Times*, May 20, 1981.

9. Ibid.

10. Paul Goldberger, "Debate Over the Proposed 71st St. Tower," *New York Times*, November 10, 1981.

11. "Commission Formally Rejects 71st St. Tower," *New York Times*, November 11, 1981.

12. "Interfaith Group Assails City's Landmarks Law," *New York Times*, March 4, 1982.

13. Paul Goldberger, "Theaters and Churches Are the City's New Battleground," *New York Times*, May 30, 1982.

14. David Lisotkin, *Landmarks Preservation and the Property Tax* (New Brunswick: Center for Urban Policy Research, 1983).

15. John J. Costonis, "The Chicago Plan: Incentive Zoning and the Preservation of Urban Landmarks," *Harvard Law Review* 85: 574. See also *Space Adrift* (Urbana: University of Illinois Press, 1974).

16. Alexander Garvin, "New York's J-51: The Program that Restored 700,000 Apartments" in *Tax Incentives For Historic Preservation* (Washington D.C.: Preservation Press, 1980).

27

Educating Architects: Pedagogy and the Pendulum

ROBERT GUTMAN

There are now 94 schools and departments of architecture in the United States that offer programs to prepare students for entry into the profession. They range in size from Cooper Union and Princeton with 75 to 150 students to the state polytechnic universities in California which enroll 1,000 or more. About 35,000 students are now enrolled in the accredited departments and schools nationwide; half of them are in professional degree programs, and half are acquiring a general education with a special emphasis on architecture as a major subject. Students who graduate with professional degrees have fulfilled the formal educational requirements of the state boards that certify architects. After three years in an architect's office, they are eligible to take the certification examination. Many of the students who go through the schools but do not get a professional degree may do so later at the masters level, but the majority follow other careers in which they may use their architectural training, including fields ranging from

From The Public Interest, *Summer 1985, pp. 67–91. Copyright © 1985 by National Affairs, Inc.*

real estate and construction to film making and the graphic arts. Of the 30–35,000 students who have been enrolled in the accredited schools on the average annually over the last five years, approximately 4,000 have received professional degrees and 2,500 have gotten non-professional degrees annually. In 1981, 2,400 candidates passed the state certification examination to become registered architects.

The number of students enrolled in professional degree programs has doubled over the last 20 years. Thus, it is not surprising that the number of licensed architects has increased by an even larger percentage. Roger Montgomery of Berkeley has argued that architecture is now the fastest-growing profession, outpacing even the lawyers. There are now some 70,000 licensed architects in the U.S. and another group of 30–40,000 people who the Census and the Bureau of Labor Statistics include among architects because they have design or technical jobs in architectural offices or have architectural training but are not certified. Some of this group are recent graduates who will be taking the state examinations in the next few years. More than the other major professions, architecture is a field in which people seem to be able to acquire clients and get work and yet be rather open about the fact that they are not licensed.

Morale is relatively high in the schools at the moment. It reflects the fact that the places available in the schools are filled, and that recent graduates have been getting jobs easily. Morale is also helped by the attention shown to architectural subjects recently by the general public. The public television networks have two series in preparation on architecture; metropolitan newspapers and the newsweeklies have added coverage of architecture in their cultural sections; many more big city art museums now include departments of architecture and design; there are commercial galleries which exhibit architectural drawings; and the publishing of architectural books has become a major enterprise, with many new presses specializing in the field as well as bookstores devoted to the subject. In many large cities and small towns the preservation of historic American buildings is often now the only evidence that the quality of the urban environment is still a political issue.

In saying that architecture students exhibit relatively high morale at the moment, however, it is important to stress the word *relatively*. Most architects and architectural educators, in my experience, are never really in good spirits or happy for very long. Indeed, even now when the profession is prospering, when there are no major unemployment problems facing architects, when construction volume—to which job opportunities are tied closely—is high, and when the nation is suddenly fascinated by architectural production, we still can pick up at random an issue of any professional monthly magazine and read an article or a letter wondering whether the profession will survive.

Four characteristics of the field are responsible for the architect's perennial disgruntlement. First, despite public interest in their field and the apparently expanding market for their services, architects are still poorly paid compared to other professions with comparable status and an ancient and noble lineage, such as law and medicine. In New York City in 1981, according to a survey of that year by the local chapter of the American Institute of Architects (AIA), the starting salary of young professionals ranged from $10–14,000 annually, with the higher salary going to the men and women employed in the larger offices—this at a time when graduates of the top law schools working in Wall Street law firms were being offered starting salaries in the $30–40,000 range. These differences between architecture and other professions persist for all ranks and age levels, except perhaps for the leading partners of the very top architecture offices, where remuneration levels are comparable to law. Within the schools the situation is similar, since the architecture faculties are at the bottom end of the pay scale of university disciplines.

A second reason for unhappiness is that even the most successful architects do not enjoy the complete control over the design and building process to which they aspire. It is important to realize that the architects who are now defined as the best in the field are artists much more than they are experts in construction, in putting buildings together, or in accommodating the needs of users. Their ambition is to design everything from the general plan of the building right down to the furnishings, including the ashtrays in a museum, the desk of the board chairman in a headquarters building, even the tablecloths and cutlery for a private house. Of course, there are very few building projects in which such full control is allowed by clients, and architects are aware that the opportunity to fulfill this aspiration is rare. Nevertheless it persists as an understandable ideal and exacerbates the sense of frustration when more modest goals are thwarted by the client.

A third problem for architects is that they are always able to point to a large number of buildings that are designed without the use of their services, either by owner-users themselves for small projects such as houses, or by competing design professionals in larger buildings. Offices, apartment houses, galleries, and other modern building types are frequently designed by engineers and interior designers. Often architects find that clients insist on a particular specialist in these fields with whom the architect must collaborate. The architectural profession has been engaged in a century-long struggle to exclude other designers from these jobs through legislation that would limit the practice of building design tasks only to architects, but the campaign never achieved its goals. The title "architect" is protected but not the exclusive right to dominate the design field. The legal arrangements for qualifying architects that the profession likes to describe as *licensing* is in fact a system of *certification* (to use Milton Friedman's distinction between the different methods advocated by occupations for achieving a monopoly over services in their field of expertise). The prospects for expanding the arrangements for architectural certification into a licensing system have become poorer in the last decade. On the contrary, the major reform efforts have been led by the clients who, in California and other states, have been attempting to substitute a system of *registration* for the certification system. Under registration, anyone who chooses to engage in design work is free to do so, providing his name is listed with the appropriate state agency.

Despite the architects' failure to institute licensing, the profession's share of the building design market continues to increase. For example, in the housing industry, which according to the lore of the profession has been especially notorious for not employing architects, the use of architects' services has doubled in the last 40 years, so that now about half of all housing units are designed with input from architects. Admittedly, in the case of mass housing, architects do not have anywhere near the degree of control over the total product that they would prefer; nevertheless, they do make some contribution to the final design, and housing has become an important source of the profession's income. It is trends like these in the housing industry that help to explain the rapid increase in the number of architects since World War II. In the face of these signs of accelerating recognition of the profession's competence, observation by architects of the many buildings under construction which they cannot affect at all may be all the more irritating.

A fourth source of continuing disappointment for many architects stems, oddly enough, from the current popularity of the field. Many architects are suspicious about what the attention architecture now receives really means, and see in it evidence that the interest of the public in their profession is only skin deep. The phrase is meant literally; in many recent and much-publicized building projects, an architect was hired to design the facade that wraps around the building, perhaps also to design the lobby areas—in the case of office buildings—and sometimes to decorate some of the interior surfaces. Meanwhile, the structure of the building, heating, ventilating, and air conditioning systems, the materials used, and the planning of interior space were all done by other professional firms. In fact, of course, this division of labor has been progressing for a century or more in response to the increasing scale of projects and also to development of more complex technologies that clients demand. But the use of celebrity architects to design only those features of the building that are more likely to be seen and visited by the public, and which therefore can help to create a favorable "image" of the client's enterprise, does seem to happen more often now than in earlier periods of American architecture. Indeed, there are relatively few building types still being constructed in which the architect who is named as the principal designer has much responsibility for making decisions about the issues relating to how the building is put together and how it is used.

Some educators worry not only that these trends will continue in practice, but also that the attitude from which the public and many clients have been approaching architecture will encourage students to regard courses and school projects about pragmatic issues as dispensable features of a program in architecture. As a result, there is a fear among faculty members who emphasize the importance of training for professional roles that students will not take seriously assignments about structure, user requirements, space planning, programming, and environmental control systems. In some schools, it is obvious from the work that students submit for their thesis projects that this is a well-grounded fear.

Underlying the recurrent displeasure, anxiety, irritation, sometimes even despair, which architects exhibit about the state of their profession, is a condition having to do with the nature of architecture itself: It is an art which only can exist in the form of an artifact that is both available to the public and useful. This combination of attributes imposes professional demands that are extremely difficult to satisfy equally well, particularly in every building that an architect designs. When a strategy for resolving these demands is made into a set of principles, and when, further, instruction in these principles becomes the obligation of an institution set in a university, the educational debate can become exceedingly complicated and factionalized. In this article, I will be discussing four issues around which the debate has focused. Since these issues have their genesis in the nature of architecture as a field of study and practice, it is hardly surprising that they are old problems. Many of them confronted architectural educators in the previous century, beginning with the decade after the Civil War, when the first three American schools were established at M.I.T., Illinois, and Cornell.

A SHIFT TOWARD DESIGN

As a result of advances in structural engineering and the growth of the building industry, the principal role of the architect since the end of the nineteenth century has been to design buildings, not to figure out how they should be fabricated, and not to engage personally in the job of constructing them. However, perhaps just because these other tasks have been played down as the job of the architect, the profession has faced the question how the design function can be integrated with the other skills required for building. These other skills include, in addition to the act of construction itself, the development and articulation of the program, the coordination of the design with code requirements and structural engineering constraints, and the supervision of the contractor to make certain that the completed building matches the design. Thus the issue for educators is how to emphasize design and still make certain that students will appreciate and use pragmatic skills in their projects.

The question reverses the issue which concerned the earliest architectural curricula in the U.S. Then the emphasis was on the role of the architect in building construction. Students were expected to concentrate on learning how to make working drawings, write specifications, and put buildings together. In the University of Illinois program, set up in 1873, for example, design was a subject studied intensively only during the last year of a three-year program. Gradually the emphasis on design became primary, but only when, around the turn of the century, several schools appointed French masters who had received diplomas from the Ecole des Beaux Arts, or selected American teachers who had received some of their own architectural education in Paris.

The move toward design as the core of architectural education is perhaps best symbolized by the development of separate programs in architectural engineering, to cater to those students whose principal ambition was to concentrate on construction. The first separate program was set up at Illinois in 1895. A further stage of this history includes the gradual disappearance in most schools of special departments of architectural engineering. Now structural engineering is taught to architects either by engineering faculty whose appointments are integrated into the architecture departments or by faculty borrowed or on joint appointments with schools of engineering.

The growing emphasis on architectural design matches developments in the practice of architecture. Although it makes sense that this should occur, the adversary relations between the schools and the profession has sometimes obscured this fact. The important change in practice is that office organization now corresponds to the complexity of building tasks. Architecture school graduates deal with overall building design, prepare working drawings, and specify design details, while engineering problems are farmed out to consultants or dealt with in-house by staff with engineering degrees. Construction review and the management of the building process also are dealt with by specialist consulting firms that are subsidiaries of large architectural practices or construction companies. The people who fill these jobs are often graduates of programs in construction management that are offered in some of the larger architecture schools, especially in state universities. Of course, it is expected or hoped that specialists of each type will be sensitive to the problems confronted by their colleagues and will also understand their way of approaching building problems. It is assumed in many departments of architecture that design students can acquire this sensitivity just by taking lecture courses in the allied subjects without actually having to solve problems in the architectural studio that raise issues of building technique or job management. Presumably, similar beliefs are held by departments that train engineers, construction managers, or environmental psychologists. For students in the latter programs who have backgrounds in architecture, the difficulty of various participants in the building process to appreciate the constraints which limit the understanding of allied disciplines is often mitigated.

How can one integrate the different specialties that are involved in professional work today? This is surely one of the most enduring issues of architectural education. The educators who believe that the faculty has minimal responsibility for integrating the specialities within the studio situation offer several different arguments in support of their view. One argument is that the student's schedule already is fully taken up by the task of learning to put forms together in a manner that one can begin to regard as architectural. Thus, it is simply not feasible to add to this requirement that the student also consider in detail the structural implications of his design. Of course, the standard rebuttal is that emphasizing design without considering practical constraints may lead to solutions that are unbuildable. This position then generates the counter-argument that the typical studio critic has had a good deal of practical experience and is unlikely to allow a student to produce a building that ignores legal and technological constraints.

Another argument made by those who favor exclusive concentration on architectural issues *per se* is that schools have specialized and limited functions in the education of architects, as they do in other professions. This view implies that the education of the architect must be seen as extending over a much longer period than the time he is enrolled in an architecture school, and that even while in school, education occurs at many places outside the school itself. These other sites and periods include the experience a student might have before reaching architecture school, learning how to draw or working at a summer construction job or taking courses in drafting; the time spent during the summer doing the modern version of the Grand Tour, visiting architectural offices, or getting construction experience—and if not in the summer, or even if done during the summer, continued during the school year. Perhaps most important, the educational process should be seen to include the period after receipt of the professional degree when the student works for three years under the supervision of a more experienced architect in order to qualify for certification. All these experiences, it is argued, provide the student with a tremendous range of opportunities for integrating in a personal way all the skills required in professional work.

Still another argument put forth in support of the view that the schools should not worry about curriculum integration is that the collaborative nature of modern architectural practice compensates for the individual architect's specialized, limited knowledge. As an educational approach, the idea of the building team is usually traced to Walter Gropius. It is interesting to note that Gropius justified the approach as a countermeasure to the over-specialization that he discovered in American architectural education which, in his view, arose from the desire of large offices for a ready supply of young architects who knew one skill well and therefore would be easier to keep in isolated, subordinate positions. In emphasizing the idea of educating students while in school to participate in building teams, Gropius was trying to guard against the possibility that this hierarchical pattern of office work would become entrenched in the profession, as he emphasized in the following statement:

> For years I have been personally concerned, through my activities as an educator, with the plight of young architects as they leave school and enter into practice. I have seen them make valiant attempts to establish themselves independently, and I have seen them more often resign themselves to work indefinitely as draftsmen in large offices which offer little or no chance of exercising individual initiative. It is sad to see so much youthful energy and talent dry up by the slow attrition of our more and more centralized working system. Democratic concepts cannot easily survive the assaults of our increasing mechanization and superorganization, unless an antidote is used which may protect the individual in his struggle against the leveling effect of the mass mind.
>
> I have tried to find such an antidote by introducing my students in Harvard, besides their individual training, to the experience of working in teams. This has become a valuable stimulant to students as well as to teachers who were all equally unacquainted with the advantages and difficulties of collaborating in groups. Now they had to learn to collaborate without losing their identity. This is to me an urgent task lying before the new generation, not only in the field of architecture but in all our endeavors to create an integrated society.[1]

Gropius's belief in the importance of group work went beyond an interest in teaching architects to collaborate as a way of assuring that young graduates would maintain their professional vitality. He also hoped that reinforcing the idea that architectural production requires team effort would open the way for architects to accept the participation of non-professionals in the design process. Studio problems should, he said, "closely follow the actual practice of the architect-designer by introducing clients, contractors and authorities concerned." Behind both of these aims was his ambition to make the school situation resemble as closely as possible the conditions which architects would encounter in practice. As I understand it, Gropius was talking about what today would be called the integrated studio, a studio which includes engineers and other specialists who work along with the architects in the supervision of student work. The underlying rationale for this studio is that design students cannot on their own achieve the integrative capacity required for the production of a total building.

In the two decades following World War II, the integrated studio was a very popular experiment. It not only attempted to incorporate faculty from many disciplines but typically also included students from the programs in landscape architecture and city planning as well. The idea was to enable the schools to prepare graduates to work in the large-scale, comprehensive form of practice which had developed among the firms that were engaged in designing defense installations during World War II. Indeed, the concept of the integrated studio became the fundamental theme of the study directed by Robert L. Geddes and Bernard Spring, which was commissioned by the American Institute of Architects in 1964 to consider the future of education in the profession. According to the text of their report:

> The study recommends three major goals that should set the pattern for the particular policies, strategies and operating procedures to be decided upon independently by the schools. The three goals are:
>   1. A student (or graduate) should be able to work effectively within the real world constraints that shape present day practice.
>   2. A student (or graduate) should be able to comprehend the continuing changes in the social, economic, political, scientific and technological setting of our society. He should be able to constantly renew and adapt his abilities in response to these changes.
>   3. A student (or graduate) should be able to formulate a concept of a better environment beyond present day constraints to give directions to his adaptability to change.[2]

The view that the schools should simulate practice is opposed to the belief described earlier that in the studio the schools should concentrate on the teaching of design to the exclusion of a focus on the pragmatic and policy issues of building. It seems, in other words, that the debate about the staffing of the studio is really also an argument about the best strategy for enabling architects to deal with the problems of the "real world" after they graduate. The "purifiers," as I will call them, are convinced that this goal is best achieved by inculcating the basic principles which are involved in the production of architecture as an ideal-type of cultural object, even if this may require assuming a hierarchy of values about building which does not correspond to the expectations and choices of clients in advanced industrial society, and even if it suggests that the student ignore the practical constraints imposed by the day-to-day organization of building production. The opposition (I will call them the "simulators") argues that the system of ideas required to support this approach has unanticipated negative effects. Students educated in a setting so divorced from the real conditions of architectural production acquire attitudes which make it more difficult for them to adjust to the building constraints they encounter after they graduate. The "simulators" also argue that in order to maintain this ideal-typical conception of architecture within the schools, faculty tend to present students only with studio projects in which the ideal-typical approach is most likely to be realized in actual building production, such as museums or art galleries. The effect of this on students, the "simulators" say, is to remove them even further from opportunities to learn how to improve the design of the ordinary, largely commercial, buildings that will constitute most of their practice, such as shopping centers, offices, and housing.

There is no doubt that in the last 15 years, despite the fact that the Geddes-Spring report advocated another position, the "purifiers" have dominated the schools. This trend is linked to the rise of "post-modernism." It is not surprising, therefore, that we should be able to find in the writings of Robert Venturi, one of the American founders of this movement, a very explicit call to architects to concentrate on the study of architecture itself. Venturi's statement is in his *Complexity and Contradiction in Architecture*, which was published in 1966, the same year that the Geddes-Spring report appeared. Venturi wrote:

> I make no special attempt to relate architecture to other things. I have not tried to "improve the connection between science and technology on the one hand, and the humanities and the social sciences on the other and make of architecture a more human social art." I try to talk about architecture rather than around it. . . . The architect's ever diminishing power and his growing ineffectualness in shaping the whole environment can perhaps be reversed, ironically, by narrowing his concerns and concentrating on his own job.[3]

I believe that the "simulators" may be on to something important. In taking their side, I do not mean to imply that the school situation can or should be identical with the world found in practice. The rationale in all the professions for moving from an educational system based on an apprenticeship in an office to a school curriculum was the conviction that lawyers, physicians, and architects, to be really professional, needed to conceive of the problems of their field from an overall theoretical perspective; and that this could be best achieved in a setting that encouraged abstraction and the analysis of hypothetical as well as real-life situations. However, many architecture schools probably have gone so far in this direction that the problems set for students are based on distorted rather than just hypothetical assumptions. What students are led to think about, therefore, is not simply biased or devoid of content, but actually is incorrect. Oftentimes I find students, for example, who do not realize that the general public does not grasp the intention behind the semiotic content of their designs, a content which the student assumes is self-evident. Or they develop plans to be used by members of social classes whose expectations are different from the groups who, in fact, are likely to use them. In other cases, students will make an effort to incorporate what they imagine to be popular iconography in their buildings, without investigating whether the symbol systems really correspond to what the average citizen desires. The biggest area of confusion seems to lie in the nature of clienteles, the building capacity of the construction industry, the development process, and how architects get jobs. Here students are oppressed by romantic beliefs. These beliefs influence both those who are oriented to elite markets and the students who are populists. They impede the ability of either to formulate designs that make sense in the twin worlds of architecture and buildings.

AESTHETICS AND OBJECTIVITY

A second issue that confronts architectural education is how teachers can impart the ideas, approaches, and methods that govern their pedagogy generally, but especially the evaluations and judgments they offer about studio projects. This has been a more serious issue in the twentieth century than ever before in the history of architectural education, largely as the consequence of two developments in the discipline. In the first place, architecture like every other profession and field has been subjected to the aura surrounding the natural sciences, in which the principle of objectively verifiable knowledge has been used as the criterion of intellectual adequacy. For those schooled in the sciences, or who take the sciences as their model, the architectural enterprise becomes suspect. Second, although all aesthetic judgments are subject to this attack, architecture is more vulnerable to the critique than the other arts just because it necessarily deals with an artifact that involves attention to subjects the knowledge about which is often based on scientific investigation: for example, building structure, heating, and lighting. Indeed, the increasing focus on the professional aspects of architecture during the past century has reinforced this emphasis, leading in turn to an interest in giving aesthetic judgments the same epistemological base that applies with respect to pragmatic considerations. Sophistication in theoretical matters, after all, is one of the features by which a profession is distinguished from a trade.[4]

I keep on wondering whether the concern for the objective verifiability of theoretical knowledge in architecture is more prominent in this country than in other advanced industrialized nations. There is some reason to think so because American architectural education was almost from its beginnings university-based, and as a university-based system was forced to adopt the standards of scientific and liberal arts disciplines, in which logical consistency and verifiability of theoretical ideas were given top priority. In the American case, the scientific mode of thought was given further weight by the adoption of the German university model as the standard for graduate education. In his presidential address to the Association of Collegiate Schools of Architecture (ACSA) several years ago, Donlyn Lyndon discussed this background and made some further points about the consequences of the university context:

> All other factors considered, I would suggest that the university setting is presently the most influential force for change in architectural education. It determines ultimately the membership of the profession; it establishes the microcosm in which young architects develop any very cohesive view of the profession and its calling, and in which many of their most exemplary learning situations are formed; it gives direction through its own internal organization to the creative energies and attention of those who have chosen careers in education; and it has fostered careers that are alternatives to that of the practicing professional.[5]

On a more mundane level, it can be said that clients expect architects to justify their proposals when making their presentations, and that this leads to an emphasis on the capability to formulate the theories which underlie their ideas. Here again the modern mentality, which in part is an outgrowth of the scientific emphasis that dominates the contemporary university, and which is represented by the rationality of industry and bureaucracies, reinforces the pressure on architects to explain their ideas in matter-of-fact terms.

It must be realized, however, that what is nonsense to some audiences is perfectly comprehensible to others, and vice versa. There are patrons and clients for whom the most important facts about buildings are their "image quality," what they stand for and signify. Indeed, it is this inclination in recent years that has encouraged the shift in skyscraper design from the glass box to neo-classicism and terra cotta ornamentation. Nevertheless, even when the expressive side of architecture is considered sympathetically (this is not to say that all art is only about expression), someone in the client's organization will worry about the pragmatic aspects of the building design. It is at this level that the architect or another member of the design team will be required to explain the building in the language that is standard in technological and scientific circles.

The resolution of the conflict between the artistic and the pragmatic sides of architecture is a major issue in practice; both the architect and the architectural firm must be capable of handling it successfully. There is no easy solution, because the relationship between art, the building, getting the job, and persuading the client is very complicated. From a marketing perspective, the feature which distinguishes architecture from other building disciplines is its aesthetic side—if architects are going to maintain a hold on work, it is wise for them to emphasize the formal and aesthetic aspects of their production. As for its implications for theory, the important fact about the aesthetic dimension is the convention of the romantic artist, shared by architects and some clients, which liberates the architect from the obligation to be articulate. The building itself is the statement and thus substitutes for many of the forms of representation on which other disciplines and professions hinge their claims for social attention. In recent years, as many intellectuals and critics, not to say some popular movements, have turned their back on technology because of its inhumane consequences for the human soul and the environment, the inarticulate artist has come to be admired just because the type of skill he demonstrates is supposed to have a natural or intuitive base. Architects sometimes capitalize on this identity, and advertise themselves in these terms; on other occasions, it is their secret, private fantasy which they hide from clients in order to appear more responsible and practical.

It seems pretty clear to me that architecture schools now face a dilemma. On the one hand, they are under pressure to make their principles explicit and to act like the educators of professionals whose skill is grounded in the sciences—pressures that stem from the university community of which they are a part. In the typical university, for example, the personnel review process is more welcoming to a promotion packet from an architect who specializes in computer aided design and whose work is carried out in the language of mathematics and engineering, than it is to the dossier of the standard design teacher whose case for tenure is based on some premiated buildings (the merits of which seem to be arguable, judging by the range of opinions about them in the professional press and among his fellow architects). At the same time, of course, the educated designer and critic knows that the architectural disciplines grounded in the sciences can do no more than support the exercise and application of the architectural imagination. Architectural education is really a version of aesthetic education, and it may be that education in the other arts, rather than law or medicine, should be compared when we wonder how best to deal with problems of the schools. A comparison with the history of teaching music may be especially worthwhile since composition was accepted as a university subject in American universities before architecture, and along with architecture is now more fully established than any of the other arts.

THE DESIGN METHODS MOVEMENT

There was a flurry of interest in the years immediately following World War II in modeling the teaching of design on the sciences. The trend was part of a larger movement in many fields, including the "softer" social sciences, to substitute more rigorous, quantitative methods for an earlier dependence on historical and more intuitive methods. The architectural version of the trend was the Design Methods movement. This movement, which still has currency in some schools, attempted to formulate standard techniques which could be used by an educated professional to derive building designs from a program, or list of building functions. The Design Methods approach was accompanied by the growth of ''workshops'' in which students from architecture and allied disciplines would discuss and try to evaluate the proposed designs, using objective standards based on information from the social and technological disciplines. The workshops often became a substitute for the studio system.

As I have indicated, the dominant approach now is the reverse of what the Design Methods movement advocated. Educators have come to believe that architecture requires the intuitive method, and that there is no adequate replacement for the subjective knowledge a student acquires through the experience of trying to achieve formal order out of the chaos represented by the client's program. However, despite the restoration of the studio system to its former eminence in the schools, the critique launched by the Design Methods movement has had an enduring impact. One such impact is represented by the programs in architectural research and building research, which I discuss in the next section. The other impact, and surely more important for its influence on contemporary architectural education and discourse, is the revival and adaptation of a pre-twentieth century tradition in architectural education which linked the studio system to a program of teaching in philosophy and humanistic studies. With the burgeoning in Europe and America of critical studies in these disciplines useful for analyzing literary texts, humanistic studies today offer ripe pickings for the teacher in architecture who is looking for a method that is rational and intellectual to address to his discipline. The adaptation of analytic concepts from the modern humanistic disciplines has the further advantage that it does not require the reduction of architectural phenomena merely to the program of functional spaces that is implied by the reliance on the scientific model. Thus we find that among the most popular subjects and approaches for architects to study and talk about now are structural anthropology, hermeneutics, and semiology. When taught within the framework of the architecture schools, by architecture faculty themselves, these courses are often lumped together under the rubric ''history and theory.'' One hazard in the history/theory sequence is that its focus on sources in the humanities of formal ideas that govern design conveys a view of the architect's task that is as one-sided as the belief of some Design Methods theorists that good architecture can be achieved through the direct extrapolation from a program of building functions. Obviously the need is to keep both the humanistic and pragmatic approaches in mind at the same time. Robert Maxwell has employed the concept of structure, or structuralism, to unite the two approaches, thus exploiting the fortuitous availability of the same word in two widely separated but nevertheless relevant intellectual traditions:

> Buildings will then be treated *both* as functioning entities, to be measured against rational goals, *and* as signifying entities, to be measured within the evolving body of knowledge which we may call a critical tradition. Two theories are necessary, because in the time and space allowed to us, we are able only to do a very little at one time, and final explanation will probably elude us. But the two areas of theory are within the same concepts: that *structure* is the key to behavior and process, and by this essential fact they allow us to see design as a legitimate subject of university study and practice. The present system suffers still from a dichotomy between the paradigm of natural science and that of private intuitional judgment. Instead we are aiming at the theoretical unity of the field which is addressed to the production of artifice, the science of the artificial produced within intentionality, and the artificial produced ineluctably and unconsciously by the very process of development in history.
>
> If this theoretical unity can be perceived as underlying two quite distinct modes of analysis—*the constructing of artifacts and the construing of texts*—then we may hope that both modes will be furthered, together, within the university, and within its School of Architecture.
>
> Design teaching could then proceed by a revaluation and rationalisation of the critical mode. If it is true that we cannot teach the processes by which the intuition cuts through complexity to produce a result, it is still the case that we can examine that result and analyse it. Intuition itself cannot be taught, but what it has produced can be criticised.[6]

The method advocated by Maxwell for dealing with the nature and role of theory that is most appropriate for architecture may be unique to this discipline. However, it also illustrates an approach to defining theoretical inquiry that is consistent with the special character and function of theory in professional fields as distinguished from academic disciplines. Donald Schon and Chris Argyris have discussed the distinction in several books in which they emphasize the difference between *espoused theory*, the concepts which professionals claim to be applying in their work, and *theory-in-use*, the ideas and methods which they use in treating cases and solving problems.[7]

Argyris and Schon often illustrate the two types of theory with cases in architecture. They point out that architects are unable to provide an espoused theory of design, even though creative architects are perfectly capable of designing new and imaginative structures. Mystique, they point out, is absolutely central to such professionals. Although in practice architects may not have to concern themselves with their inability to espouse a coherent theory, difficulties do arise when these professionals begin to teach and assume the role of educators. Then they find it difficult to discuss pedagogical theories because often they have none, and indeed are worried that too much self-consciousness about education can destroy the very intuitive skills on which they are convinced their approach to practice is based. It is difficult for practicing professionals to make explicit the grounds for their actions. Every professional considers himself an artist to some degree. However, in architecture the tradition in support of the professional mystique is not as easily challenged by rational-scientific approaches as it is in medicine, say, or in law. We know, of course, that architectural education can become very "academic," but because the typical design studio is supposed to generate a proposal that is buildable, the schools have not been captured by espoused theory in the way in which this type of theory has come to dominate education in the other major professions.

I stated earlier that my concern was how teachers of architecture deal with the need to make theory more explicit—but my discussion indicates that not all faculty or schools recognize this need to the same degree. Yet it does seem that the issue cannot be avoided, if only because the university setting propels architects in this direction. The big shift that has come about is that this need must no longer be responded to only by use of the scientific model. It now can be handled by theories of interpretation that have arisen from the hermeneutic disciplines. There continues to be some difficulty in applying the theory to design projects, because of two conditions. The theory is an interpretative theory and therefore is most useful after a design has been created. Also, the theory is examined in courses and seminars, and the faculty who teach them are often not the same people as those who teach the studios.

It should not be forgotten, however, that a good deal of the energy behind the attention to theory comes from the architectural research groups which became established in the schools along with the Design Methods movement. The members of these groups are dedicated to the view that the survival of the profession and the discipline, too, depends upon moving architecture to develop methods for cumulating knowledge in the linear pattern common in the advanced sciences. Most of them are engaged in what should perhaps be called "building" research rather than research on architecture since their investigations address mainly pragmatic issues. Perhaps just because the work of the building researchers does not often address aesthetic issues, the building researchers are more at home with the scientific models than other factions in the schools. They really are trying to establish causal relations between the built environment and human action or behavior, and for this endeavor explanations based on clearly formulated and testable theoretical ideas are an absolute necessity.

RESEARCH AND DESIGN

The discussion of building research and its place in the schools touches on a third enduring issue of architectural education: the schools' responsibility for developing new knowledge. This responsibility, like some of those mentioned earlier, has been thrust upon the schools by a combination of factors, many of which have been mentioned previously. The development of knowledge is one of the hallmarks of a profession, schools for all professions are regularly engaged in the enterprise, university faculties encourage research, and the funding of it has become a method schools often use to support design teaching and other standard courses. There is no question, therefore, that architecture schools, whatever their ideological stance, are often pressed into evaluating themselves in terms of their contribution to research.

As I said earlier, the demand placed on architecture schools to foster a research tradition constitutes a greater challenge than is true for education in other professions. It is characteristic of artistic knowledge that its development proceeds more circuitously than in the sciences, indeed, it is not progressive in the sense in which we think of scientists refining conclusions developed by their predecessors. Furthermore, even though design, the product of the architect's work, may be informed and shaped by theory, it represents a corruption of the scientific notion of verification to claim that the designed artifact tests, or is intended to test, a theory. Consequently, if architecture schools wish to meet the challenge presented by the university scientific tradition, they usually have to do so outside the system of teaching design. Given the inevitable emphasis in architectural education on the studio, this means that research tends to be seen as a threat to the studio, and vice versa.

The conflict between the studio system and other pedagogical methods is a problem even for the progress of humanistic research in architecture, such as the courses, seminars, and associated programs in architectural history. As a result, there is no universal pattern for the teaching of architectural history in American schools today. In larger schools, history is sometimes taught by faculty in a separate department staffed by architectural historians. There are other schools, however, in which architecture students acquire their knowledge of history from faculty in departments of art history outside the schools. Along with separate departments of architectural history, or courses in art history departments, and sometimes in the absence of these forms of academic organization, instruction in architectural history becomes a sideline, almost an avocational interest of studio design faculty. Regardless of the organizational pattern that prevails, the big pressure in the schools is for history to be dealt with by people who can apply it to the design issues in the same terms that these issues are formulated by the studio design faculty. Design teachers usually disagree a fair amount over what they consider "good" design or "correct" architecture, and consequently also disagree about how history should be taught, and by whom. In the end most studio faculty prefer to offer their own version of the history of architecture, a version that can be used to buttress their personal theories of architecture and to provide the ground for an attack on the architectural theories they oppose. The use of history to lend an imprimatur or to forge a polemic is not the view of history that is preferred by professional historians, which of course encourages the tension between art or architectural history departments and architecture schools. The research enterprise in architectural history often loses out in the battle, so that again we find a situation in which the research tradition has a difficult time becoming established in schools of architecture.

Looking at architectural education nationwide, it is not easy to generalize about whether research is now more or less institutionalized. Viewed from the perspective of the history of the schools over the past century, probably it has become better established, but there has also been a good deal of backing and filling with the spread of the post-modernist devaluation of building pragmatics. There is less confusion now than there was two decades ago about the relationship of research to design. Each is thought of as a largely independent type of intellectual activity, operating in its own bailiwick and more likely to be creative when separate from the other. Research and design may not interact with or influence each other very much within the schools, except perhaps at the level of administration—where they compete for budgets and faculty positions—but it is important to realize that they come together in the world of practice.

The absence of a dialogue among scientifically-oriented building researchers, scholars based in the humanistic tradition, and designers does mean that architectural education currently is probably more unstable than it was even right after World War II, when it was trying to adapt to the new comprehensive practices. Most schools are very committed to the principle that the art of design must be defended in American culture which, for all its celebration of the aesthetic dimension devoid of moral and ethical content, is viewed nevertheless to be grudging in its support for the products of high culture. While preserving their idea of architecture as an advanced cultural discipline, the schools at the same time recognize the need to prepare students to serve the primary clients and users of architects, large private and public bureaucracies with their concern for the pragmatics of buildings. In an effort to strengthen its cultural roots, architecture in the university setting is actively engaged in a search for texts in other humanistic disciplines—literature and philosophy especially—to which architecture can be compared and from which it can derive theories and paradigms for the interpretation and justification of design. Despite these programs, however, the schools are forced to recognize that they cannot totally exclude the scientific intelligence from their midst, and indeed find it necessary to undertake programs of building research in order to improve their stature in the university community as a whole.

ARCHITECTURE AND PUBLIC POLICY

A fourth issue facing the schools is how the curriculum ought to deal with the policy questions that are connected to the position of architecture in contemporary America. I am thinking of such questions as whether there should be increased funding for landmarks preservation programs; what federal policy should be with respect to allocating funds between "high culture" and "popular culture" projects; the importance of awarding all government building commissions through design competitions; the measures required to make housing available to groups which cannot afford the dwelling units provided through unregulated market processes; the development of a national building code; or the advisability of a professional code of ethics for architects. The list could go on, because there are so many issues of cultural, social, and economic policy in advanced industrial societies that impinge on architectural ideas and practice. They affect not only the ways in which architects think about the problems of our field; they also have immediate effects on the market for school graduates and the skills which are in demand. If the state or federal governments, for example, are subsidizing non-market housing, it is likely that there will be many good jobs for architects dealing with this building type. If the public sector is encouraging programs in historic preservation, then there will be a demand for the kind of knowledge that is required for restoration of old buildings. On the other hand, if public investment is languishing, or there are no effective agencies to represent the public's interest with respect to the environment, this, too, influences architecture, as it has in recent decades. The narcissism that is associated with the particular version of post-modernist architectural production that has been popular recently in the United States, for example, surely owes something to the revival of rugged individualism as the dominant ethic for dealing with urban issues.

The schools are good places to examine the connections between architecture and public policy because their curriculum is more independent of the market for architectural services than are the fortunes of the AIA and registered practitioners. The schools generally can maintain some respect for the issues in the discipline that are recurrent and persistent, even though not currently in fashion. It does not always seem that way to the profession, I know—indeed, from the practitioner's point of view it is the schools that are swayed most of all by museum and magazine attention to certain architects and to swiftly changing styles. This judgment may apply to some schools whose faculty members have become culture industry heroes, but for American architectural education nationwide, it is not accurate.

On the other hand, even though schools are good places to examine the connections of architectural ideas and practice to policy, they are much less committed to this endeavor than they were in the 20 years immediately following World War II. There are very few schools now which offer students the opportunity—fairly common at that time—to collaborate with students from other design-related fields. Beginning in the early 1950s, with programs at Harvard and Penn in urban design and civic design, respectively, there was a desire to emphasize the importance of the connection between the *art* of architecture and problems of housing and urban policy. By the late 1960s there were as many as 70 "urban design" degree programs in American universities, but now there are only about 25, despite a 50 percent increase since the 1950s in the number of architecture schools and departments. Many professional degree programs in architecture in the earlier period required students to take courses in zoning and planning, urban research methods, and the behavioral sciences, but in most schools these courses, even if they are still taught under architectural auspices, are no longer required. In some of the leading schools, such as those at Harvard and Princeton, the urban planning departments have been transferred out from under the umbrella of architecture or design to other schools in the university.

The reluctance of architectural faculty to concern themselves with policy matters is consistent with the views of those I referred to earlier as "purifiers," and is quite consistent with the statement by Venturi quoted earlier, about the advisability of "narrowing" the architect's concerns. I believe, however, that some of the post-modernist architects are beginning to realize the costs involved in the wholesale adoption of this strategy. Venturi's own firm, for example, has in the last few years begun to emphasize its competence to address urban design and policy questions, partly in an effort to create a market setting for its primary service of designing buildings. Just under ten years ago when the Harvard and Princeton urban planning departments were moved out of the architecture schools, it looked as if the ejection or voluntary withdrawal of the planning departments was going to become a major trend in American higher education. However, no other major university has followed the lead of these schools, and at Harvard one big question now is how best to reinvigorate its urban design program and incorporate some of the domestic policy concerns that were abandoned when the urban planners were moved to the Kennedy School.

The practical problems that architects face in maintaining an image of professional competence when they narrow the scope of their services and eschew claims in the policy area is revealed in the following exchange between Peter Eisenman and the Houston-based developer Gerald Hines:

> *Eisenman*: Why is it that when the government wants a legal opinion it goes to the Harvard Law School or Stanford Law School for advice? Why is it that when there is a question of development or environmental concern, nobody goes to the schools of architecture for advice? They go to the practicing architects.
>
> *Hines*: Basically, one is in touch with, and in the leadership of, the field and the other is not. In architecture the practitioners are on the cutting edge and the academicians are not considered to be on the cutting edge.
>
> *Eisenman*: Why is it that in business the academicians really *are* on the cutting edge? The Harvard Business School is a very important place.
>
> *Hines*: In comparison with the Graduate School of Design, yes. It is a reflection of the leadership that the Business School has taken and how it is perceived by the business community and the government.
>
> *Eisenman*: Even practicing architects never *make* policy; they carry out policy. Philip Johnson, Cesar Pelli, I. M. Pei, and Kevin Roche

do not formulate policy. Yet the leadership in the business community or the leaders in the legal community formulate policy. Do you
think that could change or should change?

Hines: It all depends on who the people are at those institutions.
If you can assemble a group of people who are on the cutting edge,
then you might achieve what you are talking about. I do not see it
happening in the near future, however.[8]

This dialogue is a peculiar combination of sophistication and intellectual insularity. For example, Eisenman
contradicts himself when he says that people go to practitioners rather than to architecture faculty to get advice on
urban and environmental matters, and then notes that
Johnson and other architects do not make policy, but implement the policies of others. Clients and government officials do not seek out architects for advice on public issues
because they know from experience, unfortunately, that
architects generally are ignorant and inexperienced in
these areas, especially architects who were educated during the last ten years, and who take as their role models
many of the leading figures in the American post-modernist tradition. At the same time, it should be said that there
are on the faculty of many architecture schools in this
country, men and women who are knowledgeable about
"environmental concerns," but they probably are not the
breed of architect touted by Eisenman and his colleagues
in the high art culture of architecture. Furthermore, contrary to what Eisenman and Hines assume, it often *is* the
faculty members who teach in these subject areas, rather
than practitioners, who serve as consultants and write the
reports which have helped to influence housing policy,
building codes, and environmental legislation. It is probably true in the 1980s that there are relatively few teachers
within the architecture faculties who are concerned about
the public policy aspects of design and that policy-ori-
ented scholars are now teaching in their own bailiwicks, in
schools or institutes of public affairs, government and politics. Of course, the difficulty in relying on these scholars
to address architectural questions is that they usually do
not know much about the design fields and also usually
exhibit the bias—characteristic of the social science disciplines—that architecture is not a relevant and important
factor in social development and behavior. In my view, the
lack of attention to public policy issues in architecture programs and the corresponding unfamiliarity with the sub-

ject in public affairs programs is all the more reason for encouraging the design schools to introduce courses and studio problems that are deliberately focused on the relation of architecture to policy.

THE CASE FOR PERPETUAL MOTION

In the years ahead there is a good chance that the architecture schools of this country will alter the theoretical content of their curricula and even adopt new teaching methods to supplement the traditional studio system. Some changes are likely to occur if only for the reason that the issues discussed in this article, although enduring and therefore recurrent, nevertheless fluctuate in importance and saliency in response to conditions affecting professional practice and the requirements of the university setting. For example, the recent tendency to emphasize the formal and aesthetic content of buildings is much more pronounced than often has been characteristic of American schools. It has contributed sometimes deliberately, but in other case unintentionally, to contract the scope of the architect's professional competence as viewed by the client. The schools are preparing students for a practicing profession whose members are persistently concerned about whether they can hold their own in a building industry that is in constant flux. Therefore, educators can expect that they will be asked to apply greater thought and effort than they do now toward integrating design skills with other kinds of knowledge important for building construction. Shifts in the balance of curriculum subjects have occurred more than once in the history of American schools, for example, in the 1930s when curricula to train "executive architects" were the fashion of the time and again during the 1960s when the big concern was for user-oriented architecture. New versions of these earlier educational programs to assure a role for architects that is in tune with the changes in clienteles and building production systems probably are ready to surface. Pressure from university administrations in favor of fundable research is likely to reinforce an interest in broadening the scope of architecture again. The same effect is likely to follow from university development campaigns which try to tap the only major funding source that has any connection with architecture, namely, the real estate industry. The industry's leaders have become more sophisticated in the last decade at the same time that the American urban environment is being shaped by developers on a scale without precedent in the history of this country. Many of the wealthiest and most powerful developers now regard the architectural profession, and therefore its schools, as potentially useful to their ambitions.

With these changes in curriculum in the offing, I do not think that the schools can remain content with their almost exclusive reliance on the studio method for educating architects. On this subject, too, American schools have vacillated. The past decade has witnessed an uncritical celebration of the studio, even surpassing in excitement the enthusiasm which greeted the original adoption of the method at the end of the nineteenth century. But in the 1930s and after World War II, there was the widespread sentiment that the studio method was an inefficient means for teaching general principles. And there was some doubt about whether it was useful for encouraging serious thought and investigation of issues of detail involved with building, including issues of style, form, or building function. I suspect we will see a revival of some of these criticisms and renewed attention to enhancing the relevance of lecture and seminar courses and to designing case issue approaches for learning about architectural problems.

The capacity of the architecture schools to manifest the dynamic response that I envisage for them in the coming decade is, as I have suggested, confirmed by their history of facing persistent and recurring issues, but doing so with shifts in nuance and emphasis that respond to new trends in practice and the changing demands of the universities. This capacity obviously is a considerable resource. But there seems to be a corresponding weakness of the schools, at least judging by their history, and it is this: After each phase of curriculum revision is in place, and a generation of students has struggled to integrate their skills through the use of new instructional methods, the pendulum swings back. The schools concentrate on the aesthetics of design again, the profession loses once more its connection to public issues, and leadership on environmental questions passes to builders, contractors, and developers. Is this lack of a record of sustained progress a characteristic of professional education generally? Is it a response of the schools to the university, an institution notorious for rejecting, then adopting again pedagogical theories and attitudes that were advocated by previous generations? Or are the oscillation and vacillation principally a reflection of some of the unique features of architecture as a discipline and a professional activity: that buildings have both artistic significance and practical purposes; that their construction and interpretation draw on the humanities *and* the sciences; that the architect must be a highly competitive entrepreneur while upholding the standards of a profession; and that buildings, no matter how private in conception and sponsorship, are intertwined with public policy and affect the way people live.

NOTES

1. Walter Gropius, *The Scope of Total Architecture.* (New York: Collier Books, 1962), pp. 77–78.
2. Robert Geddes and Bernard Spring, *A Study of Education for Environmental Design.* (Princeton: Princeton University Press, 1967), pp. 9–10.
3. Robert Venturi, *Complexity and Contradiction in Architecture.* (New York: Museum of Modern Art, 1966), pp. 20–21.
4. It is conceivable that the tremendous hostility among the post-modernist architects to a behavioral approach to design—although it had many sources, including the association of the behavioral approach with welfare state architecture—developed in part as a resistance against the application of the scientific model to still one more area in which architecture formerly regarded itself as autonomous.
5. Donlyn Lyndon, "Architecture Education Here," *Journal of Architectural Education,* Vol. XXXI, no. 3, p. 5.
6. Robert Maxwell, *Two Theories of Architecture.* (London: University College, 1982), p. 20.
7. Cf. Chris Argyris and Donald Schon, *Theory in Practice: Increasing Professional Effectiveness.* (San Francisco: Joosey-Bass, 1974), *passim.*
8. Gerald P. Hines and Peter Eisenman, "Interview," *Skyline.* October, 1982, p. 21.

28

The Current Crisis of Disorder

JAQUELIN ROBERTSON

In 1972, after leaving the Office of Midtown Planning and Development, I wrote a critique of some of the work of my most talented architectural peers, most of whom were good friends (''The Machine in the Garden'': *Architectural Forum*; May, 1973). It contained this passage which seems as relevant now as then:

> Over the past years I have been observing ''resort'' building activity in eastern Long Island—in particular, several cottage colonies in the dunes on the outskirts of the Hamptons.
>
> Everywhere new weekend ''villas'' are rising, a good many of them, as the locals say, ''architect designed.'' In fact, ''architecture'' is everywhere. But as yet there is no promise of an attractive community to come. Indeed each year brings along with its rash of daring and individual houses, an increasing sense of bleak ugliness. There are no new villages being built, only agglomerations of units, unrelated objects of every shape and design, pockmarking a once lovely land.
>
> This grim impression is heightened by the contrast with nearby older tree-shaded villages, and their gentle, rural-domestic, homogeneous, patterns that have evolved so successfully over the past 300 years. (Admittedly manicured by recent generations of resort money.) Today these villages offer the area's only remaining amenity besides the ocean itself. In fact, these old villages provide a retreat from the glaring world of our contemporary hand. We have made a shambles of the dunes and scrub forests and can only es-

From Education for Urban Design *(Washington, D.C.: National Endowment for the Arts, 1981), pp. 35–58.*

cape them by returning to the old tribal places we have not yet destroyed.

(Such is the residue of modern design in a culture that does not provide a larger and governing vision in which to fit all the objects it produces; a culture gripped by a devastating schizophrenia that finds no mediation between specific things and their real or implied framework. We make very few successful places, only things.)

In looking back on everything that I have been trying to do professionally over the last 15 years, and have felt for much longer than that, I find one central preoccupation: a concern that healthy cultures ought to produce a man-made world in which there is a practical, perceptible, and elegant order of things, different from, but complementary to, the larger order of the natural world. And that our culture does not have such an order.

Am I wrong, I wonder? Have I failed to see and appreciate the better part of what's going on? Is what we're up to in our planning and designing and building sensible and enhancing? I don't think so. More and more I sense some basic malignancy rather than healthy growth. I understand it's important to say this kind of thing calmly and without bombast. Certainly I'm not given to pessimism; nor do I accept guilt. I do, however, feel apprehensive, and frustrated, and annoyed. For in looking around one, almost anywhere, in any country, it's hard to find anything other than signs of increasing physical bleakness and disarray. Quite simply, it seems to me on the evidence that we are hard at work at making pretty much of a shambles of a very fine piece of real estate—and doing it with a kind of apathetic vengeance which makes the flesh crawl. (Alas! we're not shy about the thing. We do it with a great deal of rationalization; with great energy and with a bland inattention which is stunning.) I believe that we and our environment are losing a great battle against ourselves; that this doesn't have to happen; that is absurd! The conclusion of a great many serious thinkers over the last hundred years, but that it is happening.

This disorder in the physical world may not kill us, mind you, but it could condemn us for a long time to come to a kind of endless Dantean purgatory; a built world of ''Mexico cities.''

An exaggeration? Perhaps. But I think close enough. Certainly there are still too few sane people—particularly political leaders and opinion makers—ready to address these issues in a dedicated and deliberate way. Even architects and planners seem to be getting on with other things; and to the extent that we come here to talk about urban design as if it were a special branch of architecture and planning—rather than the central concern of both these disciplines—seems to give strength to my argument. Perhaps the problem has something to do first with how we ourselves, urban design professionals, conceive of and speak about what we do—and only later about how we transmit our concerns and priorities to others.

When we speak among ourselves about urban design—and this is purportedly (and ironically?) a retreat for urban design educators—we are talking simultaneously about practice, education, process, product; certainly about an attitude if not a philosophy; in some cases almost about a ''way of life.'' There is still the sense of a shared, and, yes, important, mission; of professional camaraderie, of being misunderstood and a bit on the outside; of having to proselytize still; and of being frustrated, rarely treated to tangible results. Of being very young disciples of a very old faith.

This sense of clan, of special shared interests, of an urgency and of new perspectives, with respect to the design of the city—not a little unlike the spirit that existed around Team 10 in the '50s but without the formal guest list of the ''ins'' and ''uninvited''—is, I suspect, still possible because urban design in all its many definitions has not yet caught on in our culture, and we are still in the phase of having to spread the word. I say this despite the existence of urban design groups, firms, programs, manuals, magazines and awards. The phrase may have arrived, but as this retreat illustrates, we are a long way yet from comprehending urban design as the crucial and central discipline linking the planning, design, and development of our cities and countryside. Rather, and this is particularly true among educators, urban design is seen as an area of special concern, something in addition to or on top of the basic architectural and planning disciplines. Perhaps even a separate degree altogether, for those with specialized interests; certainly an area of concentration for a few.

Which, of course, misses the point entirely. For urban design is not a separate area of study or concern, an elective if you will. Rather it is precisely what architecture and planning and development are concerned with; alas, the physical product. (Oh! feared word!)

Cities have or don't have urban design because urban design specialists were or were not on hand. Cities are urban design: how they work, and look, and are perceived and used; loved, hated, ignored—whether as symbolic settings or social processing plants. Urban design is not incidental but fundamental to cities. Therefore to teach architecture, or landscape architecture, or planning—is to teach urban design. They are one and the same. Indeed these generic disciplines go to make up urban design not the other way around. (The pieces of a puzzle may have weight, thickness, shape, color, and pattern, in themselves not unimportant statistics, but without at least partial aggregation they are without meaning.)

For this reason I am always at a loss to speak, for example, about urban design as different from architecture. And I wonder why all architects aren't deeply involved in urban design; or why planners, by and large, have abandoned it so effortlessly. And why have we had to separate urban design in our academic curricula . . . when it is the point of all the rest? If *we* still feel the separation of urban design from the rest, then urban design has *not* arrived.

During the past twenty years, that is, that period when the term, urban design, gained usage and most of us here became known, at least partly, as urban designers, the entire urban design experience has been one of continuous education or rather reeducation: education first of ourselves into a profession which was always there but also didn't exist; education of our clients, our professional peers, be they architects or planners; education of critics and the public at large—politicians, community leaders, businessmen, laymen, and lawyers—and, probably last, an education even of our students, when and if we had them. Very simply all of us have been learning on the job about something we were supposed to have known all along, yet having to justify and to explain what it was that we were doing. (Can you imagine having to explain designing cities to an architect? I'm still devastated by Philip Johnson's remark: ''Oh, yes, Robertson, I know you're an architect but what on earth are you doing? All that boring planning stuff . . .'' This hurt and dismayed. Designers, after all, still hunger for design respect, and to be completely brushed aside as irrelevant is unnerving. In going to the bookshelf for support the last thing as a designer I could point to was Peets and Hagemann, *The American Vitruvius*.)

This means that urban design, the process and product of making cities, has recently been education because we were having to relearn an old discipline. And while I've never formally been an urban design educator, a large part of what I've been doing over the last fifteen years in urban design practice has been continual teaching/learning (if not always educational). I, therefore, find it as difficult to become academic about urban design practice as to remove that practice from the ongoing thrust and counterthrust of theories and facts, *i.e.* from that paradigm of the scientific method which it is. As much as any professional activity, urban design is one in which the inductive and deductive processes are at work simultaneously; in which theory and practice, teaching and learning, the real world and the creative world, are inextricably interwoven. One can only learn here from trying to do; and can only do from learning. And, nearly all the time, one is teaching—oneself and others.

Nonetheless, my comments are colored by a focus on practice and on results; on trying to produce something tangible within the usual constraints of time, money, political, and social consent, brain power and energy. And they are very much the observations of an architectural designer who has attempted to understand the larger world around him in the hope of fashioning a more practical, culturally germane, elegant, and uplifting surrounding. The physical world results from a variety of human decisions; urban design always was, and is now, an attempt to gain leverage, to influence those decisions in a beneficial way— but it is also the result of that attempt.

The prejudice here then is not as much with the mysteries of process as with the implementation of that process and those ideas; with a product. What will it be like? What kinds of places are resulting from all this activity? Are all these recently graduated urban designers going to produce nicer, richer, more interesting, more responsive cities? Are we likely to get something equal in quality to Bath, or Savannah, in Houston?

I don't know, frankly. I have, at times, real suspicions about the ability of this pluralistic, consumer-driven, democratic/capitalist society—as much as I respect so much of it—being able to produce an attractive and humane three-dimensional world. Yes, I have suspicions and doubts—but also hopes and convictions. As an optimist (and a Jeffersonian liberal), I believe we have (and still have time) to find ways to fashion a more orderly and elegant environment—even if the process of doing it seems Sisyphean. I'd, therefore, like to concentrate here first on trying to outline a few of the more obvious problems with respect to urban design practice, problems which will not go away; and then set out specifically what I believe to be the major assumptions and concerns of urban design thinking and practice today—a point of view, or idea structure if you will. Agreement or disagreement with this operating assumption might help clarify for each of you what current urban design principles are. I would add that while my own ideas about urban design have been in a continual state of amendment since I came out of school, my conviction that it was possible and desirable to build according to a more rational order of things has not.

PRACTICING URBAN DESIGN

There are a number of major difficulties in practicing urban design other than getting it right. One is time and the corrosive sense of unfulfillment associated with large-scale, long-term work; another, which is closely related to the first, is the lack of any direct pay out for the ego in work which not only takes years to achieve but is nearly always carried out by others (who, if successful, take the credit entirely and when unsuccessful blame it on the constraints imposed by the insensitivities of those who "wrote the rules"). Then again there is the enormous complexity of putting together and holding a team over time and of getting for this team the necessary economic/political support. Finally there is the question of which "models" do we use? Let's look at these for a moment.

Time. Because of the length of time required in conceiving and even partially achieving urban design work, there is no way to test one's work as one goes; the feed-back is generally delayed past the point where it is useful—at least to the person who originated the work. One is thus constantly starting things but rarely ever finishing them and as a result is escaping from the necessary (often harsh but educational) discipline of having to live with the results. (Planners are particularly adept at avoiding this kind of self-correcting education since they very rarely commit too strongly to anything. "Stay flexible" is part of their catechism.) Cities, or pieces of cities, don't come quickly; and they require vision, passion, and will, to an almost irrational extent, over time. All of this is difficult in a culture which:

a) is short on patience;
b) is committed to change;
c) is addicted to manipulating shifts in taste;
d) tests ideas constantly as to immediate popularity;
e) encourages excessive consumption;
f) is still very young and raw, with very few mature or elegant models and with little sense yet of, or value for, continuity;
g) is very rich.

Rewards: Particularly for the very best designers there are too few opportunities in urban design to feel the imprint of one's own hand (Nash, who was a developer as well as architect/planner was an exception). Process reward is usually not enough so that ultimately gifted designers fall back from trying to work at urban scale. They seem to need the more immediate lessons and gratifications of the built product—which is so much easier at the level of the single building. Thus urban design tends to drive out, or wear out, precisely those whose help it needs most (it's fine to cite urban design programs and processes and policies but what about the product?); or it forces these visionaries away from the practical world towards fanciful utopias because even sensible proposals prove too ellusive, too difficult, to achieve, to hold the artistic interest forever.

Support Systems: A key ingredient affecting the delivery or implementation of urban design ideas is the nature and complexity of the necessary support systems. First there is socio/political and economic support: a specific client (or clients), representing a commitment to certain ideas as well as to you, who has power and holds it over time (and is strong enough to take the flak). This favors single or small groups but certainly less democratic patrons over larger community clients (Haussmann had his Napoleon III and Logue his Rockefeller; Moses needed only himself). An urban design program attached to a politically neutral bureaucracy will tend to continually adjust, chameleon-like, to whomever has power—the bureaucracy's so-called objectivity being little more than bland self-preservation. In short, patronage and connections are enormously important as well as a reliable old boy network of dependable colleagues. This highlights another major aspect of the support system: The Team which is made up of people you've come to know and trust as a result of working together. The Team provides:

- *esprit* (a sense of elitism)
- variety (different people for different roles)
- depth (backstopping one another)
- strength (a number of high-quality peers)
- inter-mural competition (among peers a way to sharpen issues)
- small-scale structure (something familiar with which to face the bewilderment of the large-scale problems)
- limited focus and responsibility
- institutional status.

Urban design can't be done alone, and while keeping a good team together (*e.g.* the original Urban Design Group in New York City) is essential to getting results, it's hard to accomplish over time. Finally, and perhaps most relevant here, there are the educational and research institutions which support the practice of urban design. As I said at the outset, while there are a growing number of really excellent programs, urban design is still seen in the architectural/planning world as on the periphery—as not being the central issue. For this reason it's possible to say that creating a *separate* U.S. program may be as dangerous as not having one at all in that it frees those not in it from having urban design responsibility. I don't want to scare away good architects and planners because they think urban design is not architecture or planning but something else. I really want the point of the whole school to be a concern with urban design issues. Nonetheless our efforts have been and will continue to be helped by urban design programs and those schools which support them with their best foot forward. The need, I believe, is to try to broaden the public's and the academy's view of what urban design means.

The Model. In practice as in education the model is critical. Until very recently most of our urban design models have been drawn from non-democratic homogeneous cultures and, as a result, not only our historical examples but our Anglo/European mind-sets have not been closely matched with the nature of the American development pattern (*e.g.* the commercial strip, even the suburbs, for too many professionals seem both foreign and distasteful; or, to use another example, English-style New Towns programs don't fare too well without support of English-style governmental subsidy and long-term commitment). The loose fit, dynamic, open sprawl of our cities does not have many ancestors; and I think it's fair to say that with respect to both new land-development policies and the patterns of continued peripheral development some of our seeming ineptness can be directly traced to not having anything to study and evaluate. We were building the models that we were having to learn from; and on review these don't look very good. The basic problem with respect to three-dimensional models, to the design in urban design, is that as yet we have no commonly agreed upon typology of parts and wholes; no hierarchy of orders; of how standard things go together. Which means that most often the newest parts of our cities, particularly where new and old meet, are a mess. (This is less true in cities with strong and dense cores built on strong and dense grids *e.g.* midtown New York. But even here there is a lack of resonance, of connection between one building type and another.)

Since 1945 we've built a second America—more than half again as much as everything built up to that date—perhaps the greatest building effort in history. Yet even the staunchest advocate of our peculiar, pluralistic, quasi-capitalistic consumer democracy cannot be happy with the results; neither with the larger patterns of order (or rather disorder) nor with the amenity of specific (generic) places. The only thing we seem to be proud of or interested in are the individual objects. These we champion.

In my own view, most of what we've been building is junk. Not junk because its general quality is so low—though it is—but because it's shabby stuff put down in a shabby way; pattern defined mainly by greed, public inattention and convenience (. . . which in time is proving to be neither economical nor convenient, certainly not pleasing).

During this time of great building activity, we seem to have given up a vision of the city as an uplifting order of the whole, a better setting for better lives, in which each part plays a role, has a place and a purpose. We have indeed given up a language of the city which we believe in (and we build to try to forget this . . .). Roads and buildings, for example, instead of being seen as basic skeleton and building blocks are conceived and designed by specialists as ends in themselves; isolated systems and objects which maximize each user's, each owner's, and each designer's, private self-interest. The social contract between buildings has been lost; landscape architecture and civic art abandoned; the street becomes the strip, the square, the parking lot. Urban design little more than the *ad hoc* manipulation of real estate development. Our cities become in such a situation a display of expensive (and cheap) spare parts.

No matter what rationalizations or seductive interpretations are made of this process—and we've had extraordinarily sophisticated explanations of what things are really like out there on the strip; no matter, we still feel conned; cheap. Most of us today driving through the countryside, when we see an attractive piece of land abut to be developed, experience a great sense of *angst*, of loss. Not because there wasn't (and isn't) lots of attractive land left in this country—there is—but *because we have absolutely no confidence in our own ability not to mess things up.* The confirming evidence of which lies all around—the ubiquitous setting of our lives. We don't believe in or like very much what our culture builds (and to offset this real disappointment with the surroundings we can only lionize individual buildings and their creators). We don't believe in its "order of things."

As an argument in partial explanation of this lamentable situation, I would put these points forward as worth further investigation:

- All architectural cultures, including ours, are based on a limited number of standard building types and their variations.
- All architectural cultures attempt to develop a limited number of ways that these limited number of types can properly be put together to form larger orders (*e.g.* streets, precincts, villages, towns and cities). That is, there are not only rules with respect to the organization of the type itself but rules about relating or connecting one type to another.
- The rules about connecting types affect the rules about the types themselves and *vice versa*; but there is a hierarchy both among the types and the rules; and, in most cases, the rules which most affect the order of the whole supersede those which affect the individual type (*i.e.* the requirements of the street dictate those of the building). Any reading, and thus any understanding, is only possible when the elements have been properly put together *i.e.* according to the rules about connection—as in any crude analogue of language.
- In high architectural cultures, there is an easy fit between the order of the whole and of the parts—each seeming to reinforce and echo the other (hence Alberti's statement that the order of the house and the city are essentially the same)—and, like unto a healthy eco-system, for example, changes and variations from the generally prescribed rules and orders (particularly as it affects connection of relationship with respect of parts to one another and to the whole) these changes must always be seen as *supporting the stability of the whole order*; or when changing this order, doing so in an incremental way and from within; protecting the order against dissolution or excessive fragmentation (*i.e.* violent reordering is nearly always lethal).
- Our architectural culture has a number of highly developed building types (though not enough and not well defined because we keep changing the rules with respect to predictability: *i.e.* if a few houses are made to look like oil refineries but most of them not, how do we read house without real disorientation and confusion?) But while we have these few well-developed types, we have very few convincing or consistent rules about how the types go together. Specifically, the parts highly developed in them-

selves don't go to make up a whole. They carry no instruction about any larger order only their own ego. In short,
they are only more parts (*e.g.* Houston and the strip are
both vital and alive, indeed they flaunt their health by re-
producing. Yet, when one continues to build by the rules
of their order, which we are doing, the more convincing
the case for runaway malignancy becomes. And, of course,
while saying signs replace buildings is clarification, is observable, there remains the suspicion that this description
is little more than the diagnosis of aberrant growth).

What I am saying is that ours is not a *high* architectural
culture precisely because we don't have an understandable language of connection between all the spare parts
we've developed. In the face of this general sense of a loss,
or of a broken language, urban designers have developed
some general operating principles. Indeed, I would have to
say my own design intentions and preferences have been
sharpened by having to operate in a world where there
seemed to be so few reasonable contemporary rules. There
are trends in urban design theory and outlook which certainly structured the kinds of things all of us have been advocating and trying these last fifteen years. I've attempted
to set these out and the reasons behind them (admittedly
subjective arguments) in what follows.

CHANGING TRENDS IN URBAN DESIGN

It is fair to say that any problem will always be described in
terms of the current perceptions and prejudices of the day
and that it is, therefore, good practice to try to take account
of these prevailing views; to understand them as an inevitable editorial filter through which the seemingly objective
facts will surely pass.

Physical Plans and Changing Times: Fix and Flexibility. A
basic problem in building cities according to a pre-determined plan is that the process of achieving the plan
changes it. Since all cities take a much longer time to build
than to conceive, they rarely resemble, upon maturity, the
descriptions or the expectations of their creators. Sometimes this is for the best; sometimes not. In any event, the
recognition (more like a spectre) of this impermanency of
the physical vision sobers the designer, mocking those
who would put their stamp on the future. For change is

continual and difficult to control and radical alteration or abandonment a disease to which nearly all large-scale designs are ultimately susceptible. Time is usually not kind to the architect's dreams; and this seems to be more particularly true in modern times where political power is increasingly transitory and the ability to carry through on earlier decisions in a sustained way over time increasingly rare; indeed, where earlier decisions are, in fact, usually suspect.

Whereas monarchies and dictatorships found it easier and more politically advantageous to finish their grand schemes, both pluralistic democracies and social welfare states alike have more and more come to rationalizing (if not favoring) piece-meal development and *ad hoc* planning as an alternative to grand physical designs. Each new government, almost by definition, must have new ideas; these new views being clearly an improvement on the ones immediately preceding them, with as much put into legally amending or delaying previous plans as in achieving one's own. (When reinforced by the popular notion that change is indeed progress and that originality is more important than continuity, this relentless process of historical rejection and a new beginning renders most physical plans obsolete before they're even started.) Governments do still plan and build; but they don't seem to believe it as much as they used to.

As a result, more and more planners, in recognition of the new pace, complexity, and depth of change, of the unpredictability of political will (and in order to rationalize their seeming inability to carry out their own plans), have stressed flexibility and indeterminancy. Some have abandoned the idea of physical planning altogether (''Planning is a process'' . . . ''end-state plans are dead,'' etc.). Whereas grand schemes are still conceived (usually for non-Western or oil-rich oligarchies), fewer and fewer seem to be taken seriously; and the master builders of yesteryear, a Haussmann or a Robert Moses, are generally derided as willful and insensitive to real community needs and interests. Cities are not so much designed any more as managed.

Yet the recognition of this and an accompanying dissatisfaction with it has prompted urban designers to try again to find ways to construct flexible plans which are not totally piecemeal; plans which result in a better product not just more efficient processes. There have to be fixes as well as flexibilities, and these are physical.

THE REDISCOVERY OF HISTORY

Serious talk about city design has until very recently been out of intellectual favor. With the exception of Brasilia and Chandigarh (both more or less architectural/sculptural stage sets), most of the serious post-war new towns seemed less affected by grand design than by the decisions relating to economic and social structure, to management, marketing and network analysis. Civic design most often seemed an embarrassing after-thought and very clearly took back seat to the more pragmatic issues of transportation, land-use allocation and employment patterns with the very real expectation that through a process of rational, analytic analysis both socially healthy and physically attractive environments would result. City planning was even talked of as a science; amenity through technics (and that most designers for their part refused to try to understand the very real requirements of city building, they were seen as less and less essential). Urban cosmetics were used to thinly mask a kind of enlightened property development in too many cases—and generally with government sanction. The physical results of this approach were neither impressive nor very popular.

The public, if not the professionals, quickly sensed that most modern cities were really not very attractive places to live in, without scale, charm or soul, and literally in some cases began to tear them down. Perceptive critics argued how rational, ordered solutions had destroyed the very complex and traditional set of interrelations which characterized the urban organism. Citizens' groups rebelled. Simultaneously, and in reaction, there began to be a renewed interest in the older quarters of cities—in existing patterns of organization and linkage—and in the past. Even some professionals began to question the new scientific methods and to postulate that how things looked was somehow importantly related to how they worked (as well as being important in its own right) and that working had to do with context; the pattern of order, function, ritual enhancement, and amenity. As a result, an interest in civic design has reasserted itself—albeit in rather different clothes and utilizing very different techniques; and there is a rekindled interest in many of the very same ideas which the Modern Movement had so energetically tried to purge. Younger architects and planners have not only retreated from the polemical and apocalyptic canons of Modernism but have focused upon modern city planning theory as a central villain behind too much of the urban destruction of the last thirty years. As an alternative they have begun to look again at the models of older cities, drawing without embarrassment upon the classic devices of boulevard, square, court, arcade, landscaped esplanade, fountain and statue for their inspiration. Indeed Post-Modernism, with its self-conscious historical referencing has become a new architectural *avant garde*; historical perservation and adaptive reuse become new imperatives.

Context. Underlying this shift in outlook (and paralleled by the new directions in ecology, cybernetics and the life sciences) is a heightened awareness among urban designers of the importance of context; of the order of the whole as opposed to the order of the parts; of the status of existing pattern. Precincts, even whole cities, are becoming a focus of interest for designers and the design and interrelationship of different and often competing systems as much as that of individual buildings. Consequently, city design is being treated seriously once again as a central discipline rather than merely window dressing. It is now strongly felt that old and new together is somehow better, more culturally healthy, than the kind of brave new world posited by the Plan Voisin where the old had to be destroyed for the new to flourish. (And one of the major recognitions of this new sensibility is that great cities are as much dependent upon the quality of their open-space systems as on handsome individual buildings; that setting rather than object is more crucial to city sense.) An architecture of gradual incrementalism and of contextural responsiveness has replaced utopia; evolution rather than revolution. And what we now call urban design has not only greatly benefited from this new concern with context but helped shape it as well.

Similarly, just as there has emerged an appreciation of the inextricable interrelationship between old and new, between a building and its surroundings, the past and future, so also has it come to be seen that planning, design and development are interconnected in a complex way and that cities are not well served when these activities are too rigorously separated. Urban design, in its new form, has tended to bring planning and development together. Whereas in the recent past planners have usually preferred to try to keep their hands clean of the dirtier world of implementation, to look into the future and not compromise long-term interests with the rather sweaty regards of the moment and the marketplace, and to avoid where possible the constraints and dictates of achievability, today it is more and more apparent (especially to those exposed to both real and theoretical worlds) that when planning decisions are divorced from the realities, neither are adequately addressed. A too-often natural corollary of uncompromised long-range strategic planning is short-term *ad hocism* of the most impractical sort. Somehow, despite the amendment that the means do make upon the ends, long and short term objectives are beginning to be viewed holistically, and the shaping discipline of implementation laid upon the rather pampered and time consuming activity of postulating alternate futures. Addressing today's problems cannot be endlessly put off for want of still more and better data, though planners continually and understandably argue for more breathing space between analysis and action.

In a similar vein, a number of architects have attempted to broaden their scope of concern and not be limited merely to building design and construction problems. They have become familiar with land-use, transport, and environmental analysis, with real estate economics and marketing requirements, with legal and political problems as well as with socio/cultural and anthropological issues and have accepted that all these have design implications (especially in the pluralistic, democratic, and quasi-free-market societies of the West). They have perceived that their role is to try to mold these concerns together—from long-range planning goals to the implementation problems facing a developer—and to produce alternatives which are flexible, feasible, and aesthetically imaginative and culturally healthy.

The new context then is not just the physical setting or the methods and styles of contemporary building, or relevant historical and metaphorical references; it is also in the broadest sense an understanding of how the world around one works and the melding of this into physical patterns of order which both function and uplift. This means a much closer relation to both the front end, to planning, and to the ultimate delivery and life-cycle of a project; to development, marketing, maintenance and management. And there can be no condescension toward either end.

This expanded or amalgamated professional role, bringing planning/design/development together, is, of course, the same one employed by Haussmann, John Nash, Robert Moses and Ed Logue; indeed by nearly all the great modern quality builders.

As such, it is an attitude of mind which is different in both process and intent (and, one hopes, in result) from the more compartmentalized approach described in traditional modern planning texts and followed in most Western planning agencies and architectural offices.

What seems relevant here is that there has emerged an inclusivist, holistic mentality and a set of operational methodologies and preferences which seem better qualified to deal with the kinds of problems, both aesthetic and practical, being posed in cities today. Recent history has provided precisely enough experience in new town building together with a more mature historical perspective to allow constructive tampering to take place. So that fortunately upon the eve of the design of so many new city center projects there is an urban design attitude both tolerant and wide-ranging enough to respond constructively. (It won't be necessary to put all hope into some profound and wholly intuitive stroke of design luck as in the case of, say, the Sydney Opera House, where the site though focal was not the center of the entire city plan.) What becomes apparent is that it is the context, the setting of any building as yet undesigned, which, as much as the building itself, will determine a precinct's future quality.

Current Urban Design Concerns. This recent revived interest in old buildings, old cities, and the older parts of new cities, with existent context, together with the new professional attitudes and a general swing towards a more sympathetic public view of the city itself (especially in traditionally suburban/rural cultures such as the U.S.) has, in fact, begun to produce a recognizable urban Renaissance

in the West. Downtowns, either destroyed by war or by neglect and attrition, are being rebuilt in a much more sophisticated way than 20 years ago, and for the first time in
the century, the pedestrian, the man-on-foot, rather than
the automobile is the focus of professional concern; human
scale is being restudied and reestablished. Pedestrianization has become not only a "catch word" but a real, popular rallying cry. And despite the strength of the automobile, its economic role and vise-like grip on established life
styles, indeed its inherent sensibleness in many regards,
it's probably fair to say that some segment of public opinion has actually turned against the car. Further fuel shortages will only tend to increase this disaffection—sentiment
which will clearly affect all cities but particularly newer
American cities, essentially decentralized, low-density automobile cities of the most exaggerated kind. While syn-
thetic fuels will result in a redesigned car rather than no
cars at all, there will in all probability be a new ethic favoring both energy conservation and exercise. For the moment then, to planners and public alike, the desirable new
city, or new city precinct (*e.g.* Georgetown), is in essence a
walking city or a city of "walking precincts." And this is in
strong contrast to modernist images of the '30s: the ro-
mance of transportation—LeCorbusier, CIAM, and the
great American road-builders. (Even Houston and Los
Angeles are beginning to develop sub-centers which emphasize walking and street charm—a shift towards the
older, denser, mixed-use urban scene which modern planning theory and practice tried to kill.) We seem to be on the
verge of striking for the first time a *realistic balance between
wheel and foot* which will be the most important advance in
city design since the introduction of the car itself; a new
adjustment between the scales and patterns of the old established streets and those much larger scales of modern
buildings and transport systems. We are reacquiring street
sense—a love for the street scene.

   Accompanying the kinds of changed focus and attitudes, described above, there have evolved quite recently a
rather loose and as yet uncategorized set of urban design
principles, prejudices, and concerns which seem to have
increasing support among a growing number of professionals, critics, and using public. These vary from place to
place but taken together do represent an essentially re-

vised view of successful city design and are just now beginning to influence design decisions in major cities the world over. Listed below, in no order of priority, is a sampling of some of the current thinking—the convictions and concerns of contemporary urban designers. It is in no way an exhaustive list nor one officially sanctioned by any one group. It is, however, a list extremely relevant to the discussion of urban design issues and one which will lie behind much of the coming debate about what to do in the future in all major cities.

Whether or not one agrees with the relative merits or accuracy of these attitudes is not as important as the recognition that they exist and that it will be very difficult to assess any current civic design problem uninfluenced by them.

THE SAMPLING

• *The street system.* The street and its frontages is the city's major public arena as well as its most important ordering device. Streets are intended to carry a variety of vehicular modes, a varying volume of pedestrian traffic in selected areas, to be lined (one hopes) with interesting commercial activity, some of which has some round-the-clock life and to be attractively and thoughtfully designed. Streets vary in size and purpose but generally single-purpose or single-mode streets are not as successful as multipurpose corridors.

Streets should provide a circulation hierarchy, but circulation control is best achieved as a result of the disposition and character of the grid (*e.g.* Savannah) rather than by artificial means (*e.g.* recent traffic planning in London). Some streets will be crowded and some empty. The point is to recognize which should be which. Contrast in activity and life is normal. Very few streets in a city can support high activity but since land uses move, street design should allow for changing use.

Since streets comprise anywhere from 30 percent to 70 percent of a downtown's land area, they represent the major public open space system and should double wherever possible as strip parks, *i.e.* they should be carefully and consciously landscaped as the city's most important park system.

Continuous frontage is a street's most important physical requirement in relation to pedestrian use. Uniform treatment is desirable; piece-meal and random set-backs, charming at certain spots, tend to destroy most streets both as spaces and as successful commercial frontages. In line with this, plazas and squares only have spatial meaning when seen as a break, a relief, from a system of defined corridors. Squares and plazas which (a) are themselves undefined by buildings, walls or landscaping or (b) occur in a too loose and open street grid are usually ineffective and unattractive spatially; also unpopular.

The narrow street and alley; the arcade and through-block gallery; the court and atrium are all time-honored urban design devices which are used to thread together and reinforce the city's pedestrian circulation system. Most city grids are composed of primary systems which usually front major streets and secondary systems which run back from these into the blocks proper and connect one primary frontage with another. The employment of these tested historical devices is advisable in the future—which means studying past models carefully.

• *Parking*. Parking represents one of the most difficult modern urban design challenges. In strip developments it creates a sea of cars around island buildings and in denser downtown areas bombed-out blocks which represent an undesirable no-mans land. Parking must be rethought since the need for it won't go away. It is expensive underground and in buildings and usually ends up being the unintended central focus of nearly all designs, the most obvious and least attractive feature of the modern urban landscape; one generally ignored by the designer —with devastating results. If cities are to be made more humane an architecture of parking must be devised and buildings conceived so as to incorporate these 20th century surrounding gardens into a total city design.

• *Urban landscaping*. Alleys and groves of trees, terraces, steps, flower beds, watercourses, fountains, basins, statues, walls and pavements are relatively the cheapest and most easily manipulated urban design tool. They should be conceived as the basic architecture of the city; that device which shapes, colors, and gives character to major open space systems. Landscaping is not frills or cosmetics, but basic city architecture. Natural landscape features should be recognized and exploited; climate, wind, rain, sun, consciously employed in the development of a local and appropriate architectural vernacular. This does not mean that ideas, styles, devices as well as materials and plants and trees should not be imported (ours is after all, an international culture in which ideas were meant for travel). It does mean that any given place will amend any set of ideas, materials, or devices, and it is precisely in the amendment where lies the art. There is no better or International Style. Design is both intuitive and responsive at the same time; homegrown and foreign.

• *City buildings*. Buildings are costly and less flexible or controllable than open space and should be seen first as the containers, liners, and background walls of the city's open-space skeleton. Most buildings in cities are not intended (nor do they want or need) to be special; to be idiosyncratic. They are usually most successful as repetitive variations on a single type in which variety is in their detail and not in their overall shape, site disposition, or massing.

"One-off" buildings should occupy special locations and serve special purposes. When all or too many buildings are "one-off," the result (like the road to the airport) is urban chaos—with serious accompanying psychic dislocation and confusion. Needless to say, far too many buildings in modern cities which should be simple background buildings are in fact rather bad special performers—conceived as *objects* in themselves, with little or no regard for their surrounding context, their urban design purpose, or their civic function. (In nearly all cases this can be traced to: a) the attitude of the owner who doesn't care about the city; b) the architect who wasn't trained to understand the city and only wants recognition for doing his own thing; c) the city planner, who doesn't know what to do. This situation was exaggerated by the Modern Movement where the existing and surrounding city was considered contemptible, out-of-date, even corrupt—to be ignored or, where possible, destroyed.)

The best cities and precincts of cities are characterized by homogeneity of type, scale, detail, by variety at points of varying function and use, and by appropriate urban landscaping. In these areas, buildings are dense, spatially rather close together; open space systems defined, legible, active, and varied. Where buildings or groups of buildings have large-scale shape (*e.g.* Bath) that shaping is generally towards some larger urban design end, rarely for its own sake.

Changes in architecture *per se* are most successful when gradual and incremental; attention being paid to the manners, practices, conventions and styles of the place; to context.

• *Mixed-use precincts.* The healthiest, most interesting and most economical precincts (from a cost-benefit point of view) generally support a mix of uses, and downtowns, particularly, require some residential component to remain viable and attractive over time. Working, shopping, recreating, and living within walking distance should be encouraged at key points in central business districts. Whereas modern planning stressed the horizontal separation of uses, traditional cities have always been characterized by a variety of uses in any one area. These seem essential to an interesting, enjoyable, and viable streetscape: uses reinforcing one another.

• *The pedestrian.* The real city client is the man on foot; and while it's unfair, indeed, misleading to characterize the struggle for urban amenity as purely one of cars *vs.* people, real environmental quality in cities is directly related to the degree to which walking, sitting and viewing can be made attractive. Pedestrianization then is a major goal of urban designers. This may mean vehicle-free precincts or more appealing pedestrian rights-of-way in corridors shared with vehicles. In either case it means the designer of the system is properly an architect/planner not a highway engineer—a question of priorities. When the design of streets is seen again from this perspective, the quality of our cities will improve.

• *The car.* Although the indiscriminate use of automobiles has devastated our cities, for certain types of trips cars are practical and will for the immediate future continue to be heavily used. Except in very high density corridors they are cheaper (in total economic terms) than fixed rail transit systems, more popular and more flexible. Downtown transport systems must, therefore, seek to accommodate a variety of modes, including cars, with an increasing emphasis on how to make buses, trolleys, minibuses, moving sidewalks, taxis, and, in some cases, metros, more appealing and more effective. This is increasingly true of dispersed cities where the car is still the essential and convenient commuter vehicle. And whereas fuel shortages will tend to bring about changes in fuel, engine type, and vehicle size, it is doubtful that such a crisis will do away with the individual private vehicle itself. Therefore, ideological opposition to the automobile *per se* should be replaced by an effort to design more flexible multi-modal movement systems while consumption practices and tastes are brought into line with more realistic and disciplined energy policies.

• *City-wide circulation corridors.* Since land value is nearly always related directly to transport access, more attention is to be paid to the integrated design of transport corridors and their interchanges with particular attention given to how the so-called unearned increment of value due to the transport investment can be used to enhance public amenity.

Highways and interchanges and public transit systems are among the most prominent components of the visible urban landscape and an environment in which we spend an increasing amount of time; like the street, they are wanting of the same design attention as buildings. Landscaping treatments similar to those associated with the boulevard and the peripheral parkway must be developed for all kinds of urban motorways, transit facilities and rights of way. This is an urban design task of highest priority as these movement corridors, like Roman aqueducts, will often be the major physical structuring elements of our cities for some time to come and are today, with few exceptions, still in the hands of engineers. (The work of Robert Moses in New York should serve as a model to this design effort.)

In the same vein, water frontages—lakes, rivers, and docks—are a major amenity, loved by city dwellers since the beginning of time and worthy of the greatest attention. Where land and water meet is an area of economic value. Cities cannot really afford to ignore, abandon, or pollute such edges (Canberra, for example, has a water system as the major central focus of the urban design and is thus high among the world's cities; Griffin's genius lay in the elegant exploitation of this river into a system of lakes, basins, pools and rivers).

• *High-rise buildings*. Tall buildings are economical and, indeed, exciting. In certain central areas, they should be grouped together around nodes of highest density, use, and transport access. Taken together tall buildings create their own special scale and environment which has a very special city quality. They are also excellent three dimensional markers. In center cities, mixed-use office/residential blocks make a great deal of sense (though they are expensive to build). Thus, their abandonment is both unlikely and undesirable. On the other hand, the indiscriminate scattering of tall blocks and towers can not only destroy a city's scale and character but introduce quite irrational points of density and congestion. More and more, experience is indicating a preference, particularly among families, for low-rise residential accommodation—built around quasi-private court systems and having more traditional street frontages (bringing back into focus various 18th and 19th century urban housing solutions). Certainly, the high, residential "tower-in-the-park" seems dead in most advanced Western planning circles—if not among developers. Building heights and massing will, therefore, be increasingly controlled in cities despite the modern symbolic and commercial appeal of the "skyscraper" for both Western and Non-Western cultures.

• *Symbol and ritual*. Pomp and ceremony are an essential part of urban life so that formal areas are as important as informal ones; and markers, statues, memorials are an essential aspect of any healthy urban culture. Modern cities in playing down this aspect of city design denied a basic cultural imperative: the marking of occasions and men. Cities without ritual places are soon psychically and emotionally dead. Since such ceremonial placemaking seems more difficult and more self-conscious in democratic societies, a major concern of urban designers is to devise a new language of serious popular ritual.

• *Urban design controls*. Since cities take time to build and rebuild and always reflect a variety of tastes and styles, even the most basic design intentions are easily lost. The surest way to ensure some overall cohesion and continuity of intent over time is to develop prototypical solutions; to establish in practice models which can be sensibly replicated by other builders—(*e.g.* The Georgian Square or Parisian Boulevard). Such examples are the best guarantee of a desired goal. A major part of the urban designer's role lies in the definition of desirable examples—and the rules which allow for easy achievement.

The urban designer must design and describe and control the skeleton of the city: circulation systems, open spaces, parks, squares, boulevards, frontages, mechanical infrastructure, public works details, typical building types and the variety of land-uses associated with each. In certain areas of high activity and public importance specific urban design controls may be necessary; in other areas looser, more general rules may be appropriate. Such controls, sensitively derived and applied, can help direct and shape development in conjunction with land-use and density requirements. View corridors, arcades, set backs, mandated frontages and uses, specific colors and materials, scenic easements, height policies and connections to transport, all can be effectively built into the design rules governing building and can, in turn, strongly affect and improve the kind of environment that results from normal development.

It is important to remember that these rules should always be viewed as flexible and be administered and reviewed by gifted professionals in order to ensure their continued viability under the stresses and unforeseen opportunities offered by change. (Obviously all rules can be broken; it is the discrimination and judgment as to when this is appropriate which counts. And perhaps the only thing worse than no rules, are ordinances too constricting or too rigorously enforced.) First, however, design rules must be developed whose three-dimensional implications are understood; these rules tested, codified, and, if necessary, altered. More often than not, planned cities go wrong physically because their creators did not understand large-scale design very well; how it both shapes and derives from other needs. For the precincts we seem to remember best are comprised of some generalized model which has been repeated again and again with minor variation according to a set of rules—be they official or popularly agreed on.

• *Art and city design.* Major artists should, as in the past, become involved in the process of city design and building, and their works conceived so as to actively participate in the city's life. Artists can inform and enrich the city planning process (*e.g.* Christo and his Running Fence) as well as enhance the final surrounding city.

On the other hand, art as afterthought—as mere decoration so common in the newer parts of modern cities—does not produce city art. Artists and city designers should work together with the various commercial and community interests from the start—their client being the city-using public. The greatest urban cultures have been characterized by a city design art. Art outside of museums—art serving life—not *vice versa*.

• *Commerce*. Commercial concerns are design information; necessary working data for the urban designer which he ignores at great risk. How the city works commercially will determine how the city will be able to survive and work aesthetically. The urban design task is to maximize opportunities for healthy commercial activity and to extract from this public amenity. Urban design enjoins art and commerce and urban designers who don't welcome, understand, and enjoy this relationship miss the point of their work entirely.

• *Citizen participation*. A fact of life of recent urban planning experience has been the degree to which people, in various formal and informal constituencies, have organized to participate in choices that affect their own communities. This has both prevented undersirable projects from being imposed from above and encouraged more specifically local initiatives. It is a process which has also, unfortunately, stopped a number of worthwhile large-scale city-wide projects. This tendency to fracture central decision-making will probably continue. Thus, all urban design policies must a) involve legitimate citizen participation; b) provide real community benefit; c) find devices to protect necessary but potentially unpopular policies. Democratic pluralism, in order to produce large-scale quality environments, must work to reduce its own built-in, inhibiting tendencies; for participatory planning, while essential, is not an end in itself; nor is it always, or necessarily, enlightened.

These are some of the concerns and views influencing contemporary urban design. Though general in nature, they have specific applicability to any city, and are, I be-

lieve, strongly affecting what we are doing as urban designers today.

Whether or not these practices can help us achieve a
more orderly and humane physical world will be their test
and ours.

Biographical Notes

Hannah Arendt (1906–1975), born in Königsberg, studied philosophy in Germany until fleeing in 1933, first to France, then to the United States. Besides her collections of political essays, Arendt is best known for *The Origins of Totalitarianism* (1951) and *Eichmann in Jerusalem* (1963). Her works of philosophy include *The Human Condition* (1958)—from which this selection is taken—and *The Life of the Mind* (1978), which remained incomplete at her death.

Walter Benjamin (1892–1940) was born in Berlin and worked as a literary critic and essayist in Germany until 1933, when he fled the Nazis to live in Paris. He was connected with the "Frankfurt school" of Max Horkheimer and T.W. Adorno, fled Paris after the fall of France, and committed suicide when it appeared he could not escape to Spain. He worked intermittently on a study of nineteenth-century Paris, of which only fragments and drafts survive. The selection reprinted here is from one sketch of the intended work.

Nathan Glazer is professor of education and sociology at Harvard University, and co-editor of *The Public Interest*. Among his many books are *The Lonely Crowd* with David Riesman and Ruele Denney (1950), *Beyond the Melting Pot* with Daniel P. Moynihan (1963), *The Urban Predicament* edited with William Gorham (1976), and *Ethnic Dilemmas* (1984).

Charles T. Goodsell is professor at the Center for Public Administration and Policy, Virginia Polytechnic Institute and State University. He is author of *The Case for Bureaucracy* (1983).

Allan Greenberg, an architect whose most recent projects include a suite of offices for the U.S. Secretary of State, has written extensively on courthouses and architectural history.

Robert Gutman, visiting professor of architecture at Princeton University and professor of sociology at Rutgers University, is editor of *People and Buildings* (1972) and author of *The Design of American Housing: A Reappraisal of the Architect's Role* (1985).

499

Neil Harris, professor of history at the University of Chicago and chairman of the Smithsonian Council, is the author of *The Artist in American Society* (1966), and *Humbug: The Art of P.T. Barnum* (1973).

William Hubbard, an architect who teaches at the Massachusetts Institute of Technology, is author of *Complicity and Conviction: Steps toward an Architecture of Convention* (1980).

Jane Jacobs was born in Scranton, Pennsylvania, and now lives in Toronto, Canada. She is best known for her trilogy on the nature of urban life: *The Death and Life of Great American Cities* (1961), *The Economy of Cities* (1969), and, most recently, *Cities and the Wealth of Nations* (1984).

J.B. Jackson, who taught landscape history for many years at Harvard University and the University of California, Berkeley, was founder and editor of the influential magazine *Landscape* (1951–1968). His essays have been collected in *Landscapes* (1970), *The Necessity for Ruins* (1980), and *Discovering the Vernacular Landscape* (1984). He lives in New Mexico.

Donlyn Lyndon is an architect, professor of architecture at the University of California, Berkeley, and co-editor of the quarterly journal, *Places*.

Charles Moore, architect and critic, was born in Michigan in 1925. Among his best known public projects are Kresge College at the University of California, Santa Cruz (1973), and the Piazza d'Italia Fountain in New Orleans (1975). He is the author of *Body, Memory and Architecture* (1977) and, with Gerald Allen and Donlyn Lyndon, *The Place of Houses* (1974); he is currently professor of architecture at UCLA.

Lewis Mumford, American critic and sociologist, was born in Flushing, Long Island in 1895. After coming under the influence of the Scottish town planner Patrick Geddes in 1914, he went on to write influential books on American culture and architecture, the history of the city, and the crises of contemporary civilization. His many books include *The Story of Utopias* (1922), *Technics and Civilization* (1934), *The Culture of Cities* (1938), *The Condition of Man* (1944), and *The City in History* (1961), from which this selection has been taken.

Frederick Law Olmsted (1822–1903), the great American landscape architect, was born and raised in New England, where be began his career as a farmer. He later turned to writing, first publishing a travelogue, *Walks and Talks of an American Farmer in England* (1852), then serving as a New York newspaper correspondent in the antebellum South. With Calvert Vaux he drew up the winning ''Greensward'' plan for the Central Park competition of 1858, and worked on his masterpiece over the next twenty-five years. His other major works include Brooklyn's Prospect Park, Boston's ''Emerald Necklace,'' and the World Columbian Exposition in Chicago (1893). The article reproduced here was a contribution to Boston's debate over the need for public parks.

Jaquelin Robertson, dean of the School of Architecture at the University of Virginia, was director of the Office of Midtown Planning and

Development in New York City during Mayor John Lindsay's administration. Among his buildings is the Museum of Modern Art Tower (1978), designed with Cesar Pelli.

Joseph B. Rose, a New York native, is chairman of Manhattan's Community Board 5.

Moshe Safdie, the architect, was born in Israel in 1938. He is perhaps best known for "Habitat '67," the prize-winning housing complex he designed for the Montreal exposition of 1967. Currently a professor at Harvard's Graduate School of Design, he has major projects underway in the United States, Canada, and Israel. He is the author of *Beyond Habitat* (1970) and *For Everyone a Garden* (1974).

Roger Scruton has written a number of philosophical works, among them *Art and Imagination* (1974), *The Aesthetics of Architecture* (1979), and *The Aesthetic Understanding* (1983). He teaches philosophy at Birkbeck College, University of London, and is editor of *Salisbury Review*.

Michael A. Scully, a former staff member in the United States Senate, is consulting editor to *The Public Interest*.

Richard Sennett is founder and director of the Institute of Humanities at New York University, where he also teaches sociology. His books include *Families against the City* (1970), *The Uses of Disorder* (1970), *The Hidden Injuries of Class* (1972), and *Authority* (1980). The selection reproduced here is from his *The Fall of Public Man* (1977).

Camillo Sitte (1843–1903), architect and planner, was born in Vienna. The son of an architect, he became director of the Austrian State School for the Applied Arts in 1883. His interest in city planning, undoubtedly spurred by Vienna's monumental *Ringstrasse* projects, resulted in the publication of *Die Städte—Bau nach Seinen Künstlerischen Grundsätzen* in 1889. The selection reproduced here is taken from the G.R. and C.C. Collins translation, titled *City Planning according to Artistic Principles* (1964).

Douglas Stalker is associate professor of philosophy at the University of Delaware. Clark Glymour is chairman of the philosophy department at Carnegie-Mellon University, and author of *Theory and Evidence* (1980).

Roger Starr, a native New Yorker, serves on the editorial board of the *New York Times*. For many years the executive director of the Citizens' Housing and Planning Council of New York, he has also served as commissioner of housing for the City of New York. He has written a number of books on urban affairs, among them *The Living End* (1966), *Housing and the Money Market* (1975), and *The Rise and Fall of New York City* (1985).

William H. Whyte, born in Pennsylvania in 1917, is the author of *The Organization Man* (1956) and *The Last Landscape* (1968). He was a long-time editor of *Fortune* magazine, but later turned to urban affairs. His *The Social Life of Small Urban Spaces* (1980), from which this selection is taken, is a product of The Street Life Project, an observational study of street life that he has been conducting since 1970.

Index

H 1987 oo